Alton B. Parker

Alton B. Parker
The Man Who Challenged Roosevelt

BRADLEY C. NAHRSTADT

Cover image of Alton B. Parker, 1904, from the Library of Congress.

Published by State University of New York Press, Albany

© 2024 State University of New York

All rights reserved

Printed in the United States of America

No part of this book may be used or reproduced in any manner whatsoever without written permission. No part of this book may be stored in a retrieval system or transmitted in any form or by any means including electronic, electrostatic, magnetic tape, mechanical, photocopying, recording, or otherwise without the prior permission in writing of the publisher.

For information, contact State University of New York Press, Albany, NY
www.sunypress.edu

Library of Congress Cataloging-in-Publication Data

Name: Nahrstadt, Bradley C., 1967- author.
Title: Alton B. Parker : the man who challenged Roosevelt / Bradley C. Nahrstadt.
Description: Albany : State University of New York Press, [2024]. | Includes bibliographical references and index.
Identifiers: LCCN 2023015783 | ISBN 9781438495972 (hardcover : alk. paper) | ISBN 9781438495996 (ebook) | ISBN 9781438495989 (pbk. : alk. paper)
Subjects: LCSH: Presidents—United States—Election—1904. | Parker, Alton B. (Alton Brooks), 1852-1926. | United States—Politics and government—1901-1909. | Politicians—New York (State)—Biography. | Lawyers—New York (State)—Biography. | Judges—New York (State)—Biography.
Classification: LCC E758.P37 N34 2024 | DDC 973.9092 [B]—dc23/eng/20230811
LC record available at https://lccn.loc.gov/2023015783

10 9 8 7 6 5 4 3 2 1

*For Debby, the love of my life and my inspiration.
I am nothing without her.*

Contents

List of Illustrations		ix
Acknowledgments		xi
Foreword		xiii
1	His Early Years	1
2	His Time on the Bench	21
3	Parker's Patron: David Bennett Hill	47
4	Turn-of-the-Century Politics	59
5	The Possible Democratic Candidates in 1904	67
6	The 1904 Conventions	95
7	The Nomination	103
8	Parker's Running Mate: Henry Gassaway Davis	123
9	The Campaign Begins	133
10	The Middle Campaign	163
11	The End Is in Sight	177
12	Election Day	191
13	A Return to the Practice of Law and a Continuing Involvement in Politics	201

14	His Final Days	251
15	What Kind of President Would Parker Have Made?	257
Notes		261
Bibliography		311
Index		323

Illustrations

Figure 1.1	Birthplace of Alton B. Parker.	1
Figure 1.2	Parker as a baby.	2
Figure 1.3	Parker as a young man.	4
Figure 1.4	Parker at the age of sixteen.	5
Figure 1.5	The schoolhouse where Parker first taught school.	8
Figure 1.6	Parker's estate, Rosemount, circa 1904. Parker's grandson, Alton Parker Hall, is seated in the foreground.	15
Figure 1.7	Judge Parker's library at Rosemount.	15
Figure 1.8	A portion of the Rosemount outbuildings and grounds.	16
Figure 1.9	Parker riding his favorite horse, Tom, on the grounds of Rosemount.	18
Figure 2.1	Parker in 1879, two years after he was elected county surrogate.	21
Figure 2.2	Parker as chief judge of the New York Court of Appeals.	26
Figure 3.1	David Bennett Hill.	48
Figure 5.1	Arthur Pue Gorman, circa 1899.	69
Figure 5.2	George Gray, circa 1899.	70
Figure 5.3	Richard Olney.	71

Figure 5.4	Francis Cockrell.	73
Figure 5.5	William Jennings Bryan in 1896.	74
Figure 5.6	William Randolph Hearst, circa 1904.	76
Figure 6.1	Opening prayer, 1904 Republican National Convention.	96
Figure 6.2	Opening session of the 1904 Democratic National Convention.	99
Figure 8.1	Henry Gassaway Davis at the time of the 1904 campaign.	123
Figure 9.1	Parker and Davis meet for the first time on the porch of Rosemount, July 21, 1904.	135
Figure 9.2	Well-wishers waiting for the notification ceremony to start.	138
Figure 9.3	Judge Parker receiving the formal notification of his nomination at Rosemount, August 10, 1904.	140
Figure 9.4	Alton B. Parker poster.	156
Figure 9.5	Parker and Davis poster.	157
Figure 9.6	A sampling of Parker and Davis buttons.	161
Figure 10.1	Parker and Davis as salesmen.	165
Figure 11.1	Parker speaking in the Third Regiment Armory in Bridgeport, CT.	184
Figure 12.1	1904 Electoral Map.	193
Figure 13.1	Mary Schoonmaker Parker at the time of the 1904 presidential campaign.	242
Figure 13.2	Alton B. Parker and Amelia Day Campbell Parker shortly after their wedding.	245
Figure 14.1	Parker near the end of his life.	252
Figure 14.2	Dedication of the Alton B. Parker birthplace marker, June 11, 1927.	255

Acknowledgments

As a practicing attorney, and a lover of all things political, I have had a long-standing interest in Alton Brooks Parker, who was a lawyer and a judge and a candidate for the highest political office in the land. It has always been somewhat of a mystery to me why no one has ever published a comprehensive biography of Parker and his life. More than three decades ago, I began collecting material about Parker that I could use to correct this injustice. This book is the end result.

Writing a book is a collaborative process. No one writes a book alone. I owe a great deal of thanks to a lot of people. First and foremost, thanks to my wife, Debby, who not only encouraged me to tackle this project, but also served as my agent and ultimately got this project accepted by SUNY Press. Thank you to my boys, Benny and Josh, who also encouraged me and kept me going during the long writing process. Thank you to my parents, Bill and Nancy, who long ago inspired my love of history and politics. Special thanks to my mother for reading the first draft and pointing out necessary revisions. I owe a debt of gratitude to two of my college professors, Ira Smolensky and Jeremy McNamara, who helped me develop and hone my writing skills.

Eric Simon obtained copies of Parker's legal opinions for me, and I am grateful to him for providing the source material for chapter 2. The Library of Congress houses thirty-five boxes of Alton Parker's papers. The staff at the Library of Congress was willing and eager to assist me in my review of those papers and offered courteous service. Many thanks to my good friend, Dan Cotter, for his helpful advice concerning the publication process.

Finally, it is my pleasure to thank Richard Carlin at SUNY Press for all he has done to see this project through to fruition. He gave the initial green light for this project, oversaw the third-party review of both the initial proposal and the finished manuscript, answered all my questions and provided much-appreciated support.

Foreword

When he was a young boy, Alton Brooks Parker told his father that he wanted to be a lawyer. And he parlayed his success in the legal field into the one job he was truly happy doing: being a judge. But he was not just any judge; he was the chief judge of the New York Court of Appeals, the highest court in the state of New York. From this lofty position Parker handed down dozens of objective, logical, and forward-thinking opinions that protected the rights of all persons, big or little, rich or poor, connected or disenfranchised.

Parker was at the height of an illustrious judicial career when his party came calling. In the last few years of the nineteenth century and the early years of the twentieth, the Democrats were in turmoil. In the elections of 1896 and 1900, the South had aligned with the West to support the failed candidacy of William Jennings Bryan. As 1904 approached, many Southern leaders in the party (men like John W. Daniel, John Sharp Williams, and "Pitchfork" Ben Tillman) agreed with Eastern businessmen (men like Thomas Fortune Ryan and August Belmont) that if they had any chance of securing the presidency, a change in strategy was needed. They decided to effect an alliance of the South with the ultraconservative East.[1] For this strategy to work, the Democrats would have to nominate a candidate who could carry the South and win the electoral votes of Delaware, Maryland, West Virginia, New York, Connecticut, and New Jersey. Parker, it was eventually believed, was that candidate.

It turns out that Parker was a transition point between the "old guard" of the Democratic Party and the new progressive Democratic Party. Parker was the last Bourbon Democrat to win his party's nomination.[2] Beginning with the 1908 election, the progressive wing of the party dominated the nominating process.[3]

Given Parker's place in the history of the Democratic Party, and given that he was the pivot point between the old guard, conservative party and the new guard, progressive party, he should be a well-known figure. But he is not. Even after his nomination, Parker was not well-known outside his native New York. He was eclipsed and overshadowed by the immensely popular Roosevelt. He did not chase publicity or hold high governmental office after the 1904 campaign. In his later years he worked hard in his profession and on behalf of the American people, but he unfortunately faded into obscurity.

Alton Parker's place in history is important. His story is important. It deserves to be told.

In his seminal work on the men who ran for president and lost, *They Also Ran,* Irving Stone wrote that Alton B. Parker was the forgotten man among the forgotten men who "also ran." According to Stone, "[o]f all the unsuccessful candidates for the presidency of the United States no longer living, he alone has had no biography written about him."[4] This book aims to change that fact.

1

His Early Years

Alton Brooks Parker was born on May 14, 1852, in a roomy farmhouse situated on the farm that his grandfather settled in Cortland County, New York (see figure 1.1). That farm, which Alton's father purchased from his own father, was located approximately four miles northwest of the village of Cortland, the county seat. His father, John Brooks Parker, was a farmer who barely earned enough to support the family. John Parker's real passion was books, and he passed on to his son a lifelong love of learning and knowledge.[1] His mother, Harriet Stratton Parker, was a devout

Figure 1.1. Birthplace of Alton B. Parker. From the *St. Louis Post-Dispatch Sunday Magazine*, April 24, 1904. Public domain.

and intelligent woman, descended from hearty New England stock.[2] Even before Alton could read, his mother had taught him Bible verses as he sat in his high chair while she sewed. Later, she required him to learn seven Bible verses each week to recite in Sunday school.[3]

Alton was the oldest of five children. Although two of his siblings, Gilbert and Harriett ("Hattie"), died in early childhood of diphtheria, his sister Mary, and his brother Frederick lived to adulthood.[4]

Parker's mother described him as "a romping little fellow who loved the field"[5] (see figure 1.2). According to Mrs. Parker, "after Alton had reached the age of eight it was not necessary once for me to punish him in any way. He kept out of mischief, and was ever ready to please his father and me."[6] Even as a small boy Alton accompanied his father and the hands around the farm, "pitching hay, pulling carrots, digging potatoes and doing other work."[7] According to his mother, he was "such an athletic lad, always wanting to be on the go, that [she] had to caution him many times not to overtax his strength."[8]

In his youth Parker had bright red hair. During the 1904 campaign for the presidency he related to a visitor at Rosemount, his fashionable country estate, the trouble his red hair caused him when he was younger.

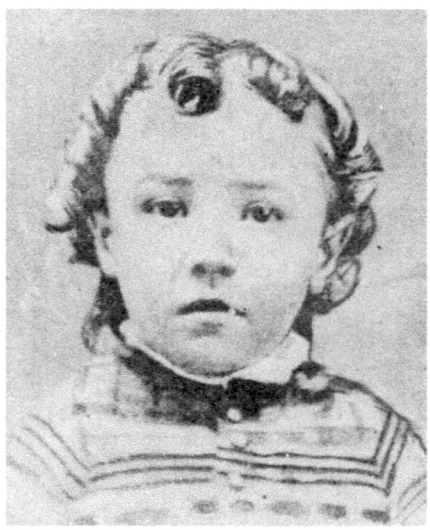

Figure 1.2. Parker as a baby. From the *St. Louis Post-Dispatch Sunday Magazine*, April 24, 1904. Public domain.

According to Parker, "when I was your age . . . my hair was redder than yours—it was fiery red, in fact, and, in consequence, my fighting instincts were over-developed while I was in school. In the country district where I learned my 'three R's,' it happened that I was the only red-haired youth. When I first attended school the boys had a good deal of fun shouting 'sorrel' and 'red-top.' It never failed to rouse my fighting blood, and I lived a strenuous life."⁹

From a very young age, Parker decided that he wanted to become a lawyer. He never thought about doing anything else long term. As he related to his friends:

> It was a little thing that led me into a choice from which I never wavered. Since I made that choice I have never thought for a moment of any other calling as possible for me. My father was a juryman during a term of court at the county seat. I used to drive him to the Court House in the morning, return to my work on the farm and then go for him with a horse at six in the evening. It happened that a celebrated breach of promise case was up for trial.
>
> The parties were of social prominence and somewhat wealthy. I remember especially that the young man was very handsome. Two distinguished outside counsel were engaged in the case—Albert Charles Sedgwick, of Syracuse, and Milo Goodrich, of Dryden, an old-time circuit rider, whose practice covered several counties. The case interested me so much that on the first day I asked my father if I could not stay and listen instead of going home to work. He consented, and I watched the trial of the case from beginning to end.
>
> The pleas of the lawyers, the examinations and cross-examinations, the speeches on either side, and, finally, the summing up, all impressed me very profoundly with one thought—that I wished to become a lawyer. My mind was made up. I never ceased to pursue this subject from that time on. Of course, it was such a boyish way in which to arrive at such a conclusion; yet it influenced my life, and I do not think that I made a mistake. I would not advise other young men, however, to act upon that sort of impression without greater determining reasons.¹⁰

Although they were modest farmers, Alton's parents valued education. He attended the local district school in Cortland, often going barefoot, until he was twelve years old.[11] At the age of twelve he was sent away to the old Cortland Academy for the fall and winter terms (he spent the spring and summer at work on the family farm)[12] (see figure 1.3). After graduating from the Cortland Academy, he attended the State Normal School in Cortland, where he trained to be a teacher.[13] Once he obtained his teaching certificate, at the age of sixteen, he began teaching school in Virgil, New York (see figure 1.4). Parker began teaching at such a young age for two reasons: to help out with family expenses and to earn money for law school.[14]

The story of Parker's first engagement as a school teacher should be told in his own words:

> I thought . . . that I ought to go away and teach, and so help out with the family expenses a little. I passed the examination and got a certificate, and then rode off across the country

Figure 1.3. Parker as a young man. From the Cortland County Historical Society. Public domain.

Figure 1.4. Parker at the age of sixteen. From the *St. Louis Post-Dispatch Sunday Magazine*, April 24, 1904. Public domain.

until I found a school with which the district magnates were willing to entrust me. When I returned I told my father what I had done, and I felt rather proud that I had found a place so promptly. But he was disappointed. He had watched young men all his life, he said, and he had always remarked that when they made a failure of any important thing at the outset they went on making failures all the way through life.

"I think you are very young for what you have undertaken," he added. "I am sorry, too, because the trustees here in our district want you to teach for them, and the pay is fifty cents a day more than you will get where you have engaged yourself."

I told my father that I would prefer to teach near home, and suggested that perhaps the other trustees would readily release me. I shall not forget the tone of his answer. "Never, never!" he exclaimed. "When you once put your hand to the plow, never turn back. But examine thoroughly hereafter anything into which you are about to enter before you do so."

That was a hard school, that first one. It was fortunate for me that my father had talked to me as he had of the meaning of failure and about never turning back from a duty undertaken. I think what he said strengthened me, prepared me for what was to come, and enabled me to acquit myself better than I would have done. He drove me over to my school. Just as I got out of the wagon at the house of one of the trustees where I was to leave my trunk, the latter came out to meet us and he said to me:

"Well, young man, one of the boys of our school saw you when you were here the other day, and said he didn't think it would take long to put you out."

I asked what was meant by this, a question, of course, which should have occurred to me before.

"Why, you see," answered the trustee, "the boys put three teachers out of the school last winter, and one of them was forty-five years old, and he went out through the window."

I saw that my father suffered when this was said to me. He had just about all he could do to keep the tears back. He thought that I was going to have a hard time at that school, and that, perhaps, I would fail in what I had set out to do. But his warning to me had given me time to think, and I had made up my mind that I wasn't going away from there except as master.

My resolution was tested on the second day of my teachership. A trustee's son was the first to rebel. He was larger than I was, although I was pretty sturdy and agile, as country boys are apt to be, if they indulge, as I had done, in wrestling and other physical sports that are common among them. This boy put an old-fashioned loco-foco match, the kind that smell of sulphur and brimstone, on the hot stove. The result was decidedly disagreeable, and the issue of discipline and order was at once raised. I stepped from the platform, where my desk was, and walked down toward the place where the boy sat, wondering what I was going to do to him.

I didn't intend anything very savage, but I knew I had to do something, or there was an end forever of all semblance of authority on my part. He solved the question as to what I was to do by his own act. As I approached, he took hold of the bench with both hands, as if anticipating that I would try to haul him off it by the collar. He had not gotten a firm hold before I leaned over, and, seizing him, stood him up on top of the bench. Then he grabbed me, and we went down together on the floor. But what followed did not last long, and there was no more question of my supremacy.

One of the little fellows came to me just as school was out and said: "Jim (that was the big boy) says he's going to tell his father, and he'll have you attended to." I thought it was about time that I began to attend to that end of the case myself. So I took a different direction from the usual one when I left the schoolhouse, walking toward the house of Jim's father. I met him just as he was crossing the road, and, Jim and several other boys being present, told him the whole story. Jim hung his head with a very hand-dog look, and the father said, "well, I think you have punished him enough; but if you have to do it again, you let me know, and after you have got through, I will do some of it myself!"[15]

At the noon recess I [often] played ball with the boys, and in that game I was more skillful than any of them. Good naturedly they were accustomed to wrestle together when not playing ball. After a time when there was snow on the ground they were anxious to wrestle and one of them proposed to wrestle with me, which I said I did not care to do as the ground was frozen hard . . . One day one of the little boys came in and said "Teacher, the boys say they believe you dasn't wrassle with them." I walked out of the school room and said to them "now I do not believe in wrestling on hard frozen ground, but if you are anxious to do it I will wrestle with the man you shall pick for side hold, square hold and back hold, and in that order." They selected Martin Coonrod who was 22 years old for the side hold wrestle. I threw him at once with, what we termed in that country, the grapevine; then with the left and under I threw him from my hips so fiercely that he was unable to come back to school again. I was not asked to wrestle the other two. Even though only sixteen, I always believed that my authority as teacher contributed toward my triumph. I had no further trouble in that school and always regarded it as a most valuable experience.[16]

Following a year spent teaching in Virgil (see figure 1.5), Alton spent some time teaching in Binghamton, where he was so successful that in 1871 he was asked by the trustees of the Accord School in Ulster County to become the school's principal.[17] While he was there he met Mary Louise Schoonmaker, the daughter of Moses and Phoebe Schoonmaker of Kingston, New York. After seven months at the Accord School, Alton moved to Kingston and accepted a clerkship at the firm of Schoonmaker & Hardenburgh.[18] The head of the firm was Augustus Schoonmaker Jr., county judge of Ulster County. The other named partner, Jacob Hardenburgh, was a member of the state senate.[19] The Schoonmaker firm enjoyed a stellar reputation in the legal profession and had a large and lucrative practice, being retained in most of the important litigation pending in that part of the state.[20] Parker's very first clients were Mr. & Mrs. Sagendorf of Hurley, New York. They hired him to draft their wills.[21] After working as a clerk for a year, Alton had saved up enough money to enter Albany Law School.[22]

Parker graduated from Albany Law School in 1872.[23] In the fall of 1873, Christopher Agar, a Kingston merchant, called upon Parker and asked him if he would accept the clerkship of the Board of Supervisors of Ulster County should he be elected to the position. Parker responded in the affirmative, and on November 11, 1873, he was elected clerk of the

Figure 1.5. The schoolhouse where Parker first taught school. From www.theclio.com. Public domain.

Ulster County Board of Supervisors. He was reelected to that position in 1874 and 1875.[24]

Soon after graduating from law school, Alton married Mary Louise Schoonmaker in Rochester, New York. The newlyweds lived in Kingston, where Alton, who had been admitted to the New York State Bar, was hired by Judge Schoonmaker to serve as the managing clerk of the firm. Shortly thereafter, Parker entered into a partnership with a law school classmate, William Kenyon, creating the firm of Parker & Kenyon.[25] Parker & Kenyon represented Ulster County and other public institutions in a wide variety of cases. In Parker's first big case, he was hired to represent Ulster County in a protracted suit against two local municipalities involving the equalization of assessments. The local press said the following about Parker's involvement in the suit: "The County is to be congratulated upon the fact that Hon. A.B. Parker has been secured as counsel by the committee of the Board of Supervisors, appointed to conduct the equalization suits. Mr. Parker has had a great deal of experience in equalization matters and the committee could not have selected a lawyer better qualified to conduct a case of this kind."[26] Parker briefed the case patiently and exhaustively and was ultimately victorious; he earned a fee of thirty-six hundred dollars.[27]

In 1877, Parker was elected county surrogate in Ulster County by a small majority (the Republican nominees for every other countywide office, including county judge and district attorney, were elected by overwhelming majorities).[28] As the surrogate for Ulster County, Parker handled probate matters and the administration of estates within the county. After he was elected surrogate, the firm of Parker & Kenyon was dissolved.[29]

Some reports in the press indicated that when Parker was starting out on his own in life, John Parker disapproved of his course and refused to offer him any aid. Parker was quick to correct this misconception. "Our home," said Parker, "was a lovely one, and our father did all he possibly could for us. In the later years he procured a piano for my sister. The only person whom he really stinted in any way was himself. His influence over us was very great. I was just as anxious to help with the work on the farm as if it had been my own. He had a way of developing the judgment of each of his children. He consulted me about everything concerning the management of the farm, as, for instance, whether such and such a field ought to be plowed, and to what crop it ought to be put, etc.," Parker continued, "in the same way he strove to develop character in us. He was never cross with us. He never punished us. When we did anything contrary to his wishes, it was quite enough punishment for us to know that he felt hurt over it."[30]

In his attitude toward human nature, Parker was a decided optimist. He invariably looked for the good qualities in people. Even when someone had personally wronged him, he was able to take an entirely impersonal view of the matter. His mind seemed to be incapable of retaining, for any length of time, feelings of ill will.[31] A story told by Arthur McCausland, Judge Parker's private secretary (and later law partner), perfectly illustrates this point.

The judge and Mrs. Parker were hosting a reception at Rosemount for many prominent people in the community. Mrs. Parker noticed the name of a man who had wronged the judge some time before on the guest list. She questioned whether the judge was actually going to invite the man to the party given the poor treatment the judge had received from the man. Parker exclaimed that he had forgotten all about the prior transgression and said that he should be allowed to come to the event if he chose to do so. Mrs. Parker remarked that she simply could not be polite to the man if he was invited. Parker told McCausland that the matter worried him. According to Parker, "it would look pretty marked; it would seem as if I were harboring resentment, wouldn't it . . . if we didn't invite him?"[32] When McCausland stated that he thought it would be petty to not invite the man, Parker insisted that he receive an invitation, noting that if the man showed up, "Mrs. Parker will relent."[33]

As an adult, Parker's outward physical appearance was described as strong and athletic. He was purported to be "broad-beamed, hard-muscled, indefatigable, weighing two hundred pounds of solid flesh and standing up six feet, in unfailing health and good spirits."[34] The journalists of the day called him a great ruddy engine of vitality.[35] He had "a big symmetrical head and a full face, with an aquiline nose, big white teeth and large brown eyes, kindly, sincere and direct in their gaze. His jaw was large and curved; he wore a generous-sized, tawny mustache. His skin was fresh and unwrinkled. Everything about him gave the impression of bigness: his strong body, his easy, straightforward manner, his moral courage."[36]

The New York Times described Parker in this way:

> In the first place the man who meets the Judge after having seen only the current pictures of him will soon make the discovery that no etching, woodcut, or anything in black and white can

give an adequate idea of what he looks like. In such a likeness his moustache and hair appear to be black. They are far from black. In fact, they are reddish. There is a good deal of color in his face, too, particularly after one of his self-imposed spells of work on his farm. The forehead is high, so high that it will undoubtedly be said that he is slightly bald over the temples. That is not the case.

There is another particular in which the black print portraits of him are misleading. They give him a certain stolidity of expression which is not true to life. Firm and square though the chin is, there is a delicacy in the face—an expression of refinement—that none of the photographers up to now has caught. There never was, never could have been anything so unfair as to depict this man as a sphinx, for instead of being anything like silent or reserved in conversation he is pre-eminently social, fond of good society, fond of taking a goodly share in the conversation, fond of listening to a good story—and telling one, too.[37]

Yet another set of commentators had this to say about Parker's physical appearance: "to a person who has never seen him before, the first meeting always causes an impression of strength and of indomitable will, expressed by the firm jaws and the formidable round chin. Brown eyes that can be both kindly and lion-like, and a symmetrical brow are other characteristics of Judge Parker to be observed, but above all there is to be seen a look of determination and honesty on his face at all times, which induces confidence on the part of his friends and a feeling among strangers that he is a man to be depended upon."[38]

Following his nomination for the presidency, the *Los Angeles Herald* provided its readers with the following description of Parker:

Physically, the Democratic candidate is as fine a specimen of manhood as can well be pictured. He stands and sits very erect, and his height of six feet does not impress one, as his body is so well proportioned. His carriage is dignified, but withal easy and not without considerable grace. The eyes are brown and sharp, and bespeak a clear analytical mind and are in excellent keeping with the lower part of the face, which is firm and full of determination.

> The jaw is sufficiently square to impress one with the belief that triflers must beware, but still not so square that there is any suggestion of brutality. The head is well poised on a full neck, suggestive of physical strength, a neck perhaps that might have been a trifle longer.[39]

Although the judge had many acquaintances, and knew many different people from many different walks of life, he had just a few really close, personal friends. To many he appeared to be a little aloof. No one ever saw him exhibit a bad temper. He adhered to the three "C's"—always stay calm, cool and collected.[40]

Parker was a man instilled with self-confidence. No matter how grim the circumstances, he believed that he could make things turn out all right. In September 1891, the Ulster County Savings Institution was forced to close its doors as a result of the embezzlement of approximately $400,000 by the bank's treasurer and assistant treasurer. The attorney general took the unusual step of appointing a temporary receiver to wind up the business and distribute the assets. After the temporary receiver was appointed, he discovered that it was impossible to wind up the affairs of the bank without substantially destroying the market value of the large amounts of farmland that the bank had under mortgage.

Judge Parker was on his farm in Accord when he got word of what was happening with the bank. As one of the trustees of the bank, Parker took the lead in trying to save the depositors from loss. He tried to get an insurance company to take an assignment of the mortgages, with some local banks acting as discount agents, but no institution was willing to take the assignment. Parker then devised a novel plan to try to save the bank. He asked the Equity Court to replace the temporary receiver with twenty-five prominent citizens as trustees. Parker worked day and night to convince the most prominent men in the county—presidents, bank officers, and other businessmen—to sign on as trustees. After the twenty-five trustees were recruited, and Parker's plan was approved by the court, a decree was issued scaling down the amount due to each depositor to his pro rata share of the bank's assets and enjoining the depositors from withdrawing more than 25 percent of the deposits without further order of court.

The leading newspaper in Ulster County, in an effort to embarrass the bank and injure some of the original trustees, began to publish a series of articles encouraging a "run" on the bank. The newspaper advised the depositors to draw out their allowable 25 percent as soon as the bank's doors opened, pointing out that it was likely all they were ever going to get.

As soon as the bank reopened for business, a large, unruly crowd of depositors crowded into the bank and spilled out onto the street demanding their twenty-five percent. Parker pushed past the mob with a bag of money he had obtained in New York. He was determined to prevent a panic. He leaped onto the treasurer's desk and cried, "Come on! We are ready to pay. Come on! Do you think we would waste our time on a broken bank?"[41] The crowd grew quiet, and someone asked how the depositors could be assured they would get their money. Parker answered, "I pledge you my word." The depositors departed with only a handful withdrawing their money.[42]

Parker was subsequently asked to become the president of the bank. He agreed to serve in that capacity on one condition: he was not to receive a salary. Parker remained as president of the Ulster County Savings Institution until the deposits of the bank were several hundred thousand dollars greater than they were before the doors closed. When the bank was finally solvent, Parker resigned and let the bank's employees regain control.[43] Parker resigned as president of the bank on January 23, 1904. He continued to serve as a trustee of the bank until March 31, 1911.[44]

Alton and Mary Parker had two children: John M. Parker and Bertha Schoonmaker Parker. When John was seven years old he was playing Cowboys and Indians with a neighbor boy when he was accidentally struck in the eye with an artichoke stalk. The wound became infected, and several days later he died of tetanus in his father's arms.[45] Bertha married the Reverend Charles Mercer Hall and had two children: Alton Parker Hall (called Parker) and Mary McAlister Hall.[46] Parker married Emmeline Grace and they had two children: Penny and Alton Parker III. Mary married Theodore Oxholm and they had three children: Mary Louise, Anne Mercer, and Theodore.[47]

Parker was exceptionally fond of his children. He loved to take his son to see new and unusual things and places, and on one occasion he took him to New York City to see Jumbo the elephant in P.T. Barnum's circus. He often showed a kindhearted nature toward punishing his kids. Once, when John had been disobedient, Bertha begged her father not to punish him. Parker, seated before the Baltimore heater in the back parlor, commended her for thinking of her brother's well-being.[48]

Parker never stopped trying to make his daughter into a proper young lady. He once offered Bertha the opportunity to pocket two brand-new dollar bills—all she had to do was walk properly down the street (as opposed to skipping, running, or hopping) and not look at her image in the big mirror over the mantelpiece every time she went into the dining room. If she did both of these things for a week, the money was hers. Parker never had to pay her the two dollars.⁴⁹

He also never failed to encourage his children's creativity. In 1892, when Bertha was seventeen years old, she came up with the idea to have a "Cobweb" Dance Party. Bertha, assisted by the judge and his brother, Fred, wound strings from the first floor of the home all the way up to the attic, around the attic railing, back down through every out-of-the-way place possible, over and over again. A quotation had been placed at the end of each string, and each quote was closely associated with every person who was attending the dance. Each of the twenty-five guests who attended the dance unwound the "cobweb" in search of his or her particular quote. Judge Parker joined in the event and even participated in a hilarious square dance that ended the evening.⁵⁰

Parker was close to both of his grandchildren, but he was especially close to his grandson Parker. Throughout the course of his life he kept up a healthy correspondence with both of his grandchildren. They addressed their letters to him "Dearest Baypsy" or "Dearest Baypa," and he often signed his letters "Love, Bayp." When Parker was in college at Princeton, the letters between Parker and "Baypa" often revolved around schoolwork, examinations, football and polo events (Parker was captain of the Princeton University indoor polo team, which captured the intercollegiate championship in 1922), and dating. Parker often visited his grandfather in New York, and the judge would treat him to lunch or dinner and, oftentimes, a show. Whenever Parker needed extra money for sporting equipment, new boots, or new clothes, the judge always sent Parker what he needed.⁵¹

In the late 1870s and the 1880s, Parker supervised and managed the Cortland farm where he was born and another farm that belonged to his wife's family in Accord. In 1898, Parker bought a fifty-acre parcel of land that sloped steeply down to the Hudson River. At the top of the property, which was located near the town of Esopus, stood Rosemount Hall (see figure 1.6). The 7,900-square-foot house was a two-and-a-half-story large square structure built in the Picturesque Italian Villa style. The oldest part of the house was standing when the British fleet anchored directly in front of it in 1777, the night before Kingston, New York, was put to the torch.⁵²

A broad hall, which served as a living room, ran through the center of the house. The walls of this hall were lined with a miscellaneous collection of photos and books. The rest of the first floor contained a kitchen, butler's pantry, dining room, and library. The library occupied nearly the whole southern half of the first floor (see figure 1.7). Floor-to-ceiling bookcases lined the walls, and revolving bookcases on the parquet floor contained

Figure 1.6. Parker's estate, Rosemount, circa 1904. Parker's grandson, Alton Parker Hall, is seated in the foreground. Public domain.

Figure 1.7. Judge Parker's library at Rosemount. From the *New York Herald*. Public domain.

reference books that the judge frequently consulted. A small, flat-top table was located in the bay window of the room, and a large director's table was located in the center of the room.[53] The spare wall space was hung with portraits of well-known and distinguished judges.[54]

The second floor of the grand house contained a spacious master bedroom and five smaller bedrooms, as well as several bathrooms. A columned covered porch ran the entire length of the east (river) façade.[55] It was on this porch that Parker would greet guests who traveled to Rosemount during the presidential campaign. A widow's walk on the roof was used as a place to observe the river.[56]

The house itself was surrounded with majestic trees, and the perfectly manicured lawn was ornamented with beautiful flowerbeds. The property contained a 1,400-square-foot guesthouse, an icehouse, a greenhouse, and multiple buildings for the raising of livestock (see figure 1.8). Judge Parker was particularly fond of his Poland China pigs. He maintained that the intelligence of pigs was superior to that of any other domestic animals and derived great pleasure from training them to answer to the sound of their names, to come to him whenever he was at the farm, and to play certain games that he had taught them. One sow in particular, named Mammy, seemed to be a favorite of Parker's. Although her eyes were almost covered by her ears, she could recognize the judge's voice and would trot up to him on command. She would often stand before him until the judge scratched her back with his cane. This action seemed to soothe her before she would trundle off to wallow in the mud and

Figure 1.8. A portion of the Rosemount outbuildings and grounds. From the Alton B. Parker Papers, Manuscript Division, Library of Congress, Washington, DC. Public domain.

take a nap.[57] Parker believed that pigs had "an instinctive preference for cleanliness" and had modern conveniences built for them, including two low stone buildings situated close to the main house.[58]

The farm was self-sustaining, producing eggs, milk, chickens, ducks, turkeys, pork, and lamb. Vineyards, peach trees, and apple trees lined the vegetable garden. Parker's apples achieved a modest amount of fame (those he kept in cold storage and brought out on July 4 tasted as delicious as the ones picked the prior October), and he experimented with new varieties of grapes that he often sent to friends and neighbors.[59]

A trail led down to the river and ended in a jetty that served as a mooring place for the judge's naphtha launch, christened the *Niobe*.[60] Judge Parker would often use this boat to ferry his family to Sunday services at the Kingston Episcopal Church, where Parker's son-in-law was the rector and Parker was a vestryman. Parker decided to serve as the local freight agent for a steamboat company so that his little private dock could be used for the convenience of the community.[61]

It was from this very same dock that Parker engaged in a daily morning ritual. Weather permitting, every day he was in residence at Rosemount he would put on a bathing suit, run down the hill from the house, leap off the dock, and go for a swim in the Hudson River. He firmly believed that good health was closely related to swimming in cold water.[62]

After his daily swim, Parker would saddle Tom, his beautiful, black, free-spirited stallion, and, regardless of the season or the weather, ride for an hour through his vineyards, fields, and orchards (see figure 1.9). During these rides, Parker would often work out the details of his cases and opinions.[63] After breakfast, which usually consisted of fruit, oatmeal, porridge, beefsteak or sausages or bacon and eggs, buckwheat cakes, maple syrup, hot cornbread, and two cups of coffee, Parker would formally begin his day's work, which often did not end before midnight. He would always put on evening dress for dinner, which normally consisted of soup and a roast, such as lamb or beef, followed by a salad and fruit or pie.[64]

Parker was an avid reader of magazines. He seldom read poetry, but he enjoyed reading a good novel. He was particularly fond of Dickens, Thackeray, and Scott. Jefferson was his favorite political writer. Any book or article on farming or animal husbandry was sure to catch his attention. He was fond of music and could often be heard singing old-fashioned ballads or hymns in a sweet tenor voice, accompanied on the piano by his secretary, Arthur McCausland.[65]

Figure 1.9. Parker riding his favorite horse, Tom, on the grounds of Rosemount. From *Harper's Magazine*, 1904. Public domain.

Judge Schoonmaker, Parker's first legal employer, was responsible for his initial entry into politics. When Schoonmaker hired Parker to work at his law firm, Schoonmaker was serving his second term as a county judge. Soon after Parker began working for him, Schoonmaker lost his bid for reelection after a difficult and hard-fought campaign. Schoonmaker was disheartened by the loss and announced to Parker that he was going to retire from politics. Parker felt strongly that his mentor had been unjustly defeated in the election and prevailed upon Schoonmaker to run for state senator in 1875. Parker managed Schoonmaker's campaign, and Schoonmaker was victorious. Schoonmaker's prestige was so well restored that he was elected New York State attorney general in 1877 and served as a member of the New York Civil Service Commission in 1882 and as one of the first commissioners of the Interstate Commerce Commission in 1887.[66]

After his success in managing Schoonmaker's campaign, Parker rose quickly in the Democratic Party ranks. As a delegate to the state convention in 1882, Parker was an early supporter of Grover Cleveland's candidacy for governor. He made a number of speeches in different parts of the state in support of Cleveland's gubernatorial campaign.[67] The next year, Parker declined the nomination to run for New York secretary of state.[68] When Cleveland ran for president in 1884, Parker was a delegate to the Democratic National Convention in Chicago. Following the convention, Parker gave speeches in support of Cleveland all over the state and was largely instrumental in delivering the state into Cleveland's column during the general election. When Cleveland won the election, a lifelong friendship blossomed between Parker and Cleveland.[69]

In 1885, President Cleveland offered Parker the post of first assistant postmaster general. Parker, at only thirty-two years of age, could have been headed to Washington, DC, to work in a popular reform-minded administration. Instead, he headed to the nation's capital to decline the president's generous offer. While he was speaking with the president, the newly appointed postmaster general, William F. Vilas, stopped by for a visit. Cleveland told him, "Parker says he doesn't want the [position], Colonel Vilas." Vilas asked, "May I inquire why?" Parker responded, "I cannot afford to give up a five-thousand dollar a year position, to take a three-thousand dollar position." Vilas retorted, "But I gave up a ten-thousand dollar practice to take an eight-thousand dollar position." "Well, Colonel Vilas," countered Parker, "if I had been making ten thousand a year for ten or twelve years, I too might afford to accept the President's offer." Cleveland was amused at Parker's logic.[70] Shortly after his encounter with Cleveland and Vilas, Governor Hill offered Parker the lieutenant governorship, which he also declined, prompting the *Ellenville Journal*, a local Republican newspaper, to label him the "great American decliner."[71]

In 1902, many of the top political operatives in the New York Democratic party, as well as a number of the state's newspapers, including the *New York World* and the *Brooklyn Eagle*, were urging Parker to run for governor. Several attorneys who knew the judge personally also urged him to run, noting that if he was elected governor, "with your wide acquaintance, your nomination for President in 1904 is very much more than probable."[72] Despite these urgings, Parker was hesitant to run. A writer for the *New York Evening Sun*, in an editorial titled, "The Call to Judge Parker," gave the reasons for Parker's unwillingness to run for governor: "It is asking a good deal of such a man to expect him to lay down the work of his life and forfeit an assured competence to lead a disorganized party which is short of issues, cash and credit. He is satisfied to be the lawgiver Moses, but the other Moses—no."[73] Senator David B. Hill encouraged Parker to run for governor, telling him, "In my judgment if you are nominated at this time for the office of Governor you will be elected. No other man is certain to be elected. In the event of your nomination and election I am confident that you will so discharge the duties of office that you will be nominated by the Democratic Party for the Presidency two years later, and I pledge you now to do everything that I possibly can from now on to accomplish that result."[74] In the end, Parker declined to be a candidate for governor, and the nomination instead went to Bird S. Coler, who lost to the Republican nominee, William Odell.[75]

Although Parker had a fondness for politics and was a successful political operative, his one true love was the law.

2

His Time on the Bench

As noted above, Parker first served on the bench in 1877, when he was elected to the position of county surrogate (see figure 2.1). At the age of twenty-five, Parker became the youngest surrogate ever to sit in Ulster County and the only Democrat on the county ticket to win election that year.

Figure 2.1. Parker in 1879, two years after he was elected county surrogate. From the *St. Louis Post-Dispatch Sunday Magazine*, April 24, 1904. Public domain.

In 1883, the Republicans nominated a particularly strong county ticket. William S. Kenyon (the father of Parker's law partner) was nominated to run for county judge; William Lawton, who had served as county judge for twelve years, was the nominee for county surrogate; and A. T. Clearwater was renominated for district attorney. The Democrats nominated John Van Etten for county judge, Parker for county surrogate, and John W. Searing for district attorney. Ulster County was a heavily Republican county at that time. The leading Republican newspaper in the county, *The Kingston Daily Freeman,* in speaking of the Democratic ticket, said, in part, "the admitted strength of the ticket is centered in Surrogate Parker. His administration of the office for six years has been satisfactory to the Republicans, and he is with all a courteous, dignified gentleman. He is an earnest Democratic partisan, but we hold that the man who can present a clean official record is none the worse for that. The difficulties that he is to encounter will arise from the fact that his opponent, Judge Lawton, is equally able, equally eminent, equally experienced in judicial service, and possesses a personal popularity much stronger and more far reaching than himself. *** The contest for the Surrogate's office will be a battle of giants, but on personal grounds, in spite of Mr. Parker's admitted popularity, the balance seems to be on the side of his opponent."[1]

The Kingston Daily Freeman, it turns out, was wrong. Parker was reelected to the office of county surrogate by a majority of 1,341 votes of 15,000 cast.[2] Once again he was the only victorious Democrat; the Republican nominees for all other county offices were elected by overwhelming majorities.[3]

In 1883 Parker declined to consider the Democrats' suggestion that he accept the nomination for secretary of state. In 1885 he declined to consider the nomination for the office of lieutenant governor proposed at a session of the state Democratic Party leaders. In both instances he said that he refused to run because he did not want to abandon his chosen profession—the law.[4]

When Supreme Court Justice Theodore R. Westbrook died of a heart attack near the end of 1885, Governor Hill appointed Parker to fill Westbrook's unexpired term, making the thirty-three-year-old Parker the youngest judge on the New York Supreme Court. In tendering the appointment to Parker, Governor Hill said, "In asking you to take this great office, I know I am taking out of politics my most efficient political friend as you have most unselfishly demonstrated. But I know that you can and will make a worthy career on the Bench and will enjoy the opportunities which will be constantly presented of working out justice under the law."[5]

Once Parker had been appointed to the supreme court bench, he had to resign his position as Ulster County surrogate. Upon learning of his resignation, C. N. DeWitt, a Republican member of the Ulster County Board of Supervisors, made the following comments:

> Mr. Parker deserves all that has been said about him. I do not mean to praise him. I wish to speak of him as he was and is. He does not need the varnish of praise to brighten the unsullied reputation he has achieved. His ability, his industry, his strict application to the performance of the duties of the office he held, his prominence as a lawyer . . . his wisdom shown in his decisions, decisions involving grave and complicated legal questions, involving large amounts of money, and from which appeals have been taken and always sustained by the higher courts—and then his kind and loving heart, his charity, in that he was the friend of the widow and the fatherless, and all these things are known and read by all men. For these things we honor and we love him. Our loss is great. Our gain is greater. We lose an able and efficient Surrogate, and we gain an upright and wise Judge.[6]

On September 23, 1886, Parker was unanimously nominated by the Democratic Party for a full fourteen-year term on the court.[7] Shortly thereafter, the Republicans met in convention to determine who would be nominated to run for various offices, including for Parker's seat on the supreme court. *The Albany Times* reported on the result of the Republican convention: "The Republican Judicial Convention for the Third Judicial District, met in this city today and declined to nominate a candidate against Alton B. Parker, the Democratic nominee for Supreme Court Justice. This is a remarkable tribute to Judge Parker's work and popularity, and assures him an almost unanimous election."[8]

In 1889, to resolve the perpetual problem of docket congestion, the New York state constitution was amended to create a Second Division of the Court of Appeals, permitting the governor to appoint seven justices of the supreme court to serve on the high court. Parker was one of the seven justices appointed to serve in the second division. He was thirty-seven years old. Parker served in the second division until it was dissolved three years later—after disposing of a backlog of 1,700 cases.[9] During that time he refused to consider Democratic Party suggestions that he run for governor or United States senator.[10]

When the Second Division of the Court of Appeals was dissolved in 1892, Parker was appointed by Governor Roswell P. Flower to the General Term of the First Department of the Supreme Court. The general term was a short-lived experiment to have supreme court judges sit in panels of three or four to review the decisions of the lower courts. Parker served as a member of the general term until the creation of the First Appellate Division in 1896. He then resumed his duties as a trial court judge until 1897, when he was appointed by Governor Frank S. Black to temporarily replace Justice George C. Barrett of the Appellate Division, First Department.[11]

In 1897, Parker's friends were urging him to run for chief judge of the New York Court of Appeals. Court of Appeals Judge Irving G. Vann said to Parker, "I want you to promise me to accept the nomination of your party for Chief Judge of the Court of Appeals this year." Parker replied, "Judge, I am grateful to you for the compliment, but I am so many years younger than any member of the Court of Appeals, being even *your* junior by ten years, and the junior of two members of your Court by twenty years, that I would not think of becoming a candidate for the office of Chief Judge. It would not be pleasant for me to preside over those great judges, some of whom are rapidly approaching the age when the Constitution prohibits longer judicial service."[12] Judge Vann's response: "If I did not know how my associates feel about the matter I would not be here urging you to accept a nomination from your party. Whether there is to be a Republican Chief, we cannot definitely say of course, but if there is to be a Democratic Chief I know that each and every one of my party associates would like to have you chosen."[13] When Parker protested that the odds were against his being elected, Vann stated, "True, there is no certainty that you can be elected. Indeed, the chances are against you, but I think you should value the compliment of the nomination for that great office by your party, even though it should happen that defeat may follow."[14]

Judge Vann, and others, continued putting pressure on Parker to run, and he eventually relented, even though he believed that his chances for election were slim given the fact that the Democratic Party had lost the state in the 1896 presidential election by more than 212,000 votes.

Governor Hill also believed that his protégé could not win, and he urged Parker not to run.¹⁵

On September 15, 1897, Parker's name was placed in nomination for chief judge of the Court of Appeals at a meeting of the Democratic State Committee in New York City. Surrogate James A. Betts placed Parker's name in nomination, calling him a "candidate favored alike by the bench, the bar and the citizen[s] [of] the Democratic party."¹⁶ The other candidates nominated for the office were Justice D-Cady Herrick, Charles F. Tabor, and Charles E. Patterson. When the roll was called and each committeeman named his choice, the vote stood at Parker, 27, Tabor, 10, Patterson, 8, and Herrick, 3. Parker's nomination was made unanimous on the motion of Mayor F. J. Malloy of Troy, and State Committee Chairman Elliot Danforth declared Parker to be the nominee of the committee amid generous applause.¹⁷

Parker's quest to win the position wasn't an easy one. In addition to battling his Republican opponent, United States Circuit Judge William W. Wallace, Parker had to deal with members of his own party who were working against his election. Following his nomination to run for the position of chief judge on the Democratic ticket, supporters of William Jennings Bryan questioned Parker's loyalty to Bryan and to the party and implied that he was not a true Democrat worthy of support at the polls. They began questioning whether Parker had voted for Bryan and Sewell, the Democratic nominees for president and vice president, in 1896. Parker went on the offensive and drafted a letter to Elliott Danforth, chairman of the New York State Democratic Committee, setting forth his bona fides. In it, he stated the following: "I can say to you frankly and sincerely that you can assure [the sincere friends of Mr. Bryan] that I voted for the last National Nominees of the Democratic party, as I have voted for all the regular Democratic nominees since I had a vote."¹⁸ Following this letter, the leadership of the Loyal Democratic League of the State of New York and the Progressive Democratic League of New York urged their members to "[work] for the election of Judge Parker."¹⁹

In addition, the Republicans decided that the probability of Parker's defeat would be considerably enhanced if an "independent" Democratic candidate could be nominated to run for the office of chief judge. At the time, a statute on the books provided that such a nomination could be made if fifty citizens of each of the sixty counties in the state signed a petition for it, made an appropriate acknowledgment before a notary public or a justice of the peace, and filed the petition with the secretary of state on or before the time prescribed in the statute. The Republicans, in conjunction with New York Democratic leader Jimmie O'Brien and others, selected "one Adams of Brooklyn" to receive the support of the independent Democrats in the state and set about obtaining the necessary petitions. Despite their best efforts, they were only successful in timely filing of fifty-nine of the sixty petitions, and Adams's name was not placed on the ballot.[20]

After a hotly contested fight against the Republican nominee, Parker was elected chief judge in November 1897 by a majority of 60,889 votes.[21] Parker was forty-six years old—the youngest man ever to be elected to head New York's judicial system[22] (see figure 2.2). Although he had counseled Parker to forego running for the position of chief judge, Hill was among the first to send his congratulations to Parker. He sent him a telegram on the night of the election that read, "Accept my congratulations. 'There is a hot time in the old state tonight.'"[23] Hill followed that telegram with a letter to Parker which read, in part, "My dear Judge: Well, it is over! Next to yourself, I was about the happiest man in the State yesterday.

Figure 2.2. Parker as chief judge of the New York Court of Appeals. Albany Art Union, 1904. Public domain.

Your candidacy kept getting better and better all the time, thanks to your intelligent and effective efforts. Your triumph is not only gratifying to all Democrats, but to many Republicans, and is a great personal victory. I am sure no one else could have obtained it."[24]

When he became chief judge of the New York Court of Appeals, the court was considered to be second, in both dignity and importance, only to the Supreme Court of the United States. Why was that the case? At the turn of the twentieth century, New York City, and New York state, were the undisputed capitals of commerce, industry and finance. New York lawyers, and the judges of its courts, were leading figures in the law's development, in the movement for greater uniformity in the law, and in the great debates over legal philosophy. The New York Court of Appeals, given its position as the court of last resort in the most populous state in the nation, was uniquely situated to weigh in on the most pressing social, political, and commercial issues of the day. And Parker, as the chief judge, was in a position to put his stamp on this emerging jurisprudence, either by drafting opinions himself or by assigning like-minded colleagues to author opinions.

Following his election as chief judge, Parker continued his lifelong habit of conducting original research on each case to come before the court, declining to rely simply on the citations provided by the lawyers.[25] He never forgot the nervousness he felt when he presented his first oral arguments as a lawyer and always went out of his way to try to make young lawyers feel at ease. As one lawyer reported, "the one trait born of his kindly nature which stands out is the consideration which, as a judge, he extended to the young men who appeared before him in the trial court and in presenting their arguments to the Court of Appeals. Particularly where it was known to him that the young lawyer was making his first appearance he would at once place him at ease and relieve him of his tremor and trepidation by the genial manner in which he spoke to him and would lend him every encouragement in the presentation of his case."[26]

Parker provided the following explanation for why he was so nice to young lawyers. In his first argument before the court of appeals, Parker, an exceptionally young lawyer, was opposing Judge Schoonmaker. He overprepared for the argument, spending most of the night before the case was called working on his presentation. According to Parker, "[My lack of sleep and overpreparation] was evidently apparent to Chief Judge Church at the very opening of my argument, for he first addressed me as Mr. Parker, and then paused, looking me in the eye as if he were trying to formulate a question, then he very slowly laid down his goose-quill pen and presented his question, slowly and clearly, which my opponent's argument had suggested to him. My nervousness was gone, my answer ready, and my argument even satisfactory to myself. Moreover it was on the winning side . . . During the many years I later served in the Appellate Courts I never failed to make ready to help out a young man with a question if he seemed to need it. Many a time in later years young men have thanked me for a word in time while they were on their feet before the Court. Without exception . . . I replied, 'If I helped you, the fact is due to that great Chief Judge of our Court of Appeals—Sanford E. Church.' "[27]

When the court was in session, Parker resided in a suite of rooms on the eighth floor of the Ten Eyck Hotel in Albany, where his practice was to rise at daybreak, mount a horse, and ride for an hour through the New York suburbs.[28] He was often accompanied on these horseback rides by Associate Justices Irving Vann and William Werner.[29] After his horseback ride was completed, Parker would return to the Ten Eyck, where he would spend a few hours conferring with the other judges at the "judges' table" over a cup of coffee and a roll. Following the morning meeting with the judges, Parker would walk from the hotel to the capitol building. The court sessions began at ten o'clock in the morning. Oral arguments were heard in the Henry Hobson Richardson courtroom located on the third floor of the capitol building. Parker, as chief judge, would occupy the middle chair behind the bench, flanked on both sides by the associate judges.

The World's Work published a colorful portrait of Judge Parker on the bench: "As he develops his thought in ready speech, colored by a magnetic, resonant voice, his eyes narrow, wrinkling at the corners, and he shoots an incisive, level gaze at his auditor. But as he rounds a sentence or reaches a climax, his powerful chin begins to project, and the last word bitten off is emphasized with a grim, decisive locking of the jaw. This, with the utmost courtesy. There is no egotism in the manner, and no lack of restraint. But there is concentration, driving power, and the air of grim persistence."[30] According to *The World's Work*, Parker simply loved the law: "There is a quick, alert conscience in Judge Parker, an unusually deep sense of responsibility, and a profound, enthusiastic conviction that no higher type of human opportunity exists than lies in administering justice. Justice is to him what beauty is to the artist or religion to the devotee."[31]

Once oral arguments were completed for the day, or on days when there were no oral arguments scheduled, the judges of the court of appeals met together at a round table in the high-ceilinged, red carpeted conference room located high in the state capitol building. Its windows overlooked the Hudson River. In a large, high-backed oak chair, Judge Parker, the youngest member of the court, would rest his arms on a red blotter that distinguished the chief judge's seat.[32]

Court adjourned at six o'clock in the evening. Parker would return to the Ten Eyck Hotel and have dinner, again at the "judges' table." After dinner, he would sit in the hotel lobby talking with friends or other judges from the court of appeals over an after-dinner cigar. Parker would conclude the evening in his room, reading law books, pouring over legal briefs, and writing opinions.[33]

Chief Judge Parker wrote approximately 190 published opinions between his investiture on January 1, 1898, and his resignation in August 1904. His judicial opinions were noted "for their forceful diction, comprehensive grasp of the fundamental questions involved, unsparing labor in citing precedents, close reasoning, and their tendency to disregard mere technicalities."[34] According to one newspaper of the day, "Judge Parker is not garrulous in his official opinions. He has a horror of superlatives and heroics. He sticks to the points before him, decides them in temperate language and refrains from sentimental essays or philosophic preachments."[35]

His philosophy of the constitutional relation of the courts to the legislatures was a strict Jeffersonian-Jacksonian one.[36] Parker persistently fought against the activist judges of his time, maintaining that only the legislatures had the right to legislate. Parker's guiding principle was the concept of judicial restraint. He insisted that the courts were "without authority to correct a statute even if in their judgment, it was founded on an erroneous view of sound principles of public economy."[37] An old friend of Parker's commented that his opinions "presented an average of eminent fairness: where he has sided with the minority he has shown himself very friendly to the workingman; where he has sided with the majority he has shown himself not hostile to the capitalist."[38]

Parker believed that citizens were entitled to have their disputes decided by the courts and that when asked to decide a dispute, the court of appeals was to be the final arbiter and decision-maker on the key issues of the day. He also believed, unlike the US Supreme Court, that the Fourteenth Amendment to the US Constitution was not meant to shield businesses from governmental regulation. In keeping with his philosophy of judicial restraint, Parker never accepted the argument that courts should use the Fourteenth Amendment to strike down government-enacted regulatory laws.[39]

Irving Vann, Parker's colleague on the court of appeals who insistently urged him to run for the position of chief judge, had the following to say about Parker's work as a jurist:

> The strongest characteristic of Judge Parker's mind, in my opinion . . . is its absolute fairness and impartiality. He is so constituted by nature that his mind is incapable of taking any but a logical view of a legal question, wholly divested of outside consideration . . . I could never see that his judgment was influenced in the least by his acquaintance with one of the parties to the action, or by the effect of a decision upon a political party, where, for instance, election questions were before us. He reasons with reference to broad general results rather than to special and particular effects. He seems to have in mind what is the best rule for all, now and for all time, rather than the effect upon the fortunes of the parties before him. He believes in a thorough separation of the functions of the three great departments of government in a free country—the executive, legislative and judicial. He appreciates the theory of the Constitution of 1789, and that its basic principle was a strong, sharp, well-defined line of demarcation between the powers of these three great departments. He has a profound reverence for law and believes in a strict obedience to law, and that each of these departments should be compelled to keep within its own sphere as defined by the Constitution; that the legislature should confine itself to legislation and never trespass upon the domain of the executive and the judiciary; that, with equal strictness, the judges should keep within their own department and confine themselves to the construction of the law and never venture into the region of the legislative or executive departments. It follows, of course, that he has the same strictness of view with reference to the duties of the executive department, and believes that it should be confined to the execution of the laws without interference with legislation or with the actions of the judges. Courage of his convictions is another strong characteristic in Judge Parker's mental character. Whether he stands alone or represents the views of the entire court, he expresses his conclusion with absolute fearlessness and without regard to anything except his honest conviction

that that is the right conclusion. In reaching a conclusion he advances slowly, and his mind is open to receive the views and listen to the arguments of others, but when he has weighed and considered them all deliberately and has made up his mind, no rock is firmer than his position from that time forward. His mind is conservative, and the rights of property and personal rights are always safe in his hands.[40]

As chief judge, Parker quickly gained a reputation as a humanitarian and a progressive, most notably in labor cases. Many times in dissent, but on other occasions able to convince a majority of the court to support his position, Parker argued for upholding laws that gave unions the right to strike (no minor issue in the early twentieth century), imposed limits on the hours of work in some industries, and prohibited the employment of children under the age of fourteen. In a case dealing with trusts, Parker held that it was immaterial whether a certain combination restraining trade was reasonable or not. In his opinion, even without a statute prohibiting such combinations, general legal principles prohibited them. In contract matters he was more conservative. The chief judge had a tendency to hold private litigants strictly to the letter of their contracts, even when they were pressured into the agreements by what later proved to be unconstitutional laws.[41]

In insurance cases, Judge Parker had a decided tendency to support enforcement of the strict letter of the policy. In *Tisdell v. New Hampshire Fire Insurance Co.*, 155 N.Y. 163 (1898), the defendant had issued a standard fire insurance policy to the plaintiff. Sometime after the policy was issued, the defendant attempted to cancel the policy by sending a letter to the insured indicating that the policy would be canceled five days hence and that the pro rata unearned premium would be returned by the company's agent, "as provided by the conditions of the policy."[42] The plaintiff's company suffered a fire loss and made a claim under the policy. The defendant denied the claim on the grounds that the policy had been canceled before the fire took place. The plaintiff sued, and the trial court entered judgment in favor of the defendant. The plaintiff appealed, and the intermediate appellate court reversed. The matter was then appealed to the New York Court of Appeals.

A majority of the court held that the plaintiff was entitled to the full amount of the loss because the cancellation of the policy was not effective since the insurance company had failed to also return the pro rata premium to the plaintiff at the time of the alleged cancellation (a fact that was admitted by the defendant). Parker filled a vigorous dissent, arguing that the plain language of the policy did not require the insurance company to return the unearned premium to the plaintiff at the time that it gave notice of the cancellation of the policy. He wrote:

> The first sentence provides for the cancellation of a policy. It declares that "it shall be canceled***by the company by giving five days' notice of such cancellation." In other words, the underwriter, by its contract, reserved to itself the right to cancel the contract of insurance by a notice of five days. Nothing else is provided to be done. Notice alone shall be sufficient says the contract. The language is unambiguous. It admits of no debate and requires no construction.

∼

> [The policy further states], "If this policy shall be canceled as hereinbefore provided"—referring necessarily to the company's five days' notice—"the unearned portions of the premiums shall be returned." When? At the time of the giving of the five days' notice of cancellation? Not at all; "on the surrender of the policy" is the occasion fixed by the contract for its return. The scheme of this portion of the contract, then, is to provide, *first*, for the cancellation of the policy—that is to be accomplished by the simple request of the insured, if he desires to cancel it, or by a five days' notice on the part of the company if it desires to terminate its obligation under the policy. The policy having been put an end to by cancellation, at the insistence of one party or the other, then the situation of the parties is such that the company has in its possession certain premiums which it has not earned, and which it does not desire to earn, and the other party has in his possession the policy of insurance, no longer, of course, of use to him, and of no particular value to the company, except that when it finally comes into the company's possession it of itself furnishes evidence that the unearned premiums have been paid to the insured.[43]

In Parker's view, the insurance contract was clear and unambiguous. The terms of the insurance contract required a reversal of the judgment in favor of the plaintiff and a remand of the matter to the trial court for a new trial.[44]

The majority of the court in *Sternaman v. Metropolitan Life Insurance Co.*, 170 N.Y. 13 (1902) held that the medical examiner on an application for a life insurance policy does not become the agent of the insured just because the policy stipulates that he does. Parker again took issue with the majority opinion and filed a dissent, arguing that the clear and unambiguous language of the insurance policy should be strictly enforced by the court. He wrote, as part of his dissent, "The decision about to be made is an unusually interesting one because it introduces a new feature into the law of contracts, by which persons of sound and open minds and honest purposes are cut off in one direction from freedom of contract, in that they may not agree that an intermediary shall for all purposes of the contract be deemed the agent of one of the parties if some court be of the opinion that he was the agent of the other."[45]

Parker's opinions were strongly favorable to the contentions of labor. He filed a dissenting opinion in one case and took a position that would limit the use of convict-made goods. In another case, the "dressed-stone case," he defended the right of the state to exclude the use, in public works, of material made outside the state.[46] In what was perhaps his most pro-labor opinion, Parker upheld a union's right to strike.

The plaintiff in *National Protective Association of Steam Fitters and Helpers v. Cumming*, 170 N.Y. 315 (1902), was a Scottish immigrant by the name of Charles McQueed. McQueed spent seven years working as an apprentice in the general engineering and steam-fitting industry in Scotland before immigrating to the United States in 1871. Once he arrived in the United States, he started his own contracting business, but it burned to the ground in 1888. He then decided to become a journeyman steamfitter. He applied for membership in the Enterprise Association of Steam-fitters, assuming, given his experience, that he would be quickly admitted.[47]

When McQueed made his application to the union, the officers took his name and a dollar registration fee and told him that he would have to go through the usual vetting process. When he failed to hear from the union and made an inquiry, he was told that the union book was closed but that it was expected to soon reopen. Sixteen months passed before McQueed was asked to pay twenty-five dollars, the first installment of his initiation fee, and to sit for an examination. After being kept waiting for six hours, he was called before the union committee at two in the morning and asked a single question—a question that was so confusing and convoluted that McQueed could not answer it. He was told that he had not passed and would not be admitted into the union.[48]

McQueed then decided to form his own union. He gathered up a number of steamfitters and steamfitter helpers who had either been kept out of the union or had never applied for admission and organized the National Protective Association of Steam-fitters and Helpers. For a time, business was good. But during the summer of 1897, the Enterprise Association, finding some of its men out of work, began a systematic attack on McQueed's union.[49]

Pressure was put on any contractor who hired McQueed's men to discharge them and hire Enterprise men. Strikes were started against any job site that employed McQueed or his union men. McQueed's efforts to join the American Federation of Labor and the Knights of Labor were stymied.[50]

With his union in peril and his livelihood at stake, McQueed turned to the courts. He had his lawyer file a request for an injunction. After the final hearing, the trial court granted a perpetual injunction against the Enterprise Association, finding that "the threats made by the defendants and the acts of said walking delegates in causing the discharge of the members of the plaintiff association by means of threats of a general strike of other workingmen, constituted an illegal combination and conspiracy, injured the plaintiff association in its business, deprived its members of employment and an opportunity to labor, and prevented them from earning their livelihood in their trade or business."[51]

The Enterprise Association appealed the issuance of the injunction to the intermediate appellate court. That appellate division reversed the decision of the trial court and ordered that the injunction be vacated. McQueed, at the urging of his counsel, appealed to the court of appeals.[52] Parker, writing for a 4-3 majority, affirmed the decision of the appellate division and ordered that judgment be entered in favor of the defendants.[53]

Parker reasoned that the defendant unions followed an appropriate legal path in their campaign against McQueed's union. He wrote:

> I know it is said in another opinion in this case that "workmen cannot dictate to employers how they shall carry on their business, nor whom they shall or shall not employ"; but I dissent absolutely from that proposition, and assert that, so long as workmen must assume all the risk of injury that may come to them through the carelessness of co-employees, they have

the moral and legal right to say that they will not work with certain men, and the employer must accept their dictation or go without their services.

∽

The defendant associations . . . wanted to put their men in the place of certain men at work who were nonmembers, working for smaller pay, and they set about doing it in a perfectly lawful way. They determined that if it were necessary they would bear the burden and expense of a strike to accomplish that result, and in so determining they were clearly within their rights, as all agree. They could have gone upon a strike without offering any explanation until the contractors should have come in distress to the officers of the associations, asking the reason for the strike. Then, after explanations, the nonmembers would have been discharged, and the men of the defendant associations sent back to work. Instead of taking that course, they chose to inform the contractors of their determination, and the reason for it.

It is the giving of this information, a simple notification of their determination, which it was right and proper and reasonable to give, that has been characterized as "threats" by the special term, and which has led to no inconsiderable amount of misunderstanding since. But the sense in which the word was employed by the court is of no consequence, for the defendant associations had the absolute right to threaten to do that which they had a right to do. Having the right to insist that plaintiff's men be discharged and defendants' men put in their place if the services of the other members of the organization were to be retained, they also had the right to threaten that none of their men would stay unless their members could have all the work there was to do.[54]

Parker's decision confirmed the right of a union, without limitation or restriction, to strike against non-union men or members of another union, and, in the process, it gave greater power and influence to the forces of labor unionism. It led, in many instances, to the formation of labor monopolies that controlled all the workmen in a given trade. In 1903, the powerful union organization of the Board of Building Delegates plunged New York City into a disastrous building trades strike. It would be unfair to charge Parker's decision in the *Cumming* case with the existence of union monopolies and their resulting labor strife, but it was undeniable that the decision strengthened the position of the labor bosses.[55]

Parker was a strong believer that the legislature had the right to pass laws for the betterment of society, and he was loathe to strike down legislation unless it was clearly unconstitutional. In a 1900 decision approving a state statute governing railroads that was admittedly dated and arcane, he explained that the courts nevertheless should not second-guess the legislature:

> Whether the legislation was wise is not for us to consider. The motives actuating and the inducements held out to the legislature are not the subject of inquiry by the courts, which are bound to assume that the law-making body acted with a desire to promote the public good. Its enactments must stand, provided always that they do not contravene the Constitution, and the test of constitutionality is always one of power—nothing else. But in applying the test the courts must bear in mind that it is their duty to give the force of law to an act of the legislature whenever it can be fairly so construed and applied as to avoid conflict with the Constitution.[56]

In 1889, the New York Legislature passed an act providing that anyone who performed any work for the state or any of its municipalities had to pay its laborers the prevailing rate for a day's work in the locality where the work was to be performed. In other words, a contractor could not contract to perform work for the state or a municipality and then pay his employees a low wage. In *People ex rel. Rodgers v. Coler*, 166 N.Y. 1 (1901), the plaintiff entered into a written contract to regulate and grade a street in New York City. Rodgers performed the work in a satisfactory manner, but the city refused to pay him for the work when it found out that he had failed to pay his employees at the prevailing rate, as required by the contract and the aforementioned statute. Rodgers sued to obtain the money he claimed he was owed.

Judge Denis O'Brien, writing for a majority of the court of appeals, held that the prevailing wage statute was unconstitutional because it interfered with the worker's right to contract with the employer at whatever wage amounts both found acceptable and thus denied the worker's substantive due process rights. Chief Judge Parker filed a dissenting opinion. He argued that the majority opinion was nothing "other than a judicial encroachment upon legislative prerogative."[57] According to Parker, nothing in the state constitution restricted "the power of the legislature to fix and declare the rate of compensation to be paid for labor or services performed on the public works of the state," and, as such, he objected to the court's desire to substitute its own judgment for that of the state's elected officials.[58] Three years later, in *Ryan v. City of New York*, 177 N.Y. 271 (1904), Parker's view became the majority view when the court, in an opinion written by Parker, upheld the constitutionality of the prevailing wage law and rejected the argument that the statute unlawfully infringed upon the rights of the contractor to liberty and property.[59] The *Ryan* decision was a vindication of Parker's belief that the courts should not second-guess the actions of the state legislature.

In *People v. Orange County Road Construction Co.*, 175 N.Y. 84 (1903), the defendant was indicted for having violated a provision of the New York penal code that made it a crime for anyone who contracted with the state or a municipality to require their employees to work more than eight hours in a day. The defendant argued that the statute was unconstitutional and, therefore, void. A majority of the court of appeals agreed, finding that the statute could not be upheld as an exercise of the police power vested in the legislature and ordered that the indictment be dismissed. Chief Judge Parker concurred in the result "on the sole ground that the indictment is insufficient because it fails to allege that the contract therein referred to was made subsequent to the enactment of the statute [in question]." Parker further dissented "from even the expression of a doubt as to the power of the state to enforce its constitutional mandate by making a violation thereof a crime, whether such violation arises under contract with the state or otherwise."[60]

In *People v. Lochner*, 177 N.Y. 145 (1904), Chief Judge Parker, writing for a majority of the court, upheld a maximum hours law as validly within the legislature's police power to "promote and protect the health of the people."[61] In the late 1890s, a number of New York newspapers published a series of exposés highlighting the unsanitary working conditions in and contaminated baked goods coming out of New York's unregulated bakeries. In response to this publicity, the New York legislature passed a bill limiting the hours of work in bakeries to ten hours per day or sixty hours per week and imposing sanitary regulations on all bakeries. Republican governor Levi Morton signed the bill into law on May 2, 1895.[62]

The law, which was inconsistently enforced, soon met with opposition. Joseph Lochner, who owned a bakery in Utica, New York, deliberately employed a baker for more than a sixty-hour week. He was arrested and fined twenty dollars. He continued to openly employ the baker above the legal limit and was fined again—this time fifty dollars for his second offense. Lochner refused to pay the second fine and appealed his conviction to the Appellate Division of the New York Supreme Court. The appellate court upheld his conviction, holding that Lochner was "subject to the police power of the State to regulate or control its use, so as to protect and preserve the public health, the public morals and the general safety and welfare of the public."[63] Lochner then appealed to the New York Court of Appeals.

The *Lochner* case reached the court of appeals in October 1903 and was decided by the court in January 1904. Parker authored the majority opinion and upheld the bakeshop law's constitutionality. Parker stated that the Fourteenth Amendment to the US Constitution, and a similar clause in the New York Constitution, were not intended to infringe upon the state's police power. He cited several Supreme Court decisions "sustaining statutes of different states which . . . seem repugnant to the 14th Amendment, but which that court declares to be within the police power of the states." New York case law, according to Parker, was in support of broad state intervention. In particular he cited an 1895 state court opinion: "laws and regulations of a police nature, though they may disturb the enjoyment of individual rights, are not unconstitutional . . . They do not appropriate private property for public use, but simply regulate its use and enjoyment by the owner."[64]

Parker also stated that changes in society and the economy warrant changing legislative requirements. He warned that the courts should be reluctant to substitute their judgment for that of the legislature and that the public interest is served by having sanitary bakeries. Unquestionably, the statute in question was designed "to protect the public from the use of the food made dangerous by the germs that thrive in darkness and uncleanness."[65] Parker closed his opinion by addressing the propriety of the legislature's regulation of a baker's work hours. He asserted that "the legislature had in mind that the health and cleanliness of the workers, as well as the cleanliness of the work-rooms, was of the utmost importance, and that a man is more likely to be careful and cleanly when well, and not overworked, than when exhausted by fatigue, which makes for careless and slovenly habits, and tends to dirt and disease."[66]

Three of Parker's colleagues concurred in his opinion. Three other colleagues dissented from the chief judge's opinion. By the close vote of four to three, the statute was upheld. Lochner appealed to the United States Supreme Court, which agreed to hear the case.[67]

Lochner v. New York was decided by the US Supreme Court on April 16, 1905, by a five-to-four vote. The majority opinion, which reversed the decision of the New York Court of Appeals and found the statute at issue to be unconstitutional, was authored by Parker's former court of appeals colleague Rufus W. Peckham. Peckham denied that bakers were "wards of the state" and ridiculed the notion that their work was dangerous. He argued that the law was not a legitimate exercise of police power and contended that it contravened Lochner's right to contract. According to Peckham, "there is no reasonable ground for interfering with the liberty of a person or the right of free contract by determining the hours of labor in the occupation of a baker . . . Clean and wholesome bread does not depend upon whether the baker works but ten hours per day or only sixty hours in a week."[68]

To this day, Peckham's opinion in *Lochner v. New York* is considered a stain on the high court's reputation. Former US Supreme Court Chief Justice William Rehnquist called Peckham's opinion "one of the most ill-starred decisions that [the court] ever rendered."[69] Judge John Roberts, in his 2005 confirmation hearing to be chief justice of the United States, said that in the *Lochner* case the Supreme Court was "not interpreting the law, they're making the law . . . Substituting their judgment on a policy matter for what the legislature had said."[70]

Parker's hostility toward trusts and monopolies actually predated his election as chief judge of the court of appeals. In 1896, when he was sitting as a trial judge on the New York Supreme Court, he decided in the case of *Cummings v. Union Blue Stone Company* that it was immaterial whether a combination in restraint of trade was reasonable or unreasonable. It did not matter if there was a statute in place outlawing the practice. In Parker's opinion, the existence of the power to restrain trade was forbidden by the common law.[71] He wrote, "the law assumes that any attempt by a combination of persons who get together to fix prices so that the community are made to pay more than they otherwise would pay is detrimental to trade and to the public interests."[72]

Twice while sitting as the chief judge on the court of appeals Parker had an opportunity to revisit the trust and monopoly issue. In a case involving a contract in restraint of trade, *Cohen v. Berlin Jones Envelope Co.,* 166 N.Y. 292 (1901), Parker wrote, "contracts by which the parties to them combine for the purpose of creating a monopoly in restraint of trade to prevent competition, to control and thus to limit production, to increase prices and maintain them, are contrary to sound public policy and are void . . . Such a contract threatens a monopoly whereby trade in a useful article may be restrained and its price unreasonably enhanced, and it matters not that the parties to it may have so moderately advanced prices that the sum exacted for the product seems to some persons reasonable, for 'the scope of the contract, and not the possibility of self-restraint of the parties to it, is the test of its validity.'"[73]

In the second case, *John D. Park & Sons Co. v. The National Wholesale Druggists' Assoc.,* 175 N.Y. 1 (1903), Parker recognized that there is a difference between an illegal combination in restraint of trade and an otherwise legal business combination. The *National Wholesale Druggist* case revolved around the sale by manufacturers of medicines or remedies covered by trademarks, copyrights, or patents that secured to the manufacturer or proprietor the exclusive right to manufacture and sell the same. The costs charged for these medicines, known in the trade as "proprietary goods," were exclusively within the purview of the manufacturers. Many of the manufacturers failed to maintain a uniform price for their proprietary goods and would often supply proprietary medicines to some wholesalers upon more favorable terms than to others, thus permitting large dealers to make a profit while a great number of smaller druggists found the handling of proprietary goods unprofitable. In an effort to address this problem, the National Wholesale Druggists Association, which represented 90 percent of the wholesale jobbing trade in the United States, adopted a plan that asked all proprietors to sell their goods only to wholesale and jobbing druggists—not the retail trade—at a fixed price and under which the NWDA agreed to furnish proprietors with lists of wholesalers and jobbers who could be depended on to abide by the prices set. The plaintiff did not agree to the plan and insisted on its right to sell proprietary goods at any price that it saw fit. When the manufacturers refused to sell or ship goods to the plaintiff, John D. Park & Sons filed suit against the NWDA seeking an injunction.

In affirming the denial of the entry of an injunction in favor of the plaintiff, Parker concluded that this was not a dispute involving a restraint of trade, but rather a business dispute between two competitors who sought the help of the courts to resolve their conflict:

> It will be seen, therefore, that this is a controversy between opponents in business, neither side trying to help the public. Nor will the public be the gainer by the success of either. The motive behind the action of each party is self-help. It is the usual motive that inspires men to endure great hardships and take enormous risks that fortune may come. In the struggle which acquisitiveness prompts, but little consideration is given to those who may be affected adversely. Am I within my legal rights? is as near to the equitable view as competitors in business usually come. When one party finds himself overmatched by the strength of the position of the other, he looks about for aid. And quite often he turns to the courts, even when he has no merit of his own, and makes himself for the time being the pretended champion of the public welfare in the hope that the courts may be deceived into an adjudication that will prove helpful to him. Now, while the courts will not hesitate to enforce the law intended for the protection of the public because the party invoking such protection is unworthy, or seeks the adjudication for selfish reasons only, they will be careful not to allow the process of the courts to be made use of, under a false cry that the interests of the public are menaced, when its real purpose is to strengthen the strategic position of one competitor in business as against another.[74]

One of Parker's earliest cases involving contract rights (decided six years before he was elected chief judge of the court of appeals) was *Hamer v. Sidway*, 124 N.Y. 538 (1891). The plaintiff in that case, Louisa Hamer, brought suit against the executor of the Estate of William E. Story, Franklin Sidway, for the sum of $5,000. When he was alive, William Story promised his nephew, William Story II, the sum of $5,000 if he refrained from drinking, smoking, swearing, or playing cards and billiards for money until his twenty-first birthday. Young Will Story agreed to abide by his uncle's wishes and did not engage in any of the prohibited activities until after he reached the age of majority. When he went to collect the money that was owed to him, his uncle stated that he would prefer to wait until Will was a little bit older before turning over such a large sum of money. Will agreed to wait. He then transferred his financial interest in the promised $5,000 to his wife, who in turn transferred it to the plaintiff. William Story I died before he paid any of the money to Will (or Ms. Hamer). Hamer then sued to collect. The defendant argued that he did not owe Hamer the money since there was no binding contract between the uncle and his nephew because of a lack of valid consideration. Parker held that the forbearance of legal rights by the nephew, namely the consensual abstinence from drinking, swearing, smoking, and gambling until the age of twenty-one, on the promise of a future benefit, namely the procurement of $5,000, constituted valid consideration for the purposes of forming a contract.[75] He also held that unilateral contracts were valid under New York law, and Sidway would have to pay Hamer the $5,000 out of the proceeds of the estate.[76]

Another notable Parker case involving contract rights was the case of *Ingersoll v. Nassau Electric Railroad,* 157 N.Y. 453 (1899). In that case, a street railroad in Brooklyn entered into a contract with a second railroad to permit the latter to use its tracks. Adjacent landowners complained about the agreement. Chief Judge Parker found that among the long-recognized rights acquired by railroads with their initial franchise was the right to permit other railroads to use their tracks. He held that any effort by the legislature to cancel those rights would be void since they were "vested as firmly and as sacredly as any of the rights we treasure and enjoy."[77] According to one commentator, "such a spiritual view of property rights helped establish Judge Parker's reputation as a conservative."[78]

Perhaps Parker's most famous opinion was *Roberson v. Rochester Folding Box Company,* 171 N.Y. 538 (1902). Abigail Roberson, the plaintiff, was a young woman whose photograph had been used by a flour company without her permission to advertise their product. Roberson claimed that after the advertising poster at issue was "conspicuously posted and displayed in stores, warehouses, saloons and other public places," people who recognized her picture subjected her to "scoffs and jeers" that were so humiliating that she "suffered severe nervous shock" and required the care of a doctor.[79] Roberson sued the company for $15,000, arguing that their unauthorized use of her likeness violated her common law right to privacy. The supreme court in Monroe County found in Roberson's favor. The intermediate appellate court agreed with the supreme court and held that the defendants had violated "the right of property which everyone has in his own body."[80] The case was then appealed to the New York Court of Appeals.

Parker could have assigned another judge to write the *Roberson* opinion but decided to do it himself for three reasons. One, he was concerned with the repeated tendency of the courts to overreach and decide questions that should be left to the legislature. Two, privacy was an undecided area of the law and one where more and more people were looking to the courts for some guidance. Three, a strong, decisive opinion in the case would boost his reputation as a leader and, indirectly, help to advance his efforts to secure the Democratic nomination for president in 1904.[81]

Judge Parker, in a case of first impression, dismissed Roberson's claim, holding that there was no right to privacy under New York law. He distinguished the cases relied upon by the intermediate appellate court in finding in favor of the plaintiff, noting that most of the cases really pertained to property rights, not to the right of privacy. He stated that there were no readily identifiable cases that would support Roberson's claim for invasion of privacy. He also posited that supporting the plaintiff's claim would open the floodgates to litigation. He insisted that "the attempts to logically apply the [privacy] principle will necessarily result, not only in a vast amount of litigation, but in litigation bordering on the absurd . . . The right of privacy, once established as a legal doctrine, cannot be confined to the restraint of the publication of a likeness but must necessarily embrace as well the publication of a word-picture, a comment upon one's looks, conduct, domestic relations or habits. And were the right of privacy once legally asserted it would necessarily be held to include the same things if spoken instead of printed, for one, as well as the other, invades the right to be absolutely let alone."[82] According to Parker, if legal redress were to be afforded for invasions of privacy, it was up to the legislature, not the courts, to create such a cause of action.[83]

Three judges dissented from Parker's opinion. Judge John C. Gray wrote a powerful opinion in which the other two dissenters concurred. Although he conceded that no court had specifically and unequivocally acknowledged a right to privacy, he argued that such a right "is a proposition which is not opposed by any decision in this court and which, in my opinion, is within the field of accepted legal principles."[84] He also argued that the law needs to keep pace with societal changes: "that the exercise of the preventive power of a court of equity is demanded in a novel case, is not a fatal objection . . . In the social evolution, with the march of the arts and sciences and in the resultant effects upon organized society, it is quite intelligible that new conditions must arise in personal relations, which the rules of the common law, cast in the rigid mould of an earlier social status, were not designed to meet. It would be a reproach to equitable jurisprudence, if equity were powerless to extend the application of the principles of common law, or of natural justice, in remedying a wrong, which, in the progress of civilization, has been made possible as the result of new social, or commercial conditions."[85]

According to one commentator, "although based primarily on a lack of existing precedent and a reluctance to open the floodgates of litigation, Parker's *Roberson* opinion also reflected the paternalistic chauvinism of its time."[86] Referring to the plaintiff's claim, Parker wrote that "others would have appreciated the compliment to their beauty implied in the selection of the picture for such purposes."[87] The *Roberson* decision resulted in a flood of criticism, and the press began calling for immediate legislative action. In response to the *Roberson* case, the New York legislature quickly enacted a statute allowing for a private right of action when a plaintiff's name or likeness was used for commercial purposes without the plaintiff's written consent.[88]

In the case of *People v. Place,* 157 N.Y. 584 (1899), the judges of the court of appeals, including Chief Judge Parker, upheld the murder conviction of Martha Place, who had been found guilty of killing her stepdaughter, Ida Place. Until that time, no woman had ever been executed in the state of New York, and the Hearst newspapers, in particular the *New York American,* began demanding that her sentence be commuted to life in prison, asserting that "womanhood should be spared the disgrace of the execution of one of their number."[89] The *New York American* threatened to print in the paper every day a description of Governor Roosevelt as a "woman killer" if he refused to commute her sentence. Roosevelt sought the counsel of Chief Judge Parker. Parker advised Roosevelt to convene an inquiry into Place's sanity and counseled him that if Place was pronounced sane, it would be Roosevelt's duty to carry out the sentence. After an examination by a committee of experts, Mrs. Place was found to be sane, and she was duly put to death.[90] Under the circumstances, the people approved of the decision, and the *New York American* did not carry out its threat.

Interestingly, this was not the only time that Parker's future rival for the presidency communicated with Parker or sought his advice. In early 1900, both Roosevelt and Parker were being mentioned as possible nominees of their respective parties for the office of the vice presidency. Roosevelt sent a letter to Parker about the rumors, and Parker replied. Roosevelt's letter, dated May 25, 1900, said: "My dear Judge: There are evidently two vice-presidential pebbles on the beach and each pebble cordially advises the other 'Don't!' "[91] Parker's reply: "My dear Governor: I note what you say about the two 'pebbles on the beach' and their advice to each other. It is very easy for one of them to heed the advice when it is so agreeable to its own inclinations, but how is it with the other?"[92] In accordance with their correspondence, Parker rebuffed any effort to make him William Jennings Bryan's vice-presidential running mate in 1900; Roosevelt failed to heed his own advice and joined the ticket with William McKinley.

In the spring of 1901, Roosevelt was inclined to speak pessimistically of his political position and prospects. "I intend studying law with a view to seeing if I cannot go into practice as a lawyer when my term as Vice-President ends," he told Leonard Wood. "Of course I may go on in public life, but equally of course it is unlikely . . . What I have seen of the careers of public men has given me an absolute horror of the condition of the politician whose day is past . . . and then haunts the fields of his former activity as a pale shadow of what he once was."[93] In light of his statements to Wood, Roosevelt sent inquiries throughout the nation to judges and lawyers, seeking advice concerning the best way to secure, over the succeeding four years, proper legal training and admission to the bar. One such letter was sent to Chief Judge Alton Parker of the New York Court of Appeals.[94]

Roosevelt's March 16, 1901 letter to Parker stated, in part:

> May I bother you about my personal affairs? . . . As you know, I want to study law during the next four years with a view of being admitted to the New York Bar. So far as the fates will permit I wish this to be done as quietly as possible, for if the newspapers get hold of it there is certain to be a cycle of preposterous and possibly humiliating stories. In Washington while I was there I was so busy I was only able to talk with a couple of justices of the Supreme Court and not to any practicing lawyer. From the two justices I got wholly conflicting views . . . Can you tell me what the facts are? Can I be admitted to the District of Columbia Bar without losing my residence here in New York, where of course I shall continue to vote and pay taxes, though my actual physical abode will for most of the year be in Washington? Can I then be admitted to the New York Bar, and in what way? Finally, during this summer

while I am out here at Oyster Bay, would you mind telling me what books I ought as a beginner to read?[95]

Parker responded to Roosevelt, urging him to attend the District of Columbia Law School.[96] Roosevelt wrote to Parker on May 31, 1901, thanking him for his advice:

> I am under great obligations to you. You have given me the very information I want. As soon as I get back to Washington I shall begin to attend the law school there, and when I have completed my two years' course and feel myself fit I shall apply for the examination. In all probability I shall then take advantage of your very kind offer (which it is unnecessary to say I shall treat as strictly private), to get an examination by myself, as it does not seem to me it would be advisable to court the inevitable newspaper sensation which would be worked up by the yellow press, if I appeared in public. But I shall openly identify myself with the Washington law school.
> Let me thank you again, my dear Judge. You are the first man of the two or three to whom I have applied who has given me the exact information I wanted.[97]

Roosevelt never got a chance to go back to law school. McKinley was assassinated just three months after Roosevelt wrote to Parker, and Roosevelt found himself with a country to run.

Those who tried to understand what kind of a chief executive Alton Parker would make by reviewing his jurisprudence would observe the following. He was no radical. Appeals to emotion did not sway him. He was a firm believer in the Constitution and the rule of law. When faced with an issue, he studied it carefully and took as much time as he felt necessary to reach a deliberate decision. Unlike Roosevelt, he was not brash, impetuous, or quick to act.

3

Parker's Patron

David Bennett Hill

No biography of Alton Parker would be complete without at least some discussion of the man who originally put him on the bench and who was most responsible for his run for the presidency: David Bennett Hill.

Very little is known about David Bennett Hill's early life. He was born in Havana, Chemung County, New York, on August 29, 1843. The Hills were a family of modest means. Caleb Hill, a Connecticut farmer who moved to New York in the early 1800s, was also a skilled carpenter, and he earned enough to support the family comfortably in a modest home located on Genesee Street.[1] According to one commentator, Hill's "mother was a woman of rare intelligence and force of character, and her example and training had much to do with the success of her son in [later] life."[2] David was the youngest of five children. He received his formal education at the district school and the academy at Havana, where he was apparently a somewhat better-than-average student.[3]

In his youth, David was weak and looked too sickly to all who met him. People would often say about young David, "Poor boy: he will not be with us long, but I suppose he will be better off among the angels." Hill would denounce his detractors, firmly stating, "I don't want to be an angel!"[4]

A book published in support of the 1904 Democratic nominees contains the following description of Hill as an adult:

> In stature Mr. Hill is rather below than above the average height, and, although somewhat sparsely built, he is a man of

physical strength and capable of enduring a large amount of labor and fatigue. Being a bachelor and unencumbered with domestic cares and concerns, he can devote himself exclusively to the affairs of State. He shows an intimate acquaintance with the history of his party, he is far-seeing and shrewd, is a master of debate, a sturdy antagonist when encountered, is perfectly cool and self-possessed, is skillful in the use of invective.[5] (See figure 3.1.)

His poor health as a child made Hill a studious boy, and he developed a distinct talent for composition and public speaking; he was known for his brightness and ambition.[6] He was the pupil always selected to read a composition or deliver a speech at school celebrations, and when he was still a child, many of his neighbors predicted that there were big things ahead for young David Hill. When he was seventeen, Hill attended a political rally at Watkins Glen. The scheduled speaker failed to show up, and Hill, at the urging of the committee that had scheduled the rally, took to the stage. His speech was full of good sense and displayed more than

Figure 3.1. David Bennett Hill. From *Booklover's Magazine*. Public domain.

a passing familiarity with local politics. The audience was surprised and delighted, and one of the men in the crowd was heard to remark, "He's made of the right stuff; he'll be heard from again."[7]

When he was younger, Hill helped out his family by selling newspapers and candy on the New York Central Railroad. It is said that it was during this time that an incident occurred from which originated Hill's famous and oft-repeated phrase, "I am a Democrat." Hill, in his role selling newspapers, was asked by a rider for a certain Republican paper. Hill responded, "No sir. I will not sell you that paper. I am a Democrat."[8]

Once Hill graduated from primary school he decided that he would pursue a career in law. He was promptly hired to work in the law office of Marcus Crawford, one of the two attorneys in Havana. When he was not sweeping the floors, tidying up the office, or filing papers, he studied law with his employer. To supplement his modest income, he also acted as the local agent for two New York insurance firms.[9]

When Hill turned twenty, he moved to Elmira, New York, about fifteen miles south of Havana. Once there he continued his work and studies in the offices of Thurston, Hart & McGuire, where he received an annual salary of one hundred dollars plus board. He proved to be a quick study, and in 1864 he was admitted to the New York bar. As soon as he was admitted to the bar, he received an offer to form a partnership with Judge Gabriel L. Smith, a prominent Elmira attorney. Within a few years, the firm of Smith & Hill was recognized as one of the top firms in the southwest New York area.[10]

The rapid rise of the Smith & Hill firm was due in no small part to the work of its junior partner. Hill did not possess a brilliant legal mind. Instead, his success was based on the thorough preparation of his cases, meticulous attention to detail, and, in court, "cogent arguments based upon a realistic understanding of human nature."[11] Hill's preparation was said to be so thorough that it almost cost him his life. An irate defendant in a marital suit, frustrated by Hill's masterful presentation of the plaintiff's case, attacked him with a penknife, slashing him across the neck just under the left ear. Hill proudly bore the scar from that encounter for the rest of his life.[12]

After acting for some time as assistant to the district attorney, in 1865 Hill was elected city attorney for the Village of Elmira. His work in the office drew widespread attention for the "aggressive, skillful and able manner in which he conducted his cases."[13] Having made his mark in his chosen profession, Hill turned his attention to his other great love: politics.

In 1868 Hill was selected as Chemung County's delegate to the Democratic state convention. In 1869 he became secretary of the new Chemung County Democratic Committee. At only twenty-six years of age, Hill was recognized as one of the prominent party leaders in his part of the state.[14]

In 1870, when he was only twenty-seven years old, Hill was elected to the New York state legislature from Chemung County. While serving in the legislature, he was appointed member of the Committees on Judiciary, Railroads, and Privileges & Elections.[15] He was easily reelected to the legislature in 1871 and served on the same committees. There were only two Democrats on the Judiciary Committee: Hill and Samuel J. Tilden. Tilden and Hill were instrumental in securing the impeachment of the corrupt Tammany Hall judge George G. Barnard.[16]

Although Hill had performed good work in the legislature (he had introduced, among other legislation, an ill-fated bill to abolish contract labor in prisons), he decided to return to private life and devote himself to his law practice and a newspaper he had purchased in the summer of 1870, the *Elmira Gazette*. Although it would be more than a decade before he again ran for office, he was not idle. Hill intensified his political activities and expanded his political network throughout the state. He continued to serve as the Chemung County delegate to the annual state Democratic conventions and wielded a great deal of influence in local party politics.[17] He also played a prominent role in the Democratic National Conventions of 1876 and 1884, "where he began to command attention as a leader, shaping to some extent the policy of [the Democratic] party."[18]

At the same time Hill was excelling in politics, his law partner, Judge Smith, decided to abandon the law and turn his attention to some industrial ventures. Hill then formed a new partnership with William Muller, an old friend who would go on to become a trusted political aide. Several years later, John Stanchfield, a future mayor of Elmira and Democratic candidate for governor, joined the firm. The Hill, Muller & Stanchfield firm was highly successful, and its partners did quite well financially. Hill's standing in the legal community was cemented when he was retained as lead counsel for the contestants in the Fiske-McGraw will case, a contest over the legality of a bequest of several million dollars to Cornell University.[19] Hill ultimately won the suit in the United States Supreme Court.[20] The most notable criminal case in which Hill was involved was that of Albert T. Patrick, a New York lawyer who had been convicted of murdering William Marsh Rice, an aged millionaire, in 1900. New York

County paid Hill $10,000 to represent the prosecution before the court of appeals. Thanks to Hill's fine work, the conviction was upheld on appeal.[21]

In 1881 Hill decided to once again run for public office and was elected alderman from Elmira's Third Ward. Encouraged by this small victory, Hill decided to seek his party's nomination for mayor of Elmira in the spring of 1882. Hill obtained the nomination and, ultimately, the office. He won by 352 votes of 3,650 cast.[22] Hill only occupied the mayor's seat for six months. On September 22, 1882, Hill was nominated by acclimation to run for lieutenant governor. Grover Cleveland was nominated to run for governor. Hill threw himself heartily into the campaign, giving speeches in support of the ticket all over the state. On November 7, 1882, Cleveland and Hill, the bachelor mayors of Buffalo and Elmira, were elected with a plurality of more than 192,000.[23]

For the next two years Hill spent his time working in the relative obscurity of the lieutenant governorship. Although his term was "uneventful and inconspicuous," he continued to be active in party circles. He spent a great deal of time with several other rising young Democrats, discussing politics and party strategy and always keeping an eye on his political future.[24]

The year 1884 was a presidential election year. Hill, sensing an opportunity to advance his own career, was among the first to urge support for Grover Cleveland's bid for the presidency. Hill arrived at the Democratic National Convention in Chicago, Illinois, with a large group from the southwestern part of New York to lend vocal support to Cleveland's candidacy. Once Cleveland secured the nomination, Hill campaigned for the Cleveland-Hendricks ticket and was delighted when Cleveland was elected president.[25]

Cleveland resigned as the governor of New York on January 6, 1885, clearing the way for David B. Hill to take over as governor.[26] There was a general feeling of guarded confidence concerning the future of the state and the party under the new governor. Indeed, Hill found warm and cordial support from a number of influential newspapers and periodicals.[27]

Hill's first annual message to the legislature struck a conciliatory note by urging the Republican legislature to "sink partisan differences in behalf of good government."[28] He urged the legislators to consider introducing legislation to bar the use of prison labor, introducing more flexibility in the voter registration laws for naturalized citizens, implementing and extending the principle of freedom of worship, and enacting several measures in the interests of labor. Not surprisingly, the Republican-led legislature did little to act on Hill's suggested legislation.[29]

On September 24, 1885, Hill received the Democratic nomination for governor and the opportunity to move past the claim that he was a "backdoor governor."[30] When Hill captured the nomination in the fall of 1885, he turned to the thirty-three-year-old Alton B. Parker to be his campaign manager. At Hill's insistence, Parker was made chair of the New York State Democratic Committee—the youngest person ever to hold the post. Much like the work he had performed for Judge Schoonmaker a few years earlier, Parker made Hill's campaign a personally exhausting one. He worked tirelessly to get Hill, and the rest of the Democratic ticket, elected. He visited every region of the state, orchestrating a vigorous series of organizational meetings and campaign speeches.[31] He became acquainted with the Democratic leaders in the state, talked to voters, and pushed home the Democratic arguments.

Largely as a result of Parker's masterful work, all of the Democratic candidates were elected to office. Hill was elected governor by a plurality of fifteen thousand votes. Parker had managed a brilliant, successful campaign.[32] The *New York Sun* proclaimed, "Congratulations are especially due to Hon. Alton B. Parker. He has borne the burden of the fight, and proves himself a political leader of very high quality."[33] The *New York Daily Graphic* said, "[Parker] was alert, vigorous, positive and strong; quick in perception and instant and inflexible in decision . . . Parker proved just the man for the exigency, exactly suited to reconcile the new element of the situation with the old methods in which, like Governor Hill, Tilden trained him."[34]

Although Hill was elected governor in his own right, the Republicans maintained firm control of the outrageously gerrymandered state legislature. As a result, Hill spent most of the next three years battling to get things accomplished in Albany. In 1888, Hill was once again selected by the Democrats to be their nominee for governor. Although Hill was heavily involved in his own campaign for reelection, he devoted a great deal of time to campaigning for the national ticket of Cleveland and Thurman. He wrote dozens of letters to friends and political acquaintances, urging them to get as many voters to the polls as possible to "pull straight for the whole ticket." He gave dozens of speeches in New York, Connecticut, and Indiana on behalf of the national slate. He did all of this at his own expense, refusing to be reimbursed by the national committee.[35]

At the end of the day, Hill was sent back to the governor's mansion; Cleveland was sent packing. Although Hill played no part in Cleveland's defeat and had labored tirelessly to prevent it, many laid the blame for the national ticket's failure to carry New York squarely at Hill's feet. When the results of the election were announced, and it was clear that Hill carried New York and Cleveland didn't (thereby costing Cleveland the election), Hill wrote to his friend Alton Parker:

> This ends me as a presidential candidate, whether for nomination or election. No explanation either by myself or my friends can make headway against the logic of events. Unjust as these inferences are, nothing will ever convince the party that I was not to blame in some way, either direct or mysterious, for the result in this State which showed my election and the defeat of the Presidential ticket with Mr. Cleveland at its head. It is one of the penalties of politics that no man must succeed at the expense of his associates on a party ticket—whether this success comes with or without his procurement or knowledge.[36]

Hill's second full term as governor played out much the same as the first. The Republicans continued to have control of the legislature, and they fought Hill at almost every turn. Despite the difficulties he faced in the legislature, Hill was able to get a number of things accomplished during his two terms as governor, including the recognition of Labor Day as a state holiday, institution of the Saturday half-holiday, insurance of the right of religious liberty in public institutions, the establishment of a "Forest Preserve" and the creation of a commission to supervise the same, expediting the final disposition of murder cases by allowing for direct appeal to the court of appeals, replacing hanging with electrocution as the means of execution in the state, originating legislation to outlaw child labor, requiring certain classes of corporations to pay wages on a weekly basis, introducing industrial training in schools, and requiring state arbitration in disputes between employers and employees.[37]

The New York Democrats had a big year in 1890. After eight years in the minority, the Democrats won a majority in the state legislature—and the right to select the next senator from the state of New York. The Democratically controlled legislature elected Hill to the US Senate in January 1891. Hill accepted the Senate seat despite being advised by Parker, William Sheehan, and his personal secretary, T. S. Williams, to refuse the position (they all feared that taking the Senate seat would hurt his chances to obtain the Democratic nomination for president in

1892).³⁸ Hill decided that he would finish out his term as governor and, as a result, did not take his seat in the Senate until January 7, 1892. For the last twelve months of his term as governor, Hill was derisively called "Governor-Senator Hill."³⁹

During the greater portion of his term in the Senate, Hill served as chairman of the Committee on Immigration and as a member of the Judiciary, Fisheries, Interstate Commerce and Organization of the Executive Department Committees.⁴⁰ He was soon known as "an indefatigable and effective working member" of those committees.⁴¹ His knowledge of the law, politics, political economy, and the statecraft of foreign countries allowed him to play a prominent role in the discussion of all the great national questions of the day. As a senator, he was instrumental in the repeal of the Sherman Silver Purchase Act (which provided for the issuance of legal tender notes sufficient in amount to pay for 4.5 million ounces of silver bullion each month at the prevailing market price). He introduced, and after a long contest secured, the enactment of a law allowing Confederate veterans to be eligible for appointment in the US Army or Navy. He also was an earnest advocate of the repeal of the Federal Election Laws, which had long allowed unfair interference with the conduct of state elections.⁴² He argued against the constitutionality of the proposed income tax law, and after its passage, he drafted a brief that, when used in the US Supreme Court, resulted in a decision that the law was unconstitutional.⁴³

While serving in the Senate, Hill wrote his protégé a letter outlining his political philosophy. According to Hill, "I believe in <u>some</u> <u>one</u> looking after details: I believe that eternal vigilance is the price of being on top in politics: I believe in organization: I believe that state leaders must be in close touch & in constant communication with local leaders."⁴⁴ Good advice that, as we shall see, was largely ignored during the general election of 1904.

In 1892, Hill was the leading contender for the Democratic presidential nomination, running on a platform of bimetallism. He had apparently broad support in the South and the Midwest and the eastern part of the country. Two things derailed his chances of obtaining the nomination: his decision to call the New York State Democratic Convention for late February (when it was normally held in the late summer months) and Grover Cleveland's decision to once again run for the presidency. Not surprisingly, the "Snap Convention" in February 1892 pledged all seventy-two delegates to Hill, but most considered it to be "machine politics in its most naked form."⁴⁵ Rank-and-file Democrats were outraged at the unsavory methods employed by the senator from New York to try to capture the nomination. And Cleveland's decision to reenter the political arena gave those who were looking for an alternative to Hill their champion.[46]

Just prior to the start of the 1892 Democratic National Convention in Chicago, Hill was hopeful that enough uncommitted delegates could be convinced to support him and he would win the nomination. Hill's advisers arrived at the convention and set to work trying to get the uncommitted delegates to throw their support to Hill. Their efforts were largely unsuccessful. Cleveland won the nomination on the first ballot; Hill managed to win only 114 votes.[47] Hill's presidential aspirations were over.

In the aftermath of his loss, Hill declined an invitation to attend Cleveland's notification ceremony, and he refused to serve on the national advisory committee. His long silence following the conclusion of the Democratic National Convention led Cleveland and his campaign managers to believe that Hill was either planning to sit out the campaign or, worse, was plotting some form of treachery.[48] In the end, Cleveland had nothing to worry about. On September 19, Hill broke his long silence. In a speech to a mass meeting of Brooklyn Democrats, Hill delivered a blistering indictment of the Republican administration and a vigorous appeal for support of the Democratic ticket.[49] He then embarked on a speaking tour up and down the length of the state, extolling Cleveland's virtues and impugning President Harrison's record. In the November election, New York gave Cleveland a heavy majority and returned him to the White House.[50]

In 1894, while still serving in the Unites States Senate, Hill was pressured into once again running for governor of New York. All signs in 1894 pointed to an overwhelming defeat for the Democrats in the fall elections. Hill was nominated at the state Democratic convention, and when he declined the nomination, the delegates refused his declination and adjourned the convention with him as their nominee. When Hill pleaded with the state committee to substitute another candidate, he was rebuffed. Tammany Boss Charles Murphy told Hill, "You run in the fat years and now you must take your chance in the lean year."[51] Hill knew he was being sacrificed, but he agreed to run. On election day, the Republican nominee, Levi P. Morton, bested Hill by 150,000 votes.[52]

By 1896, Hill was recognized as one of the "political giants" of the Democratic Party. A profile of Hill published in that presidential election year noted that he was extremely popular with his own party and had reached the pinnacle of party politics through a combination of "study, hard work . . . and . . . natural ability."[53]

On July 6, 1896, the Democratic National Committee met at the Palmer House Hotel in Chicago, Illinois, to decide the temporary roll of the upcoming Democratic National Convention and select the temporary officers of the convention. Hill was selected as the choice of the committee to be temporary chairman of the convention.[54] On the first day of the convention, July 7, 1896, immediately after the opening prayer, William F. Harrity, chairman of the Democratic National Committee, recognized Alabama delegate Henry D. Clayton, who presented a minority report recommending that Virginia senator John W. Daniel be chosen as temporary chairman in lieu of Senator David B. Hill.[55] The reason: the convention was dominated by William Jennings Bryan's pro-silver delegates, and Hill, an avowed gold Democrat, allegedly was not acceptable to a majority of the delegates.[56] New Jersey delegate Allen L. McDermott gave an impassioned speech in support of Hill (as did Connecticut delegate Thomas M. Waller, New York delegate John R. Fellows, and West Virginia delegate J. W. St. Clair).[57] In the end, the eloquence of Hill's supporters failed to carry the day, and, by a vote of 556 to 349, John Daniel was elected temporary chairman of the convention.[58]

Although Hill was not elected temporary chairman, he did play a big role at the convention. The delegates who supported the gold standard wrote a minority report on the platform (which stated flatly that the gold standard was "not only un-American but anti-American") and insisted on debating that issue—and others—on the floor of the convention. Hill was the first orator to speak on behalf of the minority report—and it was apparent that the silverite platform filled him with contempt. "It smacks of Populism and Communism," he had written in an article that appeared in the July 9, 1896, issue of the *New York World*. He told the delegates, "I am a Democrat, but I am not a revolutionist." He questioned whether the delegates really wanted to force longtime stalwarts out of the party "to make room for a lot of Republicans and Populists and political nondescripts who will not vote your ticket at the polls." No Democrat, Hill suggested, could be elected without carrying New York; only one ever had (James Buchanan in 1856). According to Hill, the Democrats would surely taste defeat in 1896 if bimetallism became "a question of patriotism" or "bravery" instead of a question of "business" and "economics."[59]

Hill's comments fell on deaf ears. It did not help that they were followed in close succession by Bryan's "Cross of Gold" speech, recognized by most historians as one of the greatest political speeches of all time.

The minority report was voted down. The free coinage of silver would be the central issue of the Democratic platform of 1896.[60]

Following the convention, Hill was undecided as to what role he would play in the campaign. He was asked by Daniel Lamont to join him, and many others, in the new Gold Democratic party. Hill refused to bolt the Democratic Party, knowing that the Gold Democrats would be beaten. According to Hill, "I do not like the martyr business as a steady job."[61] Although Hill did not join the Gold Democrats, he refused to campaign for Bryan. When asked if he would support the Democratic ticket in the fall, Hill stated, "I am a Democrat still—very still."[62]

Hill's Senate term was set to expire on March 3, 1897. On January 14, 1897, Hill was nominated to run for reelection by the New York Democratic caucus. The Republicans nominated Thomas C. Platt, who had briefly been a US senator in 1881, for the seat. Because senators were not directly elected by the people, but rather by the state legislature, Hill's fate was in the hands of the Republican-controlled assembly in Albany. On January 20, 1897, by a vote of 147 to 42, Thomas Platt was elected senator from New York.[63] David B. Hill would never again hold elective office.

Hill attended the 1900 Democratic National Convention in Kansas City, Missouri, as a delegate at large from New York.[64] Although he did not campaign for William Jennings Bryan in the 1896 presidential contest, he seconded Bryan's nomination for president at the Kansas City convention, noting, in part, that "from the closing of the polls four years ago until this very hour there never was a possibility of any other nomination being made."[65] On the third day of the convention, New York State Senator Thomas F. Grady placed Hill's name in nomination for the office of vice president. Hill was recognized by the chair and indicated that he was not interested in being a candidate. He stated, in part:

> While I greatly appreciate the unexpected action of the delegation from New York, it is proper for me to say that it is without my approval. I appreciate also the manifestations of friendliness on the part of the delegates from other States, but I feel that it is my duty to rise here and now and say to you that for personal reasons, and good and valid reasons, I cannot accept this nomination.
>
> I have not been a candidate. I do not desire to be a candidate and I must not be nominated by this convention.

There are gentlemen here whose names have been or will be presented to this convention, any one of which names are stronger and more satisfactory than my own.[66]

Despite Hill's statement that he could not—and would not—accept the nomination, he received 207 votes on the first ballot.[67] Ultimately, the nomination went to Adlai E. Stevenson, Grover Cleveland's former vice president (and the grandfather of Adlai E. Stevenson II, the 1952 and 1956 Democratic nominee for president).[68]

Although Hill wasn't able to capture the Democratic nomination for president, he was intent on making sure that Alton Parker would be able to succeed where he had failed. In 1903 and 1904 he began promoting Parker as the ideal candidate to carry the party past the failed experiment of Bryanism; he wanted to reunite Clevelandites and Bryanites under new leadership and on new issues.[69] He urged Parker to come down from the bench and deliver remarks designed to highlight his potential candidacy. He lined up support for Parker from Democratic financiers such as August Belmont and Thomas Fortune Ryan. He committed the New York delegation to Parker prior to the Democratic National Convention and was instrumental in drafting the New York platform—a platform that he hoped would serve as the basis for the national Democratic platform.[70] And he attended the Democratic National Convention in St. Louis as a New York delegate at large, determined to do whatever was necessary to see Parker win the nomination.[71]

4

Turn-of-the-Century Politics

In the 1880s, big businesses, and the men who ran them, were benefiting from high protective tariffs. The tariffs, which were essentially taxes on foreign goods entering the country, served two purposes. One purpose was to raise revenue for the federal government. The second purpose was to protect domestic manufacturers—and their workers—from foreign competition.[1]

The Democrats, fashioning themselves as "tariff reformers," wanted to enact a reduction in import duties. The Republicans, by contrast, argued that lower tariffs would expose American industry and workers to foreign competition and, in the process, jeopardize the economic well-being of the country.[2] The stage was set for a showdown over the tariff.

In December 1887, Grover Cleveland, the first Democrat to be elected president since James Buchanan in 1856, risked his political fortunes by devoting his entire annual address to Congress to a dramatic demand for a downward revision of the tariff. The Republicans, who favored the high tariff, accepted the challenge to end Cleveland's tenure in the White House and nominated Benjamin Harrison for president. The 1888 election became a campaign of education on the tariff. The Republicans did a better job of selling their policies in the press, and Harrison won a clear victory.[3]

Harrison quickly found out that running the country was not an easy job. He became involved in party squabbles over patronage. Republican support for prohibition and a push for the exclusive use of the English language in public schools alienated many voters. The introduction of a new protective tariff alienated many more. The Democrats won back the House of Representatives in the midterm elections of 1890. In that year, the Democrats and the Republicans managed to put party politics aside and agreed to pass two pieces of economic legislation with at least some symbolic value: the Sherman Anti-Trust Act of 1890 was designed to curb the excesses of big business, and the Sherman Silver Purchase Act of 1890 proscribed the coinage of at least some silver.[4]

The presidential election of 1892 turned out to be a rematch of 1888. This time, Cleveland bested Harrison, and in the process he became the only president to serve two nonconsecutive terms in office.[5] By the time Cleveland was elected to his second term, the country was in turmoil on various fronts. The workplace had become a battleground between business and labor. Workers fought their employers for higher wages, the right to organize, and some control over their working conditions. Railroad workers, miners and mill workers were striking across the country. At the same time, the nation's farmers were hurting. In the South, they were exploited by landlords and suffered under the inequalities of the crop lien; in the West they lived with high mortgages and even higher marketing costs. Everywhere they lived with low prices for their crops. The anger of the laborers and the farmers flowed into a broad national fear about the unchecked growth of the giant corporations that seemed to monopolize trade.[6]

President Cleveland, never a fan of the Sherman Silver Purchase Act, was determined to repeal it—and to lower the tariff. Then disaster struck. The Panic of 1893 turned into what was the worst economic depression in US history (even today, it stands second only to the Great Depression of the 1930s). Amid rampant unemployment and economic turmoil, Cleveland's policy backfired. The tariff revision, badly handled by the administration, pleased almost no one. Repeal of the Silver Purchase Act alienated the farmers and western ranchers and failed to have any real impact on the floundering economy. Cleveland decided to send federal troops to Chicago to keep the railroads running during the Pullman Strike of 1894—a move that pleased conservatives, but understandably alienated labor.[7]

By 1894, President Cleveland's policies in support of the gold standard had split the Democratic Party in two. Debtors, laborers, and farmers wanted more money put into circulation regardless of its base, and they joined with western silver miners in demanding a return to bimetallism. In theory, dramatically increasing the money supply by minting silver coins would be inflationary and assist those who were suffering from stagnant or falling wages, increasing debt loads and falling crop prices. Conservative business interests continued to advocate for the gold standard, fearing that unlimited silver coinage would destroy the value of the dollar.[8]

By the time the two major political parties met in convention in 1896, the year was shaping up to be the "Battle of the Standards"—the Republicans calling for strict adherence to the gold standard, but many Democrats arguing that the country should return to bimetallism and the prior established relationship between silver and gold at the ratio of 16 to 1 (meaning that sixteen ounces of silver were to be equal in value to one ounce of gold).[9] This fervent belief in bimetallism caused southern and western farmers to rally in 1896 around William Jennings Bryan's populist call for the free coinage of silver. In his famous speech at the 1896 Democratic National Convention, Bryan, his arms raised like a crucified Christ, proclaimed to the approving roars of the crowd, "You come to us and tell us that the great cities are in favor of the gold standard. We reply that the great cities rest upon our broad and fertile prairies. Burn down your cities and leave our farms, and your cities will spring up again as if by magic, but destroy our farms, and the grass will grow in the streets of every city in the country . . . Having behind us the producing masses of the nation and the world, the laboring interests, and toilers everywhere, we will answer their demands for a gold standard by saying to them: You shall not press down upon the brow of labor this crown of thorns! You shall not crucify mankind upon a cross of gold!"[10]

Bryan, who was a former two-term congressman and unsuccessful Senate candidate, was not considered a serious contender for the Democratic nomination in 1896. The leading candidates for the nomination were Richard P. Bland, US representative from Missouri; Robert E. Pattison, governor of Pennsylvania; and Horace Boies, governor of Iowa.[11] But Bryan's "Cross of Gold" speech won him the nomination on the fifth ballot.[12]

Bryan had very little money, and even less newspaper support. As a result, he traveled more than eighteen thousand miles by rail, speaking to audiences in big cities and small towns. He crisscrossed the country, urging his listeners to vote their ideals and their consciences rather than their fears and their wallets. His Republican opponent warned his followers that Bryan would repudiate the Supreme Court, wreck the economy, and tear the nation apart, class by class and region by region. McKinley promised every voter a full dinner pail, advanced prosperity, and social harmony.[13]

For a time, it seemed as if Bryan might actually win. His instant celebrity was galvanizing white workers, including many who had taken little interest in politics before the 1896 election. Unions across the country were overwhelmingly supporting "The Boy Orator." But, ultimately, the money pouring into the Republican campaign coffers from corporations afraid that Bryan and his policies would wreak financial havoc on the country began to stem the tide (the Republican campaign fund was $7 million; the Democrats only had $300,000 to spend).[14] The Republicans used that money to hire union officials to stump for McKinley, hire fourteen hundred speakers to canvass the nation on McKinley's behalf, and publish and distribute some two hundred million pamphlets to remind the voters that joblessness was tied to Democratic policies and that the protective tariff was their friend.[15]

In the end, McKinley received 51.1 percent of the popular vote to Bryan's 47.7 percent. He won with a plurality of more than six hundred thousand votes. In the Electoral College, McKinley received 271 electoral votes, Bryan 176. The heavily populated industrial states of the Northeast and Midwest cast most of their votes for McKinley. Bryan was able to carry only the solid South and the Great Plains and Mountain West states.[16] Despite campaigning extensively in the Midwest, Bryan was unable to carry the critical states of Wisconsin, Illinois, and Indiana, which Cleveland had managed to win four years earlier.[17]

The 1900 election largely amounted to a replay of 1896. The Republicans renominated President McKinley and hammered away again at their message of pro-business conservatism.[18] The Democratic platform of 1900 was a virtual duplicate of their 1896 document, and William Jennings Bryan was renominated without any real contest.[19] Despite evidence that the gold standard had improved the nation's economy, Bryan's views remained unchanged. He had a tendency to see all issues in terms of a struggle between good and evil, and there was little flexibility in his philosophy.[20] This suited the Republicans just fine. When Bryan tried to revive the free silver issue, Republican operative Mark Hanna gloated, "Now we've got him where we want him. Silver, silver, silver, that's our target."[21] Bryan again attacked the Republican "plutocracy" and charged that McKinley's protective tariff and gold standard policies had caused explosive growth of the big business trusts.[22]

But 1900 was not a total repeat of 1896. A new issue had emerged: foreign policy. Starting in the mid-1890s, thanks in large part to the "yellow journalism" of William Randolph Hearst and Joseph Pulitzer, a majority of the country found itself moved by the plight of the Cubans, who were desperately fighting to free themselves from Spanish rule. By the time McKinley took office in 1897, the fervent clamor to "free Cuba" posed a political and diplomatic problem for his administration. When the USS *Maine* blew up and sank in Havana Harbor on February 15, 1898, the demand that the United States go to war against Spain reached a fever pitch. McKinley eventually gave in to the pressure and led the country into the Spanish-American War. The United States not only claimed victory within two short months, with very few casualties, but it also gained a new hero: Theodore Roosevelt, who led his regiment of "Rough Riders" in a glorious charge up San Juan Hill. As a result of the war, the United States unexpectedly obtained three new colonial possessions: Puerto Rico, Guam, and the Philippine Islands.[23]

Bryan and the Democrats adamantly opposed acquisition of the Philippines as a colony and attempted to make Republican imperialism an issue in the 1900 campaign. The Republicans simply ignored the issue and continued to waive the flag. By the time the election rolled around, foreign policy was not the divisive issue that the Democrats had hoped it would be. One farmer who listened to Bryan rail against imperialism reportedly stated, "Price of hogs is 60 cents a pound. Guess we can stand it."[24]

In the end, the country was prosperous, and the voters saw no reason to turn their backs on McKinley and the Republican party. Although Bryan retained the Democrats' base in the South and border states, he lost five western states that he had carried in 1896 and even lost his home state of Nebraska.[25] McKinley increased his majority of the popular votes by one hundred thousand.[26]

McKinley did not have long to savor his electoral success. On September 6, 1901, President McKinley was shot by anarchist Leon Czolgosz while attending the Pan-American Exhibition in Buffalo, New York. He died eight days later. After McKinley's death, Theodore Roosevelt, at the age of forty-two, became the youngest man ever to serve as president. Roosevelt, who was essentially placed on the ticket with McKinley to remove him from New York state politics, began an energetic pursuit of domestic and foreign policies that set the stage for the 1904 election.[27]

On the domestic side, Roosevelt breathed new life into the Sherman Anti-Trust Act. Although the Act had been intended to combat the growth of monopolies during the late nineteenth century, lax enforcement and narrow interpretations of the act had rendered it toothless. Roosevelt ordered the Justice Department to invoke the act against financier J. P. Morgan and his attempts to consolidate his railroad holdings. Roosevelt also intervened in a threatened coal strike in Pennsylvania and helped to broker an agreement between labor and management. He surprised many on the labor front by backing away from the outright hostility shown by the federal government toward unions and the working class in previous strikes. He also committed the federal government to a program of conservation by expanding the National Park System.[28]

Roosevelt also built a dynamic foreign policy record. He ended the Filipino insurrection and reiterated America's claim on the Philippines and a continued commitment to imperialism. He aided the rebels in Panama who were fighting for independence from Colombia and, once an independent Panamanian government was established, negotiated for the building of the Panama Canal. The idea of carving a canal through Central America to link the Atlantic and Pacific Oceans had been the dream of many Americans for dozens of years, and Roosevelt had made that dream a reality.[29]

William Jennings Bryan had obtained the Democratic nomination and had campaigned and captured popular and electoral votes based on an alliance of states in the South and West. His populism had attracted farmers and ranchers, laborers, miners, and mine owners to the Democratic ticket. In 1896, Bryan captured all of the southern states and all of the states west of the Mississippi River except for Iowa, Minnesota, North Dakota, Oregon, and California. In the 1900 rematch with McKinley, Bryan again carried the solid South but yielded some of his 1896 western gains to McKinley, losing Kansas, Nebraska, South Dakota, Utah, Washington, and Wyoming in the process.

Following Bryan's back-to-back defeats, the conservative members of the Democratic Party (including Hill, William Sheehan, John Sharp Williams, Richard Olney, and August Belmont) were intent on regaining control of the party. The Old Guard Democrats were committed to reorganizing, and they wanted to move the party beyond the dead issue of free silver and return it to the pro-business philosophy and urban North/rural South base that had twice elected Cleveland to the presidency.[30]

The May 4, 1904, issue of *Puck,* the country's first successful humor magazine, contained a cartoon centerfold that depicted the reorganization efforts. In the cartoon, an ornately decorated camel, draped in a blanket emblazoned with the word "REORGANIZATION," gallops through the desert of Bryanism. Parker is holding the reins of the camel and is turned backward waving to Bryan, who has dug his heels into the sand while pulling on the camel's tail, trying desperately to get the camel to stop. A tiny, yellow-clad William Randolph Hearst has his arms wrapped around Bryan's waist, also trying to stop the forward progress of the camel. David Hill, John Sharp Williams, Arthur P. Gorman, Richard Olney, and Grover

Cleveland sit astride the camel, directly behind Parker, headed for the oasis of "Sane Democracy."[31]

As the *Puck* cartoon made clear, the reorganizers were united in their desire to make sure that Bryan was not the standard bearer in 1904. The question they had to answer was, who would that standard bearer be?

5

The Possible Democratic Candidates in 1904

Toward the end of 1903, the field of potential Democratic nominees was beginning to solidify. For many months, Democratic party operatives and editorialists were urging former President Grover Cleveland to seek the nomination for a fourth time.[1] On November 25, 1903, Cleveland sent a note to St. Clair McKelway, the editor of the *Brooklyn Eagle*, emphatically declaring that he would not, under any circumstances, accept the nomination or be a candidate for president.[2] Cleveland wrote:

My Dear Mr. McKelway:

I have waited for a long time to say something which I think should be said to you before others.

You can never know how grateful I am for the manifestation of kindly feeling toward me, on the part of my countryman, which your initiative has brought out. Your advocacy in the *Eagle* of my nomination for the Presidency came to me as a great surprise; and it has been seconded in such manner by Democratic sentiment that conflicting thoughts of gratitude and duty have caused me to hesitate as to the time and manner of a declaration on my part concerning the subject—if such a declaration should seem necessary and proper.

In the midst of it all, and in full view of every consideration presented, I have not for a moment been able, nor am I now able, to open my mind to the thought that in any circumstances, or upon any consideration, I should ever again become the nominee of my party for the Presidency. My determination not to do so is unalterable and conclusive.

This you, at least, ought to know from me: and I should be glad if the *Eagle* were made the medium of its conveyance to the public.

Very sincerely yours,

Grover Cleveland[3]

Upon receiving Cleveland's declaration, McKelway immediately declared his preference for Judge Parker.[4] Cleveland, who liked the judge's court record and conservatism, also endorsed Parker, calling him "the very best candidate in sight" to lead the Democratic party in the right direction and also noting that "I do not believe that the closest scrutiny of Judge Parker's entire course will develop a single instance of cowardice or surrender of conscientious conviction."[5]

With Cleveland's withdrawal from consideration, the potential Democratic nominees were essentially divided into two camps: those who were loyal to Cleveland and his ideals and represented the more traditional elements of the party and those who wished to push a more liberal and progressive agenda. Maryland Senator Arthur Pue Gorman was certainly in the first camp, and in many political circles it was privately expressed that he would probably obtain the Democratic nomination[6] (see figure 5.1). Gorman was born in Howard County, Maryland, on March 11, 1839. He received a public school education, and in 1852 he became a page in the United States Senate. He held that position until 1866, at which time he became the Senate postmaster.[7]

On September 1, 1866, Gorman was appointed collector of internal revenue for the Fifth District of Maryland. He held that office until March 1869. Three months later he became a director in the Chesapeake & Ohio Canal Company. He became the president of Chesapeake & Ohio in 1872. In November 1869, Gorman was elected to the Maryland legislature. He was reelected to the legislature in 1871 and was chosen to serve as Speaker of the House. He was elected to the Maryland Senate in 1875. In 1880, he was chosen to serve as one of Maryland's United States senators. He was reelected a US senator in 1886, 1892, and 1903.[8] Gorman was the first cousin of Henry G. Davis, the former senator from West Virginia (and the ultimate Democratic nominee for vice president in 1904).

Figure 5.1. Arthur Pue Gorman, circa 1899. From Walter Neal, *Autobiographies & Portraits of the President, Cabinet, et al.* Public domain.

Many thought Gorman would be the nominee based on his high profile in the states that typically furnished the bulk of the Democrats' electoral votes—the solid South. Reports were circulating in the fall of 1903 that James K. Jones, chairman of the Democratic National Committee; Senator William J. Stone of Missouri; Pennsylvania State Senator J. K. P. Hall; and John R. McLean, the owner and publisher of *The Washington Post* and *The Cincinnati Enquirer* were quietly advocating for Gorman's nomination.[9] However, Gorman's chances came to a crashing halt on February 23, 1904, when he voted in opposition to the Panama Canal Treaty (a treaty that was endorsed by almost all US Senate Republicans and almost half of all US Senate Democrats).

George Gray was born on May 4, 1840, in New Castle, Delaware. His father, Andrew C. Gray, was a lawyer, banker, businessman, and public official. Gray attended the common schools in New Castle and received an AB degree from the College of New Jersey (now Princeton University) in 1859. He received a master of arts degree from the College of New Jersey in 1863 and then enrolled at Harvard Law School. He left Harvard to read law with his father and was admitted to the Delaware bar in 1863.

Upon admission to the bar, Gray hung out his shingle in New Castle and was engaged in the private practice of law for the next sixteen years.[10]

In 1879, Gray was elected attorney general of Delaware, a position he held until 1885. In 1885, Gray was elected to the United States Senate to fill the vacancy caused by the resignation of Senator Thomas F. Bayard. He was reelected to the Senate in 1887 and 1893. Gray lost his bid for reelection to the Senate in 1899. While he was in the Senate, he served as chairman of the Committee on Patents, chairman of the Committee on Privileges and Elections, and chairman of the Committee on Revolutionary Claims.[11]

On March 29, 1899, Gray received a recess appointment from President William McKinley to the United States Court of Appeals for the Third Circuit and the United States Circuit Court for the Third Circuit (see figure 5.2). He was nominated to the same positions by President McKinley on December 11, 1899, and was confirmed by the Senate on December 18, 1899. President McKinley appointed Gray to be a member of the Permanent Court of Arbitration at The Hague in 1900.[12] Gray's dual appointments by a Republican president and his open abandonment of the

Figure 5.2. George Gray, circa 1899. From Walter Neal, *Autobiographies & Portraits of the President, Cabinet, et al.* Public domain.

party and its nominee during the 1896 election worked to his disadvantage in trying to establish himself as a legitimate nominee.[13]

Richard Olney was another serious contender from the conservative wing of the party. Olney was born in Oxford, Massachusetts, on September 15, 1835. His father, Wilson Olney, was a textile manufacturer and banker. Shortly after Richard's birth, Wilson Olney moved the family to Louisville, Kentucky, where Richard lived until he was seven years old. The family then moved back to Oxford, and young Richard was sent to the Leicester Academy. Upon completing his course of study there, he enrolled at Brown University, where he graduated with high honors in 1856. He then attended Harvard Law School, graduating in 1858. He was admitted to the Massachusetts bar in 1859 and began working for Benjamin Franklin Thomas, a well-respected and highly influential former judge. Olney quickly made a name for himself and won high praise as an authority on matters of probate, trusts, and corporate law[14] (see figure 5.3).

His political life began when he was elected to the Massachusetts House of Representatives in 1874. He served one term in the legislature and refused to accept renomination. In 1876 he was the Democratic

Figure 5.3. Richard Olney. Courtesy of G. G. Bain, 1913. Public domain.

nominee for attorney general in Massachusetts.[15] In March 1893, Olney became the attorney general in the cabinet of President Grover Cleveland. In this position, during a strike of railroad employees in Chicago, Olney instructed the district attorneys to secure writs of injunction from the federal courts to prevent the strikers from engaging in acts of violence. This action set a precedent for "government by injunction."[16] He also advised President Cleveland to send federal troops to Chicago to quell the labor disturbances that were occurring in the city (over the objections of the governor of Illinois) on the grounds that the government must prevent interference with the mail and the general railway transportation between the states.[17] On June 10, 1895, Olney became the thirty-fourth United States secretary of state, a position he held until the end of the Cleveland administration in March 1897.[18]

Intellectually superior to Cleveland, but possessed of many of the same qualities—"the brow of a Chief Justice with the jaw of a bulldog, set . . . upon a short thick neck and shoulders square as a yard arm"—Olney was deeply interested in rehabilitating the Democratic Party following Bryan's ignominious defeats in 1896 and 1900.[19]

The arguments advanced in favor of Olney's candidacy largely coincided with those made on Cleveland's behalf. Olney, like Cleveland, was a known personality who could rally the Cleveland wing of the party and hence could "beat Roosevelt." Many felt that when he criticized the coal mine operators in one of his rare public speeches in the fall of 1902, the corporate lawyer proved anew his impartiality and sense of justice. Recurring troubles in the Caribbean, which stirred up memories of his militancy in regard to the Monroe Doctrine, enhanced his appeal in the eyes of others.[20]

But there were many who doubted Olney would be able to prevail in the November general election. Opinion was divided on whether Olney's devotion to civil service reform would outweigh, among "independent" voters, his refusal to associate himself with anti-imperialists on the issue of Philippine independence. *The World's Work*, arguing that Olney's plea for railroad unionists in the Reading Receivers' case[21] and his denunciation of the coal barons had only partially atoned for his past offenses against labor, thought the hatred of the "populist and labor and socialistic element" in the party made his nomination and election all but impossible.[22] Others believed that Olney destroyed his chances to capture the nomination by his attitude toward William Jennings Bryan—ignoring him in one campaign

(1896) and supporting him in the other (1900)—thereby incurring the enmity of both the free silver and sound money Democrats.[23]

Senator Francis Cockrell of Missouri was also discussed as a potential candidate. Cockrell was born on October 1, 1834, in Warrensburg, Missouri, the son of Nancy and Joseph Cockrell, the sheriff of Johnson County. Francis attended the common schools in Warrensburg and then enrolled at Chapel Hill College in Lafayette County, Missouri, graduating in July 1853. He studied law and was admitted to the Missouri bar in 1855. Cockrell practiced law in Missouri until the outbreak of the Civil War[24] (see figure 5.4).

In 1861, Cockrell was made the captain of a Missouri company. He rose steadily through the ranks, ultimately attaining the rank of brigadier general before the war's end.[25] He commanded a brigade in the Vicksburg campaign and distinguished himself on the battlefield at the Battle of Champion Hill. He also took part in the Battle of Big Black River Bridge, leading his brigade in a daring escape just before Union troops seized the bridge.[26]

Figure 5.4. Francis Cockrell. Courtesy of M. B. Brady, 1870. Public domain.

Cockrell went on to fight in many battles of the Atlanta campaign and participated in Hood's Tennessee campaign.[27] He was severely wounded by a bursting shell at the Battle of Franklin. Cockrell was captured at Fort Blakely, Alabama, on April 9, 1865, and paroled on May 14 of that year.[28]

Following the end of the Civil War, Cockrell returned to his law practice. He was elected to the United States Senate in 1874 and reelected to the Senate in 1880, 1886, 1892, and 1898.[29] Given Cockrell's service in the Confederate Army during the Civil War, most did not think it was likely that Cockrell would be able to garner the northern support necessary to capture the nomination.

The progressive wing of the party was represented by two possible contenders: William Jennings Bryan and William Randolph Hearst. As early as May 1902, William Jennings Bryan intimated that he would not be an active candidate when, likening himself to Aaron who had helped lead the children of Israel out of the wilderness, he declared that he was perfectly willing to let someone else take up the role of Moses. But in the fall of that same year, he stated that if the Democratic Party should choose him again as their nominee, he could not honorably refuse the nomination[30] (see figure 5.5). Bryan's flip-flopping claims left many unconvinced that he would remain a non-candidate.

Figure 5.5. William Jennings Bryan in 1896. Courtesy of George H. Van Norman, Library of Congress. Public domain.

On April 23, 1904, Bryan gave a speech in Chicago, Illinois, condemning the platform endorsed by the Democratic Party of New York at their recent convention and urging that Parker not receive the Democratic nomination for president. Bryan picked apart each plank of the Albany Platform, claiming that each was too broad in subject matter and lacking the detail necessary to provide an actionable response. He lamented the fact that the Albany platform lacked an anti-imperialism plank and was silent on the issues of labor arbitration, an eight-hour workday, imposition of an income tax, and direct election of senators. According to Bryan, "the New York platform is a dishonest platform, fit only for a dishonest party. No one but an artful dodger would stand upon it."[31] Bryan concluded his remarks with the following statement against both the platform and Parker:

> The New York platform is ambiguous, uncertain, evasive and dishonest. It would disgrace the Democrats of the nation to adopt such a platform, and it ought to defeat as an aspirant for a Democratic nomination any man who would be willing to have it go forth as a declaration of his views on public questions. In Illinois, in Wisconsin, in Michigan, in Minnesota, in Indiana, in Ohio, and in every other state that has not acted it behooves the Democrats to arouse themselves and organize to the end that they may prevent the consummation of the schemes of the reorganizers. Their scheme begins with the deception of the rank and file of the party. It is to be followed up by the debauching of the public with a campaign fund secured from the corporations, and it is to be consummated by the betrayal of the party organization and of the country into the hands of those who are today menacing the liberties of the country by their exploitations of the producers of wealth.[32]

Colonel Henry Watterson, the owner and editor of *The Louisville Courier-Journal*, published an editorial on June 23, 1904, perhaps in response to Bryan's Chicago speech, strenuously arguing against a third nomination for Bryan (and urging the nomination of Parker). He assailed Bryan's attack on the New York State Democrats and their platform, writing that Bryan's Chicago speech meant one thing only: Bryan was intent on creating as much mischief as possible for the eventual Democratic nominee. If Bryan could not be the nominee—and could not himself win the presidency—then he was determined to make sure no other Democrat captured the office.³³

William Randolph Hearst was born on April 29, 1863, in San Francisco, California, the only child of George and Phoebe Apperson Hearst³⁴ (see figure 5.6). Hearst was educated mainly by private tutors, and in the fall of 1882, at the age of nineteen, he matriculated at Harvard University.³⁵ Hearst was a mediocre student at best, and in the spring of 1885 he was expelled from Harvard without quite having finished his junior year.³⁶ Hearst spent what would have been his senior year at Harvard working as a reporter for the *New York World*.³⁷

George Hearst had made a fortune in the mining business (unbelievably, he had a stake in three of the most profitable mines ever operated in the United States: the Ontario silver mine, the Homestake gold mine, and the Anaconda copper mine), and, to promote his efforts to become one of California's senators, had purchased a failing newspaper in San Francisco, the *San Francisco Examiner*.³⁸ The younger Hearst, firm in his belief that

Figure 5.6. William Randolph Hearst, circa 1904. Courtesy of B. M. Clinedinst, Library of Congress, Washington, DC. Public domain.

he could make his mark in the world of publishing, continually asked his father for ownership of the *Examiner*. The elder Hearst steadfastly refused to give it to him, stating at one point, "Great God! . . . I took [that paper] for a bad debt and it's a sure loser. Instead of holding it for my own son, I've been saving it up to give to an enemy."³⁹

In 1887, George Hearst was elected to a six-year term in the United States Senate. That same year, he reluctantly gave in and wrote his son that he could have the *Examiner*.⁴⁰ Hearst took over the floundering paper and turned it into a thriving success. He then parlayed that opportunity into a chain of eight major newspapers around the country, including *The New York American, The New York Evening Journal, The Chicago American, The Los Angeles Examiner,* and *The Boston American*. In 1895, Hearst's mother sold her stake in the Anaconda Copper Mining Company to the Rothschild family for $7,500,000 and then promptly handed the money over to her son, making him an instant multimillionaire.⁴¹

In May 1900, Hearst was elected president of the National Association of Democratic Clubs.⁴² The NADC was composed of some twelve thousand clubs all over the nation, with an estimated three million members. Hearst used his position with the NADC to further his own political aims.⁴³

Hearst was elected to Congress in 1902 from New York's Eleventh District.⁴⁴ While in Congress he was a member of the House Labor Committee.⁴⁵ Hearst introduced a number of reform-minded measures that ultimately died in committee, including direct election of senators, an eight-hour workday, more federal control over trusts, increased salaries for the Supreme Court justices, and federal ownership of a complete telegraph and cable system.⁴⁶ Many of these proposals made Hearst popular with organized labor, and dozens of Hearst clubs sprung up across the country.⁴⁷ The president of the very first Hearst club, in Ithaca, New York, sent out a letter asking for Democratic support of Hearst's candidacy on the grounds that Hearst was well educated, a graduate of Harvard University (actually not a true statement), an able businessman, a practical philanthropist, a firm friend of the workingman, and an enemy of the trusts.⁴⁸ By the beginning of 1904, there were numerous, strong Hearst clubs in Rhode Island, Connecticut, New Jersey, Virginia, Georgia, Texas, Missouri, Colorado, and California.⁴⁹ Hearst was so intent on capturing the nomination that he spent $1.4 million of his own money (equivalent to $42.2 million in 2021) on his campaign.⁵⁰

Hearst was a polarizing figure. The conservatives in the Democratic Party regarded him as a semi-socialistic hybrid whose movement was destructive to party ideals and party unity. His work for labor and his talk of government ownership of railroads made him, in their minds, a dangerous radical. His quarrels with Democratic stalwarts in Congress and his fostering of discord as a leader of dissident factions of the party enraged the old-timers.[51]

On the other hand, Hearst's supporters boosted him with sincere and even fanatical loyalty. They included labor leaders from all over the country, the more radical elements of the Democratic Party, and party men, mostly in the West, who remembered his full-out support of Bryan and who were concerned about domination by the eastern "reactionary" wing of the party.[52]

And then there was Alton Parker. What made Parker an attractive candidate? As a judge, Parker had not been involved in the bitter factional party struggles of the prior decade, and that made him particularly attractive to those whose greatest object was the attainment of party unity. His support of Bryan in 1896 and 1900 was expected to satisfy those who were still looking to the Nebraskan for leadership. As one commentator has noted, "his judicial career had left him untainted by political [scandal or] dealmaking. [He] was a proven Democratic vote-getter in a predominantly Republican state. He had made no political enemies. His solid, well-reasoned opinions gave him an aura of authority and reliability."[53] And all of these things stood in stark contrast to Bryan, whose populist and anti-business rhetoric had led to a Democratic defeat in the prior two elections.[54]

But Parker, of all the potential nominees, was the most reluctant to seek the nomination (he most definitely wanted to be the Democratic nominee, but he refused to actively campaign to obtain the nomination).[55] In fact, despite the party's focus on him, at no time prior to his receiving the nomination at the July 1904 national convention did he ever announce that he was seeking the presidency.[56] In various ways he indicated that he would run if nominated, and serve if elected, but he steadfastly refused to make any pronouncements on public issues while he was a judge.[57] He explained, "I am a judge on the Court of Appeals. I shall neither embarrass the court by my opinions nor use the dignity of the court to give weight to them. I shall do nothing and say nothing to advance my candidacy. If I should receive the nomination, I shall then resign from the Bench and state my views as a private citizen."[58]

Parker could find no one to sympathize with this stand. His friends and supporters told him that since he was virtually unknown outside the state of New York, if he was going to permit himself to be drafted as the Democratic nominee for president, he had to take the opportunity to discuss public affairs and earn some nationwide publicity. They told him that only by stating his political views could he secure backers and gather supporters; that only by criticizing the Roosevelt regime could he "weaken its hold on the electorate."[59]

Parker stood firm. At the beginning of 1903, he received a letter from the New England Anti-Imperialist League asking whether he, as a leader of the Democratic Party, was in support of and would advocate in favor of independence for the Filipino people.[60] On January 17, 1903, Parker sent the following response to Erving Winslow, the secretary of the New England Anti-Imperialist League: "I beg you to be assured of my appreciation of the compliment inspired by your inquiry of January 15th, but as I am not ambitious to become a party leader, it is my rule not to state my views upon public questions, where the effect of a statement may be to create a contrary impression."[61]

Parker was the guest of honor at a dinner at the Manhattan Club on February 6, 1904. At three different points during the course of the evening, the two hundred guests who had assembled to fete Parker demanded "three cheers for the next President of the United States!"[62] John G. Carlisle, former secretary of the treasury, turned and faced Parker and said, "If we go into battle with a strong and fearless leader, who stands for the best principles of our party, we cannot be defeated in the approaching national contest."[63] P. H. McCarran, the Democratic boss of Brooklyn, said it was fitting that the Manhattan Club should be the first to name the Democratic candidate for the presidency and "seconded" the nomination of Parker.[64] When Parker was called upon to speak, he made a few brief remarks but refused to refer to his alleged candidacy and sat down without making a single reference to the scenes of support displayed that evening.[65]

Because of his silence on the issues, he was accused publicly of being a coward. He was charged in the press with being afraid to express himself for fear of losing the nomination. He was called a weakling, a kept politician, a nincompoop without any opinions.[66] A popular cartoon of the day depicted Judge Parker as the Sphinx, with the heading "Why Doesn't He Say Something?" Another cartoon, published in the *Detroit Journal*, showed Ms. Democracy shopping in a pet store for a "rare parrot bird." She is stopped in front of a perch labeled "Parker" and, while admiring a bird with Parker's likeness, removes some money from her purse.

William Jennings Bryan leans in through the window and says, "You'll be cheated if you take him, madam; he can't talk." Bryan, always seeking an opportunity to try to keep the nomination out of Parker's hands, criticized Parker's silence on the issues. He called Parker "an interrogation mark" and accused him of being "the muzzled candidate of corrupt Wall Street adventurers and sinister politicians."[67]

One of the newspapers of the day published a poem about Parker's refusal to speak titled "A Heart's Desire":

> I would not give a deal to hear
>   Demosthenes declaim,
> Altho' as one with scarce a peer
>   Is handed down his name;
> Nor would I budge for Plato's wiles,
>   Altho' a worthy Greek,
> But I would gladly go for miles
>   To hear Judge Parker speak.
>
> Ulysses owned a cunning tongue,
>   From history I know,
> That made him great all men among,
>   And so did Cicero;
> Of all their fame I'd little reck,
>   Nor e'en their rostrums seek,
> But I would almost break my neck
>   To hear Judge Parker speak.
>
> Afar on Egypt's plains doth stand
>   An image made of stone;
> The Sphynx for years upon the sand
>   Has mutely gazed—alone!
> I'd like to hear her ope her head,
>   But 'twould be more unique—
> When everything is done and said,
>   To hear Judge Parker speak![68]

In May 1904, Elliott Danforth, a good friend of Parker's and an advisor to David B. Hill, provided an interview to the *New York Times* purporting to state the views of Judge Parker on a wide variety of issues.

Danforth claimed that he had recently visited Parker at Rosemount and, while there, Parker had shared his opinions about multiple topics that would be of interest to the voters. According to Danforth, Parker was in favor of reducing customs duties whenever they worked in favor of the trusts and wherever they enabled corporations to wring extortionate prices from consumers; he was in favor of revising the tariff; he was an advocate of states' rights and would insist that the "rights of the States that are guaranteed by the Constitution be jealously safeguarded"; he would insist on the use of state powers to regulate the trusts whenever a trust was located entirely within a state's borders and would enforce the federal anti-trust laws whenever a violation of those laws occurred.[69] Parker never confirmed or denied Danforth's comments about his views on the issues of the day.

The *New York World*, which was one of Parker's most vocal supporters, published a series of articles and editorials demanding that Parker speak out because his silence was destroying his candidacy. James Creelman from the *World* wrote to Parker urging him to address the pressing issues of the day and outlining the gravity of the situation if he continued to refuse to do so. Parker replied from Albany on June 17, 1904, a little over three weeks before the Democrats were to meet in convention in St. Louis: "You may be right in thinking that an expression of my views is necessary to secure the nomination. If so, let the nomination go. I took the position that I have maintained—first, because I deemed it my duty to the court; second, because I do not think the nomination for such an office should be sought. I still believe that I am right, and therefore expect to remain steadfast."[70]

Not everyone believed that Parker's silence was a bad thing. The *New York Evening Telegram* published a cartoon in its June 29, 1904, edition contrasting the different styles of William Jennings Bryan and Alton B. Parker. The cartoon shows the Democratic Party, depicted as an elderly lady, turned away from Bryan in 1900 as he leans over her shouting. In 1904, she is on her knees, facing Parker, touching his arm while he stands silently in his judicial robes. With Bryan, the Democratic Party was "talked almost to death," while Parker "won't speak a word." The caption: "What a Difference!"

Although he did not openly seek the Democratic nomination in 1904, Parker, at the urging of Hill, agreed to give two speeches in 1903 in an effort to advance his "unannounced" candidacy.[71] Parker gave his first speech at a banquet arranged in his honor by the Colonial Club of New

York City in mid-February 1903. The remarks of the opening and closing speakers were sufficiently rousing, but the methodical and uncharismatic remarks of Parker left the audience wanting more. Parker confined himself to a description of the work of the state courts and declared that, though many could see but "a treadmill of existence" in the process, others "in love with the work thought nothing so attractive" as the requisite endless investigation, thought, and joy of consultation.[72]

Parker delivered his second speech on July 3, 1903, before the Georgia Bar Association. His address was centered on the Fourteenth Amendment, one of three amendments passed during the Reconstruction era to abolish slavery and establish civil and legal rights for black Americans. Section One of the Fourteenth Amendment, which was adopted in 1868, reads, "All persons born or naturalized in the United States and subject to the jurisdiction thereof, are citizens of the United States and of the State wherein they reside. No State shall make or enforce any law which shall abridge the privileges or immunities of citizens of the United States; nor shall any State deprive any person of life, liberty, or property, without due process of law; nor deny to any person within its jurisdiction the equal protection of the law."[73]

This section of the Fourteenth Amendment was of great political concern to the people living in the southern states. It had been a political powder keg ever since it had been enacted into law and remained a political powder keg at the turn of the twentieth century. Northern congressmen never moved on the legislative floor to push across the needed acts to enforce full compliance with the Fourteenth Amendment. Southern congressmen never mentioned it, because to do so would have meant immediate defeat at the polls. Southern blacks, and those sympathetic to their plight, were unable to make any headway in getting southern political leaders to make the Fourteenth Amendment work in theory or in practice.[74] Against this backdrop, any individual who was running for president, and hoped to carry the solid South, had to treat the problem of mistreatment and disenfranchisement of black Americans, designed to be eliminated by passage of the Fourteenth Amendment, with kid gloves.

Much like his speech in New York earlier in the year, the address to the members of Georgia's bar was uninspired and scholarly. Although his southern audience may have had second thoughts about the delivery (after the speech reports drifted to New York that many southerners believed Parker lacked personal "magnetism")[75], they certainly had no quibble with the content of his remarks. At one point in his speech, Parker stated:

At no time in the history of this country could this amendment have been adopted prior to the so-called reconstruction period; and if it were not now a part of the Constitution, it is not probable that it could be incorporated into that instrument. It is doubtful if it would have been adopted had it been then understood to confer upon Congress the power to enforce the restrictions on State powers contained in the amendment, and upon the Supreme Court power to set aside provisions of a State Constitution or statute which in the judgment of the court abridge the privileges or immunities of citizens of the United States.[76]

Parker essentially argued in this speech that the Fourteenth Amendment to the US Constitution was not originally understood as granting Congress or the Supreme Court the authority to restrict states' rights (and he concluded his remarks by predicting that the current Supreme Court would continue to moderate the "restraining power of the Fourteenth Amendment as against the States.").[77] In doing so, he played well to the Democratic Party's white base by refusing to criticize the denial of black suffrage in the South.

At the same time Parker was giving his speeches, Maurice Minton, a former editor of *The New York Herald*, and James W. Gerard, a rich, young New York banker, initiated an organized propaganda campaign to get articles containing favorable commentary on Parker into the country's newspapers. According to Gerard:

> Alton Parker had a pontifical manner. He had a good reputation as a judge. He was respectable, and he was conservative. Indeed, he had everything needed in a candidate for that particular race except the colorful personality that would get him elected . . . I gave numerous interviews to the Press explaining the superior qualifications of Judge Parker. With Minton's help, we saw to it that country newspapers received appropriate half-tone cuts in boiler plate, all ready to be inserted at no cost to the newspaper. They represented Parker in his library with his dog; Parker playing lovingly with his grandchild; Parker (dressed in a cutaway) raking hay at his country place in Esopus. He was chastely portrayed in all the stock situations that the voters seem to desire—or have been led by long custom to expect of their candidate.[78]

Their efforts worked. At the beginning of 1903, and with increasing frequency as the year progressed, newspaper editors throughout the country began discussing Parker as a presidential candidate. *The Baltimore Sun* published an interview with Tennessee Senator Edward Carmack on January 2, 1903, in which he said: "There has been a great deal of talk about David B. Hill, Arthur P. Gorman and Richard Olney, but I place little faith in the predicted success of the party should either of these gentlemen be selected. *** I look rather favorably on the effort to nominate Judge Alton B. Parker of New York."[79] *The Boston Herald*, on January 13, 1903, said, "To Chief Judge Alton B. Parker of the New York Court of Appeals, the Democrats throughout the country are looking forward to as their nominee for president. From East, South and West come demands that he be the candidate . . . His candidacy seems to be acceptable to Mr. Cleveland, to Senator Hill, to Mr. Bryan, to Senator O'Gorman, and to many others of the powerful and representative leaders."[80] On February 8, 1903, a writer for the *New York Sun* said that Parker had come to the fore "without ostentation, without the gingles and cymbals that accompany many political movements."[81] On February 15, 1903, the editor of the *Brooklyn Daily Eagle*, St. Clair McKelway, editorialized that Parker was the only Democrat who could win the presidency in November 1904. After dismissing Olney, Gorman, Edward Shepard, and David B. Hill as potential nominees, McKelway noted:

> The Democratic movement toward Judge Parker is honorable to the party, creditable to him and auspicious for the country. Should he be nominated and not elected, the party would have atoned for the unfitness of its action in 1896 and 1900. The standard of presidential nomination by the party would be restored to what it was, and could afterward be maintained at what it should be. Should he be nominated and elected, the presidency would be placed in the hands of a clean and able politician, of a sound and accomplished jurist, of a scholar of respectable attainment, with a fondness for great Democratic principles, as well as with a belief in them, and of a man who understands men and who could command the services of a Cabinet of commanding abilities and of broad, patriotic principles.[82]

Just a month later, Randolph Guggenheimer, the former president of the New York Municipal Council, gave an interview to a reporter from *The*

New York World. He warned against the reaffirmation of the Kansas City platform, noting that it had twice been repudiated at the polls and calling a third endorsement of Bryan's free silver plank "political suicide" and "financial heresy." In regard to Parker, Guggenheimer stated:

> The man who, in my opinion, can by his strong personality and intellect most successfully represent . . . Democratic principles and win back the confidence of American voters is Alton B. Parker of New York.
>
> His loyalty to the Democracy cannot be challenged, and in this respect he can harmonize the party, which has been disunited for the last six years. He will not lose the votes of the organization Democrats, who always support Democratic nominees. But he will gain the enthusiastic cooperation of the men who believed it was their manifest duty to their country and themselves to vote for the Republican candidate at the last two national elections. The reunion of these two classes will insure a Democratic victory next year, because it is, I think, a political truism that a majority of the American people are in sympathy with the party which traditionally safeguards popular rights and liberties.
>
> Judge Parker's personality is magnetic. That was proved by the immense plurality of votes he received when he was elected Chief Judge of the Court of Appeals. He is not merely liked, however; he is respected. His fellow citizens admire his fine qualities of mind and character. They know him to be a man of excellent judgment, of conspicuous legal acumen, of discretion and moderation both in speech and conduct. His nomination for the Presidency is necessary, if the Democratic party wishes to return to power, because the candidate who receives the electoral vote of the state of New York will, in all human probability, be the next President of the United States.
>
> Alton B. Parker, and no other Democrat, in my opinion, can obtain the vote.[83]

The Parker boom continued throughout the rest of the year. On November 20, 1903, a writer for the *Buffalo Enquirer* noted that "this rallying of Democratic preference about Judge Parker is not marked by noise or display, nor by any of those characteristics which have taught the American voter to recognize and suspect the factitious and short lived boom. It is, on the contrary, a firm, quiet massing of opinion in many sections—a concentration of belief whose complete elimination of the element of sensationalism gives it impressiveness."[84] On December 1, 1903, J. M. Page, the editor of the *Jersey County Democrat,* a southern Illinois newspaper, wrote Parker a letter stating, in part, "February fifth, 1903, the Jersey County Democrat placed your name at the head of its editorial columns as the democratic candidate for President of the United States, and it has remained there Daily and Weekly ever since."[85] And on December 20, 1903, a journalist writing for the *Houston Post* stated that Parker's "strength has steadily increased for more than a year since he was first proposed. His cause lacks the ebullient enthusiasm which makes a campaign noisy, but by that very token it commends itself to the sober sense of the people who are weary of the spectacular and the declamatory."[86]

To be sure, not everyone was a Parker supporter. Given his New York pedigree, one would assume that Parker had the backing of all of the important New York political operatives—but that was not the case. "Silent" Charlie Murphy, the boss of Tammany Hall, was not a fan of Parker's and did not support his quest for the nomination.

Any discussion of New York politics at the turn of the last century must include at least a brief discussion of Tammany Hall. The organization formally known as The Society of St. Tammany or Columbian Order was founded in New York City in 1788 (or 1789) as a political-fraternal order.[87] The organization took its name from a chief of the Lenni-Lenape tribe, Tamanend. According to legend, Tamanend (or Tammany) greeted William Penn when he landed in the original thirteen colonies in 1682.[88] The Tammany Society's "grand sachem" presided over a council of district leaders called "sachems." The rank-and-file members were known as "braves," and the society's headquarters was known as "the Wigwam."[89]

Aaron Burr, who famously killed Alexander Hamilton in an 1804 duel, was predominantly responsible for transforming the society into a political machine. Tammany members acted as agents of the Democratic-Republican Party in 1800, throwing their support to Thomas Jefferson in that year's closely contested presidential election.[90] In 1805, recognizing the power to be gained from dominating and controlling elections, the Tammany Society established a separate political organization, the General Committee of the Democratic-Republican Party (later shortened to the Democratic Party), with smaller committees established throughout Manhattan's wards.[91] The General Committee soon became better known by its meeting place, Tammany Hall (which, at the turn of the twentieth century, was located on 14th Street).[92]

Although the Tammany Society and Tammany Hall were technically two separate organizations housed in the same building, the separation was, for all intents and purposes, a complete fiction. The society's leaders controlled the General Committee and limited access to the Wigwam. Over time, the grand sachem became little more than a ceremonial figurehead. The real power rested in the hands of the party's boss, who was selected by the General Committee.[93]

Beginning in the 1860s, Tammany Hall was under the control of a series of powerful bosses. William Marcy Tweed was the boss from 1861 to 1871.[94] "Honest John" Kelly ran the organization from 1872 to 1886.[95] Kelly's protégé, Richard Croker, was boss from 1886 to 1901.[96] "Silent" Charlie Murphy took control of Tammany Hall in 1902 when Croker left the states for his native Ireland and held the reins of power until his death in 1924.[97]

Bosses Tweed, Kelly, Croker, and Murphy turned Tammany Hall into a political juggernaut in Manhattan and the state of New York. It dominated and controlled party nominations and political patronage in Manhattan and Albany, the state capital. If a Democrat was running for office in New York (or needed New York's assistance to secure a national office), Tammany's support was essential. Case in point: Murphy himself was responsible for the election of three mayors of New York City, three governors of New York State, and two US senators from the Empire State.[98] Somehow, some way, if Parker wanted the Democratic nomination in 1904, he and his handlers would have to figure out a way to outwork, outsmart, or outflank Murphy.

Unlike today, when the eventual nominee knows that they have the nomination sewn up after the long and arduous primary season, there were relatively few party primaries held in 1904. State party conventions were the real battlegrounds. And one of the earliest battlegrounds was Parker's home state of New York.

The New York State Democratic Convention was scheduled to take place beginning on April 18, 1904, in Albany, New York. "Silent" Charlie Murphy had made it known prior to the start of the convention that he did not want the unit rule adopted (meaning that all delegates had to cast their votes as one unit), and he did not want the state's delegation to the national convention to be instructed for Parker (meaning that any New York delegate who attended the national convention would be required to cast their votes for Parker for president).⁹⁹ Opinions differed as to why Murphy refused to support an instructed delegation for Parker. Some believed Murphy's refusal stemmed from his personal dislike for the judge and his belief that Parker would be a weak national candidate (several years after the election Murphy referred to Parker as "that boob from Esopus.").¹⁰⁰ Others thought that Murphy's opposition to an instructed delegation was designed to infuse new life into "the fading candidacy" of William Randolph Hearst.¹⁰¹ Most believed Murphy's opposition was fueled by his fear that if Parker were nominated and elected president without a definitive pledge to Tammany that federal patronage would not be used to build up Hill and State Senator Patrick McCarren ("boss" of Brooklyn's Democratic organization) to the detriment of Tammany Hall, Murphy would lose his political power. Unable to compel a pledge from Parker that Tammany would be treated "fairly," Murphy dug in his heels in opposition to an instructed delegation.¹⁰²

In light of Murphy's opposition, Hill made it his mission to do everything he could to ensure adoption of the unit rule and an instructed delegation for Parker. Nine days before the start of the convention, Hill and the leaders of the Democratic State Committee decided that George Raines, a staunch Parker advocate, would serve as chairman of the state convention.¹⁰³ As chairman, Raines would oversee the parliamentary procedure of the convention, recognizing some speakers, ruling others out of order, and determining the order and presentation of business before the delegates. He would also deliver the keynote address of the convention. Hill also worked tirelessly to shore up support for Parker and adoption of the unit rule and to ensure that a majority of the delegates to the state convention were Parker men.

At the same time Hill was battling Murphy and the Tammany contingent, he was battling the presumptive nominee—over the content of the proposed state platform. Hill wanted the state platform to contain planks designed to elicit support for Parker's candidacy from the "radical" element in the party, such as government and municipal ownership of all utilities. Parker was adamantly opposed to any compromise with the radical element in the party and insisted "on the adoption of an ultra-conservative platform as most likely to bring the Presidential nomination his way."¹⁰⁴ He further believed that adoption of a radical platform by the state convention of his home state would "seriously embarrass his candidacy and would work harm in the National Convention."¹⁰⁵ Ultimately, Parker's arguments won the day.¹⁰⁶

The State Democratic Convention was called to order at three o'clock in the afternoon on April 18, 1904, by State Chairman Frank Campbell. Chairman Raines took the podium and delivered a rousing keynote, attacking the tariff and the trusts, assailing the power-hungry Republican governor, Benjamin Odell, and excoriating the colonial doctrines of the Republican Party and its "vociferous, spectacular and adventurous" leader.[107] Following Raines's speech, the committees were appointed and the convention adjourned for several hours to allow the committees to conduct their business.[108]

Senator McCarren, another Parker man, chaired the Committee on Resolutions. In committee, he read a set of resolutions outlining the proposed platform of the convention:

> The Democrats of New York, in renewing their pledge of fidelity to the essential principles of Jeffersonian Democracy, as repeatedly enunciated in our National and State platforms, make these further declarations upon the National issues of the hour, reserving an expression upon State issues until the Fall Convention, when State candidates are to be nominated.
>
> 1. This is a Government of laws, not of men; one law for Presidents, Cabinets, and people; no usurpation; no executive encroachment upon the legislative or judicial department.
>
> 2. We must keep inviolate the pledges of our treaties; we must renew and reinvigorate within ourselves that respect for law and that love of liberty and of peace which the spirit of military domination tends inevitably to weaken and destroy.
>
> 3. Unsteady National policies and a restless spirit of adventure engender alarms that check our commercial growth; let us have peace, to the end that business confidence may be restored, and that our people may again in tranquility enjoy the gains of their toil.
>
> 4. Corporations chartered by the State must be subject to just regulation by the State in the interests of the people; taxation for public purposes only; no Government partnership with protected monopolies.

5. Opposition to trusts and combinations that oppress the people and stifle healthy industrial competition.

6. A check upon extravagance in public expenditures; that the burden of the people's taxes may be lightened.

7. Reasonable revision of the tariff; needless duties upon imported raw materials weigh heavily upon the manufacturer, are a menace to the American wage-earner, and by increasing the cost of production shut out our products from the foreign markets.

8. The maintenance of State rights and home rule; no centralization.

9. Honesty in the public service; vigilance in the prevention of fraud, and firmness in the punishment of guilt when detected.

10. The impartial maintenance of the rights of labor and of capital; no unequal discrimination; no abuse of the powers of law for favoritism or oppression.

The Democracy of New York favors the nomination for President of the United States of that distinguished Democrat and eminent jurist of our own State—Alton Brooks Parker, and the delegates selected by this convention are hereby instructed to present and support such nomination at the approaching National Convention.

That the said delegates are hereby further instructed to act and vote as a unit in all matters pertaining to said convention, in accordance with the will of the majority of the said delegates; and the said delegates are further authorized to fill any vacancies which may arise from any cause in said delegation, in case of the absence of both the delegate and alternate.[109]

Tammany delegate Bourke Cockran offered an amendment to the resolution regarding the instruction of the delegates for Parker "by proposing that they be sent uninstructed, and to take counsel at St. Louis with the other delegates from the different States, the delegates then to state their choice as Judge Parker if he should be found to be the choice of the other states."[110] Following a great deal of heated debate, Cockran's amendment to send the delegation to St. Louis uninstructed was defeated by a vote of twenty-seven to twelve. A vote was then taken on McCarren's proposed resolutions, and they were adopted as a whole.[111] Hill one, Tammany zero.

The convention reconvened at 9:00 p.m. After a report from the Committee on Contests, Chairman Raines recognized Senator McCarren. McCarren read the report of the Committee on Resolutions and moved the adoption of the proposed platform. Senator Thomas F. Grady, another Tammany man, asked for and obtained recognition from the chair, saying, "On behalf of the minority of the Committee on Resolutions I present the following substitute, there being no objection on the part of the minority of the committee to the adoption of the unit rule."[112] Grady's proposed minority resolution read, in part, "The Democracy of New York believes that the result of the Presidential election now pending involves the very existence of constitutional government in this country, and in such a grave crisis it has no favor to ask of the party in the Nation except the privilege of serving it. That this service may be most effective the delegation here elected is left free to take such action at St. Louis as a majority thereof may consider most likely to insure the success of the candidates selected by the National Convention."[113] After a series of speeches for and against the minority resolution, Hill rose and called for a vote. The minority resolution was defeated 301 to 141. The platform as originally reported was adopted by a *viva voce* vote.[114] The New York delegates to the Democratic National Convention would be voting as a unit, and they would be voting for Parker. Hill two, Tammany zero.

A little more than a week after the New York State Democratic Convention concluded, William Jennings Bryan gave a speech before a large crowd in Chicago, Illinois. During his remarks he said, among other things, "Judge Parker is not a fit man to be nominated either by the Democratic party or any other party that stands for honesty or fair dealing in politics."[115] In response to Bryan's speech, J. T. Woods Merrill, a close friend of Bryan's, told a reporter for *The World* that he was surprised by Bryan's comments because Bryan himself wanted Parker to be his running mate in 1900 and referred to Parker at that time as "an able and energetic statesman."[116] In response to Merrill's comments, Bryan doubled down on his criticism of Parker, vehemently denying that he ever considered naming Parker as his running mate and saying of Parker, "I did not think much about him, my general impression of the man being that he had no strong convictions on any political questions or matters that vitally affected the interests of the people."[117]

Thanks to Hill's hard work and dedication, and despite Bryan's derogatory comments, Parker took an early lead in the pledged delegate count. Close votes in eastern and midwestern conventions in late April and May broke Parker's way (on May 6 and May 13, respectively, Connecticut and Indiana instructed their delegates to vote as a unit for Parker), and after that the southern states began to fall into his column.[118] The Georgia Democratic Convention in June narrowly adopted the unit rule, giving all of its votes to Parker.[119] But the Illinois delegation had pledged to support Hearst, and several other states and territories, including the Arizona territory, California, the territory of Hawaii, Idaho, Iowa, Nevada, the New Mexico territory, Rhode Island, South Dakota, and Wyoming, were also pledged to the millionaire publisher.[120] When the Washington State Democrats met in convention on May 5, 1904, Hearst men were in charge, and, although no specific instructions regarding candidate support were issued, the adoption of the unit rule effectively ensured that Hearst would receive the entire vote of the state's delegation, which was predominantly composed of members who were loyal Hearst supporters.[121]

Heading into the national party conventions, it was unclear whether any candidate—Parker, Hearst, or someone else—would have the necessary support to obtain the nomination on the first ballot. Some commentators were predicting that Parker would enter the convention with no more than 250 pledged delegates; Hearst with no more than 150.[122] *The Outlook*, in its Saturday, May 21, 1904, issue, noted, "Most of the talk as to Judge Alton B. Parker's being the inevitable choice of the Democratic National Convention for President has ceased, and it is now admitted even by advocates of his nomination that he will not only fail to have two-thirds of the delegates on the first ballot, but that he will fall short of having a majority."[123] But Parker's supporters could argue persuasively that their candidate, and their candidate alone, had shown his strength in New York, Connecticut, and Indiana—the three northern states, which, together with one or two others in that section of the country and those of the solid South, provided the most certainty of a Democratic victory in the fall.[124]

The editors of *Puck* magazine recognized that not everyone in the party appreciated Hill's efforts to obtain the nomination for Parker. Hill's reputation as a political manipulator made his early support of Parker controversial. The centerfold cartoon in the May 25, 1904, issue showed Parker sitting in a chair strapped to the back of David B. Hill, who was carrying him up a narrow, treacherous, rocky trail on the edge of a mountain on the way to the St. Louis convention. Hill's walking stick, which is labeled "treachery" and "peanut politics," has been broken and mended back together with tape and twine. The cartoon is titled "A Rocky Road and a Bad Guide," and the caption has Parker stating, "I think I'll get out and walk."[125]

Although some in the Democratic Party clearly did not like Hill's methods and chafed at the prospect of having a nominee "rammed down their throats," the idea of having Hearst as the Democratic nominee in the fall so frightened the conservative wing of the party—most southerners considered him "a grotesque and horrible hobgoblin"—that they renewed their efforts to do everything they could to prove the pundits wrong and get Parker nominated on the first ballot.[126] As *The Outlook* noted in its July 16, 1904, issue, "The universal dread of Hearst's success, as long as it appeared a possibility, had the effect of consolidating all the elements in the party opposed to this one man and his methods; and albeit these elements scattered their support somewhat over the field, the largest single volume of it crystallized about Parker."[127]

6

The 1904 Conventions

Many people believed, heading into the conventions, that Roosevelt was practically guaranteed to be reelected as president. The editors of *The World's Work*, in making the following proclamation, recognized Roosevelt's popularity: "The mass of voters in Republican States are pleased with the administration. In fact, it would be impossible to recall a presidential candidate in the White House . . . of whom so little serious criticism was heard a month or two before the nominating conventions. Mr. Roosevelt is personally very popular, and there is effective opposition to him neither in his own party nor among independent voters."[1]

A popular cartoon that was published in the weeks before the Democratic National Convention showed a number of Democrats, including Alton B. Parker, William Jennings Bryan, David B. Hill, Arthur P. Gorman, George B. McClellan, William Randolph Hearst, and Grover Cleveland, in an eight-oared racing shell. The Democratic boat is engaged in a losing race with President Theodore Roosevelt, who is rowing as a single sculler in an identical boat. The Democrats are depicted as exceedingly poor rowers, unable to manage their oars, as Roosevelt easily pulls ahead.

The Republicans were the first of the major parties to meet in convention: from June 21–23 in the Coliseum in Chicago, Illinois.[2] US Postmaster General and Chairman of the Republican National Committee Henry C. Payne called the convention to order at 12:16 p.m. on June 21. The Reverend Timothy P. Frost, pastor of the First Methodist Church in Evanston, Illinois, gave the opening prayer (see figure 6.1). Former Secretary of War Elihu Root was chosen as temporary chairman of the convention and gave an opening address to the delegates. After Root ended

Figure 6.1. Opening prayer, 1904 Republican National Convention. Courtesy of S. L. Stein, Milwaukee. Public domain.

his speech, the remainder of the first day was devoted to the appointment of the committees.[3]

The second day of the convention began with the report from the Committee on Credentials. Speaker of the House Joseph Cannon was then appointed permanent chairman of the convention. Cannon gave a lengthy speech to the assembled delegates that contained flashes of his well-known sarcasm and keen sense of humor. Following his remarks, Massachusetts Senator Henry Cabot Lodge, chairman of the Committee on Resolutions, read the proposed platform, which was adopted by the delegates.[4] The Republican platform was moderate and pointed to the party's accomplishments and urged a continuance of the policies started by McKinley and adopted by Roosevelt.[5] As one periodical of the day pointed out, "Conditions were such that the Republican platform could not contain any innovations or set forth any bold proposals looking toward changes of policy or important new legislation. So far as the party in power is concerned, it can do little else but present the McKinley-Roosevelt administrations to the country and ask for a vote of confidence and a renewed lease of power."⁶ John Hay, Roosevelt's secretary of state, admitted that the Republican platform "was lacking in novelty, [was] certainly not sensational, and [was] substantially the platform upon which the party had won its two previous victories."⁷

The third day of the convention, June 23, was the "day of nominations." At 10:30 a.m., Chairman Cannon brought an immense wooden gavel down on the table in front of him and directed the delegates to take their seats. Following an opening prayer, Cannon announced that the next order of business would be the roll call of states for the nomination of president of the United States. When the clerk called Alabama, Oscar R. Hundley mounted a chair and announced that Alabama requested the honor and privilege of yielding its place on the roll to the state of New York. Ex-Governor Frank Black of New York then took the stage and placed Theodore Roosevelt's name in nomination.⁸

In concluding his nomination of Roosevelt, Black stated the following:

> And in the man whom you will choose, the highest sense of every nation in the world beholds a man who typifies as no other living American does, the spirit and the purposes of the twentieth century. He does not claim to be the Solomon of his time. There are many things he may not know. But this is sure, that above all things else he stands for progress, courage and fair play, which are the synonyms of the American name.
>
> There are times when great fitness is hardly less than destiny, when the elements so come together that they select the agent they will use. Events sometimes select the strongest man, as lightning goes down the highest rod. And so it is with those events which for many months with unerring sight have led you to a single name which I am chosen only to pronounce: Gentlemen, I nominate for President of the United States the highest living type of the youth, the vigor and the promise of a great country and a great age, Theodore Roosevelt of New York.⁹

Roosevelt's name had barely left Black's lips when the crowd erupted in wild celebration. Chairman Cannon advanced to the front of the platform holding an American flag faded with age and riddled with holes. It was not until later that Cannon explained that the flag was the property of the Lincoln-McKinley Association of Missouri and had originally been waived at the very moment that Lincoln was nominated in 1860. It had also been waived at the moment that every subsequent Republican nominee for president had been announced. The demonstration lasted a full twenty-three minutes before Indiana senator Albert J. Beveridge took to the stage to second the nomination of Roosevelt. Roosevelt was unanimously nominated for president on a roll call of states. Iowa Senator Jonathan P. Dolliver nominated Indiana Senator Charles W. Fairbanks for vice president. That nomination was seconded by New York Senator Chauncey Depew. At the close of the speeches in favor of Fairbanks, Chairman Cannon called for any other nominations. There were none, as all the other favorite son candidates had been withdrawn. As a result, Fairbanks was unanimously nominated for vice president by acclamation.[10]

The *New York Sun*, a paper that had long been loyal to Roosevelt, quickly editorialized for Roosevelt's election, saying, "Resolved: that we emphatically endorse and affirm Theodore Roosevelt. Whatever Theodore Roosevelt thinks, says, does, or wants is right. Roosevelt and Stir 'Em Up. Now and Forever; One and Inseperable!"[11] Roosevelt and Fairbanks basked in the glow of the good press and waited to see whom they would be running against in the fall.

Just a few weeks prior to the Democratic National Convention, William Jennings Bryan published an "open letter" in opposition to Parker's candidacy. He declared in his letter that "burglarious methods are now being employed to foist upon the party a speechless candidate and a meaningless platform."[12] He added: "It is the first time, in recent years at least, that a man has been urged to so high a position on the ground that his opinions are unknown. Surely the Democratic party is in desperate straits if among all of its members it cannot find a trustworthy man who has ever been interested enough in public questions to give expression to his opinion. In the great contest between democracy and plutocracy our party should take a positive and aggressive stand, and it should present a standard-bearer who will infuse courage and enthusiasm among the masses."[13]

Bryan followed his open letter with a speech before The Cooper Union. He spent most of his time lambasting Hill and Parker. He declared Parker to be a hypocrite and "the weakest candidate the Democrats could put before the country" and called the New York Democratic platform "a cowardly straddlers' platform that can only appeal to cowards and straddlers."[14] He predicted that if Parker was elected "he would be a great disappointment to those who believe in Democratic principles."[15]

A total of 1,006 delegates attended the Democratic National Convention in St. Louis, Missouri from July 6–10.[16] The convention took place in the St. Louis Coliseum, a cavernous space where McKinley had been nominated for the presidency just eight years before. The convention hall was an oblong room where ten thousand spectators could "look down upon a platform projecting into the pit, a kind of peninsula from one long wall of seats."[17] A dingy yellow cloth ceiling hid from public view the iron rafters that held aloft the high, arched roof. The coat of arms of the various states were hung just below the yellow ceiling, and festive bunting covered the columns and festooned the woodwork of the great hall.[18]

The Democratic National Convention of 1904 was one of the liveliest party battles in American history.[19] The choice by two previous Democratic conventions of William Jennings Bryan as the presidential candidate, and back-to-back defeats, had set the stage for a vigorous factional struggle at this convention.[20] Not only did the party leaders want to get a new candidate, they also wanted to drastically modify the party platform that had been shaped by the free-silver Bryan forces.[21]

The convention was called to order at twelve noon on Wednesday, July 6, 1904, by James K. Jones, the chairman of the Democratic National Committee (see figure 6.2). An opening invocation was offered by the Reverend John F. Cannon, pastor of the Grand Avenue Presbyterian Church

Figure 6.2. Opening session of the 1904 Democratic National Convention. Courtesy of George R. Lawrence Co., 1904. Public domain.

in St. Louis. John Sharp Williams of Mississippi was named temporary chairman of the convention.[22] Upon taking the chair, Williams gave an extended opening address. Following Williams's speech, members of the convention's standing committees were announced. The Committee on Platform and Resolutions included several Democratic heavyweights, including Williams, David B. Hill, Henry G. Davis, William Jennings Bryan, Tennessee Senator Edward Carmack, and California attorney Delphin M. Delmas.[23] The convention then adjourned until 10:00 a.m. on Thursday, July 7, for the committees to conduct their business.

Parker, as was the custom of the day, did not attend the Democratic National Convention. He sent Hill and his closest political advisor and future law partner, William F. Sheehan, to work the halls, count the noses, and deliver him the nomination. As a result, on the opening day of the convention, Parker watched his hayfield being plowed and rode on horseback through the woods near Rosemount.[24] He got caught in a severe thunderstorm and returned to the house, soaking wet. He then went for a swim in the Hudson, picked wildflowers for his wife, worked on some court opinions, and even found time to discuss a recently published book on Thomas Jefferson. He did not seek any word on how the convention was proceeding, nor did he receive any. It was past eleven o'clock in the evening before any word reached him by phone of the day's proceedings.[25]

On the second day of the convention, William Jennings Bryan was determined to make his presence felt. He took to the stage to address the convention in a battle over credentials. Bryan spoke out against the Illinois delegation headed by Roger Sullivan and tried, instead, to convince the delegates to seat a group of Bryan followers. Although the Illinois delegation led by Sullivan was pledged to Hearst on the first ballot, Bryan knew that the Sullivan group was not above switching to Parker if momentum was seen to be shifting his way. This was a test for Bryan—if he could win this seemingly small confrontation, he just might be able to control the nomination in favor of himself or his handpicked candidate.[26]

Bryan's speech lasted approximately a half-hour. It was listened to in relative silence, generating only a smattering of applause. Bryan's speech was interrupted by the roll-call vote to decide the credentials question and, very possibly, the outcome of the convention. The delegates ultimately ignored Bryan's pleas and seated the Sullivan delegation by a vote of 647 to 299. This convention, it seemed, was not going to be a Bryan-controlled one.[27]

The Committee on Platform and Resolutions appointed a subcommittee to draft the party platform.[28] This subcommittee was composed of

John W. Daniel, Benjamin T. Cable (a former congressman from Illinois), John P. Poe (a prominent Baltimore attorney), William Jennings Bryan, Benjamin F. Shively (a well-known attorney from South Bend, Indiana), Charles Sumner Hamlin (former assistant secretary of the treasury), Robert E. Pattison (former governor of the state of Pennsylvania), Henry G. Davis (former senator from West Virginia), Francis G. Newlands (senator from Nevada), and Fred T. DuBois (US senator from Idaho).[29] In several marathon sessions over the course of two days, the subcommittee hammered out the party's formal position on a wide variety of complicated topics and issues. As a whole, the platform was "anti-imperialistic, anti-militaristic, and anti-internationalistic in tone."[30]

The original draft of the platform contained a so-called "gold plank," which recognized the existing gold standard and reasoned that in light of the large amount of recent discoveries of gold, the money question was no longer an issue. Bryan objected to the gold plank and proposed the insertion of the silver plank contained in the Democrat's 1900 Kansas City platform (which reiterated the demands for free and unlimited coinage of silver). When Bryan's proposal was voted down, Bryan then moved to add a plank demanding an income tax. Several members of the subcommittee vehemently opposed the addition of a plank calling for the imposition of a federal income tax, but Bryan refused to budge.[31] After a great deal of back-and-forth, during which several members argued that the retention of the gold plank would make electoral success in their state in the fall all but impossible, it was agreed that the gold plank would be removed from the platform and Bryan would drop his efforts to include an income tax plank.[32]

So the Democratic national platform failed to address the gold standard. What did it address? Favorable enactment of laws giving labor and corporations equal rights; liberal appropriations for the care and improvement of the nation's waterways; substantial reductions in federal expenditures; a prohibition against contractual relations between the executive branch and "convicted trusts or unlawful combinations in restraint of . . . trade"; reduced imperialism; independence for the Filipino people; enactment of meaningful tariff reform; enlargement of the powers of the Interstate Commerce Commission; irrigation and reclamation of arid lands in the West; construction of the Panama Canal "speedily, honestly and economically"; protection of US citizens at home and abroad (including universal recognition of duly authenticated government-issued passports); direct election of US senators; statehood for Oklahoma, Arizona, and New

Mexico; extermination of polygamy; liberal trade agreements with Canada; maintenance of the Monroe Doctrine, reduction in army expenditures; enactment of generous pensions for retired military; and comprehensive civil service reform. The Democratic platform closed with a detailed condemnation of the "spasmodic, erratic, sensational, spectacular, and arbitrary" Republican administration.[33]

On Friday, July 8, John W. Daniel of Virginia, the chairman of the Committee on Platform and Resolutions, read the proposed platform to the assembled delegates in a low, monotonous voice, while many of the delegates read papers, walked up and down the aisles, or chatted loudly with friends.[34] The actual reading of the platform could not be heard more than ten feet away from the speaker's rostrum.[35] Immediately after he finished reading the platform, Daniel moved that the platform be adopted. It was, without objection.[36]

In the aftermath of the platform fight, Bryan was quite pleased with himself. He had convinced the delegates to draft a platform that was completely silent on the monetary issue to which Bryan had wed himself and which had served as the main issue of contention in the 1896 and 1900 elections. This was equivalent to a practical repetition of the old free silver platform of the last two campaigns.[37] No one thought that Parker would comment on the platform's silence concerning the gold standard. Bryan himself was telling anyone who asked that Parker had no opinions concerning the money issue section of the party's platform.[38] But, it turns out, Bryan was wrong.

7

The Nomination

The platform, with its nonexistent money stand, weak antitrust, plank, and lack of an income tax plank was hardly the type of platform that would sway independent voters. It denounced "protectionism as a robbery of the many to enrich the few" and favored a tariff for revenue only; it condemned colonial exploitation and imperialism; it included a stern censure of "executive usurpation"; and it declared that the racial question was not an issue in the 1904 election. But the conservative and southern members of the party seemed happy enough. Now on with the selection of a presidential nominee![1]

Eight men were presented to the convention for the presidential nomination. Nominating and seconding speeches were made throughout Friday evening and into early Saturday morning. As dawn approached, it became necessary to limit the seconding speeches to four minutes each.[2]

William Randolph Hearst's name was placed into nomination by Delphin M. Delmas of California. In making the nomination, Delmas emphasized Hearst's allegiance to Democratic principles, his support for prior Democratic nominees (Grover Cleveland in particular), and his willingness to support populist ideas that other candidates were loath to embrace.[3] Hearst's political advisor, Clarence Darrow, the well-known lawyer from Chicago, seconded his nomination.[4]

Chairman James Beauchamp "Champ" Clark placed the name of five-term US Senator Francis M. Cockrell into nomination. He stated three reasons why he chose to place Cockrell's name before the convention: because he not only admired, but loved him; because Missouri was backing Cockrell by unanimous vote; and because Clark was largely responsible for Cockrell being a candidate.[5] Clark told of parallels between President

Roosevelt and Senator Cockrell. When he stated, "They say Roosevelt is brave, but old Cockrell—" the delegates and onlookers interrupted Clark, stood, cheered, and waved small American flags for thirty minutes.[6]

William Jennings Bryan took to the stage, ostensibly to second the nomination of Senator Cockrell. Bryan gave what many contemporaries believed was one of the finest political speeches of his career. Often referred to as the "I Have Kept the Faith" speech, Bryan began with a reference to the prior two presidential campaigns. He told the delegates, "Eight years ago a Democratic national convention placed in my hands the standard of the party and commissioned me as its candidate. Four years later that commission was renewed. I come tonight to this Democratic national convention to return the commission. You may dispute whether I have fought the good fight, you may dispute whether I have finished my course, but you cannot deny that I have kept the faith."[7] He asserted that he had done all he could to bring success to the party, and as a private citizen he felt "more interested in Democratic success today than [he] ever did when [he] was a candidate."[8] He promised that he would not sit out the coming campaign but rather would campaign vigorously for all of the Democratic candidates. He then seconded the nomination of Cockrell.[9] In closing, he could not resist one more attempt to stop Parker from obtaining the nomination. He stated, "If it is the wish of this Convention that the standard shall be placed in the hand of the gentleman presented by California, a man who, though he has money, pleads the cause of the poor; the man who is best beloved, I think I can safely say, among laboring men, of all the candidates proposed; the man who more than any other represents opposition to the trusts—if you want to place the standard in his hand and make Mr. Hearst the candidate of this Convention, Nebraska will be with you in the fight."[10]

The nominations continued as former Delaware congressman Irwin L. Handy nominated Delaware's "favorite son," Judge George Gray. Milwaukee Mayor David S. Rose presented the name of former Wisconsin state Assembly Member Edward C. Wall. Boston Mayor Patrick Collins took to the stage to nominate Richard Olney. Former Kansas gubernatorial candidate David Overmyer placed the name of General Nelson Appleton Miles, a hero of the Civil and Spanish-American wars, into nomination. North Dakota delegate E. E. Cole nominated Minority Leader of the US House of Representatives John Sharp Williams.[11]

Martin W. Littleton, the president of the Borough of Brooklyn, placed Alton Parker's name in nomination. In doing so, Littleton said, in part:

Gentlemen of the Convention, we come together in the historic valley of the Mississippi, at a time when uncounted millions are making a patriotic pilgrimage to a shrine erected by Democratic wisdom and foresight. Surely, as you gather here, with the present breaking upon your enraptured vision and the past filling your hearts with songs of praise and joy; surely, as you contemplate the commonwealths filled with happy homes that stretch out in bewildering succession to the southern seas, and recall with unaffected pride that your party gave this kingdom of wealth and courage to the world's advancing reach; surely, here, close to the quickened pulse of the great Southwestern giant as he comes to strike hands across the years with the spirit of the Old Dominion; here, swept by the thrilling and ennobling memories of the long ago, and inspired by a spectacle which makes these memories dearer and nobler still, surely you are urged by every impulse and entreated by every recollection to forever sink the differences that distract and the causes that confuse and gathering afresh from this exhaustless headwater our hope the spirit of fifty years of ascending party faith, resolve to restore our party to its place of power and pride in the hearts and affections of our countrymen.

∽

The country called upon New York for the best of its brain and blood, and New York answers with a man who cut his way through poverty and toil until he found the highest peak of power and honor in the State . . . The country called upon New York for a Democrat free from factional dispute and New York answers with a man friendly to all factions, but a favorite, or afraid of none; a man who will take counsel and courage of both, but who will take the bitterness of neither—a man who will not stir the hatred of the past nor share the acrimony of the present, but who will lead us up toward the future into a cloudless atmosphere of party peace. The country called upon New York for a man who measured up to the stature of this lofty place, and New York answers with a candidate who grew from youth to man in the humble walks of life; who lived and learned what all our common folks must live and learn; a man who ripened with advancing years in the rich attainments of the law until he went, by choice of those who knew him best, to hold the heavy scale of justice at the highest point of our great judicial system, where, with the masters who molded State and Nation, and the men who drive commerce o'er the wheel of Time, he surveyed the very ground every inch of this great Republic and saw with expanding vision the material growth and glory of his State.

The country called upon New York for a man to fit this, the critical hour and place in our national life, and New York answers with a man who puts against the strenuous sword play of a swaggering administration, a simple faith in all the perfect power of the Constitution; a man who puts against an executive republic the virtue of a constitutional republic; a man who puts against executive usurpation a knowledge of and a deep love for the poise and balance of its three great powers; a man who puts against the stealthy hunt "with the big stick" a faithful observance of constitutional restraints.

The country called upon New York for a man of stainless character in private and public life, and New York answers with a man whose path leads from the sweet and simple fireside of his country home where he enjoys the gentle society of his family, to his place of labor and honor at the head of one of the greatest courts of Christendom. And nowhere through his active and useful life has aught but honest praise found utterance on the lips of those who know him best. If you ask me why he has been silent, I tell you it is because he does not claim to be the master of the Democratic party, but is content to be its servant. If you ask me why he has not outlined a policy for this Convention, I tell you that he does not believe that politics should be dictated, but that the sovereignty of the party is in the untrammeled judgment and wisdom of its members; if you ask me what his policy will be, if elected, I tell you that it will be that policy which finds expression in the platform of his party.

With these, as some of the claims upon your conscience and judgment, New York comes to you, flushed with hope and pride.

> We appeal to every Democrat from everywhere to forget the bitter warfare of the past; forget the strife and anger of the older, other days; abandon all the grudge and rancor of party discontent, and, recalling with ever increasing pride, the triumphs of our fifty years of a constitutional government of Liberty and Peace—here and now resolve to make the future record that resplendent reach of time in which Liberty and Peace went up and down the nations of the earth, building their kingdom in the hearts of men and gathering the harvest of genius and toil; in which reason struck from the hand of force the sword of hate and plucked from the heart of war the germ of greed; in which conscience smote the thoughts of wrong and filled the mind with mercy's sweet restraint; in which power grew in the human brain, but refused the shelter of a glittering crown; in which the people of all lands and tongues, awakened to hope by the inspiration of our example, turned their faces toward the light of our advancing civilization and followed with the march of years the luminous pathway leading to a destiny beyond the reach of vision and within the providence of God. In this spirit New York nominates for President of the United States Alton B. Parker.[12]

At the mention of Parker's name, all hell broke loose. Florida led the state delegations in parading through the convention hall. A large portrait of Parker was brought to the stage and turned to face the crowd. A delegate stood near the stage and, with the help of a megaphone, chanted, "Parker, Parker, Alton B. Parker!" More than twenty-five minutes of demonstrations precluded any further oratorical activity.[13]

When order was finally restored, Tennessee Senator Edward W. Carmack took to the stage to second Parker's nomination. Carmack said, in part,

> It may be, sir, that our candidate is not as voluble and vociferous as some would have him, but I have yet to learn that laryngeal activity is the supreme test of statesmanship. I have yet to learn that the width of a man's mouth is commensurate

with the breadth of his understanding, or that the length of his tongue measures the depth of his wisdom.

∼

The democracy of Tennessee has declared that in this crisis the party should present a candidate of judicial temper, one imbued with a deep reverence for the Constitution, with a respect for law, with a just regard for established precedents and traditions, with a sane conception of the duties and responsibilities of his office, a candidate, in short, whose whole life and character will be in vivid contrast with the recklessness, the lawlessness, the epileptic and convulsive strenuosity of this Administration.

∼

Gentlemen of the Convention, in the name of the Andrew Jackson Democracy of Tennessee, I second the nomination of Alton B. Parker of New York![14]

Following the nominating and seconding speeches, it was time for the delegates to choose their nominee. The clock on the wall showed 5:00 a.m. when the actual voting started.[15] The first ballot result gave Parker 658 votes; Hearst 200; Cockrell 42; Olney 38; Edward C. Wall of Milwaukee 27; Gray 12; Williams 8; and General Nelson Appleton Miles 3.[16] Former Pennsylvania Governor Robert E. Pattison received four votes, New York City Mayor George B. McClellan Jr. received three votes, former Minnesota Senator Charles A. Towne received two votes, Maryland Senator Arthur Pue Gorman received two votes, and former nominee for governor of the state of New York Bird S. Coler received one vote.[17] Parker controlled a majority of the eastern states and all of the southern states. Hearst won the votes from mostly western states.[18] Parker's vote total fell only nine votes shy of the required two-thirds, or 667 votes, needed to win.[19] Before the result could be announced, twenty-one votes from Idaho, Nevada, and West Virginia were transferred to Parker, and the nomination was his.[20] The Missouri delegation was then recognized by the chair, and Governor Alexander M. Dockery moved that Parker's nomination be made unanimous.[21] The motion was passed without opposition.[22] Following a conservative twenty-minute demonstration, the long day of nominations was over. The convention adjourned at 5:29 a.m. on Saturday morning.[23]

Parker gave his first speech as the Democratic nominee on July 9—to his neighbors. On that day, a crowd of Parker's fellow townsmen gathered at Rosemount to congratulate him on his nomination. Parker responded to their words of regard and praise in part as follows:

> I welcome you all tonight as citizens of the county of Ulster—the county of whose men and women, of whose natural beauty, and of whose history we are so proud.
>
> ~
>
> Every citizen of this county is justly proud of its early history, and of the part taken by it in the struggles for independence, and in the formation of the government and its preservation. A long list of names is found on its rolls of honor, placed there because of patriotic and distinguished services, both in war and peace, in addition to the first governor, who held the office for a longer period than has any of his successors.
> The county had many prominent men in its early history, and in later years has enjoyed the faithful and able public service of such men as Senator Hardenburgh, Judge Schoonmaker, Gen. Sharpe, Judge Westbrook, and Judge Kenyon, whose names are treasured in the hearts of appreciative neighbors, and if we were to consider men now living we should add to the list a goodly number of men who have contributed in no small degree to the fame of the county.
>
> ~
>
> Among such a people was my lot fortunately cast many years ago, and to them my Ulster county neighbors and friends, my heart always goes out in thankfulness for the confidence so generously and often reposed, a confidence that I have tried to deserve in the only way I could, by as faithful a discharge of the trust confided in me as I am capable of.
> And now, my neighbors and friends, to whom I am deeply indebted for many kindly and neighborly deeds in the years that have passed since I came among you, I beg leave to render you my grateful and hearty thanks for the honor you do me by this visit to Rosemount.[24]

The delegates reconvened at 2:00 p.m. on Saturday, July 9, 1904. Following an opening prayer by Reverend John T. M. Johnston, a telegram from Francis M. Cockrell was read to the convention. In his telegram, Cockrell thanked the Missouri delegation for placing his name in nomination and approved the selection of Parker as the Democratic nominee. A telegram from William Randolph Hearst was then read to the assembled delegates. Hearst's telegram stated: "I wish to thank my friends for their unfaltering support. I think I can best express my appreciation of their loyalty by continued devotion to the principles of true Democracy, for which we have fought, and by loyal support of the man chosen by the Convention to lead the Democratic party."[25]

North Dakota delegate Siver Serumgard introduced a resolution noting the untimely death of fellow North Dakota delegate Jacob P. Birder. E. L. Russell of Alabama moved for a recess out of respect for the deceased. That motion carried, and the convention was recessed until 5:20 p.m.[26]

When the convention reconvened on Saturday evening, the delegates turned to the task of nominating a vice-presidential candidate. As the convention progressed, several men were under consideration for the second place on the ticket. Former Washington Senator George Turner was an early front-runner for the position, but his past political record (he was a Republican during Reconstruction) worked against him.[27] Missouri Governor Alexander M. Dockery, Kentucky Governor J. C. W. Beckham, and North Carolina Governor Charles B. Aycock were also mentioned as possible early candidates, but none of them seemed to generate any enthusiasm among the delegates.[28] Parker's managers were leaning toward Judge George Gray, the former senator from Delaware.[29] Several delegates opposed Gray's selection based on his "geographical situation" (he was from an electorally insignificant state); the fact that he held, and had held, offices under Republican appointment; and the fact that he had not always been a supporter of the Democratic ticket.[30] Gray was dropped from consideration, and attention turned to Ohio Supreme Court Justice Judson Harmon. Harmon was dismissed as a candidate based on the hostility and factional differences existing between Harmon and John R. McLean (the owner of the influential *Cincinnati Enquirer* and the *Washington Post*).[31]

Marshall Field, the founder of the famous Chicago department store, was then seriously considered for the spot. He emphatically refused to accept the nomination under any circumstances if it were given to him.[32] David S. Rose and Edward C. Wall, delegates-at-large from Wisconsin; James Kilbourne, a wealthy manufacturer from Ohio; John W. Kern, an unsuccessful candidate for governor of Indiana; and Benjamin F. Shively, a prominent Indiana attorney, were then seriously considered as candidates.[33] It was agreed by all involved that none of these men was satisfactory.[34]

The delegates from New York were concerned that the elimination of the gold plank from the party platform had seriously undermined the Democrats' chances to win the presidency in November. They believed that the only chance the party had to prevail in the general election was to nominate a vice president who "was a pronounced gold man and who would command the support and confidence of the great business interests of the country and the gold wing of the party."[35] But who would fit this bill? According to Virginia delegate Thomas F. Ryan, Henry Gassaway Davis met all the important criteria. Davis was a man of national reputation, a former US senator, an avowed gold man, a man of very large means, a Democrat who had always supported the ticket, and probably the only living person who could carry the state of West Virginia for the Democrats.[36]

Davis had left the convention on the morning of July 9 and had begun his return trip home. Every effort was made to contact Davis to gauge his enthusiasm for the nomination. Late in the day on Saturday, July 9, Davis expressed his willingness to serve as the nominee.[37]

Ultimately, the names of four men were placed before the delegates. Free Morris of Illinois nominated US Representative James Robert Williams. Washington delegate F. C. Robertson nominated former Washington Senator George Turner. Former Kansas state Representative David Overmyer nominated former Kansas Senator William A. Harris. And John D. Alderson of West Virginia nominated former West Virginia Senator Henry G. Davis.[38]

Before a vote could be taken on the nominees for vice president, Texas Senator Charles Culberson was recognized by the chair. Culberson, who stood holding a newspaper in his hands, made the following motion: "Mr. Chairman, for reasons which are obvious to all the delegates here, it seems to me we ought not to proceed to nominate a candidate for Vice-President at this time. I therefore move that the Convention take a recess."[39] When the delegates started shouting, "Why?" Culberson continued: "I think the delegates understand what I mean. And I repeat that, in the present exigency confronting the Convention, it ought not to proceed to the nomination of a candidate for Vice-President. We want to know, before a candidate for Vice-President is nominated, who will be the nominee of this Convention for President. I therefore move that the Convention take a recess until eight-thirty tonight."[40] That motion carried.

The "obvious reason" for Culberson's motion for adjournment could be found in the day's newspapers. Several were reporting that Parker had sent a telegram to Tennessee Senator Edward Carmack demanding that the gold plank be returned to the party's platform. The telegram, as reported in the papers, allegedly read, "Senator E.W. Carmack, Tennessee delegation: The Gold Standard is established by law, and I cannot accept the nomination unless that plank is contained in the platform. Alton B. Parker."[41] If the telegram turned out to be true, multiple delegations believed that they had been misled into supporting Parker. They had refused to adopt a platform that contained a plank on the gold standard and were outraged that Parker was apparently dictating terms to the convention. They saw the reported telegram "as a piece of arrogant presumption and . . . a treacherous attack upon his own party at a critical moment."[42] Several of the delegates from the southern part of the country denounced Parker in very strong terms and demanded that he decline the nomination.[43] South Carolina Senator "Pitchfork" Ben Tillman ran up to Virginia Senator John Daniel, who had done much to swing Tillman over to Parker, and shouted that he had been "deceived, seduced, maltreated and horswoggled."[44]

Bryan, upon hearing of the telegram, helped lead the call for a new nominee. Since the convention had not yet adjourned, there was time for the Bryanites to demand a review of the party's nominee for president.[45] Cooler heads prevailed, and a majority of the delegates voted for another temporary adjournment. This gave everyone time to think matters over, under much quieter circumstances, rather than on the hustle and bustle of the convention floor.[46]

During the recess, Chairman Clark returned to his hotel room, where he found a message from the Missouri delegation waiting for him. It requested that Clark immediately come to the Missouri delegation headquarters in the Southern Hotel. When Clark arrived at the hotel, he was met by a group of concerned delegates. Their main thought was if the reported telegram was real, then the nomination should be taken away from Parker. They asked Clark how they could go about making this happen. Clark told them that because a two-thirds majority of the delegates was needed to give Parker the nomination, the same number of delegates was required to rescind the nomination. The delegates then asked Clark if the two-thirds requirement could be changed to a simple majority. Clark indicated that it only took a simple majority vote to change the rules of the convention.[47]

The delegates from Missouri worked out a plan. When the convention reconvened, Clark would recognize Governor Dockery, the chairman of the Missouri delegation, who had moved to make Parker's nomination unanimous. Dockery would then move to rescind the previous nomination. Former Missouri Lieutenant Governor David A. Ball would then move for the repeal of the two-thirds rule. Assuming the motion passed, Clark would then announce that only a simple majority would be necessary to accomplish the intended task.[48]

It turns out that Parker had indeed sent a telegram to the convention. But instead of sending it to Senator Carmack, he had sent the telegram to Sheehan. Why did Parker feel compelled to send a telegram to the convention? At the start of the convention, Parker believed that everyone understood his views on the money question. The Democratic Party was divided into two factions—the conservatives and the radicals—and the fight was between those two factions at the opening of the convention. Parker believed that his nomination "hinged upon the ascendancy of the conservatives, who were in favor of the recognition of the gold standard."[49] According to Parker, the thought never occurred to him that neither faction would win a complete victory, that there would be a compromise on the money question, and that the platform would omit all mention of such a vital matter.[50]

On Saturday morning, July 9, Parker thoroughly read the papers, ascertaining, for the first time, the full extent of the fight over the platform and the compromise and consequent silence concerning the money plank and his own subsequent nomination. Parker saddled his horse and went for a ride in the Esopus countryside, pondering how to solve the problem that his previous silence and the lack of a gold plank in the platform had created. He decided that he had to issue a statement concerning his unequivocal support of the gold standard lest Bryan and his supporters say that he had concealed his views on gold in order to trick them and obtain the nomination. Although the presidency might be lost, Parker believed that sending a message to the convention would allow him to retain his self-respect. He decided to telegraph the convention before it adjourned, make known his views, and urge the convention to nominate another if his views on the gold standard were not acceptable to the delegates.[51]

When he returned from his ride, Parker dictated the contents of a telegram to his secretary, Arthur McCausland; and Alvah S. Newcomb, the assistant state reporter. He asked both men for their opinions concerning the contents of the proposed telegram, and when both enthusiastically concurred with the contents, Parker instructed Newcomb to go to the local telegraph office and personally see to the transmission of the telegram to William F. Sheehan at the St. Louis convention.[52]

The telegram that Parker sent to Sheehan read: "I regard the gold standard as firmly and irrevocably established, and shall act accordingly if the action of the convention today shall be ratified by the people. As the platform is silent on the subject, my view should be made known to the convention, and, if it is proved to be unsatisfactory to the majority, I request you to decline the nomination for me at once, so that another may be nominated before adjournment."[53] Contrary to what the papers were reporting, Parker was not demanding that a gold plank be inserted in the party's platform, and he was not threatening to decline the nomination if that was not done. He was, however, stating his view, which previously had not been publicly expressed, that Bryan's support for free silver was an untenable position. Parker believed that his telegram laid to rest the money question—it was now a dead issue. He knew that the Democrats had to turn toward other concerns if they had any chance of regaining control of the White House.[54]

During the recess, Parker's telegram was shared with a cadre of Democratic leaders who had hastily met to decide what should be done about the party's nominee for president.[55] After reading Parker's actual telegram, and a lengthy conference, the leaders of the party decided that a new candidate and a new platform were not the answer.[56] They concurred that the campaign against Roosevelt was going to be tough enough without splitting the party further apart. They accepted Parker and his courageous act of sending the telegram.[57] The party bigwigs were convinced that Parker's stand could work for them, since a gallant play always has appeal, especially in politics.[58]

Following the meetings and the consensus that Parker's nomination would stand, the delegates decided that a reply to Parker's telegram was in order.[59] A reply was drafted, and the party leaders returned to the convention floor. Chairman Clark did not, in fact, recognize Governor Dockery. Instead, he introduced Mississippi Congressman and House Minority Leader John Sharp Williams.[60] Williams took to the stage and made an explanatory statement to the delegates.[61] He told them that a muddled and incorrect account of Parker's telegram had been published in hostile newspapers, in which it was reported that Senator Carmack had received a telegram from Judge Parker demanding the restoration of the gold plank, and threatening to resign if it was not done.[62] Williams further explained that Senator Carmack had never received a telegram from Parker and that Parker had made no demand that any changes be made in the party's platform—he had merely indicated that if the party intended the platform to be a free silver platform, and if his views on the money question were offensive to the delegates, his resignation was at their disposal since he did not want to hold on to a nomination made under a misapprehension.[63] These remarks seemed to not only satisfy the delegates, but also filled them with enthusiasm and admiration for their nominee, as evidenced by their loud and continuous applause.[64]

Williams then read Parker's telegram to the delegates and caused it to be reread by Mississippi Governor James K. Vardaman.[65] Williams then offered a resolution to send the previously drafted reply to Parker's telegram.[66] The reply was twice read to the convention, and South Carolina Senator Benjamin Tillman made a speech in favor of the resolution.[67] At that moment, Bryan took the stage and, despite the best efforts of Williams to convince him to say nothing, launched into a fiery speech "designed to distract, confuse and break up . . . [the] Convention, to misconstrue Parker's action, to criticize and discredit his party's nominee, and to give all the aid and comfort to the enemy he could."[68]

Bryan's efforts were to no avail. By a vote of 794 to 191, the following resolution was authorized to be sent to Parker in reply to his telegram: "The platform adopted by this convention is silent on the question of the monetary standard because it is not regarded by us as a possible issue in this campaign, and only campaign issues were mentioned in the platform. Therefore, there is nothing in the views expressed by you in the telegram just received which would preclude a man entertaining them from accepting a nomination on such platform."[69] Some commentators praised Parker's decision to send his telegram to the convention. James Creelman, a leading political journalist and an avid Parker backer, wrote the following concerning Parker's telegram in the August 1904 issue of the *American Monthly Review of Reviews*:

> There is no parallel to that act in American history. It may be that journalism is entitled to some credit for its quick warning; but under such circumstances, would President Roosevelt, Grover Cleveland, or William J. Bryan have accepted the hint and acted upon it so swiftly and fearlessly? Not every hero will take advice, even when it is obviously sound. Judge Parker

can listen as well as speak. That is one of his strong traits. He comes before the nation as a leader whom the wise and the brave can safely follow. A great genius? Probably not. But a sane, courageous, unselfish patriot of the old, pure, Democratic type—that he is beyond all questions.[70]

New York representative Bourke Cockran proclaimed:

[Parker's telegram] has revealed him to the people of this country almost in an instant as a great leader—the greatest of this generation; an honest man—the most impressive in displaying that virtue that I have ever known either through experience or reading; a courageous man—of such incomparable courage that he was willing to throw away not merely the hope or prospect of a nomination, but an actual nomination for the Presidency, rather than stoop to an evasion or equivocation on a matter of principle.[71]

Writers for the *New York Evening Post* stated:

A real man appeared above the American horizon on Sunday. Judge Parker had been represented as a veiled candidate; but at an intensely dramatic moment the curtain was dropped, and he was revealed as a figure of heroic proportions . . . We suspect that the Republicans will not hereafter be so eager to challenge comparison of personalities. It appears that your charging colonels are not the only ones in whom civic courage may be bred. That product seems to thrive even better on the banks of the Hudson than on San Juan Hill . . . Already it is plain that the kindling hope and zeal put into the hearts of young men by Grover Cleveland are to be renewed under the inspiration of Judge Parker's leadership.[72]

And consider this from the editors of *The World's Work*: "[T]he convention's indirection gave Judge Parker an opportunity to show, by a single telegram, that he is a man of uncommon courage and frankness, fit for the highest and greatest responsibilities. It won the world's admiration instantly; and he has given to his party leadership with character such as it has had but once before within the memory of living men."[73] According to the *New York Times*:

> In Alton B. Parker the Democratic Party has a leader who leads . . .

~

> Never in our political history has a candidate for President, already nominated by his party, shown greater courage, a finer fidelity to principle, or stronger elements of leadership than Judge Parker did in this dispatch. That his position was indorsed by the convention by a vote of 774 to 191—more than a hundred larger than the vote by which he was nominated—was a gratifying proof of the respect felt for sanity and courage when the matter was brought to the test . . .

~

> The party can now enter upon the campaign with courage and hope. It has a candidate who is the antithesis of Roosevelt in temperament and opinion, and quite the equal of the strenuous President in moral courage and political sagacity.[74]

Roosevelt himself believed that Parker's bold act in sending the telegram to the convention was a shrewd move. Roosevelt remarked that Parker had "become a formidable candidate and opponent; for instead of being a colorless man of no convictions he now stands forth to the average man . . . as one having convictions compared to which he treats self-interest as of no account . . . I think that this act gave him all of Cleveland's strength without any of Cleveland's weakness, and made him, on the whole, the most formidable man the Democrats could have nominated."[75]

But not everyone believed that sending the telegram was a good idea. Champ Clark, the chairman of the 1904 Democratic National Convention, surmised that Parker's chances to win the presidency evaporated when he sent his telegram to the convention: "Perhaps Colonel Roosevelt would have been elected no matter what the Democratic candidate, for the tide was running strong in his favor; but many think to this day that until Judge Parker sent his 'Gold telegram,' his chances of success were no means hopeless. However, that may be, it unquestionably put a damper on Democrats in West and South, and brought him no additional strength in the East."[76] South Carolina Senator "Pitchfork" Ben Tillman told David B. Hill, in response to Parker's gold telegram, "the Democratic party can always be relied on to make a damn fool of itself at the critical time."[77]

Not surprisingly, the editors of the Republican and western independent press depicted Parker as an "opportunist," not a hero. Editors of the *San Francisco Bulletin* remarked that "Judge Parker is a respectable man whom nobody outside of his own State ever heard of until he was put forward as Dave Hill's man for the nomination and who will be as respectable in defeat as he was in obscurity."[78] The editor of the *Cincinnati Times-Star* said of Parker's nomination that "no political party ever sought before a man who represents nothing, voices nothing, who is nothing."[79] The editor of the *New-York Tribune,* in an editorial titled "Simply a Sharp Political Trick," said that Parker had "played a shrewd game of politics. By maintaining his own silence and permitting his accredited agents to create an erroneous impression of perfect docility on his part . . . we cannot concede that the final dramatic act in a skillful performance entitled him to be acclaimed as a man of heroic mould."[80]

The *Oklahoma Law Journal*, in making a prediction that turned out to be entirely true, said the following about Parker's gold telegram:

> We must say from an independent standpoint and without partisan prejudice that he has placed his party in a very awkward position. In doing so he may have acted from honest motives; but whether from honest convictions or otherwise the result will be the same and the blow inflicted on his party will prove none the less fatal to his election. His party stood uncompromisingly opposed to the gold standard. One half of the party is still absolutely opposed to it and idolized their grand and gallant leader Bryan who like the Spartan boy had the courage to endure the pain of the wolf gnawing at his heart without discomposure, but will never indorse the gold standard. Mr. Parker does not only endorse it but says it is "settled and fixed." An admission that the Republicans were right in the past and in establishing it, and that his party was wrong. If his party was wrong then by his own admission, how will he convince the voters of the country that his party

is right now? Especially in the face of the fact of not only this admission, but of the evasion of the money question in the platform—another admission that his party does not dare tackle it. The voters will ask "why a distinction without a difference? Why leave the Republican party that established the gold standard to vote with you for a gold standard?" And will the western Democrats stultify themselves and say "We were fools, our great leader was not great at all; greatness and ability is only to be found with our enemies of 1896 and 1900, and we must help them out now so they can enjoy it hereafter, and not only tell us 'I told you so,' but that when they get control of all National political affairs they can relegate us to the rear and give us seats with the infant classes where we can't hurt any one." The human heart must change its nature, and the day of miracles return between now and next November, if Mr. Parker is to be elected, however good and worthy a man he may be, under the surrounding and attendant circumstances.[81]

Having laid the monetary issue to rest, for better or for worse, the delegates turned their attention to electing their candidate for vice president. On the first ballot, Henry Gassaway Davis was selected as the Democratic nominee for vice president of the United States. Davis received 654 first ballot votes, James R. Williams received 165 votes, George Turner received 100 votes, and William A. Harris received 58 votes.[82] Kentucky Secretary of State C. B. Hill moved to make Davis's nomination unanimous. That motion passed unanimously.[83] Davis, at eighty years of age, was the oldest person ever nominated by a major party for the office of the vice presidency. The Democrats believed Davis was the ideal candidate for vice president—he was from the South (his nomination bolstered the East-South coalition), he was from a state that the Democrats needed to win if they had any hope of capturing the White House (West Virginia), and he was exceedingly wealthy (a deep pocket to help defray campaign expenses).

Colonel Watterson, who had issued the scathing editorial lambasting Bryan's actions leading up the Democratic National Convention, wrote a second editorial, on July 10, 1904, the last day of the convention, in an effort to rally the troops in support of Parker as the Democratic nominee. He emphasized that Parker was the very antithesis of Roosevelt, in character, temperament, and political conviction. He predicted that Parker would carry New York, which in turn would carry New Jersey and Connecticut. He correctly predicted that the South would be solidly behind the Democratic nominee. And he ended his editorial with the following exhortation: "Fools to the rear. Braves to the front! March."[84]

Grover Cleveland, who had early on endorsed Parker, published an article in *Collier's Weekly* at the end of July promoting Parker as the ideal candidate. Cleveland wrote, in part, that "forbidding portents were seen in the Democratic sky when a platform deliverance intended to pass as a recognition and approval of the gold standard was rejected after discussion in the platform committee, leaving no substituted expression of any kind in its place" and, as a consequence, "trepidation and disappointment . . . immediately supervened among the masses of the expectant Democracy." But "at this critical moment the sun appeared and scattered every evil portent"; "a leader came to the Democratic hosts"; and "while the Democratic rank and file trembled and waited, the voice of this quiet, reserved, and able man rang out above all convention clamor, drowning the roisterous hum of convention diplomacy," and giving his message "in tones of authority and leadership."[85] According to Cleveland, as a result of Parker's telegram, and its subsequent approval by the delegates, "the National Democracy enters upon the campaign, not in gloom and fear, but in hope and confidence."[86]

The Republicans, for their part, wasted no time in calling the Democratic ticket "an enigma from New York and a ruin from West Virginia."[87] Republican Senator Henry Cabot Lodge of Massachusetts seriously questioned the motives of the Democrats in nominating Davis. "To nominate a man 81 years old for Vice-President is strange," he wrote to President Roosevelt on July 12, "but I suppose it means money and a desperate bid for West Va."[88]

Bryan, who had been a perpetual thorn in Parker's side during the convention, issued a statement in the days following the convention that he intended to vote for Parker and Davis for the following reasons:

> First—Because the Democratic ticket stands for opposition to imperialism, while the Republican ticket stands for an imperialistic policy . . . Second—Mr. Roosevelt is injecting the race question into American politics, and this issue, if it becomes national, will make it impossible to consider economic questions that demand solution . . . Third—Mr. Roosevelt stands for the spirit of war . . . The Democratic ticket stands for peace, for reason, and for arbitration rather than for force, conquest and

bluster. Fourth—The Democratic platform declares in favor of the reduction of the standing army, and, as this plank was unanimously adopted, there is reason to believe that a Democratic success on this subject would bring some advantage to the people.[89]

Despite proclaiming his support for the ticket, Bryan could not help but address the money issue. Bryan claimed that there was no hope for the Democratic Party so long as it was controlled by the Wall Street element and that "on the money question Mr. Parker is as thoroughly converted to the side of the financiers as Mr. Roosevelt."[90] He then attacked Parker's decision to send his gold telegram to the convention:

> If he had sent to the Albany convention the telegram that he sent to the St. Louis convention, he would have had very few instructed delegates from the South, and no possible chance for the nomination. But he and his managers adroitly and purposely concealed his position until the delegates had been corralled and the nomination assured. Then his friends attempted to secure a gold plank, which was overwhelmingly defeated in committee. After the party had rejoiced over the harmony secured by the omission of the question, and after he had secured the nomination, he injected his views upon the subject at a time when he could not be taken from the ticket without great demoralization. The nomination was secured, therefore, by crooked and indefensible methods, but the Democrat who loves his country has to make his decisions upon conditions as he finds them, not upon conditions as he would like to have them.[91]

Bryan concluded his statement by putting everyone on notice that after the election he intended to organize a campaign for 1908 for "a radical and comprehensive policy within the Democratic party against 'the plutocratic element that controls the Republican party and, for the time being, the Democratic party.'"[92]

The *Philadelphia North American* published a cartoon in the days following the convention that ridiculed Bryan's "support" of Parker. Bryan is depicted as an old woman sitting in a rocking chair. Parker is draped over his knee and is being swatted with Bryan's oversized slipper. A sign on the wall recites several of Bryan's public statements about Parker: "Parker is controlled by Wall Street"; "Parker's nomination nullifies the anti-trust plank"; "Nothing good can be expected from Parker on the money question"; and "Parker got the nomination by deceit!" Underneath the quotes it says, "P.S. I'll vote for Parker." The caption of the cartoon reads, "Auntie Bryan: You know, Alton, this pains me as much as it does you!"

The Democrats left their convention, and entered the campaign, "with a conservative candidate, a platform that was neither one thing nor the other, an octogenarian for second place, and the radical wing as disgruntled and disaffected as the conservative wing had been before."[93] Their standard-bearer in the prior two elections was unenthusiastic about the nominee. Campaign contributions were scarce. Winning in November was going to be a decided challenge.

There was one other interesting issue that the Democrats were going to have to wrestle with in the coming campaign. In most elections, the nominee counts on name recognition and favorite son status to win his or her home state. The election of 1904 marked the first time that the presidential nominees of both parties hailed from the state of New York (it would happen again in 1944, when Franklin Roosevelt ran against Thomas Dewey, and in 2016, when Hillary Rodham Clinton ran against Donald J. Trump). Unquestionably, Parker would have to fight incredibly hard to win votes away from New York's most famous citizen, Theodore Roosevelt.

8

Parker's Running Mate

Henry Gassaway Davis

Henry Gassaway Davis (see figure 8.1) was born in the village of Woodstock, Maryland, a few miles from Baltimore, on November 16, 1823, the third child of Caleb Davis and Louisa Brown Davis.[1] He had an

Figure 8.1. Henry Gassaway Davis at the time of the 1904 campaign. Courtesy of George Prince, Library of Congress, Washington, DC. Public domain.

older brother, John, and an older sister, Elizabeth. He had a younger sister, Eliza Ann, and two younger brothers, Thomas and William.[2] His mother's ancestors served in the Continental Army during the Revolutionary War. His father was a soldier in the War of 1812, and after the war he became a successful merchant and lived on a farm in Howard County, Maryland.[3]

Davis's father was one of the founders of the Village of Woodstock, Maryland.[4] In Henry's early years, the Davis family was prosperous and happy. They had a comfortable home, a nice carriage, and ponies for the children to ride, and they always provided generous hospitality for friends and relatives.[5] Henry was described as "a carefree lad, with a love for the out-of-doors and a real liking for farming."[6] According to his early acquaintances, "he went 'possum hunting with . . . [the neighborhood boys] and roamed the woods and went fishing in the streams."[7]

In the late 1820s, Caleb Davis closed his store and, despite having no experience, decided to help build the Baltimore & Ohio Railroad (the B&O). In the early 1830s he suffered severe financial losses, both because of his own venture in contracting to grade a section of the B&O and because he had signed notes for other contractors who had failed and defaulted.[8] When the "Panic of 1837" hit, Caleb Davis lost all of his property—even the children's ponies were sold to cover his debts.[9] At about the same time, he suffered severe mental and physical infirmities, and Louisa Davis became his primary caretaker. To support the family, Louisa remodeled her home and opened a school for young girls.[10]

Henry Davis was fourteen when his father became incapacitated. He had received some home schooling and perhaps a year of actual educational instruction. His love for his mother, and his inclination to do his part in supporting the family, caused him to abandon any idea of continuing his formal education and to look for employment.[11] He obtained a job as a water boy in the Woodstock quarries, carrying water in stone jugs to the laborers when they became thirsty. He also did seasonal work for neighboring farmers, helping with planting, harvesting, and haymaking.[12]

In 1838, former Maryland governor George Howard, who knew the Davis family well, asked Louisa if Henry could go to work for him at Waverly, his family plantation. Louisa readily agreed, and Henry went to Waverly to live and work. Henry worked hard, and within two or three years he was given supervision of the accounts, made responsible for distributing supplies to the slaves, and given considerable oversight of the farmwork.[13] Davis stayed with Governor Howard until some time in 1842, when he was about twenty years of age.[14]

By 1842, the B&O had extended its railroad line to Cumberland, Maryland. The increase in traffic on the B&O once it reached Cumberland led to a need for more railroad employees. The superintendent of the B&O, a Dr. Woodside, knew Henry Davis from his work on Governor Howard's estate. He offered Davis a job as a brakeman on a freight train. Physical strength and mental judgment were the prime qualifications for a brakeman—Davis had both in abundance. In the railway parlance of the day, the "armstrong" brakeman was the most important component of the freight train, since the train had to be stopped by forcing the brake shoes against the wheels by sheer manual power.[15]

In due course Henry was promoted from brakeman to conductor on the freight line. He was then promoted to supervisor of the B&O line between Baltimore and Cumberland. By the late 1840s, Davis had been promoted to a conductor on the passenger trains.[16]

Sometime in the early 1850s, Henry Davis met Katharine Ann Bantz of Frederick, Maryland. Katharine and Henry, who was six years her senior, wed on February 22, 1853.[17] Henry and Kate had seven children: Mary Louise ("Hallie"), Kate Bantz, Anderson Cord, Ada Kate, Grace Thomas, Henry Jr., and John Thomas. Anderson and Ada Kate both died in early childhood.[18] Henry was drowned off the coast of South Africa in 1896. Hallie married Stephen B. Elkins, a Republican who served as secretary of war under President Benjamin Harrison and as a US senator from the state of West Virginia.[19] Kate married Lieutenant Robert M. G. Brown.[20] Grace married Arthur Lee, a member of the famous Lee family of Virginia.[21] John married Bessie Armstead of Brooklyn, New York, and was involved in several of his father's business concerns.[22]

After Henry and Kate got married, Henry was offered the position of station agent and superintendent of motive power at Piedmont, Virginia, a job he readily accepted. As station agent, he was responsible for sending the trains up over the Divide, designating the engineers and the train crews, and adjusting their labor.[23] Shortly after Henry began his duties at Piedmont, Kate's father died, leaving her approximately fifty thousand dollars. Henry used that money to start a general store and invest in large tracts of timber and coal lands.[24] When the general store first opened, Henry, and his brother Thomas, who had joined him in the business, sold groceries, hardware, and dry goods to the farmers in the upper reaches of the North Branch of the Potomac River. Soon, however, the company, known as H.G. Davis & Company, was primarily engaged in supplying the B&O with lumber and in shipping coal and oil. The Davis brothers opened lumber camps and built sawmills and began mining coal. They organized and incorporated the Piedmont Savings Bank, with Henry as the president and brothers Thomas and William as directors.[25]

By 1858, Davis was an accomplished and successful entrepreneur. His business ventures demanded his full-time attention and were supplying him with a sizeable income. As a result, he resigned his position with the B&O Railroad Company. He would never again be an employee of anyone else.[26]

With the election of Abraham Lincoln as president in 1860, the southern states had the excuse they needed to secede from the union. Shortly after the Civil War began, the northwestern counties of Virginia separated from Virginia, and in 1863 the new state of West Virginia was admitted to the Union. Davis was thirty-eight years old at the start of the war. H.G. Davis & Company obtained contracts to supply the Union army with foodstuffs, horses, and other supplies. The company was also kept busy supplying lumber and coal to the B&O Railroad. To meet the insatiable demand for lumber, Davis bought extensive tracts of timber and built additional sawmills and lumber camps.[27]

When the war ended, H.G. Davis & Company had made substantial profits and had accumulated a considerable amount of capital. Davis and his brothers used that capital to purchase several thousand acres of fine timberlands in West Virginia and Maryland.[28] These lands, when harvested of their timber and stripped of their coal, would make Davis a multimillionaire and help catapult him into the upper echelons of West Virginia society.

The political career of Henry Davis began in 1865. Within six months of the end of the war, Davis was elected from Hampshire County to the West Virginia House of Delegates as a member of the Union-Conservative party.[29] Davis's second act in the legislature was to carve a new county, Mineral County, out of Hampshire County. Soon thereafter he played a leading role in getting a bill enacted to carve Grant County out of Hardy County. During that same session he succeeded in obtaining passage of a bill to charter the Potomac & Piedmont Coal and Railroad Company (Davis was one of the original incorporators of the railroad). Before the end of the legislative session, Davis was successful in obtaining passage of a bill providing for the incorporation of Piedmont as a town.[30] Having succeeded in fathering two counties, obtaining a charter for his railroad company, and incorporating his hometown, Davis chose to not seek reelection in 1866.[31]

In 1868 Davis was elected to the West Virginia State Senate. He took the oath of office as a state senator on January 19, 1869. He was assigned to the Committees on Finance and Claims, Internal Improvements, Navigation, and Auditing.[32] While a state senator, Davis was instrumental in securing the repeal of test oaths and other laws that limited the suffrage of or otherwise discriminated against former supporters of the Confederacy. He also played a leading role in the framing and passage of revenue and appropriation bills and in settling the dispute involving West Virginia's share of Virginia's pre–Civil War debt.[33]

Henry Davis served with distinction in the West Virginia State Senate until 1871, when he was elected by the West Virginia legislature to the US Senate.[34] When Davis took his seat in the Senate on March 4, 1871, he joined some of the giants of that body, including Republicans Roscoe Conkling of New York, Charles Sumner of Massachusetts, Hannibal Hamlin of Maine, Simon Cameron of Pennsylvania, and Lyman Trumball of Illinois; and Democrats Allen G. Thurman of Ohio and Thomas F. Bayard of Delaware.[35] Davis was assigned to the Committee on Claims (an important committee dealing with claims of various sorts from individuals and companies for government payment for services or damages connected with the Civil War), the Committee on Agriculture, and the Committee on Engrossed Bills.[36]

When Davis became chairman of the Senate Committee on Agriculture, he earnestly advocated the formation of a new executive department devoted to the interests of those engaged in farming. He introduced bills to grant cabinet status to the Department of Agriculture and to establish the Department of Commerce (neither of which passed during his time in the Senate).[37] In 1873, Davis was appointed to a much-coveted seat on the Appropriations Committee. He eventually became chairman of the committee when the Democrats gained control of the Senate in 1879.[38]

Davis was reelected to the US Senate on January 27, 1877. He began his second term on March 4, 1877.[39] During his two terms in the Senate, Davis was involved in votes on some of the most pressing issues of the day, including the Ku Klux Klan Act of 1871, which authorized the president to suspend the writ of habeas corpus and to use military force to suppress the Klan (Davis voted against it); the Treaty of Washington, which settled all disputes against Great Britain arising out of its conduct during the Civil War (Davis voted against it); the "Salary Grab" of 1873, a bill that doubled the president's salary and increased by 50 percent the salaries of the vice president, the Supreme Court justices, and members of

Congress (Davis voted against it); the "Inflation Bill" of 1874, which was designed to increase the amount of currency then in circulation (Davis voted for it); the impeachment trial of Secretary of War William Belknap (Davis voted to convict on all counts); establishment of the Electoral Commission to decide the outcome of the disputed 1876 presidential election (Davis voted in favor of establishing the commission, which eventually gave the presidency to Rutherford B. Hayes, despite the fact that Samuel J. Tilden had received a quarter of a million more votes than Hayes); the Bland-Allison Act, which provided for increased coinage of silver dollars and set their value in gold at the ratio of sixteen to one (Davis voted for it); and the Pendleton Act, which mandated that most positions within the federal government be awarded on the basis of merit instead of political patronage (Davis voted for it).[40]

On November 18, 1882, Senator Davis sent a letter to the *Wheeling Register* stating that he would not be a candidate for reelection to the Senate. He stated that "business is more agreeable to me than politics, and I am now engaged in lumbering, mining, banking and farming . . . These and other private matters are reasons which forbid my being a candidate for reelection."[41] Davis's last day in the Senate was March 3, 1883.[42]

When Davis retired from the US Senate, he devoted his full time and attention to the construction of the West Virginia Central and Pittsburgh Railway (the C&P). This railroad was designed to provide transportation for north central West Virginia and to serve as a means to transport to market the timber and coal located on and under the vast tracts of land Davis had purchased in the region.[43] Several of Davis's close friends from the Senate became stockholders and directors in the railroad, including Thomas F. Bayard, James G. Blaine, J. N. Camden, Jerome B. Chaffee, Stephen B. Elkins, Arthur Pue Gorman, William Pinckney White, and William Windom.[44] Ultimately, the C&P would stretch for 112.1 miles, from Cumberland, Maryland, to Elkins, West Virginia, and would allow Davis to exploit and monetize the natural resources of large swaths of the West Virginia countryside.[45] Davis sold the C&P in 1902 for several million dollars and immediately organized the Coal & Coke Railway Company. He was the sole owner of that railroad and ultimately supervised the laying of 175 miles of track from Elkins to Charleston, West Virginia.[46]

In 1889, President Benjamin Harrison appointed Henry Davis to be one of the US delegates to the First Pan-American Conference. The purpose of the conference was to promote closer relations with the other nations of the Western Hemisphere. John B. Henderson of Missouri, a former senator and an expert on international law, served as the chairman of the US delegation. Other delegates included William H. Trescott of South Carolina, Cornelius N. Bliss of New York, Clement Studebaker of Indiana, T. Jefferson Coolidge of Massachusetts, Andrew Carnegie of New York, M. M. Estee of California, John F. Hanson of Georgia, and Charles R. Flint of New York.[47] Davis was asked to serve on the Pan-American Railway Committee and the Committee on Custom Relations.[48] President Harrison also appointed Davis to be one of the three US commissioners on the Intercontinental Railway Commission, a body that was tasked with investigating the feasibility of building a railroad from the United States to all the independent countries of Central and South America.[49]

In 1901, President McKinley named Davis as a delegate to the Second Pan-American Conference, which was scheduled to meet in Mexico City on October 22, 1901. The other US delegates to the conference were W. I. Buchanan, the former minister to Argentina; Volney W. Foster, an Illinois businessman; journalist Charles M. Pepper of the District of Columbia; and John Barrett, the former minister to Siam. Davis was selected by his associates as chairman of the delegation.[50] At his suggestion, a Committee on Committees was formed, and he was named as chairman. Under his leadership, this committee prepared a number of proposals that provided for continuity of Pan-American conferences well into the future. Davis also served as the chairman of the Pan-American Railway Committee and was instrumental in drafting a report that provided for the establishment of a permanent Pan-American Railway Committee.[51] Davis served as chairman of the permanent committee, along with Andrew Carnegie; Don Manuel de Azpiroz, Mexican ambassador to the United States; Manuel Alvarez Calderon, Peruvian minister to the United States; and Antonio Lazo Arriaga, Guatemalan minister to the United States.[52]

For decades before and after his service as a US senator, Davis was active in national politics. Between 1868 and 1904, he attended eight Democratic National Conventions. He was a delegate from West Virginia to the 1868 Democratic National Convention held in New York City.[53] He was a delegate from West Virginia to the 1872 Democratic National Convention in Baltimore, Maryland.[54] He was a delegate from West Virginia to the 1876 Democratic National Convention held in St. Louis, Missouri.[55] He was a delegate from West Virginia to the 1880 Democratic National Convention in Cincinnati, Ohio.[56] In 1884 he attended the Democratic National Convention in Chicago, Illinois, as a delegate from West Virginia.[57] He was asked to accept the nomination for vice president at the 1884 convention, but he declined to allow his name to be placed in nomination.⁵⁸ He did serve as a member of the Committee on Resolutions and was a member of the subcommittee that formulated the Democratic platform in 1884.⁵⁹ In 1888 he attended the Democratic National Convention in St. Louis, Missouri, as a delegate from West Virginia, and in 1892 he attended the Democratic National Convention in Chicago as a West Virginia delegate.⁶⁰ He did not attend the 1896 or 1900 conventions but was back as a delegate, representing West Virginia, at the Democratic National Convention in 1904.⁶¹

Davis was a noted philanthropist throughout his life and used his immense fortune to help those who were in need. He provided the funds for a new high school in Piedmont, West Virginia, in 1886. In 1893 he gave a nine-acre park to the city of Elkins, West Virginia. He and his brother, Thomas, erected the Davis Memorial Presbyterian Church, in Elkins, in memory of their mother. He also paid for the erection and outfitting of a church for the African-American residents of Elkins. He established the Children's Home in Charleston, West Virginia, and endowed the place with a yearly annuity of one thousand dollars for maintenance of the home. He provided sixty-five thousand dollars for a YMCA site and adjacent park in Charleston, West Virginia; contributed to a YMCA building in Parkersburg; and helped his daughter, Hallie Elkins, build and furnish a YMCA in Elkins. He erected the Davis Memorial Hospital in Elkins in honor of his eldest son, Henry G. Davis Jr. Along with his son-in-law, Stephen B. Elkins, he provided the land and the funding for the establishment and continued maintenance of Davis & Elkins College.⁶² He also built a home for the president of the college.⁶³

Although Davis was eighty years old at the time of his nomination, he appeared to be much younger. He was described as hearty, "six feet tall, as straight as an Indian, without an ounce of fat, rugged in countenance and a grip that is reminiscent of the days when he was a railroad brakeman. His face is illuminated by a hearty smile whenever he greets anyone. But his countenance has no soft lines. He wears a close-cropped beard, with the upper lip shaved, and dresses fashionably . . . Ex-Senator Davis, though in his eighty-first year, is as spry as a man of 60, and a good deal spryer than many."⁶⁴ Another writer observed that "Davis's face features are regular and bold. His nose is aquiline. His eyes gray and sharply penetrating, but withal kindly in expression and set wide apart . . . The whole bearing of the man denotes an alert, vigorous interest in life . . . He is of a kind disposition. He laughs easily. He is the soul of good nature, and he is essentially democratic. One short sentence really describes the man. He's a Southern gentleman of the old school."[65] Yet another set of commentators provided the following physical description of Davis at the time of his nomination:

> Standing six feet in height, lean and loose-jointed, the observer would estimate his age at from fifty-eight to sixty years. If he were to declare himself sixty-two, the listener would make mental reservations regarding his veracity. He has a healthy brown skin, but not the ruddy complexion of Andrew Carnegie. His upper lip is clean-shaven. His hair and close-cropped beard show jet black alternating with white. Both are typically iron-gray.
>
> No man can surpass Mr. Davis in amiability. His clear brown eyes are always laughing. He is invariably pleasant and approachable. He is democratic by profession and practice. His voice is ordinarily keyed to a low, soft, musical pitch, but when occasion requires he can give it the most surprising force and volume. The vehemence of these infrequent utterances belie the surface indications of under-strength. He is in no sense a rugged-looking man. His step is not firm or elastic. It never was either. He walks with an easy, sliding motion. He is never garrulous, but always conversational . . .

~

> The physical endurance of Mr. Davis is surprising, and almost irritating to younger men who do not possess his untiring vitality. He seems never to become tired. He is always fresh and vigorous. His capacity for hard work is unlimited. Neither loss of sleep nor hardship impairs his energy . . .[66]

David would need all of that endurance for the campaign ahead.

9

The Campaign Begins

Parker knew that in the aftermath of the convention he needed to try to unify the party. To that end, he reached out to Bryan to try to solicit his help during the campaign. Three days following his nomination, Parker invited Bryan to visit him at Rosemount. On July 23, Parker sent a letter to Bryan thanking him for a copy of Bryan's last acceptance speech, delivered four years earlier, in which he had spelled out his opposition to the Republican policy of imperialism. Parker indicated to Bryan that he would incorporate some of Bryan's thoughts on imperialism into his own attacks on the subject in the current campaign. And on August 12, 1904, he sent another letter to Bryan outlining his hope that the Nebraska legislature would elect Bryan to the US Senate. These overtures did little to bring Bryan into the Parker camp and even less to unify the party.

On July 14, 1904, former President Cleveland pledged his assistance to Parker's campaign and reminded Parker that he was anxious to see the Democrats triumph in November:

> Our best campaign material just now is—<u>You</u>. I mean "You" as you are manifested to your countrymen in the despatch you sent to St. Louis. The spirit and sentiment aroused by this utterance of yours, should be kept alive and stimulated from time to time during the campaign. Occasions will present themselves when you respond probably to the Committee on notification and when you write your letter of acceptance . . . For myself I do not think expediency demands of you the distortion of anything your judgment suggests, in deference to the South

or the radicals of our party. Bryan is doing the cause much good in his present mood; and I for one hope it will continue.[1]

Nine days later, Cleveland published an open letter in *Collier's* magazine to the party faithful titled "Steady, Democrats, Steady!" In it he recounted the discouraging failure of the platform committee to include a plank affirming the gold standard and the resulting "trepidation and disappointment which immediately supervened among the masses" of expectant Democrats who were eager to eliminate "any further free silver or double standard vagaries."[2] Amid the gloom and doom, a quiet, able, and reserved man strode forth and pronounced "in tones of authority and leadership" an irrevocable adherence to the gold standard. According to Cleveland, Parker's gold telegram to the convention "filled the blank in a disabled platform . . . gave leadership to the Democratic cause, and rallied supporters by thousands and tens of thousands to the Democratic standard."[3] Cleveland ended his letter by reminding all Democrats that the party was entering "upon the campaign, not in gloom and fear, but in hope and confidence . . . [Parker] has reminded all who profess Democratic principles that they also have work to do if they, like him, would do the patriotic political duty the time demands."[4] His final words of encouragement: "Let the Democratic lines be steadied at every point; and let our splendid leadership be followed with genuine Democratic zeal and stubbornness."[5]

Less than two weeks after the conclusion of the Democratic convention, on July 21, 1904, Henry Gassaway Davis traveled to Esopus, New York, to meet his presidential running mate for the very first time (see figure 9.1). Upon meeting, "both men clasped hands warmly, exchanged greetings, and in a few minutes former Senator Davis was as much 'at home' as though Rosemount had long been on his visiting list."[6] Indeed, Davis noted in his diary that he "spent several hours with the Judge—like him very well."[7] Davis and Parker spent a significant amount of time together at Rosemount talking about the issues of the day and the impending campaign. After a five-hour consultation, the candidates made one official announcement: both Parker and Davis would be notified separately of their nominations at their respective homes (there had been some speculation that both would be notified of their nominations while Davis was visiting Rosemount).[8]

Within ten days of his nomination, Parker had grown tired of the constant attention of reporters and press photographers. He issued a statement demanding that the constant photography of Parker and his

Figure 9.1. Parker and Davis meet for the first time on the porch of Rosemount, July 21, 1904. Courtesy of G. V. Buck, Library of Congress, Washington, DC. Public domain.

family must stop: "I reserve the right to put my hands in my pockets, and to assume comfortable attitudes, without having to be everlastingly afraid that I shall be snapped by some fellow with a camera."[9] He thereafter refused to be photographed.[10]

Shortly after Parker issued his demand that he and his family not be photographed, the *New York Times* published on its front page an open letter to Judge Parker from Abigail Roberson, the plaintiff in the *Roberson v. Rochester Folding Box Co.* case. "I take this opportunity," Roberson indignantly wrote, "to remind you that you have no such right as that which you assert. I have very high authority for my statement, being nothing less than a decision of the Court of Appeals of this State, wherein you wrote the prevailing opinion."[11] Then, having pointed out that Parker, a candidate for the highest office in the country, was asserting the very same right that he had denied to a "poor girl" who "never had courted publicity," Roberson observed that her plea for privacy was exceedingly more plausible than his.[12]

The Democratic National Committee met on July 26, 1904, to elect a national chairman. Thomas Taggart, an Irish-born Indiana hotel proprietor and a member of the committee, was unanimously elected to the position. Upon being notified of his election, Taggart stated, "I thank you for the great honor which you have done me in selecting me for your Chairman. I realize fully the responsibility that goes with the honor. I feel that with our candidates and our platform we can win the coming election, but we can do it only by the united efforts of the members of the committee and every Democrat. I ask you for your help in the future. I will fill the duties of my office faithfully, and, I hope, intelligently."[13] Urey Woodson, a Kentucky newspaper editor and publisher, was elected secretary.[14]

A week later, Taggart announced the appointments of those who were to assist him in managing the campaign. New York lawyer De Lancey Nicoll was appointed vice chairman of the national committee. George Foster Peabody, a southern-born New York banker and philanthropist, was named national treasurer. August Belmont; Colonel James M. Guffey, a Pennsylvania oilman; Virginia Senator Thomas S. Martin; John R. McLean, owner and publisher of the *Cincinnati Enquirer*; Wisconsin attorney Timothy E. Martin; William F. Sheehan; and former New Jersey senator James Smith Jr. were named to the executive committee. Sheehan was asked to serve as the chairman of the executive committee.[15] Daniel McConville of Ohio resumed management of the Speakers' Bureau, a position he held during the campaigns of 1896 and 1900. Grover Cleveland's friend George F. Parker (no relation to the candidate) served as the head of the Literary Bureau, as he had during the campaigns of 1888 and 1892. Parker's early advocate, Maurice M. Minton, headed the Press Bureau.[16]

On August 5, 1904, a little less than a month after the Democratic convention, the New York Court of Appeals held a rare and unannounced session in Albany to dispose of a large portion of the court's outstanding docket. Parker traveled by train to Albany from Rosemount that morning, and by late afternoon the judges had performed the official acts necessary for the release of sixty-six opinions.[17] Once the court adjourned, Parker gave up his duties on the New York Court of Appeals, despite receiving a unanimous opinion from his fellow judges that his resignation from the bench was unnecessary.[18] After twenty-seven years on the bench, doing the one job he truly loved, Parker sent the following succinct letter to New York Secretary of State John F. O'Brien:

Hon. John F. O'Brien

Secretary of State, Albany, N.Y.

Sir: I hereby respectfully resign my office as Chief Judge of the Court of Appeals of the state of New York, and such resignation to take effect immediately.

Alton B. Parker

Rosemount, Esopus, N.Y.

August 5, 1904[19]

By resigning before August 8, Parker eliminated the possibility, should he be defeated in the presidential election, of being reelected to the chief judgeship in November 1905. Had he waited until August 12 to resign, there would not have been enough time, under the relevant statutes, to elect a successor to a full term of fourteen years.[20] Always committed to doing the right thing, Parker insisted on a timely resignation so the people (as opposed to the Republican governor) could decide who should replace him—even though that decision likely meant that he would never be a judge again.

Once he resigned from the court, Parker waited to be formally notified of his nomination.[21] Notification ceremonies were special occasions for the candidates, full of pomp and ceremony and marked by both notification and acceptance speeches. In the case of Parker, who had remained steadfastly mum about his positions on the pressing issues of the day, it was the first opportunity for the citizenry to hear his stand on the issues.

The notification committee for Judge Parker was chaired by Champ Clark. Clark, along with several other members of the notification committee, including the chairman of the Democratic National Committee, Tom Taggart, visited Parker at Rosemount on August 10, 1904. In the hours before the committee members arrived, Esopus was shrouded in fog, and rain fell in sheets on Parker's steep lawn, causing mud to cascade down into the river.[22]

When the notification committee arrived at Rosemount, they disembarked at the Rosemount pier from the small steamer that had brought them north from New York City and looked with trepidation at the slippery path up to the house. An authoritative escort lined them up two abreast and shouted "Forward, march!"[23] Almost immediately, the carefully orchestrated formation disintegrated as the party officials floundered and lost traction on the treacherous slope. One of the special guests, bent almost double, was heard to say that the hero of San Juan himself "couldn't climb this hill!"[24] August Belmont's shoes raced on a patch of slimy mud, and he tumbled backward. Fortunately, someone quickly caught him, or the party's richest benefactor would have ended up in the Hudson River.[25]

Parker waited on Rosemount's porch until the dignitaries came up, drenched and puffing, to shake his hand. He then led the way to a small stage in the garden draped with patriotic bunting. About two thousand friends and townspeople, as well as the notification committee, crowded around to hear the candidate's first words on the important issues of the day[26] (see figure 9.2).

Champ Clark began his notification address by emphasizing that the Democrats emerged from their St. Louis convention "a reunited party"

Figure 9.2. Well-wishers waiting for the notification ceremony to start. From the Alton B. Parker Papers, Manuscript Division, Library of Congress, Washington, DC. Public domain.

looking to prevail in the fall elections. He praised the "absolutely free and . . . great debates" that took place at the convention and emphasized that out of this openness "there grew such unity as encourages lovers of liberty and of pure government everywhere." He then turned to the aims and purposes of the Democratic party: "to serve the whole American people without discrimination; faithfully and well; to distribute the benefits of the Federal Government impartially to all . . . citizens; to lighten the burdens of Government by reducing taxation to the minimum . . . ; to administer the powers conferred by the Constitution justly, wisely, fearlessly, vigorously and patriotically . . . ; to maintain freedom of thought, freedom of speech and freedom of the press; to promote the sacred cause of human freedom everywhere . . . ; to vindicate and glorify the theory and the practice of representative government."[27]

Clark expressed his hope that Parker and Davis would have the support "not only of every Democrat in the land, but also of every voter by whatever political name called who believes that the Constitution of the United States is a living reality, and that it is binding equally on high and low, great and small, public official and private citizen."[28] He then reminded everyone in attendance (and everyone who would eventually read his words) that the Democratic nominee for president was a learned man of the law, duty bound to follow its mandates:

> The most marked characteristics of the bulk of the American people are reverence for the Constitution and obedience to law. Your long and conspicuous career as a jurist in one of the highest courts in the world—the period which you have spent in expounding constitutions and statutes—causes your countrymen to believe that into that more exalted position to which they are about to call you, you will carry with you that profound respect for the Constitution and the law which with you has become a confirmed mental habit, and upon which depends the perpetuity of our system of government—the best ever devised by the wit of man—a system whose beneficent results have made us the most puissant nation on the whole face of the earth.[29]

Before turning the podium over to Parker, Clark handed Parker the formal notification of his nomination and a copy of the platform unanimously adopted at the convention (see figure 9.3).

Figure 9.3. Judge Parker receiving the formal notification of his nomination at Rosemount, August 10, 1904. From *Harper's Weekly Magazine*. Public domain.

Parker's acceptance speech was a mirror of the man himself: dignified, judicial, and cautious. It was conservative and matter-of-fact and contained not a single dramatic flare.[30] *The Outlook* described his speech in this manner: "Judge Parker in this address spoke as a lawyer: dispassionate, disinterested, almost without partisanship; but there was not a flash of inspiration or a note of leadership in the address throughout. Those who attempt to find either must read them into this orderly, characteristic utterance of a straightforward, methodical and eminently trustworthy man whose mind is legal rather than forensic, and who speaks as a judge rather than as a statesman."[31]

Parker began his address using judicial language:

> Liberty, as understood in this country, means not only the right of freedom from actual servitude, imprisonment or restraint, but the right of one to use his faculties in all lawful ways, to live and work where he will and to pursue any lawful trade or business. These essential rights of life, liberty and property

are not only guaranteed to the citizen by the Constitution of each one of the several States, but the States are, by the Fourteenth Amendment to the Constitution of the United States, forbidden to deprive any person of any one of them without due process of law."[32]

After emphasizing the importance of the constitutional guarantees of due process, Parker warned against the dangers of misuse of power, a common Democratic theme against the "imperial" Roosevelt. He quoted a letter written by Thomas Jefferson to William C. Jarvis, "If the three powers of our government maintain their mutual independence of each other, it may last long, but not so if either can assume the authority of the other."[33] He continued: "If we would have our government continue during the ages to come, for the benefit of those who shall succeed us, we must ever be on our guard against the danger of usurpation of that authority which resides in the whole people, whether the usurpation be by officials representing one of the three great departments of government, or by a body of men acting without a commission from the people."[34]

He condemned recent violence on both sides of a labor dispute, lamenting the fact that the reign of law had given "way to the reign of force."[35] In his estimation, "these illustrations present some evidence of the failure of government to protect the citizen and his property, which not only justified the action of [the] convention in this regard, but made it its duty to call attention to the fact that the Constitutional guarantees are violated whenever any citizen is denied the right to labor, to acquire and to enjoy property, or to reside where his interests or inclination may determine; and the fulfillment of the assurance to rebuke and punish all denials of these rights, whether brought about by individuals or government agencies, should be enforced by every official and supported by every citizen."[36]

After spending several minutes outlining his conservative judicial philosophy, the Republican misuse of power and the rise of force over law, Parker turned his attention to the issue of the tariff. He began by noting that the present tariff law was "unjust in its operation, excessive in many of its rates and so framed in particular instances as to exact inordinate profits from the people."[37] Although many prominent members of the Republican party agreed with that general sentiment, Parker pointed out that the Republicans never seemed to be able to include a plank in their platform that did anything more than admit that revision of the tariff "may from time to time be necessary" and was written in such a nebulous way that it was satisfactory to "those in favor of an increase of duty, to those who favor a reduction thereof, and to those opposed to any change whatever."[38] And although Parker was in favor of a reasonable reduction of the tariff, he was a realist. He knew that the Democrats had no "hope to secure a majority in the Senate during the next four years," and hence, even if elected, he would be unable to secure any modification in the tariff, "save that to which the Republican majority in the Senate may consent."[39]

He then turned to the second contentious "T" issue—the trusts. He said:

> The combination popularly called trusts which aim to secure a monopoly of trade in the necessities of life as well as in those things that are employed upon the farm, in the factory and in many other fields of industry, have been encouraged and stimulated by excessive tariff duties. These operate to furnish a substantial market in the necessities of eighty millions of people, by practically excluding competition.
>
> With so large a market and highly remunerative prices continuing long after the line of possible competition would naturally be reached, the temptation of all engaged in the same business to combine so as to prevent competition at home and a resulting reduction of prices, has proved irresistible in a number of cases. All men must agree that the net result of enacting laws that foster such inequitable conditions is most unfortunate for the people as a whole, and it would seem as if all ought to agree that the effective remedy would be to appropriately modify the offending law.[40]

Parker, as a student of the law, was quick to note that the courts were not to blame for the growth of the monopolies: "the fact that they have multiplied in number and increased in power has been due, not to the failure of the courts to apply the law when properly moved by administrative officials or private individuals, but to the failure of officials charged with the duty of enforcing the laws to take necessary procedure to procure the judgments of the courts in the appropriate jurisdiction."[41] The remedy, according to Parker, was the passage of a statute revising the tariff duties to a reasonable basis and the election of officials with "both the disposition and the courage to enforce the existing law."[42]

At the time of Parker's speech, the Philippines, which the United States had wrested from Spanish control during the Spanish-American War, were being administered as a protectorate of the United States. Although he wondered aloud how long the United States could maintain the Republican policy of imperialism toward the island nation, and he said it was hard for him to visualize one country wanting its freedom and another holding on to that country, thus denying that country its rights, he did not offer any realistic plan for Philippine independence. Instead, he simply said that the islanders should be prepared "as rapidly as possible" for self-governance and should be given "the assurance that it will come as soon as they are reasonably prepared for it."[43]

Toward the end of his remarks, Parker took further aim at Roosevelt's desire to engage the United States in the affairs of other nations. He said, "I protest . . . against the feeling, now far too prevalent, that by reason of the commanding position we have assumed in the world, we must take part in the disputes and broils of foreign countries; and that because we have grown great we should intervene in every important question that arises in other parts of the world."[44] In Parker's view, peace should be the nation's aim, and the government "should confine our international activities solely to matters in which the rights of the country or of our citizens are directly involved."[45]

Parker concluded his acceptance speech with an absolutely astounding claim: that if elected, he would serve only one term. In his words: "I accept, gentlemen of the committee, the nomination; and, if the action of the convention shall be endorsed by an election by the people, I will, God helping me, give to the discharge of the duties of that exalted office the best service of which I am capable, and at the end of the term retire to private life. I shall not be a candidate for, nor shall I accept a renomination."[46]

Parker's stated reason for limiting himself to one term: he believed that no president should ever be placed in a situation of possible temptation to "consider what the effect of action taken by him in an administrative matter of great importance might have upon his political fortunes."[47] In other words, Parker believed that executive independence—and public knowledge of that independence—outweighed executive continuity.

In reality, no one can know, when they begin their quest for the White House, what national, or international, conditions may exist at the time their first term is drawing to a close. Circumstances may not allow for the changing of horses in midstream. And yet Parker committed himself to just such a course of action (despite being reminded by August

Belmont the night before the speech about the possible importance of a second term for an administration that found itself, at the end of its first term, in the middle of developing important policies).⁴⁸

There was nothing exciting in this acceptance speech—nothing to get the electorate worked up or to get the faithful to the polls. Following the address, Hill growled that the judge would be out of politics by the end of the year.⁴⁹ Adjectives such as "impersonal," "sober," "labored" "tame," "dull," and "heavy" recurred in editorial columns from Boston to San Francisco.⁵⁰ The editor of the *New York Sun* remarked that "instead of rising above the [Democratic Party] platform, Judge Parker has crawled pretty ignominiously beneath it . . ."⁵¹ On August 27, writers for *Harper's Weekly* had the following to say about Parker's acceptance speech:

> The fact becomes increasingly evident that Judge Parker's speech of acceptance fell upon his party like a wet blanket. The dramatic element injected into the campaign by his telegram to Mr. Sheehan had raised expectations too great, perhaps, to be realized, but not too great, from the viewpoint of his supporters, to be reached for. The Judge, however, either could not, from force of habit or temperament, or did not consider it the part of his wisdom to strive to enhance the enthusiasm which his own act had created. The net result was a wholly unobjectionable but also a wholly uninspiring utterance.⁵²

Not surprisingly, the Republican press was even more brutal in its assessment. Editors for the *Philadelphia Press* remarked that Parker's speech "does not fulfill the promise of the gold-standard telegram. That exhibition suggested the possibility of bold, vigorous, dominant personality. The speech suggests nothing above decorous and respectable mediocrity." ⁵³ Writers for the *Boston Evening Transcript* had this to say:

> He is indeed a man who walks safely, but does not carry a big stick. We are fortified in this conclusion by the treatment now accorded his speech of acceptance by the certain newspapers which but a few weeks ago were industriously booming him as the man for whom the nation has yearned. *Harper's Weekly*, the *Springfield Republican* and others in that category are plainly of the opinion that he is not the man they thought he was . . . In common with others, some of

these critics may have thought Judge Parker was a strong, silent man, with great utterances in him which he withheld out of deference to his judicial position . . . Hence it was held by many that something novel, striking and forceful might be expected of every utterance of the Democratic candidate. His famous telegram lent a certain measure of support to this estimate. Since then, however, Judge Parker's utterances have been cloudy commonplaces.[54]

Hearkening back to Parker's earlier days when he refused to discuss any of the issues, *The Chronicle Telegraph* in Pittsburg, Pennsylvania, published a poem about Parker's acceptance speech titled "The Sphinx Speaks":

A wondrous thing has happened
    At old Esopus town;
'Tis certainly amazing,
    A thing for wide renown.
For Parker, so long silent,
    And on all questions mum,
The strongest proof has given
    That he's not always dumb.

Men entertained the notion,
    Because he always balked
And dodged all leading questions,
    His lips were tightly locked.
They classed him, for this reason,
    With Egypt's famous sphinx—
Bereft of speech entirely,
    No matter what he thinks.

But up to old Esopus
    A big committee went
To tell the Judge they'd picked him
    To run for President.
They served the notice calmly,
    Convinced that they'd be heard,
But none, of course, expecting
    That he would say a word.

> And then the strange thing happened,
>   For Parker took the floor
> And soon reeled off an answer,
>   A yard in length, or more.
> He gratefully accepted
>   The honor thus conferred,
> And all who heard him speaking
>   Were to their centers stirred.
>
> Of course it was amazing
>   To all who gathered there
> When Parker's studied phrases
>   Went floating through the air.
> But maybe 'twas excitement
>   That opened lips long dumb,
> And after the reaction
>   He may again be mum.[55]

To be sure, not everyone was unhappy with Parker's comments. A week after Parker delivered his remarks, *The Nation* published a piece full of praise for Parker's speech. They began by stating that his speech of acceptance was "the utterance of a man who does his own thinking, who has something to say, and who says it with the utmost frankness. The country will pronounce him a man worth listening to, and will gladly hear him further."[56] In commenting on Parker's single-term pledge, *The Guardian* praised his desire to be above suspicion and wondered if many of Roosevelt's recent actions might lead "thoughtful men" to question his true motives:

> The very reasons that Parker gave for [limiting himself to one term]—which so astonished the professional politicians—have made thoughtful men run over in their minds the actions of President Roosevelt within the last year or year and a half. Why the rapprochement with Addicks? Why the readiness to sign the famous pension order merely to save Congress the trouble of legislating? Why the installation of Senator Quay's notorious son in the Naval Office in Philadelphia? And, since the nomination, why the reconciliation with "Lou" Payn and the appointment of Gov. Odell's white-haired civilian neighbor to a majority in the regular army over the heads of hundreds

of officers of long and faithful service? Do these and many similar acts bespeak the President who is, in Judge Parker's words, "unembarrassed by any possible thought of the influence his decision may have upon anything whatever that may affect him personally"?[57]

The Guardian framed the upcoming election in stark terms:

> The speech at Esopus makes it plain to all that Judge Parker was the right candidate with whom to oppose President Roosevelt. The two men stand for antithetical ideals, and it is for the nation to make its choice between them. It is Constitutionalism versus Imperialism. It is law against impulse. It is the man of calm and poise and judicial habit against the impetuous meddler who leaps first and asks afterwards what the law is, who violates a treaty and thinks it defence enough if he says his own "sense of honor" was satisfied.[58]

Parker and the Democrats were counting on the nation to choose law and order over impulse and chaos, calm and judicious over animated and impetuous. As we shall see, that was not to be the case.

The August 1904 issue of *The American Monthly Review of Reviews* contained a detailed character sketch of Alton Parker authored by James Creelman. Creelman recognized that the public needed to learn all it could about Parker since he was a relatively unknown figure outside the state of New York. He set out, through his piece, to inform the voting public of the type of candidate Parker was and what kind of president he would make.

Creelman took great pains to try to distinguish the steady, reliable Parker from the rash and impetuous Roosevelt. He wrote, in part:

> With the nomination of this strong, brave, sober American . . . the Democracy once more takes its place as the advocate and guarantor of government according to the written Constitution and written laws, as against the personal and radical policies which inspire and control the Republican party today.
>
> At the root of Judge Parker's candidacy is the contention that a just government exists only for public purposes, and that the use of public powers for private ends—as in the tariff

laws—not only violates the spirit of our institutions, but leads to favoritism, corruption, and a perilous disruption of the conditions which are necessary to the equal development of the moral, mental, and material interests of the American people.

∾

There is a simple, unpretending dignity about the man that fits his massive physique and easy, upright carriage. He is sober, sincere, unselfish, decent. Men in every walk of life turn to him instinctively with confidence. There is neither exaggeration nor self-consciousness in his speech or manner. He does not boast. He has a hearty scorn for heroics. Firm in spirit, even-tempered, charitable in his judgment of others, loyal in friendship, loving work for its own sake, seeing in law only the means of justice and order, he unites the virilities and the sobrieties in his strong, modest character . . .

∾

Judge Parker comes before the country as a Presidential candidate at a time when his characteristic qualities are especially needed in the executive direction of national affairs. A fanatical high tariff policy, breeding domestic monopolies and encouraging national extravagance, has brought about high prices, so that the increase in the cost of living in the United States is out of all proportion to wages. Even President McKinley, in his last public utterance, confessed the need for a change to the plan of commercial reciprocity. He died with a protest against the "stand pat" policy on his lips. Articles made in the United States are sold cheaper in foreign countries than at home. Even from the original protective-tariff standpoint, many great industries have outgrown protection. The task to which the Democratic party sets itself is substantially the elimination of favoritism in taxation . . . What man in the country is better fitted to lead in this movement against tariff favoritism and its concomitant corruption than Judge Parker? What man is more likely to insist that changes shall be made with a common-sense regard for existing conditions, however artificially and unjustly produced? His character and record are guarantees against rash, headlong policies."⁵⁹

Creelman quoted extensively from Parker's court opinions to support his claim that Parker—not Roosevelt—was the man to take on the trusts and reminded the audience that although Roosevelt had persuaded the courts to dissolve the Northern Securities Company, "the coal trust, the beef trust, and other like combinations still flourish."⁶⁰ He closed by urging his readers to vote for Parker, "a sane, courageous, unselfish patriot of the old, pure, Democratic type."⁶¹

Around the same time that Creelman published his character sketch of Parker, Albert Stickney, a prominent New York lawyer, published a pamphlet titled "The Records." Stickney spent most of the pages of the pamphlet assailing President Roosevelt and the Republican Party. Stickney labeled Roosevelt a "dangerous man," a "man on whose judgment we [cannot] safely depend for the wise and discreet conduct of national affairs."⁶² He questioned Roosevelt's war record, writing that, "during the advance by the United States forces against the hill of San Juan, [Roosevelt] was guilty of a violation of orders, which might have had serious consequences; and might easily have resulted in great disaster, if there had been any severe contest."⁶³ Stickney quoted extensively from military reports and Roosevelt's own book about the Rough Riders before concluding, "The fire from the rear, which Col. Theaker speaks of as being 'unaccountable,' is now clearly accounted for. That fire was coming from the disorganized men under the command of Mr. Roosevelt, who, being a portion of the 'reserve,' abandoned his position in violation of orders, directed an advance through the regiments of Regulars in his front, carried them along with him by his mad impestuosity, disorganized the entire plans for the engagement, and ended by firing on our own troops 'from the rear.'"⁶⁴ Stickney also accused the Republican Party of engaging in massive pension fraud related to the Civil War, failing to properly prepare for the recent war against Spain, and spending exorbitantly on the army and navy after the war with Spain ended. He concluded his discussion of Roosevelt's record, and the record of the Republican Party, by stating, "Theodore Roosevelt, under existing conditions, constitutes a standing menace, to the peace, and well-being, of the entire civilized world. To make him the Chief Executive of our national government, to make him our War Lord, by the process of popular election, would be to put a brainless boy in charge of a powder magazine."[65]

At the end of his pamphlet, Stickney said the following about Alton Parker's record:

> Alton Brooks Parker, it has been frequently said of late, is a man without a record.
>
> A graver error of statement is hardly possible. For upwards of thirty years, Judge Parker has been making his public record. It is spotless. His complete integrity has never been questioned, by either proof, or assertion, that deserves serious consideration. His large ability is universally conceded. His soundness of judgment, his discretion in high public place, have always been acknowledged. From his earliest years, he has commanded the unbounded confidence of the men of his own vicinage, who have been his judges, and who have been mainly instrumental in placing him in the public positions which he has filled with much dignity and honor.
>
> To say that such a man has no public record, is to make a grave misuse of language. His public record consists in the absence of adverse criticism of his public conduct, by any competent authority. That fact concedes, and proves, the ability, and integrity, with which he has discharged all the duties of the high offices which he has filled from early manhood.
>
> The calm decorous dignity, born of the consciousness of power, which he has always displayed on the bench of his native State, constitutes evidence above question, of his qualifications for the highest office in the United States.[66]

After formally accepting the nomination for President, Parker sent a letter to the Democratic organization in each county in New York, asking for a list of the names and addresses of all of the officers and members. Each county organization responded, supplying Parker with the information he requested. Parker then took each list and sent a letter to the members of each county organization, encouraging each man to "co-operate with [the] chairman and undertake the work assigned to you with such a measure of enthusiasm and public spirit as will ensure complete success."[67] At the same time Parker was corresponding with the county organizations and encouraging hard work and enthusiasm to "ensure complete success," his campaign managers were telling reporters that they felt sure of carrying New York State, but could not "yet see where Parker is to get a majority of the electoral college and win the battle."⁶⁸

On September 8, 1904, Parker was visited at Rosemount by a steamboat-load of Democratic newspaper editors from different parts of the country who had been brought together to consider how best to promote the interests of the party in the upcoming campaign. Parker had prepared a written address to the editors. His principal theme was the extravagance of Republican governmental spending. He did not mention any specific instances of improper appropriation of public money, but merely compared the size of the federal budget under Roosevelt to its average size in Cleveland's first term. Parker noted that in 1903, the federal government spent $582,000,000 and then said, "there is an inevitable result to such extravagance."⁶⁹ According to Parker, the result of such profligate spending "is now a deficit of forty two million dollars, instead of a surplus in the annual receipts of about eighty million dollars, which the present Executive found on assuming control."⁷⁰ Parker's advice to the editors was that they take this theme of wasteful spending and bring it up with some frequency during the course of the campaign.⁷¹

Joseph Pulitzer, an avid Parker supporter, wrote to the Democratic newspaper editors before they met with Parker (they were meeting as a group and attending a banquet in New York City prior to making the journey to Rosemount). Pulitzer's note to the editors stated, in part, "It is because I so strongly desire Judge Parker's election, that I speak so plainly on this subject. I admire his judicial temperament. I appreciate that great personal sacrifice he has made in accepting the nomination. But having accepted it, I earnestly beg of you, when you see him tomorrow at Esopus, to urge that he accept also the full responsibility of his position, and that he will not permit the campaign in New York, the pivotal state, to be mismanaged by the small politicians who beset him. That he will in the next sixty days be even more heretofore the peoples leader and teacher, their tribune and advocate."⁷² If they relayed Pulitzer's request to Parker, there is very little indication that he acted upon it.

Parker supplemented his acceptance speech by issuing a formal letter of acceptance to the Democratic National Committee on September 26, 1904. The letter, much like his acceptance speech, was unexciting. In addition to addressing many of the topics covered in his acceptance speech, his formal letter of acceptance touched upon other matters not mentioned in his August 10 remarks.

Parker outlined his belief that it was essential that a passport issued by the United States to an American citizen must be accepted the world over as proof of citizenship. He discussed the need for civil service reforms and the just and impartial enforcement of the Civil Service Act. He called upon the Interior Department to honestly and capably develop the infrastructure necessary to reclaim the arid lands found in the western portion of the country. He demanded that the Panama Canal be completed "with all reasonable expedition."[73] He called for a drastic increase in the capacity of American shipping. He promised, if elected, an honest and thorough investigation of every department of government and an end to military promotions and appointments based on favoritism instead of merit. He advocated the passage of legislation that would provide a pension, without reference to disability, to the surviving heroes of the Civil War. And he called for an investigation into rampant Republican spending and the inauguration of a "policy of economy and retrenchment."[74]

Parker concluded his formal letter of acceptance with the following statement:

> I solicit the cordial co-operation and generous assistance of every man who believes that a change of measures and of men at this time would be wise, and urge harmony of endeavor as well as vigorous action on the part of all so minded.
>
> The issues are joined and the people must render the verdict.
>
> Shall economy of administration be demanded or shall extravagance be encouraged?
>
> Shall the wrongdoer be brought to bay by the people, or must justice wait upon political oligarchy?
>
> Shall our government stand for equal opportunity or for special privilege?
>
> Shall it remain a government of law or become one of individual caprice?
>
> Shall we cling to the rule of the people, or shall we embrace beneficent despotism?[75]

He claimed that he would await the people's verdict with "calmness and confidence."[76]

The Democratic leaders were neither calm nor confident. Many believed that Parker's letter, "with its platitudinous indirections and total lack of anything resembling vigorous assertion," would contribute more than any other cause to the party's defeat in the November election.[77] Party leaders "expected something better than a cold douche from [the] alleged author of that gold telegram."[78] One leader, who seemed to give voice to what many were thinking, stated, "Thank goodness a candidate for President is not expected to write more than one letter of acceptance. [Parker's letter] has about as much character as a jellyfish."[79]

Henry G. Davis was formally notified of his nomination for vice president of the United States by Mississippi Representative John Sharp Williams, chairman of the Democratic National Committee, at White Sulphur Springs, West Virginia, on August 17, 1904. Williams, in discussing the personality of the Democratic nominee for vice president, said:

> ... The people see in you one of the best products of the best period of American institutions, a period whose salient characteristics were local self-government, individuality, equal opportunity and freedom—freedom to work, freedom to buy and sell, freedom to compete in industrial life, resulting in self-dependency; freedom to develop as one's own master and not merely as the well trained and well managed industrial servant of another. They see in you what Oliver Wendell Holmes said is a rare thing, "a self-made man who is yet not proud of his maker."

∼

> In real conclusion, Mr. Davis, it is a sincere pleasure indeed to know and to be able to help place in high position a man of your character and sense and modesty; a man who, as the result of a life of continence, temperance, self-containment and usefulness and honest industry, presents a picture in virile though advanced age of *mens sana in corpore sano* which is a delight to the eye, a satisfaction to the soul, and was thought by wise ancients to be the *summum bonum* of individual earthly existence.[80]

In his speech accepting the nomination, Davis remarked on the fact that this was the first time since the Civil War that a nominee of a major party ticket had been selected from south of the Mason-Dixon line. He lamented the fact that in the preceding four years of Republican rule, many factories, mills, and mines had closed, and those that were open were being operated with reduced workforces and shortened hours. He railed against perceived Republican extravagance, highlighting the federal budget deficit of $41,000,000.[81]

Toward the end of his acceptance speech, Davis lavished high praise on his running mate:

> I congratulate your committee, and the constituency it represents, in the selection by the delegates to the National Convention of the nominee for the Presidency. He is a man of courage, yet prudent; of high ideals, yet without pretense; of the most wholesome respect for the Constitution and the majesty of the laws under it, and a sacred regard for their limitations; of the keenest sense of justice, which would rebel against compounding a wrong to an individual or to a nation; positive in conviction, yet of few words; strong in mental and moral attributes, and yet, withal, modest and reserved; possessed of a sturdy constitution and magnificent manhood, and yet temperate in his actions and dignified in his demeanor. It is not the orator or man of letters, but the man of reserve force, of sound judgment, of conservative method and steadiness of purpose, whom the people have called to the office of the Presidency; notably in contests between Jefferson and Burr, Jackson and Clay, Lincoln and Douglas, Grant and Greeley, Cleveland and Blaine.[82]

He concluded by predicting a Democratic victory in November: "With a candidate whose personality appeals to the good sense and sound judgment of the American people, a platform whose principles are for the greatest good to the greatest number, and a reunited party, earnest for the restoration of good and economical government, we should succeed and the principles of Democracy again triumph."[83]

On August 28, David B. Hill dropped a political bombshell. He announced that he would retire from politics, no matter the result of the presidential election, effective January 1, 1905. Most believed that Hill's announcement was designed to silence talk that Hill would be appointed secretary of state (or some other important position) in Parker's administration—talk that was deemed by many to be prejudicial to the national ticket (especially to those who feared Hill's possible domination of national affairs).[84]

In September, Davis also issued a formal letter of acceptance of the nomination for vice president. In it he criticized the increasing cost of government under the Republican administration (always an item of consternation for Davis). A paragraph of the letter was devoted to the topic of imperialism, which he noted had a tendency to drift toward absolutism and centralized power. Imperialism, he insisted, was always dangerous to liberty. Concerning the tariff, "he declared that he was in favor of a wise, conservative and gradual change that would equalize the burdens of taxation and make honest competition possible; but expressed the opinion that in making such a change, due regard should be had for [the] capital and labor involved in industrial enterprise." Davis reiterated his conviction that local self-government could be maintained only by strict adherence to the federal constitution. He also discussed in some detail civil service and the race issue, and he renewed his tribute to Judge Parker.[85]

In the aftermath of his nomination, Mr. Dooley, the fictional Irish bartender created by newspaper columnist Finley Peter Dunne, poked fun at Davis's age and considerable assets:

> Hinnery Gassaway Davis is a fine ol' Virginia (West) gintleman. Through his middle name, he is related to Willum J. Bryan . . . Mr. Davis is eighty-wan years old an' has forty millyon dollars, or is forty millyon years old an' has eighty-wan dollars, I'm not sure which, but, anyhow, th' figures passes belief. He is a good man, and it is thought that his ripe judgment an' still riper fortune will add great strength to th' ticket. I see in th' pa-apers that he looks twenty years younger than his years, an' I'll bet before the campaign is over he'll feel three millyon dollars younger in his bank-roll . . .
>
> [His Republican rival Charles Fairbanks] is not quite the statesman that Hinnery is. He misses it by about thirty-nine millyons . . .[86]

As Mr. Dooley suggested, the Democrats hoped that Davis would spend lavishly on the campaign. They would be sorely disappointed. In total, Davis contributed a mere $140,000 to the campaign, $50,000 of which was spent inside the state of West Virginia. His cousin, Arthur P. Gorman, wrote him in September 1904, urging him to send more money for the campaign, saying that the Democratic National Committee chairman was "very much disappointed indeed" with what Davis had contributed outside West Virginia.[87] Gorman's words had little effect on Davis's pocketbook.

Between the nomination of the candidates at the national convention, and the ultimate notification of their respective nominations, the Democratic Party began churning out all of the campaign paraphernalia typically used to try to convince the voting public to support their candidates. Posters and broadsides were printed in a variety of shapes and sizes to be distributed to state and local campaign headquarters to be given out to voters who wanted to advertise their candidate of choice (see figure 9.4).

Some, like the poster depicted in figure 9.5, proclaimed a return to Jeffersonian principles and included select excerpts from the Democratic Party platform.

At least five different individual campaign songs were created in an effort to rally the faithful. E. O. Fletcher composed a Democratic Presidential March. George Haydn Bromby wrote the Democratic National Campaign song "Pull Together Boys." Paul West and J. W. Bratton wrote a song titled "Good-Bye Teddy! You Must March! March! March!" The chorus of that song:

Figure 9.4. Alton B. Parker poster. Courtesy of George Prince, 1904. Library of Congress, Washington, DC. Public domain.

Figure 9.5. Parker and Davis poster. Courtesy of Kurz & Allison, 1904. Public domain.

> Good morning, Mister Roosevelt, permit us to present
> Just the man that we've selected
> And who's going to be elected in your place as President.
> Go wash the White House china and all the linen starch,
> Have a clever metal marker.
> Stamp the door plate "A.B. Parker."
> Good-bye Teddy! You must march, march, march![88]

Paul Dresser wrote a piece titled "Parker! Parker! You're the Moses Who Will Lead Us Out of the Wilderness." Dresser's composition contained lyrics such as "Oh, the eighth of next November, Is a day you must remember, There will be a great uprising of the people—know you why? We searched the country over, And from out the fields of clover comes a leader of the people—'by the people'—hear the cry!" The refrain of that song: "Parker, Parker, the days are growing darker, Your country needs you badly in its hour of distress . . . Parker, Parker, you're not a sideshow barker, You're the Moses who will lead us out of the wilderness."[89] The Iroquois Campaign Song was sung to the tune of "Good bye, My Lover, Good Bye" and substituted the words "Dear Teddy" and "King Teddy" for "My Lover." A sample verse:

> Your military tactics are so plain,
>   Good bye, Dear Teddy, good bye,
> That we know you want to be our King,
>   Good bye, King Teddy, good bye!"[90]

There was also a Parker Campaign Songster, authored by Logan S. Porter and published by The Home Music Company of Logansport, Indiana. The Songster, which had a red cover emblazoned with the pictures of Parker and Davis, contained such memorable numbers as "Lay Them in the Tomb," "Vote for Parker," "They'll Have to Go," and "We Pity Them, Don't You?"[91]

John J. Beekman, an obvious fan of Parker's, wrote a rousing poem in support of the Democratic nominee that originally appeared in the *Brooklyn Eagle* and was subsequently reprinted in *The Evansville Courier*:

> Alton Parker,
>   Here and there—
> Alton Parker,
>   Everywhere.
> Alton Parker
>   Fills the air—
> Man of excellent repute,
> His chaste name none can dispute.
>
> Alton Parker,
>   Just and right—
> Alton Parker,
>   Wholly white,
> Alton Parker'll
>   Win the fight—
> Man he is for all the mass—
> Takes no bribes from any class.

Alton Parker
    Our land needs—
Alton Parker
    Will sow seeds.
Alton Parker
    Won't reap weeds—
Acorns of justice they will be,
Effective soon from sea to sea.

Alton Parker,
    For the throng—
Alton Parker
Alton Parker
    Won't do wrong.
So, men, on election day
Your just duty to him pay.[92]

Another supporter, L. M. Hazen from Lewiston, Montana, wrote the following sonnet about Parker:

A noble leader of a mighty host,
Without base fears, and far too great
        to boast
Of aught he may achieve, or know,
        or say,
Yet doing well his duty day by day.
In him the toiling masses find a
        friend,
Strong, wise and safe, and steadfast
        to the end.
He does not wish the people's vote to
        win
By loud-voiced bluster, or a war-like
        din;
And silent, 'till the time is ripe to
        speak,
He shows his strength where foes
        have called him weak.

He does not yield to every passing
    whim.
No master mummer's arts are used
    by him
To win a cheap renown. Unmoved by
    hate,
Will not this man guide well the Ship
    of State?[93]

Even religious figures got in on the action. Rabbi Joseph Leisen, the spiritual leader of Temple Emanu-El in Kingston, New York, authored the following poem about Parker:

The man we hail, oh, he is not
    A prince of royal fief,
But from the school of daily toil
    He comes to be our chief.

Unblazoned is his stainless name
    On the heraldic page,
But he has worn a nobler badge—
    The toiler's honest wage.

No blusterer he, no lord of war,
    On either land or sea,
Uplifted by his deeds of blood,
    To bear our sovereignty.

But well he knows of patient toil,
    The weight of want and care,
For he has shared the common lot,
    And ate the poor man's fare.

Like Lincoln, he, like every son
    That greatly serves the State,
A man must live the people's life
    To shape the nation's fate.

We trust him. He is wise and just.
    One of the people, he.

On them is based our country's hope,
 The love of liberty.

A farmer, teacher, lawyer,
 A plain, God fearing man,
Our leader stands the kin and type
 Of hearts American.[94]

In addition to the posters and songs and poems, hundreds of different campaign buttons were produced in support of the candidates. The buttons came in all different sizes, from large three-and-a-half-inch ones down to those that were a mere three-quarters of an inch in diameter (see figure 9.6). Many contained formal, sepia-toned portraits of Parker and Davis (or Parker by himself) or depicted Parker and Davis (or again, just Parker) with Lady Liberty, the eagle of the republic, or above a lucky horseshoe or wishbone. Some had a gold background, reminding those who saw it of Parker's stand on the monetary issue.

Figure 9.6. A sampling of Parker and Davis buttons. From the author's collection.

10

The Middle Campaign

Most people believed that Wall Street was going to throw its support behind Parker and Davis. Conventional wisdom was that Roosevelt's efforts to bust the trusts would be scaled back or dropped completely by a President Parker—something that the country's business leaders would presumably pay big money to guarantee. For months prior to Parker's nomination, William Jennings Bryan was beating the Wall Street drum, arguing that Parker was already bought and paid for by the Wall Street tycoons. As it turned out, very few of the Wall Street bigwigs entered the Parker camp. To be sure, August Belmont (head of the Belmont Banking House and builder of the original New York City subway), Thomas F. Ryan (owner of the American Tobacco Company), and Daniel S. Lamont (vice president of the Northern Pacific Railway Company) stayed with the Parker campaign, but the large, big-business contributions from the likes of the Union Pacific Railroad, the New York Central Railroad, Western Union, General Electric, Standard Oil, and the New York Life Insurance Company found their way into the Republican coffers. Limited funds meant a limited campaign.

Why, with Roosevelt's reputation as a "trust buster," did Wall Street support the Republican nominee for president? One commentator has suggested that there were several factors that brought Roosevelt Wall Street's support in the 1904 campaign. To begin with, the Democrats failed to offer a more satisfactory candidate. The strength of the "radical sentiment" in the Democratic Party (Hearst and Bryan and their supporters) not only weakened it politically, but also frightened conservatives away. Roosevelt was sufficiently cautious, both in his election-year policies and campaign arrangements, to convince all but the most hostile business executives that he was the more "conservative" candidate. In addition, Roosevelt had the constant help of loyal friends in Wall Street circles, chief among them Cornelius Bliss (owner of one of the largest wholesale dry goods businesses in the country, former secretary of the interior, and treasurer of the Republican National Committee); Henry Clay Frick (founder of the H.C. Frick & Company coke manufacturing concern and chairman of the Carnegie Steel Company); Elihu Root (Andrew Carnegie's attorney and former US secretary of war); and Henry White (a prominent US diplomat), who tactfully spread his message that business interests were better off under a Republican administration.[1]

Other than the notifications of the candidates in both parties, and the release and publication of their follow-up letters of acceptance, there was very little other campaign activity that took place during the summer of 1904. That was because both campaigns agreed, coming out of their respective conventions, that there should be a minimum of political activity in the months of July and August and "that the campaign ammunition should be expended very sparingly until the beginning of September."[2] Later on, the date for campaigning in earnest was postponed until September 15. Finally, in the first week of September, the Republican campaign managers agreed on a further postponement, and the first day of October was fixed as the date for the beginning of the period of active campaigning.[3]

As noted above, the Parker campaign was not off to a very good start. Parker was a tepid and colorless campaigner, in marked contrast to the colorful and dynamic Roosevelt. Parker's neighbor described his oratorical skills in the following fashion: "On the platform Judge Parker is capable of effective public speech; but he is not a 'spellbinder.' The hypnotizing power of the orator or the rhetorician is in his case apparently preoccupied by directness; he appeals simply to one's sense of the truth of things, and leaves on the mind an impression of sanity which is not liable to be distorted by any refracting influence in our modern atmosphere."[4] Certainly not the type of description that would give one hope that impassioned speeches and forceful calls to action would be emanating from the Democratic nominee!

A cartoon that appeared in the *Philadelphia Inquirer* perfectly encapsulated the issues that the Parker campaign was grappling with (see figure 10.1). The cartoon depicts Parker and Davis, dressed in full formal wear, as salesmen at the "Democratic Rummage Sale." A sign near Davis's head claims that there is "Something to Suit Everybody—We Aim

Figure 10.1. Parker and Davis as salesmen. From the *Philadelphia Enquirer*, 1904. Public domain.

to Please." Cans of "Grover Soup" are stacked neatly on a shelf. A sign on the back wall advertises a "Full Line of Imitation Republican Goods (in reference to the lack of any real difference between the Republican Party platform and the Democratic Party platform) Much Cheaper, Safer, Saner and Almost as Good." The manufacturer is listed as the "Safe & Sane Manufacturing Co.—St. Louis & Esopus" (a reference to the site of the Democratic National Convention and Parker's hometown). Another sign on the back wall says, "Get a Democratic Blanket (a sure reference to Parker's "wet blanket" acceptance speech) They Make You Go to Sleep True Enough, If You Sleep You Can't Eat." The table in front of Parker and Davis is piled high with Democratic wares. Parker has his finger on a bolt of cloth labeled "Gold Standard Parker Ribbon." Davis has his finger on a bolt of cloth labeled "Protection." Other bolts of cloth on the table are labeled "Army & Navy We Are Closing Out This Line of Goods," "Free Silver," "Philippines," "Pensions Revoked," "Free Trade—Protection is Robbery" and "16 to 1 Bryan Cloth Just One Bolt Left." Both Parker and Davis are covering their mouths to stifle deep yawns. The caption at the bottom of the cartoon reads, "Business is frightfully dull, considering the great variety of cheap goods they are offering to the public."

Further compounding the issue of Parker's colorless oratorical skills, Parker did not believe that a candidate for president should "actively" campaign for the position. To him, the tranquility of the law was more appealing than the hurly-burly of politics. Stumping was "undignified"; "personalities and innuendos" were irrelevant.[5] Indeed, he bluntly told one visitor to Esopus that "the campaign itself must be conducted by others . . . [and that he had] told the leaders that he proposed to be a passenger . . . that he [would] not follow any recent pernicious example by clamoring for an election."[6] Parker made this pronouncement despite being urged by his campaign managers to make a speaking tour of the West "in order to turn the drift of sentiment in [that area].'"[7]

Parker believed that a front porch campaign, like the one conducted by President McKinley in 1896, was the only way to seek the office. He also believed that elections should be quiet, dignified, and truthful and that the "masses" should come to him. So, unlike William Jennings Bryan, who had traveled thousands of miles and given hundreds of speeches in his quest for the presidency in 1896 and 1900, Parker refused to leave Rosemount, calmly remarking, "if the people of this country want me to be president, they will elect me."[8]

A cartoon that was published in the *Cleveland Leader* illustrates the problem associated with Parker's approach to campaigning. It shows Parker kneeling in front of a stump, nervously eyeing several voters who surround him. As sweat drips down his brow, Parker tacks a piece of paper to the stump that contains the following message: "I will follow the course of every successful candidate and will not go on the stump—Judge Parker." Beneath the cartoon was this caption: "Voters (to candidate Parker): 'Yes, Judge, but we knew what they would say!' "[9]

Although William McKinley (and others before him) had waged a popular and highly successful front porch campaign for president, Parker had five disadvantages that McKinley did not. To begin with, Parker had no great propagandist, like McKinley's campaign manager, Mark Hanna, to get him large doses of free publicity from the media. Second, Esopus, Parker's hometown, was a relatively small, isolated village, whereas Canton,

Ohio was a moderate-sized city in the center of multiple railroad lines that could easily bring enthusiastic supporters out to meet the candidate. Third, McKinley was already a nationally well-known politician at the time he received the nomination; Parker was an obscure state court judge. Fourth, McKinley had the image of being a winner, while Parker had the image of being an uncharismatic candidate with a hopeless candidacy. Finally, while the battle of the monetary standards was fought with ardent fervor on both sides during the prior two campaigns, there was no major issue in 1904 that could sufficiently rile up the electorate.[10]

Perhaps the editors of *Puck* magazine best addressed the problem of Parker's front porch campaign when they wrote, "We are sorry for Judge Parker's decision not to show himself to the public or to make speeches from any other rostrum than that of the Rosemount front steps at Esopus. It is all very well for him to cite the precedent of Mr. McKinley in 1900, but the circumstances are by no means parallel. To begin with, Mr. McKinley was tolerably well known to the people of the United States at that time as a President who had served his country well through an unusually trying period. His name had been heard by every man, woman and child in the land some days prior to his nomination. There was no question as to his politics or as to his identity. If he were mentioned in Kalamazoo, Kamschatka or Kennebunkport the mere use of the word McKinley conveyed a definite idea to the mind of the listener. Such is not the case with Judge Parker, and PUCK's view of it is that the people whose favor he seeks have a right to see him, to hear him and to ask him questions on points concerning which they wish to know his opinions. So far, to a vast number of American citizens, he is a mere abstraction."[11]

The American Monthly Review of Reviews commented on the perceived lack of enthusiasm from voters on both sides of the aisle. According to the publication, even after October 1, "the public maintained its calmness, persisted in giving its attention to the ordinary affairs of life, and did not clamor at all for the spellbinders, torchlight parades, or political documents . . . Day after day spent upon the exposition grounds at St. Louis, with hundreds of thousands of men passing under inspection, failed to discover half-a-dozen campaign buttons or badges. In the trains, on the street cars, and in places where men congregate, there was almost as little political talk to be overheard as in an off year. Heated discussions like those of 1896 or 1900 were hardly to be heard anywhere . . . The chief topic [at national campaign headquarters] was the apparent total lack of political interest."[12]

This same publication, in the same issue, discussed the fact that this was a campaign not of questions, but of personalities. The voters knew Roosevelt—he had been their president for three years already. They had heard him speak, they had seen almost daily pictures of him, they knew about his exploits during the Spanish-American War, they followed the comings and goings of his family. Parker, on the other hand, was known to most members of the legal profession in the state of New York, but was not known personally to any considerable number of people outside of the state. And that was a very real problem:

> [Parker] could not in three or four months have penetrated to every nook and corner of the country, but he could easily have attended political receptions and gatherings in very many places, leaving to other people the debating of points raised by him in his speech and letter of acceptance, but responding in a brief way to the greetings of his fellow citizens, and impressing upon hosts of influential men throughout the country his very agreeable and reassuring personality. The Roosevelt campaign had really been made in advance of the convention that nominated him, and there remained nothing for the Republican National Committee to do except to use due diligence to take care of the party situation and to see that the voters were registered and brought to the polls.
>   The opposition, on the other hand, had not only to push the negative side of its campaign—namely, that of attack upon Republican candidates, policies, and record—but it had also to spare no effort in pushing the positive side—that of enthusiasm for its candidate as a personal leader. This positive side it has sadly neglected, with injustice to its candidate, and with what seems to be practical loss to its cause . . . The Democrats seem to have forgotten that it was not enough for them to attack Rooseveltism, but that they were also expected to build up at the same time a warm and convinced support for their own candidate.[13]

Unfortunately, because of Esopus's remote location and the campaign's lack of funds to bring in delegations to meet with him, Parker received very few visitors.[14] Those who did manage to make their way to Rosemount heard the same "safe and sane" speeches, which were mostly about returning to the old ways, reducing the size of the federal government, reigning in the power of the presidency, giving deference to the courts when dealing with the trusts, and returning to a more isolationist foreign policy.[15]

Because Parker refused to leave Esopus, he had to rely on others to take to the hustings on his behalf. Although the Democrats' key campaigners, Bryan and Hearst, supported the ticket, they only provided a half-hearted effort (Hearst told acquaintances, "I did, as a matter of fact, shut my eyes, hold my nose, and support Judge Parker . . . But I am not proud of having done so. It is the one act of my political career that I am heartily ashamed of.").[16] Bryan gave speeches on behalf of Parker and Davis, but they were few in number (particularly when compared with the number of speeches Bryan gave when he himself was running for president), they occurred late in the campaign, and they lacked any real punch or enthusiasm for the Democratic nominee. Bryan's speeches were more notable for their zestful attacks on Roosevelt for campaign financing, his militarism, and other lapses than for their attention to Parker. When he did get around to Parker, Bryan was "hardly a spectacle of quivering enthusiasm."[17] Bryan referred to himself and Parker as a kind of Aaron-Moses tandem, reserving the glory for himself and insulting the actual candidate: "the Lord selected Aaron as his speech maker. I am willing to be the Aaron of the party if our Moses, who has been slow of speech, will but lead the people out of the wilderness."[18] Hearst's papers contained very little about the Parker candidacy (no doubt partly because of the decree that had gone out from Tammany Hall at the end of July that it would actively oppose the publisher's renomination as congressman from New York's Eleventh District).[19] Most of the headline stories in his papers centered around Hearst's congressional reelection campaign and the Russo-Japanese war. Thomas E. Watson, the Populist Party candidate for president, was given more space in Hearst's papers than Parker was.[20]

Unlike Parker, Henry G. Davis did hit the campaign trail. Unfortunately for the Democrats, the trail was very short. Davis gave between eighty and ninety speeches during the closing month of the campaign, but except for a handful of speeches that were delivered in neighboring Maryland, all of Davis's orations took place in his home state of West Virginia.[21] Unquestionably, he campaigned vigorously in the Mountain State. But so did his son-in-law, Stephen B. Elkins—for the Republican candidates. Journalists had a field day trying to find out whether Elkins would actually vote for his father-in-law and business partner. One journalist captured Elkin's divided loyalties when he penned the following ditty:

> Eenie, Meenie, Meinie, Mo!
> What's the answer, yes or no?
> Ought I vote for Theodore?
> Or cast my slip for Pop-in-law?
> Pop-in-law's a Democrat,
> Hence, I'm not for him, that's flat!
> But, even though a Democrat, he
> Has always been a Pa to me.
> How I'd hate to hear him say,
> "Steve, you knifed your Gassaway!
> Pop-in-law or Theodore?
> Eenie, Meenie, Meinie, Mo—
> Why does fate pursue me so?[22]

Although Roosevelt followed tradition and kept close to the White House, he did send surrogates out to campaign for him. Future President (and current Secretary of War) William Howard Taft proved to be an able campaigner and, as the former governor of the Philippines, was particularly effective in countering the Democrats' assertion that the Philippines were being mismanaged. Republican vice-presidential nominee Charles Fairbanks embarked on an extended campaign tour, speaking from one end of the country to the other. He opened his party's campaign by traveling through Connecticut, New Jersey, New York, West Virginia, Maryland, and Delaware.[23] In mid-October, Fairbanks was reported to have made 113 speeches within a two-week span.[24] In all, Fairbanks visited thirty-three states and gave hundreds of speeches on behalf of the Republican ticket.[25]

There was something else that the Republicans—but not the Democrats—were doing very well. They were reaching out to various ethnic voting blocs and actively courting their votes. Roosevelt's campaign organized committees to appeal specifically to Irish, Catholic, Jewish, black and German-American voters.[26] For example, the Republicans published "A Pamphlet for Americans of Irish Birth and Irish Descent." It opened with a poem titled "The Irish Vote" by John Boyle O'Reilly and contained a collection of articles and speeches authored or given by Roosevelt that would be of particular interest to Irish-Americans.

Thirty-seven Armenian-Republican clubs had sprung up in 1904. The Republicans also took an active interest in the formation of an innumerable number of Czech, Polish, Hungarian, Croatian, and Slavonian clubs.[27] Frank L. Frugone, the Genoese-born editor of the *New York Bolletino,* organized a Latin-American Republican National League. The league founded clubs and distributed literature with a strong emphasis on Roosevelt's labor record among both Italian- and Spanish-speaking Americans.[28] Very little similar outreach occurred on the Democratic side.

The Republicans took serious steps to court the African-American vote. The Republican Inter-State League, which was composed of African-American Republicans from around the country, issued for distribution a *Supplementary Republican Text Book*. The purpose of the book was to place before the African-American voters facts as to why they should cast their ballots for the Republican candidates, to impress upon the African-American voters in the doubtful states and close congressional districts the importance of working for the success of the Republican candidates, and to encourage the African-American voters to study the questions of public concern to be addressed during the election.[29]

With regard to the Jewish vote, Nathan Bijur, an American Jewish lawyer and judge, financed an elaborate campaign that Philip Cowen, an American Jewish newspaper publisher, organized after consultation with Republican National Committee chair George Cortelyou. Cowen planned to distribute literature to the Jewish press, engage representatives to appear in social centers to stimulate discussion about the merits of Roosevelt and the Republican administration, establish Roosevelt headquarters in the major Jewish centers, and hold a rally in each of those centers in the last week of the campaign where prominent Jews would speak in favor of Roosevelt and the Republicans.[30] For his part, Roosevelt, following the April 20, 1903, Kishinev pogrom, in which 25 Jews were killed and another 275 wounded, agreed to receive the bearers of a petition calling on the Russian czar to redress the grievances of the Jews in his country. These gestures gave Jewish voters an impression of genuine feeling even though they had very little real effect.[31]

Although the Democrats adopted a strong plank in their platform in favor of insisting on the protection of the rights of all citizens traveling under an American passport, a declaration directed principally against Russian refusal to recognize the rights of American Jews, serious Democratic blunders during the course of the campaign helped to alienate the Jewish vote. *Harper's Weekly* contributed little to the Democratic cause when it announced that Oscar Straus, a prominent New York Jew, was going to vote "for Mr. Rosenfeld." Even worse, Richard Olney chose his single campaign pronouncement at the Cooper Union to denounce in scathing terms the Kishinev petition and Roosevelt's handling of the matter.

Republican speakers in Jewish districts joyfully lambasted the outspoken former secretary of state.[32]

As a symbolic gesture toward the Roman Catholic vote, Roosevelt named a Catholic, James F. Smith, as one of the governing commissioners of the Philippines. When the civil government was set up in the Philippines, Roosevelt appointed another Catholic, John T. McDonough, to sit on the supreme court of the islands.[33] He also appointed two Catholics to the Board of Indian Commissioners.[34] These actions on Roosevelt's part certainly helped pave the way for a series of important endorsements. The *New York Sunday Democrat*, an Irish-American and Catholic newspaper, which for more than thirty years had consistently supported the Democratic Party, endorsed Roosevelt for president. *The Boston Pilot*, which had supported the Democratic nominee for president for more than seventy years, soon followed suit. John A. McCall, president of the New York Life Insurance Company, and John M. Byrne, a well-known New York banker, were among a number of prominent Catholic laymen who gave vigorous support to the president. Archbishop S. G. Messmer of Milwaukee demonstrated that there was support for Roosevelt among German Catholics by declaring publicly that he would like to see Roosevelt elected to a second term.[35]

In an effort to win the labor vote, the Democrats circulated a pamphlet containing six of Parker's pro-labor decisions, including his opinions in the *National Protective Association* case and the *Lochner* case. David Hill, giving speeches on behalf of the Democratic ticket, condemned "government by injunction." William Jennings Bryan, speaking in Indiana, advocated for a system of arbitration in labor disputes and for a universal eight-hour workday.[36]

The Republicans circulated a document reviewing Roosevelt's work in the labor field, from the introduction of "sweat shop" legislation to the measures the president took to end the anthracite coal strike in 1902. The Republicans also depicted Henry Davis as "a most bitter enemy of union labor."[37] These reports were so persistent that Davis felt it necessary to publish a letter "in which he denied having ever in his long business career fired a union man or sought an injunction against a strike or, indeed, had any but two short strikes, both peaceably settled."[38]

When it came to the youth vote, the Republicans again outworked and outorganized the Democrats. The National Association of Democratic Clubs (NADC) sent out a circular exhorting its members to "begin earnest campaign work immediately," but the sheet strangely omitted the names of the candidates on whose behalf young Democrats were to labor, and "included a whole list of objectives to which neither Parker nor Davis—nor even the St. Louis convention—had given endorsement."[39] Even more perplexing, the NADC refused to hold a convention in the month prior to the election, depriving Parker of an opportunity to address this important voting bloc.[40]

The Republican counterpart to the NADC, the National League of Republican Clubs (NLRC), was incredibly active in stirring up the enthusiasm of Republican youth. J. Hampton Moore, president of the NLRC, estimated that at least two million young men and first voters had been brought into the league by the time of the election. And unlike the NADC, the NLRC did hold a national convention in Indianapolis in October. Keynote speakers included William Howard Taft, Indiana senator Albert Beveridge, Treasury Secretary Leslie M. Shaw, and prominent California Republican George A. Knight.[41]

Try as they might, the Democrats just could not come up with an issue that would differentiate the two parties. The proposed building of the Panama Canal and Roosevelt's trust-busting actions against J. P. Morgan and Northern Securities were good points in the president's favor. The monetary issue from the prior two campaigns had been laid to rest and taken off the table. Other issues, such as tariff reform and Philippine independence, never caught the attention of the general public. Only Roosevelt's way of doing things could be assailed. The president was labeled as "arbitrary," "lawless," or "dictatorial." He was a "man of blood and thunder," a "swaggering" bully who might easily involve the nation in an "era of blood and fire."[42]

Bryan criticized Roosevelt for "sword waving and militarism." Henry Watterson, the editor of the *Louisville Courier-Journal,* referred to the president as "as sweet a gentleman as ever scuttled a ship or cut a throat." The Parker Constitutional Club, which was composed of forty high-ranking New York attorneys, looked unfavorably upon the president's "arbitrary usurping of legislature functions and his massing [of] enormous power in his own hands." They wanted a president who had "safe tendencies."[43] Their formidable talents produced a series of "briefs" for the Democratic campaign. In one such report, they found that the president's executive order lowering the age of "presumptive disability" for Union veterans from sixty-five to sixty-two violated the constitutional requirement that appropriations be made by law. In another, they concluded that Roosevelt's use of repeated recess appointments to continue W. D. Crum as collector of the Port of Charleston was a "usurpation" of the appointing powers of Congress. In a third, they alleged that the assumption by the United States of responsibility for the payment of debts owed by Latin American nations to European creditors was a "grotesque, preposterous and dangerous perversion" of the Monroe Doctrine.[44] Despite their stellar work, their constitutional criticisms failed to incite the ire of the voting public.

In early September, Carl Schurz, former Republican senator from Missouri and former secretary of the interior under President Rutherford B. Hayes, published "An Open Letter to the Independent Voter." Schurz opened his letter by proclaiming that if Americans meant to preserve their free institutions, they must always remember that "[the] Government of this republic must be a government of law, not a government of adventure; [it] must be a Government for the general benefit, not a Government of favor for the promotion of special interests; [it] must be a Government not permanently controlled by one political party, but by different parties alternating in the possession of power."[45] He stated that he was an enthusiastic member of the Republican Party from its "earliest days," when it proudly called itself "the party of moral ideas."[46] Now, according to Schurz, the Republican Party was something altogether different—it was a party enraptured with material prosperity and growing wealth, and boastful of its policies that allegedly produced such bounty. Schurz took issue with Republican support for high tariffs and the public corruption they engendered. He lambasted the Republicans for increasing American armaments and pursuing a policy of "conquest . . . arbitrary dominion over subject populations" and unabashed imperialism.[47] He attacked Roosevelt's repeated dealings with party machines and bosses, his failure to adequately address the issue of the trusts, his temperamental inclination to choose "the use of force," and his hasty recognition of the independence of Panama, an act that "could hardly fail to inflame the distrust of our Southern neighbors with regard to our possible designs with regard to them."[48] Schurz closed his open letter with a plea that independent voters support the Democratic Party in general, and Alton Parker in particular, since Parker was "a man who knows the law; who reveres the law; who will never permit his emotions to make him overlook the law; who will never presume that his will is law, and who will constantly keep in mind that a democracy will drift into chaos as soon as its government ceases to be a government of law."[49]

Much like Schurz, *Puck* magazine understood the marked difference between the bellicose and combative Roosevelt and the steady and disciplined Parker. The magazine published a cartoon setting forth the stark choice for the voters. The cartoon, titled "Take Your Pick Gentlemen," shows Puck, the magazine's eponymous protagonist, pointing out the differences between the two candidates: Roosevelt, dressed as a Rough Rider, standing on the Constitution while raising the sword of "militarism," and Parker, wearing his judicial robes, standing on the sword of "militarism" while holding the Constitution.

Around the same time that Schurz published his open letter to the independent voter, Parker published an article in *Success* magazine titled "Educated Men in Politics."[50] In his article, Parker argued that whenever a great question of public importance has arisen in this country, it has been presented and championed by "the educated, thoughtful, unselfish and independent man in politics."[51] He gave as examples Samuel Tilden's implementation of civil service reform on the local and state levels in New York and Abraham Lincoln's campaign to abolish slavery. According to Parker, "It is service of this character, prompted solely by an unselfish desire to serve the country, patriotic service that seeks no other reward than the consciousness of helping in even a humble way toward bettering the condition of government in town, city, county, state, or nation, that is most needed [today]."[52] And those who could best appreciate the opportunities through which the public interest could be advanced were "the men possessed of trained minds, broadened by sound reading, careful study and association with men of thought and action."[53] Parker's pronouncement: educated men needed to get involved in local politics and "contribute as much unselfish effort toward the betterment of local conditions as circumstances and [their] environment permit."[54] In that way, "wise measure[s] boldly and persistently presented by unselfish, public-spirited citizens" become law and policy.[55] Although he didn't specifically say it, Parker was undoubtedly hoping that the educated men he was writing to would support him and the Democratic ticket in the fall.

As the campaign wound its way to a close, the campaign managers on both sides were dismayed to find that their long lists of speakers were essentially unwanted. They convinced themselves that speakers were not in high demand because people were reading more and were able to acquaint themselves with the issues without going to meetings. As a result, they redoubled their efforts to distribute political literature to the voting public. Both the Democratic and the Republican literature focused on the issue of "Rooseveltism." Together with pamphlets on the tariff and the rising cost of living under the Republicans, the Democrats widely circulated Joseph Pulitzer's scathing condemnation of Roosevelt's speech of acceptance, Arthur Pue Gorman's Senate attack on "executive usurpation," and statements gleaned from Roosevelt's "unconventional youthful pronouncements on American life and history."[56] Aside from a somber picture book containing distressing scenes of American life during President Cleveland's second administration, the Republican campaign literature consisted entirely of material designed to highlight Roosevelt's record and enhance his presidential reputation.[57]

By the end of September, the only major journalistic comment on the campaign was how dull it was. One journalist wrote, "I was afraid when the campaign began that possibly Parker might develop some unexpected strength, but so far he appears to be a blank cartridge."[58] Albert Shaw observed that "this is the most apathetic campaign ever heard of since James Monroe's second election."[59] It was clear, as the campaign headed into its final month, that the Democrats would need "some brilliant play that [would] captivate the audience and rally the party."[60]

11

The End Is in Sight

That "brilliant play" arrived on September 28, when the *Brooklyn Eagle* published a long, front-page article charging that "every trust, corporation, and moneyed interest in the country was being 'held up' by Republican fundraisers, and successfully so due to the peculiar methods employed."[1] According to the *Eagle*, corporate solicitations were being coupled with promises of a continuation of the administration's present "quietness" in the matter of trust prosecution. George Cortelyou, the chairman of the Republican National Committee, was alleged to be engaged in the active solicitation of campaign donations—a task that was said to be facilitated by Cortelyou's previous opportunity, as secretary of commerce, "to learn all the fears and funds of the business magnates of the country."[2]

The very next day, Democratic attorney Edward Shepard, during a speech at the Brooklyn Academy of Music, charged that Roosevelt, when he knew he was a candidate for reelection, created the Bureau of Corporations; appointed Cortelyou, his private secretary, to head the same; and then, by his own fiat, made Cortelyou chairman of the Republican National Committee. Although Shepard did not explicitly state it, the implication was clear. The amassing of corporate contributions designed to finance Roosevelt's reelection campaign was "the outcome of a consciously-devised scheme of extortion engineered by Roosevelt long in advance of his nomination."[3]

Daniel S. Lamont, the former secretary of war for President Cleveland, the vice president of the Northern Pacific Railway Company, and a very good friend of Parker's, came to visit Parker on October 23, 1904. After shaking hands with Parker, he said, "Well, you are going to be licked old fellow, but brace up and make the best fight you can, and when it is over come down [to New York] and practice law."[4] Parker asked, "How do you know I am to be defeated?" Lamont replied, "Why they have underwritten it just as they would underwrite building a railroad to San Francisco!"[5] Parker asked Lamont for the source of his information, but Lamont replied that he could not give it. On the train ride from New York City to Rosemount that afternoon, Parker decided that if he could not win the election, he would start a campaign against corporate contributions to campaign funds that would help ensure cleaner elections in the future.[6]

The very next day, Parker received a delegation of about four hundred people at his home in Esopus. He took the opportunity of that visit to deliver his first utterances concerning the insidious dangers associated with the corporate bankrolling of political campaigns—and in particular the campaign for the reelection of President Roosevelt. Parker said, in part:

> Many years have passed since my active participation in politics. In the meantime a startling change has taken place in the method of conducting campaigns—a change not for the better, but for the worse; a change that has introduced debasing and corrupt methods, which threaten the integrity of our Government, leaving it, perhaps, a republic in form, but not a republic in substance, no longer a government of the people, by the people, for the people, but a government whose officers are practically chosen by a handful of corporate managers . . .

~

> The excessively protected interests, which formerly poured out their treasure in order to continue existing and procure the passage of new laws permitting its further accumulation, have been joined by the combinations popularly called trusts. Their plan is to perpetuate the present Administration. Such of the combinations or trusts as do not profit by the aid of the tariff secure their profits by the exercise of monopolies . . . When such forces unite to furnish the money which they are promised will control the election, their purpose is as clear as noonday; it is to buy protection, to purchase four years more of profit by tariff taxation, or four years more of extortion from the people by means of monopoly . . . A corporation will subscribe to a

> political party only because the corporation expects that party, through its control of public officers, executive or legislative, to do something for the benefit of the corporation, or to refrain from doing something to its injury. No other motive can be imagined. In the nature of things no other motive can exist.

∽

> Whether there were real difficulties between [the corporations and trusts] and the Administration—difficulties which have since been settled to the satisfaction of all parties concerned—or whether there were no difficulties to be compromised and adjusted, their action being but a play to deceive the voters, the fact remains that the trusts are not now opposed to the continuance of the present Administration. On the contrary, it is common knowledge that they have determined to furnish such a sum of money to the Republican National Committee as it is hoped will secure the "floaters" in the doubtful States for the Republican ticket.[7]

Parker would return to this theme with greater zeal as the campaign wound to a close.

On October 28, 1904, Parker spoke to two thousand farmers who visited Esopus. His opening words: "No more satisfactory evidence of the widespread public interest in the attempt to control the election by moneys of great corporations and trusts need be looked for than that furnished by the President and his late Attorney General, Knox. Knox was bidden to the presence of the President for a consultation. About what? About the iniquity of the large contributions being made by gigantic corporations and trusts? Not at all. But rather to devise means by which the force of the statement of this commonly accepted fact could be parried."[8] The remainder of the speech focused on Republican imperialism, administrative extravagance, and the pressing need for regulation of the trusts and tariff reform.[9]

At the beginning of the campaign, the Democrats applauded Parker's decision to avoid stumping for the presidency. The *Norfolk Landmark* voiced the traditional sentiment that the "presidential candidate who stumps in his own behalf cheapens himself." Others treated the practice of active campaigning as "old-fashioned and tiresome." The *Boston Advertiser* declared stumping obsolete because "votes are made and lost now through the newspapers." According to the *Brooklyn Daily Eagle,* "[o]ur politics [have] been over-talked by candidates"; it was much better to ponder the candidates' "deliberate utterances" without distraction.[10]

These thoughts began to change as the campaign headed into the final stretch. In the last few weeks of the campaign, Parker's campaign managers began receiving dozens of requests from state and local Democratic operatives urging Parker to get out on the campaign trail and address the masses.[11] They believed that Parker had no chance of obtaining the 239 electoral votes necessary to capture the presidency unless he went before the people and passionately stated his case. Writers for the *Chicago Tribune* asserted that Parker "must show himself to the people by injecting a personal element into the campaign and try to take it out of the slough of despond into which it fell after the first brief spurt of enthusiasm that followed his nomination."[12] *The American Monthly Review of Reviews,* in its November 1904 issue, noted that "Judge Parker, toward the end of the campaign, still remains to the great majority of Americans a man of mystery—indeed, almost a myth."[13] As a result, it was decided that Parker would make a series of campaign speeches in Connecticut, Indiana, New York, and New Jersey.[14]

Parker used these speeches to fling two criticisms at Roosevelt: first, that his treatment of the Filipinos had been unjust; and second, that in appointing George Cortelyou as his campaign manager, Roosevelt had purposely tapped his former secretary of commerce because Cortelyou, knowing the secrets of the big corporations, could extract sizable campaign contributions from them.[15] At a speech in New York City, Parker declared that although Roosevelt was responsible for enforcing the antitrust laws, he had accepted large campaign gifts from several of those big corporations. He attacked the political corruption arising from the acceptance of those gifts and called for clean elections.[16]

As part of his speeches, Parker began to repeat the "Ten Questions" originally posed by Joseph Pulitzer in the October 1 issue of the *New York World*: How much has the beef trust contributed to Mr. Cortelyou? How much has the paper trust contributed to Mr. Cortelyou? How much has the coal trust contributed to Mr. Cortelyou? How much has the sugar trust contributed to Mr. Cortelyou? How much has the oil trust contributed to Mr. Cortelyou? How much has the tobacco trust contributed to Mr. Cortelyou? How much has the steel trust contributed to Mr. Cortelyou? How much has the insurance trust contributed to Mr. Cortelyou? How much have the national banks contributed to Mr. Cortelyou? How much have the six great railroads contributed to Mr. Cortelyou?[17] He suggested that Cortelyou's rapid rise from presidential aide to secretary of commerce to head of the Republican Party had been engineered with the precise intent of shaking down the captains of industry for campaign contributions. No man in the country, Parker implied, enjoyed such equal access to privileged information in his former fiefdom, the Bureau of Corporations. Hence, Cortelyou's success in "demanding" support from business tycoons too scared to resist him. "Although this may be satisfactory to the conscience of the Republican leaders," Parker said, "it must, I firmly believe, be condemned as a shameless exhibition of a willingness to make compromise with decency."[18]

Halloween saw Parker delivering an address before fifteen thousand supporters in Madison Square Garden. In what was described as "a demonstration [the likes of] which probably never has been equaled in this city," the crowd cheered for Parker for twenty-six minutes straight before he was able to deliver his remarks.[19] In his speech, Parker "boldly charged the [R]epublican party with having entered into a combination with the tariff protected trusts to purchase the election, and he characterized the selection of Mr. Cortelyou as director of the [R]epublican campaign and the collector of the campaign fund as a 'scandalous exhibition.' "[20] Parker cautioned his audience that requiring corporations to provide limitless and unchecked campaign contributions to political parties "invite[s] the establishment of new and dangerous principles and standards for our guidance as a people" and would lead the country down "a path that is full of danger to our future."[21]

On November 1, Parker delivered three speeches in two different parts of New Jersey. He made the first set of remarks before ten thousand supporters in the Essex Troop Armory in Newark. He then addressed a crowd of three thousand at Elks' Hall in Jersey City, followed by a speech in St. Peter's Hall across town. In all three venues, Parker again assailed the Republican effort to purchase the election through significant corporate contributions, and "he arraigned 'Cortelyouism' in a tone almost of bitterness."[22]

On November 2, Parker gave two speeches within hours of each other in New York City. The first speech, which he gave before an assembled crowd of approximately two thousand at the Cooper Union for the Advancement of Science and Art, focused on imperialism under the recent Republican administrations. He criticized Roosevelt's support of the revolution that led to Panama's declaration of independence from Columbia and the adoption of the Panama Canal Treaty, the staggering increase in military spending, and the "transformation of the old republican peace power into an empire preparing for war."[23] He advocated for a return to Jeffersonian ideals. He said:

> I ask you now in all soberness, is it not best for the peace, well-being, and happiness of our people and for the preservation of our free institutions, to which we owe so much of our growth in comfort, wealth and power, that, instead of indulging our ambition in an adventurous policy of empire and dominion over foreign countries and alien populations; instead of squandering our substance in wholly unnecessary war establishments at immense cost; instead of sacrificing the great conservative principles and high ideals we inherited from the fathers to the false glitter of imperial greatness, which at all periods of human history has marked the decay and perdition of republics; instead of provoking the distrust of all mankind by the display of armed force on every possible occasion, which raise a suspicion of vague and hazardous schemes of restless ambition lurking in the background—we should return to the principles and ideals which during the first century of our National existence have proved so just and beneficial, so that government of the people, by the people and for the people may not perish from the earth?[24]

Following his speech at the Cooper Union, Parker traveled to midtown Manhattan to give an address at Carnegie Hall. Four thousand people greeted Parker with a twelve-minute ovation. His remarks at Carnegie Hall touched upon a recurring theme: the evils associated with the undue expansion of a protective tariff and the unchecked rise of the domestic trusts. He ended his speech by once again asking the audience for its support in returning to the old Democratic ways:

> Let me say to you in conclusion, and through you to the people of the United States, in reply to those who point to artificially high prices as a justification for a compromise with ideals in National life, that prosperity is not a necessary incident of national wrongdoing. And that if elected by the people to be

their President I shall do all that lies in my power to increase and not to subtract from the prosperity of the country, and to assist in our attainment of that prosperity to which, by our unique position in the world, we are entitled.

∽

I shall do all that lies in my power to see to it that we shall have peace as well as prosperity. I shall do all that lies in my power to emphasize the old-fashioned ways of thought and conduct, and in the discharge of my stewardship I shall always act as trustee responsible for my acts to the American people. I shall join with you in searching for and in finding, not prosperity secured at the expense of our good name, but that true wisdom and understanding in whose left hand is length of days and in whose right hand are riches and honor.

And the highest reward which I shall hope to gain will be that I have kept the covenant now made with you, to be your constitutional and your dutiful representative, to the end that we, the people of the United States, may live over again in experience and in result the historic days of simplicity and prosperity in this land born of high resolves and nurtured in the truth of principles.[25]

At the close, after outlining the necessity of a return to the democracy of old, Parker paused. The audience was so still that one could have heard a pin drop as Parker, tapping his manuscript emphatically with his fingers, looked out over the crowd and said, in a measured, steady voice, leaving a pause after each word, "To all this I stand pledged."[26] The crowd erupted in pandemonium, and Parker left the hall to attend a reception at the Democratic Club of New York.[27]

On November 3, Parker delivered four speeches in Connecticut. Prior to his speech in Bridgeport, Parker received a surprise visit from his mother and sister. Following lunch with his family, he delivered remarks before 2,500 people packed into the Third Regiment Armory (see figure 11.1). The crowd heard him once again assail the tariff and the trusts. Then he took aim at Roosevelt's "stand pat" policy. According to Parker, nothing good ever came from "standing pat": "In fact, the whole of modern progress has come largely from the refusal of the world to 'stand pat.'"[28]

Figure 11.1. Parker speaking in the Third Regiment Armory in Bridgeport, CT. From the *New York Herald*, November 4, 1904. Public domain.

After he left Bridgeport, Parker gave speeches in New Haven, Meriden, and Hartford. In all three locales, he spoke again about the dangers of imperialism and of the trusts and their efforts to make sure that Roosevelt was elected president. At the opera house in Hartford, before a crowd of 3,500, he again brought up the issue of Republican National Committee Chair Cortelyou's use of information gained while secretary of commerce to "shake down" corporations for large contributions to the Republican campaign coffers: "We do not want a Department of Commerce and Labor whose Secretary shall go out from it every four years, after he has filled his brain and his notebook with the secrets of all the great corporations and combinations, which depend upon the Government for business or favors, in order not to serve the people, but to raise money to corrupt them."[29]

In contemporaneous remarks delivered before his prepared speech, Parker talked about what a sacrifice it was for him to give up the pleasant and congenial life he had mapped out for himself on the court of appeals and embark on the quest for the presidency. He said, "I want to say a word for myself. I am not making this fight for myself, but I am doing what I think is right. Your Chairman said I left the bench to enter this contest. It was the saddest day of my life, for I loved the place. As the nomination came from the party I loved I believed I could not decline."[30] This was the one and only time that Alton Parker shared, publicly, just how much he had given up to fulfill what he believed was his duty to his friends, his party, and his country.

On November 2, Roosevelt wrote to Cortelyou and told him that he was going to finally come off the sidelines and issue a public denial of Parker's charges: "I am the man against whom Parker's assaults are really directed and I am the man who can give widest publicity to the denial . . . I think that it would be in keeping with my character to end the campaign with one slashing statement like this."[31] Four days before the election, President Roosevelt replied to Parker's allegations of campaign misfeasance. In a thousand-word statement that he released to the press, Roosevelt wrote:

> Certain slanderous accusations as to Mr. Cortelyou and myself have been repeated time and again by Judge Parker, the candidate of his party for the office of President. He neither has produced nor can produce any proof of their truth; yet he has not withdrawn them; and as his position gives them wide currency, I speak now lest the silence of self-respect be misunderstood.

> Mr. Parker's accusations against Mr. Cortelyou and myself are monstrous. If true they would brand both of us forever with infamy; and inasmuch as they are false, heavy must be the condemnation of the man making them . . .

> The assertion that Mr. Cortelyou had any knowledge gained while in any official position whereby he was enabled to secure and did secure any contributions from any corporation is a falsehood.
> The assertion that there has been any blackmail, direct or indirect, by Mr. Cortelyou or by me is a falsehood.
> The assertion that there has been any understanding as to future immunities or benefits, in recognition of any contribution from any source is a wicked falsehood.

> The statements made by Mr. Parker are unqualifiedly and atrociously false. As Mr. Cortelyou has said to me more than once during the campaign, if elected I shall go into the presidency unhampered by any pledge, promise or understanding of any kind, sort or description, save my promises made openly to the American people, that so far as in my power lies I shall see to it that every man has a square deal, no less and no more."[32]

Parker was under pressure to prove his claims that large sums of money from corporations had found their way into the Republican campaign coffers and to reveal his sources. He could do neither. As noted above, Parker had received specific information about the corporate campaign contributions, confidentially, from Daniel Lamont. During their October 23 conversation, Lamont had related to Parker that Roosevelt had convened a secret conference with businessmen including Edward Harriman, James Stillman, Henry C. Frick, and George W. Perkins. The purpose of that conference was to obtain much-needed campaign funds from the titans of industry. Lamont swore Parker to secrecy during their October meeting, and Parker never betrayed the trust that Lamont had placed in him.[33]

Instead, two days before the election, and lacking any factual predicate, Parker's final words on the charges were published:

> The President placed at the head of this great department—empowered to probe the secrets of all the trusts and corporations engaged in interstate commerce—his private secretary, who held that position for some months, when he resigned and was made chairman of the National Committee.
>
> Now, these facts are not challenged in the statement of the President, nor can they be. The statute was passed and money was appropriated to probe the trusts; Cortelyou was appointed at the head of it. He was without experience in national politics, and yet the President says in his statement, "I chose Mr. Cortelyou as chairman of the National Committee."
>
> Now that this intended crime against the franchise has been exposed in time, now that the contributions of this money by these great monopolies looking for the continuance of old favors, or seeking new ones, stands admitted, now that these

contributions have been made in such sums as to induce and permit the most lavish expenditures ever made, we, as a people, will fail in our duty if we shall not rebuke at the polls this latest and most flagrant attempt to control the election—not for legitimate business conducted for proper ends—but in order that the few may still further strengthen their hold upon our industries. We shall rue it, if, as a people, we do not make this rebuke so emphatic that the offense will never again be repeated.[34]

One commentator remarked that Parker, "being unable to respond by giving names, amounts and the place . . . was at a complete disadvantage. Most of the public considered Parker's attack a last-hour campaign roarback and it undoubtedly injured [him]."[35]

Editors of the Republican and independent press commented enthusiastically about Parker's failure to prove his charges. The *Chicago Tribune* stated that the "argument, the logic, are characteristic of the man and the candidate. They mark the descent of Parker from a high plain . . . to the level of the cheap politician. It is not pleasant to note the fall of even a sparrow."[36] The *New York Sun* wrote, "Democratic enthusiasts were sure that Judge Parker 'had something up his sleeve' . . . One hardly knows which to admire the more, the Judge's self-denial or his confidence in the impeccable purity of his campaign fund."[37] In December 1904, the *Review of Reviews* added that, "as against the President's emphatic denial, Judge Parker's repetition of his charges without a single citation of fact to support them produced a veritable consternation in the ranks of his followers, and undoubtedly contributed not a little to the completeness of his defeat."[38]

Several years after the election, as a result of a congressional investigation in which Roosevelt admitted, under oath, that he had not told the truth in his campaign, it was disclosed that large corporations had indeed contributed heavily to the Roosevelt campaign.[39] According to the evidence produced at the hearing, one week before the election was to take place, Roosevelt himself summoned E. H. Harriman, the president of the Union Pacific Railroad, to the White House and asked him to raise money to help carry New York.[40] Harriman was happy to oblige. He contributed $50,000 to the Republican campaign coffers and leaned on several of his Wall Street colleagues to do the same. J. P. Morgan gave $100,000 and followed that up with $50,000 more. Chauncey Depew removed his senatorial hat, donned his hat as chairman of the New York Central Railroad, and kicked in $100,000. Henry Clay Frick donated $50,000 (Frick, in the years after the election, angrily complained, "We bought the son of a bitch and then he didn't stay bought!").[41] George Perkins wrote three separate checks on behalf of himself, the House of Morgan, and the New York Life Insurance Company for a total of $450,000. George J. Gould, of Western Union and the Great Northern Railway, contributed $1.5 million. Other donations were made by executives from Standard Oil, National City Life, General Electric, American Can, the Equitable Life Insurance Company, the Mutual Life Insurance Company, and International Harvester.[42] Roosevelt always claimed that the money Harriman raised had been used to elect New York Governor Frank Higgins, as if it were possible to separate the gubernatorial campaign from the presidential contest in a presidential election year.[43]

Unfortunately for Parker, this information was too little, too late. His revelation during the campaign that the president had taken money—vast sums of money—from Wall Street financiers caused only a slight reaction from the public. The president had appealed directly to the voters and then pushed the matter aside without a second thought. The public was simply too enamored with their "Rough Rider" to believe that he could be caught up in any wrongdoing.[44]

At the same time Roosevelt was issuing his scathing denial of Parker's charges, New York Governor Benjamin O'Dell dropped a bombshell of his own. O'Dell, a Republican, gave a speech in the Murray Hill Lyceum in which he claimed that Parker owned shares in the Shipbuilding Trust at the same time he was rendering a decision in the court of appeals that affected the value of his holdings of trust stock.[45] According to O'Dell, Parker could not complain about the involvement of the trusts in the current campaign or purport to be a "trust buster" when he himself had profited from involvement in the trusts.[46] Parker refused to comment on O'Dell's claims. Instead, Samuel Untermyer, an attorney in the receivership case involving the Shipbuilding Trust, issued a statement that Judge Parker had "never been concerned or taken part in a decision affecting any aspect of the [Shipbuilding Trust] litigation."[47]

While Parker was slinging accusations at Roosevelt and Cortelyou, Parker's friends in politics and the media continued to pen articles and editorials and give speeches in support of his bid for the nation's highest office. On October 11, 1904, Colonel Watterson published his last editorial in support of Parker's candidacy. He titled it "He of the Big Stick." Watterson opined that the election of Parker would guarantee at least four years of tranquility at home and abroad. According to Watterson, Parker's election would lead to the elimination of wasteful government spending, check the tendencies of absolutism, and assure the adoption of practical government reforms. And most importantly, it would place control of the federal government in the hands of "a just and sensible man, not a theorizing experimentalist."[48]

David B. Hill spent the week of October 17 campaigning for Parker in the battleground state of Indiana. In the span of five days, he spoke on behalf of the Parker-Davis ticket in Indianapolis, Lafayette, Terre Haute, Fort Wayne, and Evansville.[49] Bourke Cockran spoke on behalf of the Democratic ticket in New York and Chicago. "Pitchfork" Ben Tillman stumped in Chicago; John Sharp Williams campaigned in Brooklyn; Adlai Stevenson spoke in Princeton, Indiana.[50]

Former President Grover Cleveland spoke to a standing room only crowd at Carnegie Hall on October 21, 1904. He spent most of his time castigating the Republicans, noting at one point that never "before has it been so distinctly claimed that all the virtues, all the patriotism and all the governing ability of our citizenship are found among the members of one political party . . . [Never] . . . before have those of our citizens, not among the chosen, been so boldly considered as aliens in their own land, who should be cast into outer political darkness as unworthy to be entrusted with the power and responsibility of a government established by the people and for the people."[51] Cleveland concluded his remarks by urging the crowd to send Parker to the White House and D-Cady Herrick to the governor's mansion.[52]

Just a few days before the election, Cleveland penned an article in *McClure's Magazine* supporting the Parker candidacy and urging Americans to cast their votes for his longtime friend. Cleveland reminded voters that Parker, unlike Roosevelt, was deliberate in his thinking and conservative in his political philosophy. He spent several paragraphs discussing Parker's devotion to duty above all else—a devotion that led him to decline federal appointments and refuse to run for statewide political offices. And when, in the end, Parker was summoned by his fellow citizens to accept the responsibility of national party leadership, that same devotion to duty required him to continue to discharge his judicial obligations until his docket was cleared and he could resign his judgeship so that the tribunal he had led with fidelity and steadfastness would be "untouched by the atmosphere of political contest." He closed by urging the American people to make Parker president.[53]

On November 4, 1904, Cleveland was the keynote speaker at a meeting of the First Voters' Democratic Association of Essex County in Newark, New Jersey. Seven thousand people packed into the Essex Troop Armory to hear the former president's remarks. The majority of Cleveland's speech failed to mention either Parker or Roosevelt. Instead, he spent the bulk of his time castigating the Republicans for failing to address the tariff issue and providing a "scathing arraignment of the trusts."[54] At the very end of his speech, Cleveland folded his prepared remarks, waited for the applause to die down, and when the audience became hushed, he said, "Heaven grant that the aroused sense of justice of the American people and the pure American love of country may bring the best sentiment of that country to the support of this contest, and that such sentiment may be an ever-present encouragement and promise of victory for our noble standard-bearer, Alton B. Parker."[55] At the mention of Parker's name, the crowd erupted in wild cheers, "handkerchiefs and flags were waved, [and] men and women hurrahed like mad."[56]

Cleveland's written and spoken endorsements of Parker's candidacy did little to generate enthusiasm for the candidate or swell the campaign bankroll. The Democratic National Committee announced that it was $900,000 in debt.[57] Urey Woodson, the committee's secretary, reported this fact to Thomas Fortune Ryan and August Belmont. Ryan did not seem concerned about the debt, telling Belmont, "That's very reasonable. Gussie, you send your check for $450,000 and I'll send mine for $450,000. We'll pay these bills and let Mr. Woodson and the boys go home." Belmont was hesitant to contribute any more funds, stating that he had already given $200,000 to the campaign. Ryan reminded Belmont, "Yes, Gussie, I know that, but remember, Parker was your candidate."[58]

At the end of the campaign, Mr. Dooley, the fictional Irish bartender, delivered his final observations about the election: "Manny people ar-re opposin' [Parker] because they think he . . . if ilicted, wud plunge th' country into a great and disastrous sleep." Roosevelt, however, with his boundless energy and dynamic personality, was providing excitement. "Th' issues ar-re clearly marked. There are none . . . Th' counthry, me boy, is swimmin' on its back smokin' a seegar an' havin' th' time iv its life. Annywan who thries to save this counthry is in f'r a good lickin'."[59] Parker got just that.

12

Election Day

The weather was favorable throughout most of the country on November 8, 1904. Despite this fact (and the fact that there had been a rise in voter registrations), nearly half a million fewer voters showed up at the polls to cast ballots than they had four years earlier.[1] Neither the candidates, nor the issues, could convince more people to vote.

On election day the two candidates voted in their home districts. Roosevelt, who left Washington, DC, by train shortly after midnight, arrived at his Oyster Bay polling place at 9:45 a.m. to vote. Parker drove his buckboard into Kingston by a back road and cast his ballot an hour later. Following his election day custom, Parker then paid a visit to his dentist to have his teeth examined.[2]

At the Democratic National Headquarters in the Century Building on 5th Avenue, while guests of the national committee received returns on the lower floors, William Sheehan, De Lancey Nicoll, August Belmont, and Urey Woodson gathered in a private room shortly before 6:00 p.m. These four managers of the Parker campaign gave up hope of a Democratic victory almost immediately. At 7:15, Belmont announced his conviction that Roosevelt had won the election and left for home.[3] By 8:30 p.m., Parker knew that he had lost. He sent a telegram to Roosevelt at that time: "The People by their votes have emphatically approved your administration and I congratulate you. Alton B. Parker."[4] Roosevelt replied: "I thank you for your congratulations. Theodore Roosevelt."[5]

At the very outset of the campaign, the Republicans conceded that several states, with 162 total electoral votes, were firmly in the Democratic camp. Those states were Alabama, Arkansas, Delaware, Florida, Georgia,

Kentucky, Louisiana, Maryland, Mississippi, Missouri, North Carolina, South Carolina, Tennessee, Texas, and Virginia.[6] The states regarded as most certainly Republican, and virtually conceded as such by the Democratic campaign managers, were California, Iowa, Kansas, Maine, Massachusetts, Michigan, Minnesota, Nebraska, Nevada, New Hampshire, North Dakota, Ohio, Oregon, Pennsylvania, Rhode Island, South Dakota, Vermont, Washington, and Wyoming.[7] The electoral vote total for those states was a combined 180 (239 Electoral College votes were necessary to win the presidency in 1904).[8] That left eleven states essentially "in play" at the start of the 1904 campaign, with a total of 134 electoral votes: Colorado, Connecticut, Idaho, Illinois, Indiana, Montana, New Jersey, New York, West Virginia, Wisconsin, and Utah.[9]

In the end, the Republicans had little to worry about. One writer remarked that the little Dutch boy with his finger in the dyke was the greatest example of human fortitude until "Parker ran for the presidency against Theodore Roosevelt and was defeated by acclamation."[10] Roosevelt garnered 7,630,557 votes to Parker's 5,084,537 votes—a plurality of more than 2.5 million votes.[11] Roosevelt's plurality of 2,546,020 votes was the greatest in any presidential election up to that time.[12] Roosevelt outpolled McKinley's vote total in 1900 by more than 400,000; Parker dropped almost 1.3 million votes from Bryan's 1900 total.[13]

Roosevelt carried every northern and western state and two states that were traditionally in the "southern" camp: Missouri (the first time since the Civil War that a Republican presidential candidate had carried the state) and West Virginia (Henry Davis's home state).[14] Parker and Davis only managed to win the solid South, Kentucky, and Maryland (the latter by only fifty-three votes)[15] and in doing so failed to gain even 40 percent of the popular vote. In the West, Parker hardly made any showing at all. In seventeen Western and Great Plains states, he failed to carry a single county.[16] The vote that Parker received was described by a writer for the *New York Times* as follows: "Judge Parker has received, with few exceptions, the vote of the Eastern independents, the class formerly described by the term 'mugwump.' He has received, we judge, the greatest part of the sound money Democratic vote, together with the vote of those unswerving, old-fashioned Democrats, the bone and sinew of the party."[17]

In the Electoral College, Roosevelt fattened the Republican margin from 1900, carrying thirty-three states, five more than McKinley, with 336 electoral votes[18] (see figure 12.1). This was the best showing for a winning presidential candidate in the Electoral College since the 1872

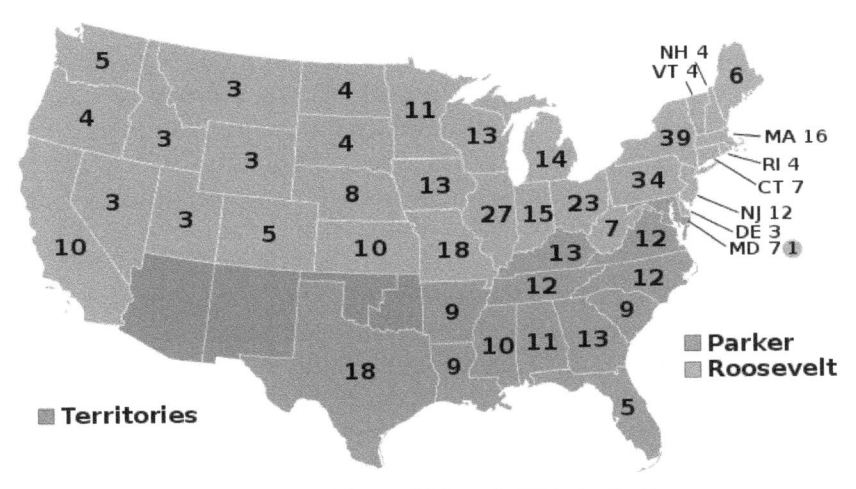

Figure 12.1. 1904 Electoral Map. © 2008 Andy Hogan.

election, when U.S. Grant defeated Horace Greeley.[19] Parker garnered only 140 electoral votes, and in the process, he forfeited the gains Bryan had made in the West.[20]

The clearest message to be read from these returns was Roosevelt's overwhelming popularity. He ran ahead of the Republican ticket in every part of the country, even in the South.[21] The people liked his energy, his frankness, and his zest for life. But the voters sent an equally clear message to the Democrats. They had only made matters worse for themselves by ignoring the policies and constituencies that Bryan had attracted to the party.[22] Two facts left this message unmistakable: the disastrous showing in the West and the more than fourfold increase in the votes cast for the second-time Socialist presidential candidate, Eugene V. Debs.[23] Debs managed to collect 402,283 votes, up from 90,000 in 1900, and he got his best percentages in the West.[24] The Prohibitionists also improved their 1900 showing, garnering more than 258,000 votes.[25] Even the Populists made a modest comeback, more than doubling their total to 117,183 votes.[26] According to one historian, "[Parker] made a lifeless, colorless campaign. He was ponderous and heavy and uninspiring."[27]

A few days after the election, the *Guthrie Daily Leader*, a top Democratic journal from Oklahoma, lamented Parker's loss and declared its allegiance to William Jennings Bryan: "We are frank to confess that we did not endorse all that Judge Parker stood for. We are of the breed of democracy represented by Thomas Jefferson in its foundation, and represented by William Jennings Bryan today, if you please."[28] Bryan fully agreed with the *Leader,* stating even before election day that "as soon as the election is over I shall . . . organize for the campaign of 1908."[29]

On election night, when the magnitude of his victory became apparent, Roosevelt issued a statement to the American people, thanking them for their support. He said:

> I am deeply sensible of the honor done to me by the American people in thus expressing their confidence in what I have done and have tried to do. I appreciate to the full solemn responsibility this confidence imposes on me, and I shall do all that in my power lies not to forfeit it. On the Fourth of March next, I shall have served three and one half years, and this three and one half years constitutes my first term.
>
> The wise custom which limits the President to two terms regards the substance and not the form, and under no circumstance will I be a candidate for or accept another nomination.[30]

Roosevelt's promise to renounce all efforts to elect him to a third term was not an impulsive or emotional gesture. It had been well thought out in advance, and it fulfilled his campaign strategy of winning by downplaying controversial issues.[31] No better way existed to give lie to the allegations that he was hungry for power (which even some Republicans believed) than to voluntarily withdraw from future consideration as a presidential candidate.[32] But this promise clearly turned out to be a campaign blunder. Noble as the gesture may have been, it helped rob Roosevelt of a dynamic and impactful second term.[33] Once it became clear that Roosevelt meant to honor his pledge to quit in 1908, a stalemate quickly developed between the president and Republican congressional leaders.[34]

Parker issued his own statement to the American public following his defeat. He wrote:

> To the Democracy of the Nation:
>
> Our thanks are due to the members of the National Committee and to the Executive Committee in charge of the campaign for the most unselfish, capable, and brilliant party service. All that

it was possible for men to do they did, but our difficulty was beyond the reach of party managers.

I am most grateful to them and wish in this general way to extend my thanks to the workers, as well as the rank and file, all over the country. I know how hard they struggled against overwhelming odds, and I only wish I could take each one by the hand and thank him.

Deeply as I regretted leaving the bench at the time of it, in the presence of overwhelming defeat, I do not lament it. I thought it my duty. In light of my present information I am now even more confident that I did right. I shall never seek a nomination for public office, but I shall to the best of my ability serve the party that has honored me, and through the party serve my country.

The party has in the near future a great mission. Before long the people will realize that the tariff-fed trusts and illegal combinations are absorbing the wealth of the Nation. Then they will wish to throw off these leeches, but the Republican Party will not aid them to do it, for its leaders appreciate too well the uses to which the moneys of the trusts can be put in political campaigns.

When that time comes, and come it will, the people will turn to the Democratic Party for relief, and the party should be ready—ready with an organization of patriotic citizens covering every election district, who are willing to work for the love of the cause—an organization supported by as many town, city, county, and State officers as we are able to elect in the meantime.

We entered this canvass with every Northern, Western, and Eastern State save one in Republican control. This gave that party a large army of office holders reaching into every hamlet, many of whom gladly followed the examples set them by the members of the President's Cabinet in devoting their time and services to the party.

To accomplish much in this direction, however, we must forget the difficulties of the past. If any one suspects his neighbor of treachery let him not hint of his suspicion. If he knows he has deserted us let him not tell it. Our forces have been weakened by divisions. We have quarreled at times over non-essentials.

If we would help the people: if we would furnish an organization through which they may be relieved of a party that has grown so corrupt that it will gladly enter into partnership with trusts to secure money for election purposes, we must not forget the differences of the past and begin this day to build up, wherever it may be needed, a broad and effective organization. And we must by constant teaching, through the press and from the platform, apprise people of the way the vicious tariff circle works. We must bring home to them, at other than election seasons, the fact that the money contributed to the Republican Party by the trusts is not only dishonest money, but it is given that the trusts may without hindrance, take a much larger sum from the people.

In the presence of a defeat that would take away all personal ambition—were it true that otherwise it possessed me—I do not hesitate to say that in my opinion the greatest moral question which now confronts us is: Shall the trusts and corporations be prevented from contributing money to control or to aid in controlling elections?

Such service as I can render in that or any other direction will be gladly rendered. And I beg the cooperation, as a fellow-worker, of every Democrat in the country.[35]

In the aftermath of the election, Parker commented on why he thought he lost. He said, "It was a defeat which was easy to foresee and predict. It was preceded by division and faction in our ranks over a period of eight years. It was emphasized by the use of governmental power for partisan purposes, by the reckless and unprecedented expenditure of money, and by demagogic appeals to interests as wide apart as the poles."[36] He also outlined what he thought it would take for the Democrats to once again savor electoral success:

This is not the first time that the party has been in what seemed a hopeless minority. But even when its condition was least encouraging, it was still the same consistent advocate of patriotic and manly policies as when it was in the full plenitude of power during the first sixty years of the last century. Rallying about its natural leaders—as courageous and patriotic as any in our political history—it was then, as always, its virtue to be a national party.* * * With us, organization, to be effective, must lie in the State, the county and the district. By the very necessity of our principles and our existence, we must protect the rights and promote the interests of communities, and carry up into federal politics only that reserve of power properly incident to our institutions and system of government.* * * All our later history has shown that it is far more important to have our full share of Governors, Legislatures, Senators, Members of Congress and of State, county and municipal officials than it is, by neglecting these, to command a long list of places under the general government. When we can once again control these training schools for the higher politics, we shall have little need to trouble ourselves overmuch about candidates for President, because we shall have laid deep and strong in the people's will, the necessary foundations. Then, and only then, may we look with hopefulness and confidence to the country at large. Then we may go North or South, East or West, for candidates, certain of their fitness for the work in hand, and of their acceptableness to our countrymen.[37]

Bryan, not surprisingly, had a different take on why the Democratic nominee had not been successful. He stated that Parker's loss "was due to the fact that the Democratic party attempted to be conservative in the presence of conditions which demand[ed] radical remedies. It sounded a partial retreat when it should have ordered a charge all along the line."[38] He added that "the Democratic party [had] nothing to gain by catering to organized and predatory wealth."[39] Champ Clark wrote to Parker two weeks after the election and offered his thoughts on why Parker lost: "I have always contended since meeting you, and do now believe, that had you made an extensive stumping tour you would have greatly enhanced our chances of success—for I am certain that you made a most favorable impression on all with whom you came in contact."[40]

Many rank-and-file Democrats were saddened by Parker's loss to Roosevelt. A popular toast began making the rounds shortly after Parker's defeat:

> It's a pardonable pride a
> Democrat feels
> For Alton B. Parker, Court of Appeals,
> He bore our standard last
> campaign,
> And although his fight was in
> vain,
> Alton B. Parker, you're alright.
> Alton B. Parker, may your skies
> be bright.

Much of the post-election commentary on Parker centered around his apparent discomfort at being placed on the changing national political stage. Writers for *The Forum,* when conducting their postmortem of the 1904 election in January 1905, stated that Parker "shifted his position with every change of tide. At one time, he would not leave Esopus or make any speeches beyond the shelter of his own porch; at another time, he was being whirled in a special train through many states, delivering addresses twice and thrice a day."[41] A writer for *Life* sympathetically added, "He made as good work of it as any available Democrat could have done, but the difficulty he had in adjusting his habits of mind and of life to the exigencies of active politics was very noticeable. It took him a long time to get limbered up, and to write speeches instead of opinions."[42]

The writers for *The Forum* also believed that the Parker campaign made a major mistake when they made the campaign all about Roosevelt (even though they themselves admitted that "there was no real vital issue involved in the contest between the parties.").[43] In their words, "the Democrats were in error when they forced a personal fight upon the President. They could not make the country believe that he was not to be trusted. The very characteristics which the Democratic orators held up to ridicule were the ones which attract the average American—the energy which does not hesitate to act even at the risk of making a mistake; the courage which does not fear to speak without regard to consequences; the instinct which exposes and condemns official misdoing with more impulsiveness than caution. The Democrats characterized President Roosevelt as strenuous, erratic, and unsafe; but they could not disguise the fact that the forcefulness of his individuality compelled admiration, and they could not question his honesty."[44]

Parker never again held elective office—and he never again served as a judge on any court—but, as we shall see, his skies were indeed bright, as he continued to be engaged in politics and became a well-respected leader of the bar.

13

A Return to the Practice of Law and a Continuing Involvement in Politics

Parker seemed to take his loss in stride. The day after the election, he got up early, dressed, and told his wife, "Now I'm going to New York to make some money."[1] And he did just that, remaining in active practice for twenty-one years, at first with Edward W. Hatch and William F. Sheehan and later in the firm of Parker Marshall & Randall.[2] On April 5, 1920, David Miller and Gordon Auchincloss merged their firm with Parker's firm to create Parker, Marshall, Miller, Auchincloss & Randall.[3] By 1921 the firm was known as Parker, Marshall, Miller & Auchincloss.[4]

As Parker once again entered the ranks of the practicing attorney, he took the time to author an article about the important role that attorneys play in the civic life of the country. In June 1905, Parker's article appeared in *The Green Bag*. Titled "The Lawyer in Public Affairs," Parker highlighted the tendency of attorneys to take part in the affairs of city, county, state, and country from the earliest days of the Republic. During the Revolution, the voice of the lawyer guided the debates, led the councils, and formulated the philosophies of the fledgling nation. Attorneys were the prominent actors in the drafting of the Constitution and had the greatest say in how that document was ultimately interpreted. According to Parker, lawyers have dominated the executive branch of our national government: eighteen of the twenty-four presidents who succeeded Washington "had devoted themselves exclusively to the study and practice of law."[5] Parker was proud of the fact that despite these positions of privilege and power, "no really great lawyer, whose reputation was both made and earned in the practice of his profession, or by experience on the Bench, has attached himself to dangerous or demagogic movements."⁶ Writing several decades before famed comic book author Stan Lee, Parker recognized that with great power and privilege came great responsibility. He concluded his article with these words:

> If, at any time it shall become apparent that the sanctity of the ballot is either threatened or assailed; if the administration of the law, whether civil or criminal, becomes either lax or careless, if the evils in any industrial movement manifest such power that they threaten monopoly or put popular rights in peril; if the executive, the legislative, or the judicial branches of our system shall, either by design or accident, tend to trench unduly or dangerously upon the rights of any of the others—the one man who should resent and resist the dangers thus threatened, is the American lawyer. The traditions of his profession, the execution of the high trust confided to him, the example set him by great leaders through many generations, all demand that he should exercise the greatest watchfulness and show the highest courage.⁷

For the rest of his career, Parker did just that.

Parker was busy with legal work almost as soon as he hung out his shingle. Within two weeks of the election, he received from some of the New York judges he knew certain appointments as commissioner in a series of condemnation proceedings.⁸ Before the close of the calendar year, he was inundated with requests that he handle appeals before his former court, that he handle an appeal before the United States Supreme Court (complete with a $25,000 retainer), and that he try a number of cases to verdict in the New York trial courts.⁹

In 1905, Parker served as counsel for New York mayor George B. McClellan Jr. in a dispute over the New York mayoralty election. McClellan's opponent in the 1905 contest was none other than William Randolph Hearst. McClellan was declared the winner of the election by a mere 3,472 votes (out of more than 690,000 total votes cast).¹⁰ As soon as McClellan was certified as the winner, Hearst filed an action for a writ of mandamus commanding the election officers to assemble and recount the ballots cast in the November 7, 1905, election. Parker convinced the New York Court of Appeals that it was without the power—or the authority—to order a recount of the ballots.¹¹

Parker was a close personal friend and counsel for Samuel Gompers, the president of the American Federation of Labor. He was often involved in representing Gompers, or the AFL, in cases involving labor disputes. One of the most famous of these cases was *Loewe v. Lawlor*, also referred to as the Danbury Hatters' Case.

In 1901, D.E. Loewe & Company, a manufacturer and seller of fur hats, was operating as an "open" shop. The owners of the company had long refused to allow their employees to unionize. As a result, the United Hatters of North America (UHU), in conjunction with the AFL, instituted a strike and a nationwide boycott of the company's hats. The boycott was ultimately successful in persuading large numbers of retailers, wholesalers, and customers to not buy from or do business with Loewe.[12]

Loewe & Company sued the UHU, the AFL, and more than 200 individual union members for violating the Sherman Antitrust Act. Loewe & Company essentially alleged that the boycott interfered with the company's ability to engage in the interstate commerce of selling hats. The United States Circuit Court for the District of Connecticut dismissed the suit on the grounds that the alleged actions of the union and its members fell outside the scope of the Sherman Antitrust Act. Loewe & Company appealed the dismissal of their case to the United States Court of Appeals for the Second Circuit, and that court certified the case to the United States Supreme Court.[13]

On appeal, the Supreme Court held, in a unanimous decision, that the defendants were acting in restraint of interstate commerce and had violated the provisions of the Sherman Antitrust Act.[14] The case was sent back to the trial court for additional proceedings. A trial was held in 1909, and the jury returned a verdict in favor of the plaintiffs and against the defendants in the amount of $74,000, which was tripled, under the act, to $222,000.[15] The verdict was affirmed by the Court of Appeals, and the case was then appealed to the US Supreme Court.[16]

Parker represented the defendants before the Supreme Court. He argued that the trial court had made multiple errors in the admission of evidence and that the defendants' actions did not amount to an unlawful restraint of interstate trade under the Sherman Antitrust Act, thereby requiring a vacation of the verdict rendered in the trial court. Justice Oliver Wendell Holmes, writing for a unanimous court, rejected Parker's arguments and held that the defendants were liable for damages, stating, in part, "we agree with the Court of Appeals that a combination and conspiracy forbidden by the statute were proved."[17] In 1917, the case was settled for slightly over $234,000 (approximately $5.6 million in today's dollars), of which the AFL was able to obtain $216,000 in voluntary contributions from union members.[18]

In 1911, Parker defended Samuel Gompers for allegedly violating an anti-boycott injunction against the Bucks Stove & Range Company. The Bucks Stove & Range Company had obtained an injunction restraining Gompers (and other members of the AFL) from boycotting Bucks Stove & Range Company or from publishing or making any statement that the Bucks Stove & Range Company was, or had been, on the AFL's "Unfair" or "We Don't Patronize" lists. Some months after the injunction had been issued, the company filed a petition to have Gompers held in contempt of court for violating the injunction by publishing statements that either directly, or indirectly, called attention to the fact that Bucks Stove & Range Company was on the AFL's "Unfair" list. Gompers was found guilty of contempt of court for violating the injunction and was sentenced to twelve months in prison.[19] Gompers appealed to the United States Supreme Court.[20]

On appeal, the Supreme Court held that the trial judge could not impose criminal sentences for contempt on the defendants in a civil proceeding and ordered that the criminal sentences be set aside.[21] It remanded the case to the Supreme Court of the District of Columbia with directions that the contempt proceedings instituted by the Bucks Stove & Range Company be dismissed, "but without prejudice to the power and right of the Supreme Court of the District of Columbia to punish by a proper proceeding, contempt, if any, committed against it."[22] The day after the US Supreme Court issued its opinion, the Supreme Court of the District of Columbia appointed a committee to inquire whether there was reasonable cause to believe that Gompers (and others) were guilty of willfully violating the December 18, 1907, injunction.[23] The committee reported and charged that Gompers and his associates were guilty of violating the injunction, and a rule to show cause why they should not be held in contempt of court was issued on the same day. A trial was held, and the defendants were once again found guilty and sentenced to prison.[24]

Parker filed a writ of certiorari with the US Supreme Court, which was granted. Parker argued that the applicable statute of limitations, which provided that "no person shall be prosecuted, tried or punished for any offense, not capital . . . unless the indictment is found or the information is instituted within three years next after such offense shall have been committed" precluded the bringing of any contempt charges against Gompers. In other words, Parker argued that Gompers could not be prosecuted for violating the injunction because all of his alleged actions in violation of the injunction took place in 2008—more than three years before the Supreme Court of the District of Columbia brought criminal contempt proceedings against Gompers. The Supreme Court agreed that the statute of limitations applied and ruled that the judgments against Gompers and his co-defendants must be reversed.[25] Parker's winning arguments kept Gompers out of jail.

In that same year, Parker also argued a significant antitrust case before the US Supreme Court. Dr. Miles Medical Company was engaged in the manufacture and sale of proprietary medicines, prepared by means of secret methods and formulas, and identified by distinctive packages, labels, and trademarks. Dr. Miles sold its medicines to jobbers and wholesale druggists, who in turn sold them to retail druggists for sale to the consumer. For each medicine, the company fixed not only the price of its own sales to jobbers and wholesale dealers, but also the wholesale and retail prices. John D. Park & Sons was a Kentucky corporation that was engaged in the wholesale drug business. Park refused to abide by the sales prices dictated by Dr. Miles and, it was alleged, induced several other wholesalers who had entered into contracts with Dr. Miles to sell their products for the previously agreed-on prices to sell Dr. Miles medicines to Park at "cut rates." Dr. Miles moved for an injunction to prohibit Park from inducing or attempting to induce any wholesaler from breaking its contract with Dr. Miles and to enjoin Park from selling any Dr. Miles medicines for less than the established retail price.[26]

The trial court and the court of appeals refused to enter an injunction, and Dr. Miles appealed to the Supreme Court. Alton Parker represented John D. Park & Sons before the Supreme Court. He argued that Dr. Miles was not entitled to an injunction because the contracts at issue, which set the minimum prices at which independent resellers could resell its products, were unlawful under the common law and Section 1 of the Sherman Antitrust Act. The Supreme Court agreed, finding that Dr. Miles' contracts were unenforceable on the grounds that all competition between the wholesalers and retailers was destroyed. It rejected Dr. Miles' argument that its restrictive covenants only prevented injurious competition between the dealers and only resulted in the maintenance of reasonable prices.[27]

In 1913, Parker was appointed lead trial counsel in the impeachment of New York governor William "Plain Bill" Sulzer. William Sulzer was a member of Tammany Hall and, under its auspices, was elected to a number of state and national offices. In 1889, at the age of twenty-six, he was elected to the New York State Assembly on the Tammany ticket. He was reelected to five consecutive one-year terms in the Assembly, and in 1893 he was elected speaker of the Assembly. A year later, after serving as the Democratic minority leader, he resigned from the legislature—but vowed to return to Albany someday as the state's governor.[28]

Sulzer was elected to the congressional district representing the Lower East Side of Manhattan in 1895. He served in the US House of Representatives from 1895 until 1912, ultimately rising to the chairmanship of the House Foreign Affairs Committee.[29] Although he had long been supported by Tammany Hall, he frequently followed his own political course—a precursor of the trouble in which he would find himself embroiled in the second decade of the twentieth century. He was, writes Roscoe Brown, "a dreamer, erratic and egotistical, inspired by a desire to serve the public, but also by an overwhelming ambition for leadership and distinction."[30]

By 1912, Tammany Hall, with pressure from Woodrow Wilson, had decided to move on from Governor Dix and throw its support behind Sulzer for the governorship. Before he took office, Sulzer told of a meeting that he had with Tammany leader "Boss" Charles Murphy. Sulzer related that:

> His [Murphy's] attitude was very friendly and confidential. He said he was my friend; that he knew my financial condition and wanted to help me out. As he went on, I was amazed at his knowledge of my intimate personal affairs. To my astonishment, he informed me that he knew I was heavily in debt. Then he offered me enough money to pay my debts and have enough left to take things easy while Governor. He said that this was really a party matter and that the money he would give me was party money . . . and that nobody would know anything about it, that I could pay what I owed and go to Albany feeling easy financially. He then asked me how much I needed, to whom I owed it, and other personal questions.
>
> As I did not want to be tied hard and fast as Governor in advance, I declined Mr. Murphy's offer, saying that I was paying off my debts gradually; that my creditors were friends and would not press me; that I was economical, that I would try to get along on my salary as Governor. Murphy countered saying, 'If you need money at any time, let me know, and you can have what you want and never miss it.'[31]

Once he took office, Sulzer was summoned to another meeting with Murphy at the home of Supreme Court Justice Edward E. McCall. According to Sulzer, "Mr. Murphy demanded from me pledges regarding legislation and especially concerning appointments to the Public Service Commission, the Health Department, the Labor Department, the State Hospital Commission, the Department of State Prisons and the Department of Highways."[32] Sulzer refused to appoint Murphy's men to state positions.[33]

After six months in office, Sulzer wrote an article detailing the amount of waste he had uncovered in state departments. He wrote, in part, "I have been in office now for six months, and in that time I have learned enough to be able to say without fear of contradiction that in the past three years $50,000,000 of the people's money has been wasted or stolen."[34] Sulzer decided to appoint a committee to investigate state graft. He appointed two men who were above reproach to spearhead the investigation: John A. Hennessy and George W. Blake. "Boss" Murphy insisted that Sulzer appoint one of his own men to the committee. When Sulzer refused, Murphy told him, "If you don't do this, I will wreck your administration." When Sulzer responded, "I am the Governor," Murphy retorted, "You may be the Governor, but I have got the Legislature, and the Legislature controls the Governor, and if you don't do what I tell you to do, I will throw you out of office."[35]

The battling back and forth between Sulzer and Murphy continued until June 1913. When Governor Sulzer called the legislature into special session to act on a proposal to adopt direct, open primaries for party nominations, Boss Murphy had had enough. At Murphy's urging, members of the state assembly voted to expand the powers of a joint committee that had been set up to investigate the finances of state-supported institutions. The committee was now empowered to probe campaign receipts and money spent by candidates for public office. Conveniently, the committee excluded from its probe assemblymen, senators, and mayors. The focus of the probe: William Clay Sulzer.[36]

On August 11, 1913, the committee issued its report to the assembly. Two days later, the assembly voted seventy-nine to forty-five to impeach Sulzer "for willful and corrupt misconduct in his said office, and for high crimes and misdemeanors."[37] Sulzer faced eight articles of impeachment, alleging that he had made and filed a false statement regarding his campaign accounts, perjured himself in verifying the statement concerning his campaign accounts, bribed witnesses and fraudulently induced them to withhold evidence from the committee investigating his misconduct, suppressed evidence by threatening witnesses, dissuaded a witness from appearing before the committee pursuant to a duly authorized subpoena, used campaign contributions to speculate in the stock market, promised and threatened to use his influence and authority as governor to affect the votes or political actions of certain members of the assembly, and used his authority and influence as governor "to affect the current prices of securities listed and selling on the New York Stock Exchange."[38]

Before the impeachment trial began, Sulzer tried to explain the most serious charges against him by saying that if he had signed campaign disclosures that were inaccurate, "it was due to haste and carelessness and not an intent to deceive."[39] Trying to clarify the rest, Sulzer stated, "Some of the moneys were not for campaign purposes at all, but were loans. They were given to me by friends who knew I was heavily in debt, and who loaned me the money to pay my debts or to use as I saw fit. These friends wanted nothing, and in the case of my election I knew there was nothing they would ask me to do, or that I could do for them. Politics had nothing to do with the matter."[40]

Sulzer's impeachment trial, which was conducted before the State Senate and the judges of the court of appeals, began on September 18, 1913. Parker was aided in his prosecution of Sulzer by former judges John B. Stanchfield and Edgar T. Brackett and attorneys Eugene L. Richards, Isidor J. Kresel, Hiram C. Todd, and Henderson Peck. Sulzer was defended by former judges D-Cady Herrick, Irving Vann, and Harvey Hinman and attorneys Louis Marshall, Austen G. Fox, Roger P. Clark, and Charles J. Herrick. Edgar M. Cullen, the man who became chief judge of the Court of Appeals when Parker resigned to run for president, presided over the impeachment proceedings.[41]

As one commentator noted, "the [impeachment] court sat in an atmosphere of tension and drama and with a sense of historic significance."[42] Sulzer's trial was billed as "the most sensational and tragic" public event "in the history of the State."[43] At the beginning of the trial, Sulzer's counsel, D-Cady Herrick, described what was happening as "the greatest" trial that "had been held in this country since the trial of President Johnson." It was, according to Herrick, a case "which is arousing the attention of the whole country."[44]

Before any evidence was presented in the case, counsel for the governor challenged the participation of some of the senators in the trial and objected to the jurisdiction of the court to even try the impeachment in the first place. In regard to the first issue, Sulzer's counsel argued that Senators James J. Frawley, Felix J. Sanner, and Samuel J. Ramsperger had been members of the committee that recommended Sulzer's impeachment and, having "taken an active part in investigating charges against him, and in formulating the report thereon," could not be fair and impartial in their deliberations.⁴⁵ They also argued that Senator Robert F. Wagner, who was president *pro tempore* of the Senate, could not participate in the impeachment trial on the grounds that he was "an interested party." If Sulzer was convicted and removed from office, Wagner would "succeed to the office, honors, dignities and emoluments of the Lieutenant Governor of the State."⁴⁶

The challenges to the participation of the senators were argued at great length by Herrick and Parker. Herrick, in urging the tribunal to remove the four senators from the court of impeachment, said, "[this] Court itself . . . is upon trial . . . you must be above suspicion in all your membership . . . There can be no question here but what the senators who participated in the investigation . . . have deliberately formed and expressed an opinion upon the guilt of the respondent."⁴⁷ He appealed to their sense of justice: "The time has come when the highest court in this State should determine, once and for all, that its members should be composed, and composed only, of these who are free from even a suspicion of bias and partiality, and that a respondent before it is to be tried upon the same principles of justice that would be applied to the trial of the meanest criminal, for the smallest offense known to the law."⁴⁸

Parker pushed back, arguing that the court was without power to exclude some of the senators from sitting in judgment of Sulzer. He said, in part, "this High Court . . . is without authority to exclude any qualified member of the Court. The people of the State of New York, our sovereign, created this Court. The Court was brought into existence by the mandate of this sovereign, and it said, and says, and has from the beginning, it shall be composed of the president of the Senate, the senators or a majority of them, and the judges of the Court of Appeals, or a majority of them. That is the mandate of the people, and you are here by virtue of that command, without power to say to any one of your members, and of any one of them, whether a judge of the Court of Appeals, whether a senator of the State of New York, 'you shall not sit in this Court.' "⁴⁹ He then provided the court with a number of detailed constitutional arguments in support of the prosecution's position that the four senators in question had every right to participate in the trial.

When it came time to decide the question, Chief Judge Cullen agreed with Parker's position. He stated that Sulzer's challenge to the participation of Frawley, Sanner, Ramsperger, and Wagner in the impeachment proceedings "cannot be entertained [as it is against] . . . the uniform current of authority. All the precedents are against it. I also think it is not sustained on principle."[50] After stating his position, Cullen called for a vote. The vote was unanimous to disallow Sulzer's challenge to the four senators' participation in the trial (Frawley, Sanner, Ramsperger, and Wagner, upon their own request, were excused from voting).[51]

Having lost the battle over the seating of the four "interested" senators, Sulzer's counsel turned to the jurisdictional argument that they hoped would end the impeachment hearing before it really began. Sulzer's counsel noted that the regular session of the legislature of 1913 began in January and adjourned on May 8. Shortly after the legislature adjourned, Governor Sulzer, by proclamation, called the legislature into an "extraordinary session" set to begin on June 16. The constitution gave the governor the power to convene the legislature on extraordinary occasions and specifically stated that at such sessions, "no subject shall be acted upon, except such as the governor may recommend for consideration."[52] It was during the extraordinary session that the assembly impeached the governor. According to his lawyers, because Sulzer did not recommend that his impeachment be considered by the legislature, the assembly was without the power to impeach him pursuant to the plain language of the constitution.[53]

Parker responded:

> Let us come to the grant of power, for it is to that grant of power that this High Court must look first to ascertain the extent of the power conferred upon the Assembly in such cases. How does it read? 'The Assembly shall have the power of impeachment.' How? By a vote of the majority of the members elected. Is there any limitation suggested in that grant of power? It is as broad as human language can make it. Add to it anything you may think of that could possibly be added to it, and you will realize that you cannot strengthen it one iota. As a grant of power, it is absolute and complete, when we consider the history of impeachment proceedings back of the time when it was first incorporated into our Constitution. Is there anywhere any suggestion of time or place or occasion when the Assembly should act? Not at all. Is there anywhere else in this Constitution any provision relating to the subject of impeachment that suggests a limitation upon the power,

upon the time, upon the occasion when action should take place? . . . Can you conceive for a moment that when the power was granted it was the intention to limit the exercise of that power to those days or weeks or months when the Legislature should be in regular session? There is no provision in this Constitution that the Assembly should consider the matter at all at regular session.

~

Our contention is that the Assembly had the power to impeach; could self-convene itself and impeach; that it was not necessary that the Senate should be present or that the Legislature should be in session at all; that in any great emergency which may arise, it will be done; and that the Court of Impeachment should not at all, unless the situation be presented where it is compelled to, interfere with what is perfectly plain . . .[54]

After hearing the arguments of counsel, the court went into private session to debate and vote on the jurisdictional issue. The final vote against the jurisdictional argument raised by Sulzer's counsel was fifty-one to one. Senator Gottfried Wende of Buffalo was the sole negative vote. His rationale for voting to dismiss the charges was that when the assembly voted to adjourn the regular session, it foreclosed any right to impeach the governor or to act on anything else not specified in the proclamation for the extraordinary session.[55]

Having lost the first two rounds, Sulzer's legal team tried one last-ditch effort to narrow the charges against the governor. They argued that the articles of impeachment alleging failure to disclose all campaign contributions, filing a false statement of account, and using campaign funds to speculate in the stock market all dealt with actions that took place *before* Sulzer was elected governor. As a result, they argued that these activities could not serve as the basis for the governor's impeachment. According to the defense attorneys, "No case of impeachment in this country has been found where a public official has been impeached for offenses prior to his assumption of office. All are cases of misconduct in office."[56]

The prosecutors argued that impeachment could lie for acts that occurred before the accused assumed office. They pointed to the fact that New York's original constitution in 1777 specifically provided for impeachment of officers for misconduct "in their office" and that this limiting language was removed from the constitution when it was revised in 1846—the implication being that the limitation to acts committed while in office no longer applied. They also argued that "the acts stated in the articles of impeachment, including the filing of a false statement of campaign contributions, were so closely related and part of the preliminary qualifications for office as to fall within the scope of misconduct in office."[57] The court overruled the governor's objections to the sufficiency of the articles of impeachment by a vote of forty-nine to seven.[58]

After several days of wrangling over procedural issues, the actual trial got underway. The proof was detailed and involved a complicated set of facts. Dozens of political donors testified at the trial—only a handful of them had their contributions reported by Sulzer. In total, $37,400 that had been given to Sulzer for his campaign was not accounted for on the governor's campaign finance disclosure forms. Sulzer did not testify on his own behalf to explain what had happened with the campaign contributions.[59]

Parker gave the closing argument for the prosecution. His closing argument, which began on October 9 and concluded on October 10, carefully laid out all the evidence the impeachment managers had produced to find "that this defendant has been guilty of misconduct so gross as to necessitate his removal."[60] In his peroration, Parker declared:

> Before this bar, this defendant stands guilty of these offenses charged by the impeachment and proven by uncontrovertible evidence. Before the bar of the court of public opinion, this defendant stands condemned on the evidence here presented, and on the further damning testimony of his shifty defenses and of his futile efforts to dodge, by technicalities, the trial of the issues before this high Court, in which evasion public opinion, with a freedom not permitted to judicial opinion, finds direct evidence of guilt. That same public opinion takes cognizance of the fact that the defendant here is suffering from such a severe attack of moral nearsightedness that even when directed by a myriad scornful fingers, he cannot discern the dishonest, criminal, and dishonored nature of the acts proved.
>
> Even justice must see through its severe eye something of the pathetic in this defendant's frantic efforts to cover the nakedness of his wrongdoing. Defiance, defense, justification, prevarication, denunciation of his accusers, attempts to suppress

and falsify testimony and efforts to cast blame elsewhere—each in turn has been stripped from his quaking flesh until he stands now naked before this Court, without a rag of his attempted vindication clinging to his deformed and mutilated manhood!"[61]

With those words wringing in their ears, the court retired to deliberate in private. On October 16 and 17, the Court of Impeachment voted on whether or not Governor Sulzer was guilty of the charges pending against him. The final vote on the first article of impeachment, making and filing a false statement regarding his campaign accounts, was thirty-nine, guilty; eighteen, not guilty.[62] On the second article, perjuring himself in verifying the statement concerning his campaign accounts, the vote was the same.[63] On the third article, bribing witnesses and fraudulently inducing them to withhold evidence from the committee investigating the governor's misconduct, the vote was zero, guilty; fifty-seven, not guilty.[64] The final vote on the fourth article of impeachment, suppressing evidence by threatening witnesses, was forty-three, guilty; fourteen, not guilty. On the fifth article, dissuading a witness from appearing before the committee pursuant to a duly authorized subpoena, the final vote was zero, guilty; fifty-seven, not guilty. On the sixth article, using campaign contributions to speculate in the stock market, the vote was zero, guilty; fifty-seven, not guilty.[65] The final vote on the seventh article of impeachment, promising and threatening to use his influence and authority as governor to affect the votes or political actions of certain members of the Assembly, was fifty-six, not guilty (Senator Frawley asked to be excused from voting on this particular article).[66] On the final article of impeachment, using his authority and influence as governor to affect the current prices of securities listed and selling on the New York Stock Exchange, the vote was zero, guilty; fifty-seven, not guilty.[67]

Having found Sulzer guilty of three of the charges, the court then proceeded to determine the punishment to be imposed on the governor. The question posed to the court was, "Shall William Sulzer be removed from his office of Governor of this State, for the cause stated in the articles, of the charges preferred against him upon which you have found him guilty?" The vote to remove Sulzer from office was forty-three to twelve (two members were excused from voting). The court voted not to disqualify Sulzer from holding any other office in the future and then adjourned.[68]

In 1915, Parker was lead counsel for the AFL during a congressional investigation, which lead to congressional modification of federal court authority to issue injunctions.[69] In 1918, Parker represented the plaintiffs in a well-publicized suit seeking repayment of $3.1 million in receivers' certificates. Parker argued that the certificates were prior liens on the Pittsburg Shawmut & Northern Railroad and that his clients were entitled to be repaid before the railroad should be allowed to pay any other debts.[70] The trial court disagreed, holding that it did not have the power to subordinate the rights of other debtors to the rights of the holders of the receivers' certificates.[71]

Parker's last major case involved a dispute concerning the estate of the late Jay Gould. At the time of his death in 1892, Jay Gould left the largest estate of any American up to that time—$82 million (the equivalent of approximately $2.3 billion in today's dollars). Gould owned a controlling interest in the Manhattan Elevated Railroad, a controlling interest in the Western Union Telegraph Company, and a controlling interest in the Missouri Pacific Railroad.[72] Gould's will required his estate to be divided into six equal shares, each share to be designated and invested for each of his six children. Four of his children, George J. Gould, Howard Gould, Edwin Gould, and Helen Gould Shepard, served as executors and trustees of the estate. Some years after the will was probated, the executors and trustees were charged with mismanaging the trusts, resulting in staggering losses of nearly $70 million.[73]

The *Gould* case attracted some of the top legal talent of the day. Former presidential candidate John W. Davis represented the estate of George J. Gould (George Gould had died sometime after the case was filed).[74] Parker represented Edwin Gould in the case. Parker argued that the trustees of the Jay Gould estate had paid $114 million to his heirs since he died, thereby negating the claims that the estate had been depleted and mismanaged. He also argued that Edwin Gould was an exemplary trustee who performed his duty in such a way that "any open minded judging of Edwin's activities as a trustee would be impressed with his conduct and realize that he was a man of the highest character, sagacity and fidelity to duty."[75]

Ultimately, James A. O'Gorman, the referee in the case, rejected Parker's arguments. He found that the actions of the executors and trustees were "tainted with self-interest" and held that the trustees were liable for a $50 million loss in the Gould estate.[76] In the end, a settlement was reached with the estate, and the four trustees agreed to pay the estate $17.5 million.[77]

In addition to his legal work, Parker was very involved in a number of bar organizations. In 1906, the American Bar Association held its annual meeting in Saratoga, New York. Parker was unanimously elected president of the ABA at that annual meeting.[78] Upon being elected, Parker provided an address to the organization titled "The Congestion of Law." In it, Parker took issue with the annual enactment of nearly fifteen thousand laws, "two thirds of them devoted to private or special questions."[79] This "congestion of law," in his mind, resulted from popular clamor "encouraged by sensational newspapers, and by the oftentimes scarcely less sensational pulpit," as well as aspiring young men seeking to make their name "as [a] stepping [stone] to something . . . better" and political bosses "who [order] legislation, in order that [they] may sell it or exchange it for personal power."[80] Instead of enacting new laws, Parker argued that people—lawyers in particular—needed to do a better job of enforcing the laws already on the books. As he noted, "it has become far more common to look for a new law for the punishment of an old offense or for defining anew the relations of individuals to each other than it is to invoke those powers or remedies by which, over many centuries, while law has been gradually taking fixed form, men have been able to punish crimes against society or to settle their own differences."[81] Parker implored his brothers and sisters of the bar to work tirelessly to curb the overabundant enactment of useless, duplicative, dangerous, and wasteful laws. In his words, "the duty of the lawyer in the premises is imperative, for he understands the dangers better than anyone else. His daily work enables him to appreciate in large measure the wrongs the people are now suffering, and to see the rocks in the distance ahead, toward which we are steadily drifting. Therefore, he ought to take up the task, and carry it on with energy, until our current legislation shall simply properly supplement such part of our present law—whether common or statute—as has justified its existence."[82]

During his term as president, Parker also represented the ABA and provided remarks on behalf of the American bar at a memorial lecture in honor of James Wilson, one of the six original justices appointed to the US Supreme Court. Parker recognized Wilson, along with John Marshall and Joseph Story, as one of the men who "laid the cornerstone of constitutional interpretation upon deep and solid foundations" and reminded his audience that "when studying [Wilson] we can understand clearly why [the Supreme Court] has stood for permanence and stability, why it has resented the agitator and demagogue, and why it has resisted tyranny and oppression."[83]

While Parker was serving as president of the ABA, he had to deal with a potentially embarrassing matter involving his former rival for the presidency. As the annual meeting in Portland, Maine, drew to a close, ABA member George Whitlock presented a resolution criticizing President Roosevelt for commenting on the trial of the Beef Trust case the prior year and adversely criticizing the presiding judge and some of his rulings. Debate on the resolution was heated and lasted for more than an hour; one attendee, who failed to get recognition from Parker, shouted, "Someone has said the American Bar Association has no right to criticize the President of the United States. I hold that when the President of the United States violates his trust it is the duty of the American Bar Association to criticize him."[84] Parker could find no technical grounds on which to rule Whitlock's resolution out of order, but he repeatedly asked Whitlock to withdraw it—to no avail. The resolution was ultimately tabled.[85]

It was at this same meeting that Parker delivered a presidential address that served as a general reaffirmation of his lifelong conviction that the material of the common law affords a remedy for most of the problems of society and diplomacy.[86] He praised the idealism of the legal profession and reminded the assembled members that the government of the United States "is one of delegated, limited and enumerated powers."[87] He urged the members attending the meeting to resist federal usurpation of the powers reserved to the states and to give more attention to the careful and cautious passage of legislation to avoid statutory law "being ground out from a legislative hopper at the rate of five hundred laws a month."[88] Echoing his 1906 address, Parker lamented that too often laws were drafted in haste, amended on the fly as they went through the legislature, and deeply flawed by the time they reached the statute books. That put a burden on the courts to interpret and apply them and, sometimes, strike them down as unconstitutional. That, in turn, led to public impatience with the courts, which irresponsible politicians latched onto to unduly criticize the courts.[89] The solution, according to Parker, was to rely on judges to thoughtfully and judiciously make common law: "The common law is expanded slowly and carefully by judicial decisions based on a standard of justice derived from the habits, customs and thoughts of a people . . . [It is] an ideal method of building the law of a people."[90]

Immediately after his term as ABA president ended, Parker was appointed a member of a 1908 ABA committee charged with drafting a code of ethics for the American bar. The purpose of the committee, according to its chairman, was to prepare "a body of rules, few in number, clear and precise in their provisions, so there can be no excuse for their violation, to be given operative and binding force by legislation or action of the highest courts of the states."⁹¹ The committee presented its final version of its draft canons of professional ethics to the membership of the ABA at the group's annual meeting in Seattle, Washington, in August 1908. The entire draft, with the exception of a proposed provision concerning contingency fees, passed without modification and with little debate from the floor.⁹² Passage of the ABA's canons of ethics opened the doors for states to pass similar rules. By 1910, twenty-two state bar associations had adopted the ABA canons.⁹³

On October 1, 1907, the *New York Law Journal* carried a front-page notice issuing a call to all members of the Bar of New York County to attend a special meeting to be held that evening at the Carnegie Lyceum located at Fifty-Seventh Street and Seventh Avenue. The purpose of the meeting, according to the notice, was "to consider what measures shall be adopted to procure the nomination of fit, capable, and reliable men to the Bench at the approaching election."⁹⁴ Approximately one hundred lawyers attended that meeting, and one of those lawyers, John Brooks Leavitt, drafted a resolution calling for the appointment of a committee to explore the formation of a new bar association, open to all lawyers, and devoid of the blackballing, high dues, and exclusiveness associated with the Association of the Bar of the City of New York (also known as the City Bar). Leavitt's resolution was unanimously adopted, and the chair of the meeting, Charles Strauss, appointed a committee of twenty-five to pursue the formation of the New York County Lawyers' Association. Alton Brooks Parker was one of the lawyers appointed to the Committee of Twenty-Five.⁹⁵

Once it became apparent that there was a great deal of interest in the formation of a new bar organization, an organizational committee was formed. The Committee on Organization met for the first time on January 20, 1908, in Parlor A of the brand-new Hotel Knickerbocker located at Forty-Second Street and Broadway. Alton Parker was a member of the Committee on Organization, and at that first meeting he was elected first vice chairman of the committee.⁹⁶ When the committee met again on February 19, 1908, work began on the drafting of a certificate of incorporation, by-laws, and a constitution. The certificate of incorporation was executed and duly notarized in April of that year (Parker was one of the original incorporators of the New York County Lawyers' Association) and filed with the secretary of state on April 23, 1908.⁹⁷ John Forrest Dillon was elected as the first president of the New York County Lawyers' Association; Alton Parker was elected as the group's first vice president.⁹⁸

The first meeting of the New York County Lawyers' Association was held on May 21, 1908, in the Assembly Room of the Metropolitan Life Insurance Company Building. By the time of the first meeting, the organization had attracted 2,500 active members. The main speaker for the evening was President John Dillon, but Parker also made some remarks to the membership.[99]

Parker became the president of the New York County Lawyers' Association at the group's annual meeting on April 27, 1909. When he became president, he quickly found himself overseeing the new organization's growth. Within two months of taking the helm, Parker and the Board of Directors approved the expansion of the group's space at 165 Broadway, appropriated money to acquire a library for use by the members, and called a special meeting to address the association's approach to the year's judicial elections.[100]

Parker served as the president of the NYCLA from 1909 to 1912. During his tenure in office, active membership rose to almost three thousand members, publications commenced, and plans were laid for the funding and erection of a building to serve as the permanent home of the association. In addition, under Parker's leadership, the association endorsed judicial candidates, provided commentary on proposed legislation, drafted a proposed code of professional ethics, and became the first bar association in the country to issue formal ethics opinions with practical responses to real questions posed by lawyers.[101]

Parker was a longtime member and leader of the Lawyers Club, a New York organization dedicated to fostering and promoting collegiality among the members of the New York bar. Lawyers and their guests who met for lunch in the club's surroundings would dine in an ornately appointed dining room dominated by a sixteen-by-eighteen-foot stained glass window that told the story of the law from its source in the Ten Commandments through the adoption of the English common law.[102] From 1916 to 1921, Parker was vice president of the club. He also served on the Lawyers Club's Board of Governors and the Committee on Meetings and Speakers, and during the First World War he served on the club's War Committee and the Sub-Committee on Finance.[103]

In an ironic twist of fate, when Associate Justice Rufus E. Peckham, the author of the *Lochner* opinion overturning Parker's finding that the New York maximum hours law was constitutional, died in 1909, it was Parker who was the principal speaker at a meeting of the Bar of the United States Supreme Court convened to honor Peckham. Parker, who held no grudge against Peckham for his *Lochner* decision, said in part, in eulogizing his former colleague, "Mr. Justice Peckham loved justice with all his heart, and his highest ambition was to devote his life to its administration . . . It was his privilege to be a member of the Court during a period when more questions of far-reaching national importance were to be passed upon than during any like period in the history of the Court, as it was also to be his pleasure to be associated with Justices whose usefulness to the Court and the country has not been surpassed in the history of the Court."[104]

In 1910, Parker and another former chief justice of the court of appeals, Morgan J. O'Brien, were seated as members of the Committee on Criminal Courts. The main task of the seventeen-member committee was to work with judges, city officials, state legislators, and members of the public to suggest reforms to the criminal justice system. One of the most important changes to come out of the committee's work was the creation of a central record-keeping system. The system enabled judges to pull the card file of a past offender and see at a glance what charges the perpetrator had faced in the past. Prior to the implementation of the central record-keeping system, the judges would have to try to keep track of each person's previous offenses by memory, an almost impossible task.[105]

At the beginning of the second decade of the twentieth century, a movement was underway in many parts of the United States to give voters the right to recall judges and even override state court decisions that declared laws unconstitutional. In 1912, at a special meeting of the New York State Bar Association, Alton Parker was appointed the head of a committee of fifteen to investigate the recall of judges and judicial decisions. Parker's committee spent the better part of a year meeting with lawyers throughout the state and in 1913 issued its report on the subject.

The Committee of Fifteen found "that the courts were sound [and] their decisions were well considered and well documented."[106] The basic problems leading to the push for judicial recall were "misstatements and misinterpretations of the decisions and attitudes of the Courts," "misapprehension of the powers and duties of the Courts and Judges," and "the fault finding of defeated litigants and their attorneys."[107] Most of the criticism leveled against the courts by the leading newspapers was "simply abuse and misrepresentation." Some critics said the courts went too far; others argued that the courts didn't go far enough. The Committee of Fifteen declared that "the United States Supreme Court is criticized for legislating, and on the other hand, our Court of Appeals is criticized because it does not legislate, and change the law as they understand it to be, in order that they may thus keep abreast of the times and facilitate progress in accordance with a supposed preponderating public sentiment."[108]

According to the committee, recall of judges or decisions "would destroy the independence of the judiciary and the impartial administration of justice and deprive all classes of the community of the protection now afforded to individual rights, by substituting for the training, intelligence and conscience of the judiciary, and settled rules of law, public clamor, agitation and constantly varying opinions of voters overruling the judgments of the courts and punishing judges for unpopular decisions."[109] The Committee of Fifteen recommended that attorneys undertake to explain the function of the courts, and the limitations imposed by the state and federal constitutions, to combat the demands for the recall of judges and judicial decisions.[110]

Parker was elected president of the New York State Bar Association on January 28, 1913.[111] He held that position from 1913 to 1914. On February 27, 1914, as part of his duties as president of the organization, he testified before the Committee on the Judiciary of the House of Representatives urging Congress to pass an act authorizing the Supreme Court to prescribe uniform rules to regulate the pleadings and procedure in common law actions pending in the district courts. Parker was joined in his endeavor to get the bill passed by William Howard Taft, Elihu Root, James D. Andrews, and Thomas W. Shelton.[112]

From the time of its founding in 1905, Parker was for several years a special lecturer at Fordham University School of Law.[113] He also traveled around the country giving lectures and speeches on US history and the US legal system. On July 11, 1907, Parker delivered an address before the state bar association of North Carolina. He returned to some of his favorite themes in his remarks, including an overabundance of legislation, the diminishment of states' rights through expansion of the federal government, and the dangerous influence of the country's corporations. He decried what he perceived as a present-day contempt for the Constitution and argued that the contempt for our central governing document was more widespread than was generally supposed.[114]

A little more than two months later, on September 17, 1907, Parker was the featured speaker at a Constitution Day celebration in Jamestown. Not surprisingly, Parker waxed poetic about the beauty of our constitutional form of government, echoing Gladstone's comment that the Constitution was "the most wonderful work struck off at a given time by the brain and purpose of man."[115] He also used his remarks to warn the audience to resist efforts by the president and those in Congress to increase the power of the federal government at the expense of the states.[116]

The following year, Parker spoke to the Law Academy of Philadelphia. The topic of his speech was "The Lawyer's Duty in the Preservation of Civil and Religious Liberty."[117] He delivered a memorial address about Abraham Lincoln in New York City on February 12, 1909, and a memorial address about George Washington at the University of Virginia on February 22, 1909. Three weeks later he delivered an address titled "The Tariff—A Moral Issue" at Princeton University. In it he traced the history of the tariff in the United States and explained how those who had benefited from the tariff had used political contributions to ensure the continued enforcement of protective duties. He called for a downward revision of the tariff and reminded his audience that such a step would not occur ". . . unless the people demand it so loudly that the Congress dare not refuse."[118]

Parker served as the keynote speaker at the annual meeting of the New Hampshire Bar Association in June 1910. The title of his talk: "The Lawyers' Opportunity for Patriotic Public Service." Returning to a familiar theme, Parker used his time before the members of the New Hampshire bar to urge them to resist augmentation of federal executive power and prevent usurpation of the "precious rights and liberties won only after centuries of effort."[119] He argued that it is incumbent upon the members of the bar, as students of history as well as law, to "lead in a movement which shall demand the maintenance in all their integrity of the constitutional safeguards of our liberties, as they now are, until the people themselves shall alter or amend them."[120]

On January 25, 1912, Parker gave a speech before the South Carolina Bar Association. He began his remarks by noting how important it is to have an independent judiciary and lamenting the fact that that independence was being threatened by a movement to allow for the popular recall of judges. Parker reflected on the fact that a number of western states had passed legislation allowing for the recall of judges and were then engaged in "stimulated advocacy of constitutional amendments taking away from the courts the power to declare void statutes enacted in violation of the Constitution."[121] What was the impetus for this movement to recall judges and amend constitutions to remove the court's power to declare statutes unconstitutional? According to Parker, it was Theodore Roosevelt, who "went out of his way on many occasions to attack [the] courts."[122] His solution to this battle against the supremacy of the courts and the rule of law? "An organized effort on the part of those members of the Bar who will place love of country and devotion to our constitutional scheme of government above ambition for political distinction or preferment."[123] He concluded his speech with this warning: "Let us take good care that some future historian shall not be able to say of us, 'the lawyers in the early part of the 20th Century saw the danger in abundant time to save the situation and they possessed the influence requisite to save it, but they were so steeped in money-making that the necessary zeal and energy were lacking.' "[124]

Parker followed that speech up a year later with an address before the Ohio Bar Association. He used his remarks to warn against the rising tide of socialism and communism, noting that the Socialist Party had polled more than nine hundred thousand votes in the prior election. According to Parker, "Multitudes are becoming addicted to the imbibing of the restless mixture of socialism, anarchy and sedition dispensed by those who seek to lead the industrial class into violence and trouble."[125] He revisited the condemnation of the courts detailed in his address the year before to the South Carolina Bar Association and again derided the growing trend to increase the power of the federal government at the expense of the states. He closed his address with this call to action: "Because the members of the bar have been trained to discern between legal right and legal wrong, because the influence of the bar politically and socially is very great, because the opinion of the bar on public questions is widely sought and accepted—it is our plain duty to refrain from petty criticism of authority and of public officials, to be found ever upon the side of law and order, to boldly condemn the wrong and as boldly defend the right, and to beware at all times the ambition, partizanship, personal interest, and all bias else [we] be barren of influence in the formation of our judgment upon public matters."[126]

Parker served as the commencement speaker at the Yale Law School graduation ceremony in June 1914. His theme: the need to be ever vigilant in safeguarding "the constitutional foundation of [this country's] liberty, prosperity and happiness."[127] Parker told the graduates:

> Of one thing, however, you may be most sure: the duty and opportunity of vigilance rests not alone upon the federal and state officials, not alone upon the courts, but primarily and most fully upon the men with the ballots. And since lawyers are well qualified to appreciate the necessity for law and to understand how imperative it is that the necessary law be respected and

obeyed—that duty of eternal vigilance lies heavily upon the legal profession.

Therefore, I call upon you to stand ever ready to do battle against every enemy of constitutional law and constitutional liberty, because you are young, because the country needs such service from you and because, as lawyers, you will have a special mission to faithfully serve in the Constitutional Army.[128]

Parker concluded his remarks with some sage words of advice, including this gem: "There are plenty of tongues that preach before they think and the man with the cool head must counteract the effect upon public opinion of all aimless, unthought and unthinkable twaddle."[129]

On October 6, 1920, Parker gave an address at the College of William and Mary as part of the celebration of three hundred years of government in this country. He traced the history of government in America from the Mayflower Compact through the drafting of the Declaration of Independence and the adoption of the Constitution. He also spent a considerable amount of time discussing the "vain effort of the Virginians to prevent the importation of slaves."[130] In that regard, Parker quoted a condemnation of King George III concerning slavery that was contained in the original version of the Declaration of Independence:

> He has waged cruel war against human nature itself, violating its most sacred rights of life and liberty, in the persons of a distant people who never offended him; captivating them and carrying them into slavery in another hemisphere, or to incur miserable death in their transportation thither. This piratical warfare, the opprobrium of infidel powers, is the warfare of the Christian King of Great Britain. Determined to keep open a market where men should be bought and sold, he has prostituted his negative for suppressing every legislative attempt to prohibit or restrain this execrable commerce.[131]

According to Parker, the debate on this provision lasted three days and, ultimately, "the influence of South Carolina, Georgia and New England was sufficient to cause those words to be stricken out [of the Declaration]."[132] He also outlined the efforts of five Virginians who became president of the United States, Jefferson, Madison, Monroe, Tyler, and Taylor, to prevent the spread and continued utilization of slavery.[133]

As 1921 dawned, Parker delivered an address to the Vermont Bar Association. The premise of his talk: lawyers are preeminently qualified to mold and shape public opinion, more so than politicians, church leaders, financial leaders, the press, and faculty members—and they have a duty to do so. He compared the lawyer to the lookout stationed aloft in a ship, able to discern the beacon lights and the dangers ahead. According to Parker, "so placed aloft, [the lawyer] must be alert, both to see and to report. With this service faithfully performed, our great nation may weather all storms, escape every danger and carry in safety the precious freight with which she is burdened."[134]

On January 14, 1922, Parker gave a speech titled "American Constitutional Government" at the dedication of the College of William and Mary Marshall-Wythe School of Government and Citizenship in Williamsburg, Virginia. He used the speech to declare that "the colleges and universities of America must teach thoroughly the principles as well as the history of our constitutional government."[135] According to Parker:

> The fact that assaults are being made upon the judiciary for deciding, as they are compelled to do now and then, that a statute is void because it violates either a State or the Federal Constitution, by an element of our population who are without roots in the revolutionary days and the formative period of our Government, makes it necessary that the colleges, and even the high schools, shall teach the youth of our land both to know and to cherish the history which inspired the fathers to build the most wonderful Government ever created by man—a Government of the people, by the people, and for the people. Such a Government, for continued success, must depend upon an educated electorate, who, because of their trained minds, can not be deceived by the ambitious and selfish leaders whose eloquent tongues seek to persuade the people to travel in dangerous paths.
>
> Never in the history of this country were there here so many descendants of non-English-speaking peoples, brought up to hate the Governments of which they were subjects, and who are wholly without knowledge of principles upon which our Government was so wisely built. If their children are made to understand, by careful instruction, the aims of the fathers, the principles which actuated them, and the wisdom which inspired their governmental building, they will come in

time to be a helpful addition to our great population. But if they are not thus educated, it is quite likely that great numbers of them will be led by the anarchists, the I.W.W.'s, the Russian Reds and others of like character to join the forces which openly seek the overthrow of our Government that they may fatten upon the fruits of the people's labors.[136]

Although Parker lost the presidential election in spectacular fashion, his loss did not end his involvement in politics. On April 13, 1905, Parker was the featured speaker at the Jefferson Day banquet of the Democratic Club of New York. More than seven hundred guests attended the lavish event at the Waldorf-Astoria Hotel in New York City. Other speakers included New York City Mayor George B. McClellan Jr., Nevada Senator Francis Newlands, Illinois Congressman Henry T. Rainey, and former New York Supreme Court Justice Augustus Van Wyck.[137]

Parker received an enthusiastic reception from the crowd, and his remarks were frequently interrupted by hearty applause. He spoke on the future of the Democratic Party, and his remarks were "replete with suggestions for harmony and urgent appeals against sectionalism."[138] Not surprisingly, Parker railed against corporate donations to political campaigns. He spent significant time warning against the continued dangers of the trusts and called for consistent and fair enforcement of the laws to keep corporate greed in check. He also berated the Republicans for failing to address and reduce the tariff, the "fertile and nursing mother of all the abuses to be found in [the] trusts."[139] Parker closed his remarks by calling for a reaffirmation of the fundamental principles on which the Democratic Party was founded. He said:

> From time to time much idle talk is indulged in about the organization or the reorganization of the Democratic party. This is to forget two things. The first is that when a party has an idea and a policy which makes appeal to half the people, they will not be long in getting together to promote this idea and this policy.
>
> The second thing to be borne in mind about organization is that it begins down in the smallest political units that compose our political life.
>
> In order, therefore, to have an organization worthy of the name we must arouse or re-arouse, down in every community, the attachment to and interest in our higher politics,

which since the days of Jefferson, have been the vivifying force of the party. This is only possible when the party stands for something, not some new fad, but the fundamental principles that underlie its life.[140]

The *New York Daily Tribune*, in its April 15, 1905, edition, mocked Parker's calls for a return to "Jeffersonian democracy." According to the paper, "The kind of Jeffersonianism that D.B. Hill wrote into the Albany platform, that ex-Judge Parker exploited on the stump and that he echoes now in his Jefferson birthday speech is not the kind of Jeffersonianism the country wants. The voters have no use for a humbug 'safe and sane' Democracy. They do not want a weak central government on the original Jeffersonian plan, which 'minded its own business' and would never have presumed to interfere with the operations of combinations in restraint of trade and commerce chartered by the States. The disastrous breakdown of Judge Parker's canvass was an evidence of the dissatisfaction of hundreds of thousands of Democratic voters with his attempt to commit the party to a sterile and colorless conservatism[!]"[141]

In April 1908, Parker served as the permanent chairman of the Democratic State Convention. In his address to the delegates, Parker returned to his favorite themes: Republican waste of public funds, the tariff and predatory wealth, combinations in restraint of trade, and the dangers associated with corporate contributions to elections. He urged the delegates to set aside past differences and work harmoniously to elect Bryan and Kern in order to secure the implementation of much-needed reforms.[142]

Three months later, Parker attended the Democratic National Convention in Denver, Colorado, as a delegate-at-large for New York.[143] As a member of the Committee on Platform and Resolutions, he helped to write the Denver platform on which Bryan made his third try for the presidency.[144] On the first day of the convention he offered a resolution honoring the life and public service of former President Grover Cleveland. As part of that resolution, he called on the Democratic members of Congress to take all necessary steps to erect a monument to Cleveland in the nation's capitol.[145]

Following the convention, Parker offered his services to the Democratic National Committee as a campaign speaker and devoted a great deal of time to making speeches on behalf of Bryan and Kern. In Los Angeles he enthusiastically spoke in favor of Bryan and Kern before a crowd of four thousand.[146] In a move that must have pained Bryan considerably, he telegraphed Parker at the beginning of October, asking him to provide the exact number of days and where he could speak, and reminding him that because his stumping on behalf of the national ticket was "of vital importance," he should "give all the time you possibly can."[147] Ultimately, Parker wound up giving speeches on the East Coast and traveled through ten of the western states speaking on behalf of the Democratic ticket.[148] In one week in October he delivered speeches on behalf of Bryan and Kern in Cincinnati, Ohio; Springfield, Ohio; Nashville, Tennessee; Indianapolis, Indiana; South Bend, Indiana; and Canton, Ohio.[149] Unfortunately, Parker's work on behalf of the ticket did not bring them victory.

On August 11, 1909, a call was sent out to newspapers throughout the state "for the purpose of inaugurating a movement to unite the Democrats of New York State so that they may once again form an effective and militant party based upon Democratic principles."[150] To do so, it was proposed that a state conference made up of representative Democrats from every county in the state be convened in Saratoga Springs, New York. According to Judge D-Cady Harrick, the purpose of the conference was "not to form a new party, but to strengthen the old; not to read any one out of the party, but to call back those who have strayed from the fold; not to discuss men, but principles."[151] Alton Parker answered the call and attended the conference as a representative from New York County.

When the conference opened on September 9, 1909, Parker was unanimously chosen as the temporary chairman. As the temporary chairman, he was the first person to address the assembly. Parker began his address to the attendees with the following call to action:

> We are here for no selfish purpose. This conference is no place for the man whose ambition for high official station is greater than his desire to render a public service. It is the place for patriotic men who are willing to make sacrifice for the public good.
>
> And who that has made a careful study of the political condition of our country can doubt that the need of the hour is the upbuilding of a party so fundamentally sound in its principles and so clean in its leadership that the people will select it as the instrument to drive from place and power the party that has seated its money-changers in the temple of liberty, where they have bought and sold the privilege of collecting from the people in one form or another the riches in which they riot.[152]

He then turned to the criticisms he had been addressing for years: "extravagant and wasteful" government spending, unreasonably high tariffs, an explosion in the number of "trusts and combinations in the restraint of trade, corporate financing of campaigns.[153] He concluded by calling on the attendees to "fight for the restoration of political interest and activity in the mass of our people, and for a departure from the methods under which the thinking and action and the direction of public affairs are left in the hands of the few."[154]

At the end of the conference, a motion was made to create a permanent organization, called the New York State Democratic League, for "the purpose of aiding and strengthening the Democratic party, bringing back to its ranks those who have been separated from it, and attracting to it the independent, and the young voters, of the State; offering a place of refuge for those Republicans who feel that their trust in their party has been betrayed, and its solemn pledges and promises to them broken, who deprecate its wastefulness and extravagance in administering the affairs of government, and look with apprehension upon the steady strides it is making towards the centralization of government at the expense of the legitimate powers of the States, and of the rights reserved to the people; and for the purpose of disseminating the principles of the Democratic party."[155] The motion was unanimously adopted.[156] Thus did Alton Parker become a founding member of the New York State Democratic League.

Harmony in the league does not appear to have lasted very long. A majority of the league's members refused, in 1911, to back the candidates for office proposed by the Democratic Party. As a result, Parker, Morgan J. O'Brien and a handful of other members publicly condemned the actions of the league in refusing to endorse and support the Democratic ticket. Said Parker, "I maintain that it is wrong for any organization, Democratic in name or spirit, to oppose such a superior ticket as the ticket named by the Democrats this year."[157]

In 1910 Parker attended the State Democratic Convention in Rochester, where he served as the temporary chairman. He used his remarks as temporary chairman to excoriate the Republicans for fifteen years of wasteful and extravagant spending and called on all New York Democrats to work tirelessly to elect men who would condemn governmental mismanagement and "the surrender of the power of the many into the hands of the few."[158] There was talk circulating throughout the state that the convention was going to nominate Parker to run for governor. Parker received a telegram from his wife, Mary, that put a stop to any further speculation. It read: "If you accept the nomination, don't come home. Mary Parker."[159]

The delegates to the state convention ultimately chose John Alden Dix as their candidate for governor of New York State. Parker agreed to manage Dix's campaign for the governorship. Dix had been chairman of the New York State Democratic Committee and was by occupation a banker and paper manufacturer.[160] His Republican opponent was Henry L. Stimson, a New York lawyer handpicked by Roosevelt to run for the top spot.[161] Parker took a page from his own campaign playbook and, sensing that 1910 was going to be a Democratic year, advised Dix to remain at home and give only two speeches during the course of the campaign.[162] Although Dix kept relatively quiet throughout the course of the campaign, Parker spent the weeks between Dix's nomination and the general election crisscrossing the state giving speeches on his behalf.[163] His hard work paid off. Dix won the election with a plurality of about 65,000 votes.[164]

The Democrats not only captured the governor's mansion; they also gained control of the Senate and the State Assembly. As a result, the Democrats would be electing the next senator from the state of New York. Several prominent New Yorkers wrote to Parker in the aftermath of the campaign and urged him to actively seek the senate seat.[165] This he refused to do, stating, "my obligations are such that I would not accept the office, even if it should be tendered to me."[166]

At the same time that Dix was campaigning for governor, Theodore Roosevelt was laying the groundwork for another run at the presidency in 1912. In a speech before the Colorado legislature in 1910, Roosevelt attacked the Supreme Court. He singled out the *Lochner* decision as an example of the courts favoring business interests and ignoring the public welfare (recall that Parker upheld a maximum hours law for New York bakers as constitutional and the US Supreme Court reversed that decision, finding that the statute violated the Fourteenth Amendment to the US Constitution). Roosevelt called for public referenda on court decisions that overturned legislative enactments as unconstitutional.[167]

Parker responded to what he believed was unwarranted criticism on Roosevelt's part:

> It is safe to assert that the attack upon the Supreme Court of the United States by Mr. Roosevelt in his address to the legislature of Colorado will not be approved by the bench and bar

and the thoughtful people of this country, who appreciate the importance of the Judiciary in our governmental system and the necessity for a continuance of the existing public confidence in and affection for our courts. It happens that in the case of *People v. Lochner,* referred to in his address as the "bakeshop case," the prevailing opinion of the Court of Appeals of this state was written by myself, with concurring opinions by Judges Gray and Vann. Judges O'Brien and Bartlett wrote dissenting opinions, so that in all five opinions were written in the Court of Appeals, showing the full appreciation by that court of the fact that the question was a very close one about which minds must differ. Indeed, this fact was made very prominent in interesting debates around the consultation table, as well as in the opinions written.

The history of this case indicates how narrow was the dividing line between upholding and rejecting the statute. The trial judge held the statute constitutional. The Appellate Division affirmed his decision by a vote of three to two. And the Court of Appeals affirmed the Appellate Division by a vote of four to three. The Supreme Court of the United States reversed the Court of Appeals by a vote of five to four.

Every Judge in every court gave to this important question his best effort, which is strongly evidenced by the differences of view of the members of the several courts. That fact should be quite sufficient to protect the greatest court in the world from offensive criticism from any source, and especially from one who heretofore manifested his dissatisfaction with a department of government which was performing the independent function conferred upon it by the Constitution so as to neither encroach upon its coordinate departments of government nor to allow them to encroach upon it.[168]

Parker's political mentor, David Bennett Hill, had passed away on October 20, 1910. On July 6, 1911, Parker eulogized his friend and adviser at a joint meeting of the Senate and the assembly held in the capitol building at Albany. Parker spent most of his address highlighting the depth and breadth of Hill's political career. He closed with these words of praise for the one man, more than any other, who obtained for Parker the 1904 presidential nomination:

This was a man, of highest ideals and clean life, fearless, incorruptible, zealous in politics, loyal to the councils and principles of his party, faithful to every public trust, conscientiously devoted to the welfare of the people, enduring calumny patiently, eager to help all in distress, never vaunting his rectitude and beneficences, and having personal qualities that made his friendship a thing to be cherished with nothing less dear and sacred than ties of home and nearest kindred.

By his death his profession loses an able, logical and scholarly advocate, his party a potent, enthusiastic and pre-eminent leader, and his country a great, far-seeing and broad-minded statesman.[169]

The year 1912 was a presidential election year. As the year dawned, a move was afoot to draft Parker as the Democratic Party nominee for president. On January 19 a large number of the leading Democrats in Delaware came out in favor of Parker for the presidency. Following a meeting at the state capital that was attended by a number of prominent party leaders, it was announced that every effort was going to be made to have the six delegates from Delaware pledge to support Parker at the Democratic National Convention in Baltimore.[170] Parker, true to his post-1904 election pledge, refused to be considered as a candidate.

From June 25, 1912, through July 2, 1912, the Democrats met in National Convention at the Fifth Maryland Regiment Armory in Baltimore, Maryland. The Democrats were excited at their prospects of finally getting back into the White House after twenty years of Republican rule. The Republicans were in disarray. Roosevelt had made an attempt to capture the nomination, but the Republicans had stuck with President William Howard Taft and Vice President James S. Sherman. Roosevelt, unwilling to accept defeat, bolted from the Republican Party and accepted the Progressive Party nomination for president.[171]

When the Democrats arrived in Baltimore, the race for the presidential nomination was wide open. Among the many presidential aspirants were Missouri representative and Speaker of the House of Representatives Champ Clark, New Jersey Governor Woodrow Wilson, Ohio governor and former US Attorney General Judson Harmon, US House of Representatives Majority Leader Oscar Underwood of Alabama, Indiana Governor Thomas Marshall, Massachusetts Governor Eugene Foss, and Connecticut Governor Simeon Baldwin.[172]

The Democratic National Committee had made it known that they intended to name Parker as the convention's temporary chairman. The position was essentially an honorary one and typically lasted only one day—until the delegates could elect a permanent chairman. Although the position was largely ceremonial, the temporary chairman was expected to deliver the opening address to the delegates.

Despite having lost a third election for president, William Jennings Bryan was still a force to be reckoned with in the Democratic Party. Prior to the convention, Bryan was still flexing his political muscle and opposing various moves. The selection of Alton Parker as temporary chairman was one of them.[173] Bryan still believed that Parker was the tool of the Belmont-Ryan-Murphy crowd and a representative of "predatory wealth." In speaking to the *New York Times* about Parker's "fitness" to serve as temporary chairman, Bryan stated, "if [Parker] does not know whose agent he is he lacks the intelligence necessary for a presiding officer, and if he does know he does not deserve the support of any man who has the right to call himself a Democrat."[174]

Bryan sent a telegram to all of the presidential candidates opposing Parker's selection as the temporary chairman. The telegram he sent to Champ Clark read as follows:

Chicago, IL June 21, 1912

Speaker Clark

Washington, D.C.

> In the interests of harmony I suggest to the subcommittee of the Democratic National Committee the advisability of recommending as temporary chairman some Progressive, acceptable to the leading Progressive candidates for the Presidential nomination. I took it for granted that no committee interested in Democratic success would desire to offend the members of the convention overwhelmingly Progressive by naming a reactionary to sound the key-note of the campaign. Eight members of the subcommittee, however, have, over the protest of the remaining eight, agreed not upon a reactionary, but upon the one Democrat who among those not candidates for the Presidential nomination, is in the eyes of the public

most conspicuously identified with the reactionary element of the party. I shall be pleased to join you and your friends in opposing his selection by the full committee or by the convention. Please answer here.

W.J. Bryan[175]

Bryan's telegram put Clark and his followers in a sticky situation. If they opposed Parker's nomination for temporary chairman, there was a good chance that the ninety delegate votes from New York would go elsewhere. If they decided to back Parker, the wrath of Bryan would descend upon them.[176]

Clark tried to stay neutral and maintain public harmony (he actually favored Texas representative Robert L. Henry for the position, but he was not about to publicly push Henry's nomination). Thomas Marshall chose to go with Parker. After hours of indecision, Woodrow Wilson joined Bryan in opposing Parker.[177] Wilson sent the following letter to Bryan:

> You are right. Before hearing of your message I clearly stated my position in answer to a question from the Baltimore Evening Sun. The Baltimore convention is to be the convention of progressives—the men who are progressive in principle and by conviction. It must, if it is not to be put in a wrong light before the country, express its convictions in its organization and its choice of the men who are to speak for it. You are to be a member of the convention and are entirely within your rights in doing everything within your power to bring that result about. No one will doubt where my sympathies lie, and you will, I am sure, find my friends in the convention acting upon a clear conviction and always in the people's cause. I am happy in the confidence that they need no suggestion from me.[178]

In a statement released to the public, Wilson claimed that his opposition to the selection of Parker as temporary chairman was not due to any personal feelings against the judge. He said, "Any real Progressive is a good man for the Temporary Chairmanship. My opposition to Judge Parker is not from personal feeling, but is due to my belief that in so much as the convention is one of Progressives, the spokesman should be a Progressive."[179] Wilson's decision to not back Parker may very well have contributed to

Parker's early decision to not support Wilson's bid for the nomination.

On the first day the convention assembled, Bryan met Parker in the convention hall and told him personally that he intended to fight his selection as temporary chairman of the convention since he felt that Parker was not in sympathy with the reforms necessary to the success of the party.[180] Shortly after that meeting, the presiding officer and chairman of the Democratic National Committee, Norman E. Mack, gaveled the convention to order and announced that he was "instructed by the National Committee to submit the name of Hon. Alton B. Parker, of New York, for Temporary Chairman of the Convention."[181] The band, on hearing his name announced, played "Oh, You Beautiful Doll." Parker, who was sitting with the New York delegation, "smiled through a slightly blushed expression."[182] As the music died down and the cheering stopped, Mack asked if there were any other nominations.[183]

William Jennings Bryan took the stage. The convention erupted again—many cheering Bryan and many others booing him. Following a fifteen-minute demonstration, Bryan insisted, in a fiery oration, that Parker be rejected as the temporary chairman. He proposed, instead, that his running mate in 1908, John W. Kern, be elected to the position.[184]

After reminding the delegates that he had thrice served the Democratic Party as its nominee for president, and in the process polled 6.5 million votes, Bryan rather disingenuously claimed that he had been working for days prior to the convention to bring "harmony" to the process of selecting the temporary chairman. After nominating Kern and setting forth his bona fides, he turned to an attack on Parker, claiming that "not every man of high character or good intent is a fit man to sound the keynote of a progressive campaign." He argued that in 1904 Parker was the candidate of the moneyed elite of Wall Street, that he was still backed by the Ryans and Belmonts of the world, and that such a man could not be relied on to adequately open a campaign devoted to progressive ideals.[185]

After Bryan's speech, Kern took to the stage. He made a personal appeal to Parker to join with him in selecting a nominee for temporary chairman who would be satisfactory to both of them. When Parker did not respond to Kern's call for a compromise candidate, Kern withdrew his name from consideration and nominated Bryan.[186]

Bryan proclaimed his readiness to support any progressive candidate for the position and then announced, "if no other progressive appears I shall accept the leadership and let you express through your votes for or against me your advocacy of or opposition to what we have fought for

for sixteen years."[187] After several speeches in support of both Parker and Bryan, Mack asked the secretary to call the roll. In the end, Parker was elected temporary chairman by a vote of 579 to 508.[188] Luke Lea, one of the delegates from Tennessee, moved that the election of Parker as temporary chairman be made unanimous; that motion was unanimously agreed to.[189]

After dinner, Parker took to the podium to deliver his keynote speech to the assembled delegates. He began by addressing the dustup over his nomination as temporary chair: "We have had a little difference here today; a question of men; but, my fellow delegates, there was nothing said, I now think, by the principal debaters on either side which was intended to wound. If, for a moment, I thought the chief speaker a bit harsh, I remembered on the other hand those three magnificent struggles that he has made in this country as the chosen standard-bearer of the Democratic party. I realize that all this has meant much—very much to him—and if he is mistaken in regard to my position, as we must assume, I believe it to be your duty and mine to forget it and to co-operate with him in furthering the highest party and public interests in this Convention."[190] Parker, unlike Bryan, was able to forgive and forget.

Parker then spent several minutes discussing the dangers associated with a presidential third term and taking Roosevelt to task for seeking that which Washington, Jefferson, Madison, and Monroe had refused. He reminded the crowd of Roosevelt's promise, on the eve of his 1904 reelection, that he would not, under any circumstances, accept a nomination for a third term. He then turned to the issue of the tariff and the trusts, discussing how the Republican Party had "geared the machinery of the government to enrich the few at the expense of the many."[191] He continued with a recitation of the Republican shakedown of corporations for political donations in the 1904 campaign and decried the use of corporate money that "debauched the electorate in every debatable State."[192] Parker ended his address with the following call to action:

> We are called upon to do battle against the unfaithful guardians of our constitution and liberties and the hordes of ignorance which are pushing forward only to the ruin of our social and governmental fabric and their own deep damnation.
>
> Too long has the country endured the offences of the leaders of a party which once knew greatness. Too long have we been blinded to the bacchanal of corruption. Too long have we listlessly watched the assembling of the forces that threaten our

country and our firesides. The time has come when the salvation of the country demands the destruction of the leaders of a debauched party, and the restoration to place and power of men of high ideals who will wage unceasing war against corruption in politics, who will enforce the law against both rich and poor, and who will treat guilt as personal and punish it accordingly.

For their crimes against American citizenship the present leaders of the Republican party should be destroyed.

For making and keeping the bargain to take care of the tariff protected interests in consideration of campaign funds, they should be destroyed.

For encouraging the creation of combinations to restrain trade, and refusing to enforce the law, for a like consideration, they should be destroyed.

For the lavish waste of the public funds; for the fraudulent disposition of the people's domain, and for their contribution toward the division of the people into classes, they should be destroyed.

For the efforts to seize for the executive department of the federal government powers rightfully belonging to the States, they should be destroyed.

And destruction will be theirs, this very year, if we but do our duty.

What is our duty? To think alike as to men and measures? Impossible! Even for our great party! There is not a reactionary among us. All Democrats are Progressives. But it is inevitably human that we shall not all agree that in a single highway is found the only road to progress, or each make the same man of all our worthy candidates his first choice.

It *is* possible, however, and it is our duty to put aside all selfishness, to consent cheerfully that the majority shall speak for each of us, and to march out of this Convention shoulder to shoulder intoning the praises of our chosen leader—and that will be his due, whichever of the honorable and able men now claiming our attention be chosen![193]

Perhaps if Parker had harnessed some of the energy, enthusiasm, and determination he expressed in his 1912 keynote during the 1904 campaign, the results may have been different!

When voting for the presidential nomination started, the front-runner was Champ Clark, who received 440.5 votes on the first ballot, versus 324 for Woodrow Wilson.[194] For the first nine ballots, Parker, and the rest of the New York delegates, cast their votes for Judson Harmon, the governor of Ohio.[195] No candidate managed to gain a majority of the votes cast until the tenth ballot, when the New York delegation shifted its allegiance to Clark (unfortunately for Clark, a simple majority of votes was not enough to capture the nomination; the winning candidate needed to obtain two-thirds of the votes eligible to be cast in order to prevail).[196] Once Tammany Hall, the powerful and corrupt political machine in New York City, threw its support behind Clark, William Jennings Bryan turned against him. Bryan delivered a speech denouncing Clark as the candidate of Wall Street and threw his support to Wilson.[197] Wilson finally received the presidential nomination on the forty-sixth ballot.[198] Thomas Marshall was chosen as Wilson's running mate.[199]

At the close of the convention, Parker was appointed chairman of the Committee to Notify Thomas Marshall of his Nomination for Vice-President.[200] Parker and the Notification Committee traveled to Indianapolis, Indiana, on August 20, 1912, to officially notify Marshall of his selection as the Democratic nominee for vice president. As chairman of the Notification Committee, Parker delivered a keynote address before tendering the nomination to Marshall.

Parker began his address by commending the nominees for president and vice president, both successful governors, men "whose lives were so clean and righteous that the people could be assured at once that the pledges made by their party and their own promises to the people would be faithfully kept and executed."[201] Ten minutes into his remarks, a slow, grinding noise began emanating from the grandstand that had been erected behind the speakers' platform. Parker stopped speaking and turned toward the sound—and in an instant the grandstand collapsed in a heap of shattered timbers and broken bodies. In all, seventy-five people were injured, several of them seriously.[202]

Once order had been restored and the injured were help out of the debris and sent off to receive medical treatment, Parker continued with his remarks. He launched into a lengthy condemnation of the tariff statutes and Republican vetoes of bills designed to reduce the tariff rates, followed by a denunciation of the rampant proliferation of the trusts under Roosevelt and the insidious nature of corporate campaign contributions. Parker closed his remarks by asserting that only the Democratic Party could be counted on to reduce the tariff, bust the trusts, and enact lasting campaign finance reform.[203]

In October 1912, Parker attended the Democratic State Convention in Syracuse, New York. John D. McMahon, the chairman of the Committee on Permanent Organization, presented Parker's name as permanent chairman of the convention, and, as in Baltimore, a challenge was presented. Delegate Frank Mott presented a minority report substituting the name of Poughkeepsie Mayor John K. Sague for permanent chairman in place of Parker. Mott, in presenting the minority report, stated, "I yield to no man in this State in my admiration for the distinguished citizen and jurist who has been named for permanent chairman by the majority of our Committee. But this is a Democratic Convention and it ought to represent the progressive sentiment of the entire State of New York . . . I claim that the majority has selected a reactionary for permanent chairman. He is most conspicuously identified with reactionary policies. In saying that I do not quote my own words, I quote the words of the greatest statesman of the republic, William Jennings Bryan, and I am substantiated in my statement by Woodrow Wilson."[204] At the end of the roll call, Parker was elected permanent chairman of the committee by a vote of 412 to 35.[205]

As permanent chairman, Parker was allowed to address the delegates. He spent the first portion of his remarks defending his record—as a judge, as a candidate and as a productive member of the Democratic Party. The remainder of his speech focused on Republican mismanagement of the federal government, the achievements of Governor Dix and the Democratic majority in the New York State Assembly and Senate, and the need to elect Wilson and Marshall to the presidency and vice presidency.[206]

Between the time that Parker lost his bid for the presidency and his death in 1926, a Democrat occupied the White House for only eight years. Woodrow Wilson was elected president in 1912 and was reelected in 1916. Wilson, as president, had three opportunities to put someone in the one job Parker really wanted: associate justice of the United States Supreme Court. He got his first opportunity to appoint a justice to the court in July 1914 following the sudden death of Associate Justice Horace Harmon Lurton. He got his second opportunity in January 1916 following the death of Associate Justice Joseph Rucker Lamar. The third opportunity arose in June 1916 when Associate Justice Charles Evans Hughes resigned from the court to accept the Republican nomination for president (and run against Wilson).

Wilson had never forgiven Parker for his early failure to support his candidacy in 1912. As a result, Wilson refused to appoint Parker to the coveted post of associate justice.[207] Instead, he nominated James Clark McReynolds for the Lurton vacancy, Louis D. Brandeis for the Lamar vacancy, and John Hessin Clarke for the Hughes vacancy.[208] McReynolds was nominated and confirmed in August 1914; Brandeis was nominated in March 1916 and confirmed in June of that year; Clarke was nominated and confirmed in July 1916.[209]

In the fall of 1916, while attending a meeting of the ABA, Parker suggested that the past presidents, other officers, and members who were present draft a letter to President Wilson urging him to appoint former President William Howard Taft to the position vacated by Charles Evans Hughes. Twenty-nine participants at that meeting signed the letter (fourteen Democrats, fourteen Republicans, and one who "supported Roosevelt in 1912") that was ultimately delivered to Wilson.[210] Wilson failed to act on the recommendation, and Taft would have to wait until Warren Harding became president in 1921 to assume a seat on the high court. When Taft was under consideration for the position of chief justice in 1921, Parker wrote a letter to *The New York Herald* stating that no one was better trained to occupy the role of the chief justice than William Howard Taft. He wrote, in part, "[Taft] was Solicitor-General under Harrison's Administration and argued nearly all of the great cases of the Department of Justice in the Supreme Court of the United States. And as a United States Circuit Judge he demonstrated great judicial ability, as every lawyer in the United States will testify. Nor should the fact be lost sight of that the knowledge he acquired as Governor of the Philippine Islands, Secretary of War and President of the United States will prove of the greatest value to the new Chief Justice."[211]

In 1915, the League to Enforce Peace was established in Philadelphia by a group of American citizens concerned by the outbreak of World War I in Europe. Former President William Howard Taft was elected permanent president of the organization, and Alton Parker was named one of the group's vice presidents.[212] The league advocated the need for an international organization devoted to the promotion of peace. It proposed an international agreement in which participating nations would agree to jointly use their economic and military force against any one of their number that went to war or committed an act of hostility against another before submitting its case to an international court or to a council of reconciliation. It also proposed strengthening international laws by hosting conferences dedicated to a discussion of the systematic arrangement of these laws.[213]

On May 7, 1915, a German U-boat sank the RMS *Lusitania* off the coast of Ireland. More than 1,100 passengers and crew lost their lives; 123 of the casualties were American. In the days after the sinking, sentiment was running high in the United States to have the country declare war on Germany. Parker issued a public statement in support of President Wilson and urged that he be left undisturbed to act in the best interests of the country:

> The attempt to persuade the public what action the Lusitania disaster requires the President to take, is unfair to him and may work injury to us. He alone must bear the heavy responsibility of decision—and greater there cannot be. No one knows it better than he. For both personal and patriotic reasons his best effort will be put forth. We all know this to be true. Why then do we not let him alone? Why not give him time? There is certainly no need for hurry. On the contrary, there is every reason for making haste slowly.
>
> Have we forgotten the Maine? Can we not see President McKinley, standing with his back to the wall in the face of the hoarse cry of angry men demanding war—and his refusal to hurry. He saw his duty to the people and performed it. True, in the end war came—but not as a result of passion—and in the meantime the sentiment of the world had come to our side.
>
> The President has information that we have not. When to announce a decision may be almost as important as what the decision shall be. Let us all pray that those who will be heard because they cannot act may be induced to desist until the man chosen by the people to decide shall have performed his great task.[214]

Ultimately, the United States would not enter World War I until nearly two years later, on April 6, 1917.

Parker followed his public statement urging restraint with attendance at the World Court Conference in Cleveland, Ohio, on May 12, 1915. The conference, over which Parker presided, advocated the formation of a league of peace and an international court of justice that would arbitrate disputes among the signatories, thereby minimizing the possibility of war. In his remarks at the conference, Parker explained how the league and the court of justice would work: "The consensus seems to be that in order to make the league fully effective each nation should be bound to submit non-justiciable disputes arising between the signatories and not settled by negotiation to a Council of Conciliation for hearing, consideration and recommendations before any declaration or act of war, the council to make and publish a report of each dispute submitted to it together with its recommendations and the reasons therefor. Moreover, it is proposed that the signatory powers forming such a league shall jointly use their military forces to prevent any one of their number from going to war against another of the signatories before the questions arising shall be submitted either to the judicial tribunal or the Council of Conciliation."[215] Parker ended his remarks by urging the people of the United States to let the government know of their interest in joining such a league.[216]

When the First World War broke out in Europe in 1914, the United States initially took a position of neutrality. Many prominent Americans, chief among them former President Theodore Roosevelt and former Chief of Staff of the Army General Leonard Wood, sought to persuade the administration of President Woodrow Wilson and the population at large of the need for American involvement in the conflict, ongoing military preparedness, and a strengthening of the country's national defenses. To that end, a series of "preparedness parades" were held around the country.

May 13, 1916, the eve of Parker's sixty-fourth birthday, marked the occasion of the Citizens' Preparedness Parade in New York City. The parade, billed as a "non-partisan demonstration" and "an act of constructive Patriotism," consisted of a continuous stream of 150,000 men and women, marching 20 abreast, in sixty-four separate divisions.[217] The parade started at 9:30 a.m. and continued until 10:30 p.m. Parker was the marshal of the Lawyers' Division, which included 2,200 lawyers dressed in silk hats and Prince Albert suits, all wearing red carnations in their buttonholes and red, white, and blue ribbons on their arms.[218] The Lawyers' Division, which was sandwiched between the Lower Wall Street Business Men's Association and the Jewelry Trades Division, stepped off at 2:45 p.m.[219] Parker did not arrive home until after 7:00 p.m. and was not the least bit fatigued. He reported that he had had a fine time and was "thoroughly warmed up." According to his daughter, "His eyes were as bright and he was as straight as if he was just starting out." At sixty-four, the judge was still in fine shape.[220]

In 1916, despite the fact that war was raging across the continent, Alton and Mary enjoyed an extended tour of Europe and Russia. While they were in Russia, the Parkers were visited by the entire cabinet of Czar Nicholas II.[221] When they returned from Europe, Parker took his sixteen-year-old grandson, Alton Parker Hall, to the 1916 Democratic National Convention. Parker did not attend the convention in any official capacity, but he watched with approval as Wilson and Marshall were renominated at the Coliseum in St. Louis, Missouri.[222] Although Mary's ill health forced Parker to decline an active role in the 1916 presidential contest, he did agree to give two speeches in the closing days of the campaign.[223]

Mary Schoonmaker Parker died on April 2, 1917, in her apartment in the Hotel Essex after a long illness[224] (see figure 13.1). She and Alton had been married for forty-four years. Together they had raised a daughter, mourned the loss of a son, built and maintained a prosperous farm, entertained the elite of New York society, and traveled the world.

In 1918, Parker's old nemesis, William Randolph Hearst, attempted to make a political comeback and set his sights on capturing the Dem-

Figure 13.1. Mary Schoonmaker Parker at the time of the 1904 presidential campaign. Courtesy of Davis & Sanford, 1904. Public domain.

ocratic nomination for governor. Parker worked to derail Hearst's bid for the gubernatorial nomination and threw his support behind former assemblyman and president of the New York City Board of Alderman, Alfred E. Smith. Smith managed to obtain the Democratic nomination and ultimately was elected to the first of his four terms as governor.[225]

Parker's rival for the presidency in 1904, Theodore Roosevelt, died on January 6, 1919. The Rocky Mountain Club of New York, an organization of western men who called New York home, held its first annual Theodore Roosevelt Day Dinner on October 27, 1919, the anniversary of Roosevelt's birth. The dinner was given at the Waldorf-Astoria Hotel. Members of the club and their guests filled the grand ballroom of the hotel and listened to a series of remarkable addresses about Roosevelt. Alton Parker served as the toastmaster for the evening.

As toastmaster, Parker had an opportunity to share some remarks about Roosevelt. He titled his remarks "Roosevelt's Americanism." Parker focused not on Roosevelt's actions as president, but rather on his services to the country as a private citizen. Parker labeled Roosevelt as the greatest preacher of preparedness and Americanism of his generation. He reminded the audience that Roosevelt aroused his fellow citizens to demand that Congress ultimately prepare for entry into World War I. He then quoted Roosevelt's comments on immigration: "We cannot have too many . . . [immigrants] of the right type, the type that is morally, physically, economically right. We should not have any at all of the wrong type. We should not admit them simply because there is a need of labor. Better go slow on labor than to bring improper men into the body of our citizenship, to dilute it, that citizenship into which our children are to enter."[226] Parker lamented the fact that "Anarchists, Bolshevists . . . and criminal broods" had immigrated to the United States "by the hundreds of thousands" and then urged that legislation be passed to "prevent any more scum of the world from coming here and [allow us to] . . . deport those already here."[227] Parker closed his remarks by noting that the current movement to erect a memorial to the late president would provide the perfect opportunity to focus the attention of the American people on Roosevelt's "many pleas and exhortations for Americanism" and "to take the needed steps to secure for the future a citizenry worthy of our glorious history."[228]

In 1919, Parker became president of the National Civic Federation, an alliance of labor, business, and political leaders that had been established at the turn of the century. At its founding it had promoted moderate progressive reforms and sought to resolve disputes between industry and organized labor. After the First World War, the organization turned its energies to fighting a perceived threat from communists, socialists, and radicals. In 1920, Parker appointed a committee to expose disloyalty, particularly in academia and religious organizations.[229] According to an article in the *New-York Tribune*, "[the] committee will make a survey of industrial, political and social progress, inquire into the extent to which the revolutionary movement has invaded the body politic and will give every support to all practical means tending to improve the general well-being of the people."[230] To accomplish these purposes, the committee dedicated itself to studying socialist doctrine and tactics, "including the preparation and distribution of literature and the organization of a training school for speakers," studying communist propaganda in the United States, and studying "the extent to which revolutionary forces have penetrated into the . . . fields [of] Labor, agriculture, church, college, public school, press, social agencies, philanthropic agencies, foreign groups, women's organizations, public employees and negroes."[231] Several of Parker's long-standing friends were members of the committee, including Bird S. Coler and Samuel Gompers.[232]

Parker, as president of the National Civic Federation, also supported immigration restrictions and deportation of alleged radicals.[233] In January 1920, during the opening of the group's annual meeting, he publicly criticized Bishop Charles H. Brent and other clergymen when they protested against the deportation of alleged "reds." Said Parker, "Do the kindly-minded clergymen expect us to stand still while the scum of the earth are roaming about the country? I wonder if these good men realize what they were criticizing?"[234]

Parker served on the campaign committee of the National Democratic Club and made a generous contribution to help elect James M. Cox and Franklin D. Roosevelt as president and vice president in 1920.[235] Following his defeat, Cox wrote to Parker to commiserate, stating, in part, "I have no apologies to make to my own conscience and none to history. Defeat has brought no sting. It is infinitely better to have a shortage in votes than in principle."[236]

On January 16, 1923, Parker, who was seventy years of age, married Amelia Day Campbell, fifty-one years of age, at a small, private ceremony conducted in Campbell's apartment in the Hotel Berkley, 170 West 74th Street, New York City (everyone in the family called the new Mrs. Parker "Amy")[237] (see figure 13.2). Arthur McCausland, one of Parker's law part-

Figure 13.2. Alton B. Parker and Amelia Day Campbell Parker shortly after their wedding. Courtesy of Underwood & Underwood, 1923. From the author's collection.

ners, served as the best man. The maid of honor was the bride's niece, Ruth Campbell Bennett.[238] Neither Parker's daughter nor either of his grandchildren attended the wedding. According to the *New York Times,* "the marriage was a surprise to friends of both."[239]

Parker had been a widower for about six years when he met Amelia at a luncheon given at the Lawyers' Club by the Sulgrave Institution (a group dedicated to the study and preservation of the ancestral home of George Washington).[240] At the time that they met, Parker was serving as the chancellor of the Sulgrave Institution (former Presidents Theodore Roosevelt and William Howard Taft and presidential candidate and Supreme Court Justice Charles Evans Hughes were members of the Sulgrave Institution's Board of Governors),[241] and Amelia was serving as the chair of the Sulgrave Institution's National Women's Committee. They met several times in their official capacities after that first luncheon, and mutual admiration and respect soon ripened into personal friendship, understanding, and love.[242] They got engaged at Mt. Vernon in December of 1922 when they took part in the planting of two trees that had been brought from Washington's ancestral home in England.[243]

Campbell was born on October 6, 1871, in Cambridge, New York, the daughter of Andrew Arthur Campbell and Amelia Day. Campbell, like Parker, had been married once before. But, unlike Parker, Campbell's first marriage was not dissolved by the Grim Reaper. Amelia Campbell's first marriage, to Edward Burton Styles, ended in divorce in 1903. At the time of their marriage, Amelia was a member of the National Committee on Foreign Relations and National Defense, a member of the Society of Mayflower Descendants, and the New York State historian of the Daughters of the American Revolution.[244]

Unlike her new husband, Amelia Parker was not a Democrat. In 1924, Judge Parker, on his way to Europe for an ABA trip, expressed regret to a reporter that the Democratic nominee for president, John W. Davis, was unable to make the trip and paid tribute to Davis's ability and suitability to serve as the standard bearer for the Democrats. Amelia Parker stated to the reporter that she would vote for Davis despite the fact that she was a Republican. When the reporter asked her if she was a Republican when Parker ran for president she smiled, nodded, and said, "I certainly was. Only I didn't have a vote then and now I have!"[245]

As soon as the happy couple got married, they left at once for Washington, DC, to attend the annual conference of the National Civic Federation. Once the conference concluded, the newlyweds honeymooned in Florida and Bermuda.[246]

In the late fall of 1923, Parker, as president of the National Civic Federation, found himself embroiled in a very public feud with Montana senator Burton K. Wheeler. Wheeler had taken a trip to the Soviet Union and was advocating for official recognition of the Soviet government. Parker took Wheeler to task, writing a series of letters to Wheeler arguing that official recognition of the Soviet government would turn "every consular office established [in the United States into] a center for [revolutionary and atheistic] propaganda in America."[247] In the end, the United States would not officially recognize the Soviet Union until 1933.[248]

In the early 1920s, a gentleman by the name of Kirby Page published a book titled *War—Its Causes, Consequences and Cure*. The book, which sought to elicit a pledge against participation in any other war, even a defensive one, was widely circulated to various religious groups and other organizations throughout the country. Parker, as president of the National Civic Federation, sent a letter to dozens of church and college officials, asking for their response to Page's proposed peace pledge. The letter he sent out read as follows:

LETTER OF INQUIRY

March 17, 1924

Dear Sir:

    The book entitled "War,—Its Causes, Consequences and Cure," by Kirby Page, which is having wide circulation among the churches, women's clubs and peace organizations of the country, contains the following pledge:
    "Let the churches of America say to their own government and to the peoples of the earth: We feel so certain that war is now unchristian, futile and suicidal that we renounce completely the whole war system. We will never again sanction or participate in any war. We will not allow our pulpits and class rooms to be used as recruiting stations. We will not again give our financial or moral support to any war. We will seek security and justice in other ways."
    As this subject will be discussed at the Twenty-fourth Annual Meeting of The National Civic Federation, to be held in New York on the 23d and 24th of April, I am addressing a number of bishops and other clergy, as well as representative laymen of the several denominations, asking their reaction upon that pledge, with the idea of reading such replies at the meeting, if agreeable to the writers.
    Will you favor us with an expression of your view?
Very truly yours,

    Alton B. Parker

    President, The National Civic Federation[249]

Parker received dozens of responses to his request for comment from church leaders, including the Bishop of Cleveland, the Bishop of Boston, the Bishop of New York, the Bishop of New Jersey, and the Bishop of North Carolina. He also received dozens of responses to his request for comment from the presidents of colleges and universities across the country, including the University of Chicago, Stanford University, Brown University, Syracuse University, and Colgate College. All of these responses showed an almost unanimous rejection of Page's pacifist pledge. Representative of many of the responses, the Vicar-General of the Diocese of Hartford, Connecticut wrote, in part, "The pledge is constructive treason. Its only redeeming quality is its transparent absurdity. If its proponents are to be taken seriously they will soon find themselves in one of the federal prisons."[250] The National Civic Federation compiled all of the responses, including the eight that were submitted in support of Page's pledge, into a printed booklet and made it available for purchase for twenty-five cents.[251]

At the twenty-fourth annual meeting of the National Civic Federation, the members unanimously adopted a declaration that condemned the ultra-pacifist movement. According to the declaration, the National Civic Federation, "while expressing the deepest abhorrence of the cruelty and frightfulness of war, unqualifiedly condemn all who ignore the inescapable fact that freedom and right may be subject to unprovoked attack and that, as a last resort, their maintenance justifies and requires a recourse to arms."[252] The declaration further stated that the Federation "[deemed] it a serious offense against the United States, for any person or organization to attempt to pledge citizens of this country to a violation of their constitutional obligations and that it warn[s] the people of this country not to be misled by the sentimental appeals of persons who, in the name of peace, seek to disarm the Nation and render it defenseless against enemies from without and disloyalty from within."[253]

Toward the very end of his life, Parker made one last trip overseas. In 1924, an ABA delegation of approximately three thousand lawyers and family members visited Europe. Among the delegation were five former presidents of the ABA, including Alton Parker, and the current president of the organization, Secretary of State Charles Evans Hughes. As part of the festivities, Parker delivered an address at Lincoln's Inn and sat on the bench with the Right Honorable Viscount Cave.[254] He and Amelia made a pilgrimage to Sulgrave Manor and presented several gifts of historic significance to the caretakers of the manor.[255] After the London activities, which included a garden party at Buckingham Palace where the royals received a representative from each of the forty-eight states (Parker and his wife represented New York), the delegation divided, some going to Paris and others going to Dublin. Alton and Amelia elected to go to Dublin and stayed there as the guests of the Honorable Timothy Healy, Governor General of the Irish Free State.[256]

In addition to all of the other things Parker had going on in his personal and professional life, he was one of the founders and a life member of the Board of Governors of the Thomas Jefferson Memorial Association for the preservation of Jefferson's home, Monticello, in Charlottesville, Virginia.[257] He also served as honorary vice president of the National Security League, as a member of the American Committee of the Kitchener Memorial Fund, and as a member of the Organizing Committee of the Stable Money League.[258] He was a member of the Citizens Committee of America, the National Committee on American Japanese Relations, the American Committee for Armenian Independence, the American Committee on the Rights of Religious Minorities, and the National Council of Religions in Higher Education; a director of the National Budget Committee; and served on the Board of Trustees of the Albany Law School.[259] In June 1923 Parker was elected to membership in the American Law Institute, an honor reserved for fewer than one percent of the attorneys practicing in the United States.[260] He was exceptionally busy with professional and civic engagements right up to the last days of his life.

14

His Final Days

In early February 1926, Parker appeared at the hospital with complaints of heart pains upon exertion and retention of urine. He was diagnosed with obesity, pulmonary emphysema, coronary sclerosis, and a distended bladder. He was advised to take nitroglycerine for his heart condition and was admitted to the hospital for his physicians to further examine and drain his bladder. Parker underwent a cystoscopy, and his prostate was found to be enlarged. On February 18, 1926, an operation was performed on Parker's bladder. The bladder wall was found to be tremendously thickened, which accounted for Parker's inability to empty his bladder. He underwent a second operation on March 9, 1926. An attempt was made to perform a prostatectomy under epidural and local anesthesia, but Parker had a seriously adverse reaction to the anesthesia and went into severe shock. He became pulseless, his "heart sounds became almost inaudible and breathing practically ceased."[1] He was ultimately resuscitated, and the decision was made to forego any further attempts to remove the prostate.[2]

On March 21, 1926, Parker suffered a mild attack of the flu, and in April he suffered from a bout of bronchial pneumonia. His battle with these illnesses left him confined to his rooms at the Ambassador Hotel in New York City.[3] On May 10, 1926, Parker was feeling better, and he decided to continue his recuperation at Rosemount. On the way to his country home, he convinced his wife, Amelia; his nurse, Ruth Belles; and his driver to take a drive through Central Park. Talk in the car covered a variety of subjects, including the death of former New York Governor Benjamin Odell earlier that day.[4] As the judge's automobile neared the reservoir in the park, Parker gasped suddenly, rose halfway out of his seat, and collapsed. The chauffer turned the car around and hastened back to the Ambassador Hotel. Parker was unconscious and was carried back to his apartment. All efforts to revive him were unsuccessful.[5] Parker died just four days shy of his seventy-fourth birthday (see figure 14.1).

Following Parker's passing, the *New York Transcript* and the *New York Times* reflected on the former Democratic nominee for president. The *Transcript* stated, "He proved disappointing as a candidate, his speeches and public appearances having none of the magnetic quality of those of his adversary." The *Times* wrote that Parker's "national fame rose and fell in a single year."[6]

Although the papers were harsh in their judgment of Parker, those who knew him well celebrated his accomplishments and his steadfastness as a jurist. The New York Court of Appeals sent a memorial to Parker's family signed by Chief Judge Frank H. Hiscock. It read, in part, "In a life so varied in its interests and so rich in its achievements, there is matter for many pages. Those who carry on his work today as members of this court must dwell with special emphasis upon his service as Judge. They remember the clarity and poise and even balance of his judgment. Not a few of these have taken rank as milestones in law."[7] John W. Davis, the 1924 Democratic nominee for president, said Parker was "one of the

Figure 14.1. Parker near the end of his life. From the Harris & Ewing Collection, Library of Congress, Washington, DC. Public domain.

outstanding figures in public life in the United States, a man of great courage, loyalty and devotion to his convictions. As a jurist he combined all the highest ideals of the bench and bar."[8] Governor Alfred E. Smith, who would himself run for president in 1928, said, when he learned of Parker's death, "The State and Nation has lost a most useful citizen."[9]

President Calvin Coolidge sent the following telegram to Amelia Parker when he learned of the judge's passing:

White House.

Washington, D.C. May 10

Mrs. Alton B. Parker

Hotel Ambassador, New York.

> Please accept my sincere sympathy on the death of your distinguished husband. As a Justice of the New York State Supreme Court, as Chief Judge of the Court of Appeals and as an officer of the American Bar Association and similar bodies, as head of national civic federations, he has rendered distinct service to the public. His prominence in public life was attested by his nomination for President of the United States. His death will be a great loss.
>
> Calvin Coolidge[10]

A memorial to Parker published in the *American Bar Association Journal* summed up the man and his life in this way:

> [Parker] was a man of impressive stature and handsome appearance, with a suggestion of power, courage and good nature.
>
> In character he was upright and true; to friends and associates he was sociable, sincere, unselfish and loyal.
>
> He was natural, honest and ambitious but he lacked conceit and pretense.
>
> He neither claimed or assumed to be over brilliant or scintillating or dramatic.
>
> He was a strong, courageous and virile man but he recognized his limitations. Never have we known anyone who

made better or higher uses of the equipment and gifts which he received from the Lord and which he wisely and prudently employed in life's work . . . To those who knew him well it matters little whether he was successful or not as a candidate for President, for we cherish the gifts of mind and heart which he possessed and shared with us and which will keep his memory green and sacred.

∼

. . . In dying, Judge Parker might well have exclaimed with Paul: 'I have fought a good fight, I have finished my course, I have kept the faith. As to the rest there is laid up for me a crown of justice, which the Lord the Just Judge will render to me in that day.'[11]

Parker's funeral took place on May 12, 1926, at St. Thomas's Protestant Episcopal Church in New York City. The Right Reverend Ernest M. Stires, bishop of Long Island, officiated at the ceremony. Among the honorary pallbearers were two former presidential nominees: Charles Evans Hughes (the Republican nominee in 1916) and John W. Davis (the Democratic nominee in 1924).[12] Other pallbearers, all personal friends, were Morgan J. O'Brien, Nathan L. Miller, James A. O'Gorman, Judge Severyn Sharp, Colonel Walter Scott, De Lancey Nicoll, Edwin Gould, Charles M. Schwab, Arthur McCausland, John G. Milburn, Gordon Auchincloss, Albert Boardman, and David Hunter Miller.[13] Delegations from the New York County Lawyers' Association, the Sulgrave Institution, the National Civic Federation, the New York State Bar Association, the Lawyers' Club, the National Democratic Club, and the Bar Association of the City of New York attended the services.[14]

Following the funeral service in New York City, Parker's body was placed on a train and traveled to Kingston, New York. Members of the Ulster County Bar Association met Parker's coffin at the train station and acted as an escort to the cemetery.[15] Parker was buried in Wiltwyck Cemetery under an imposing granite tombstone. This monument to Parker's life memorializes many of his greatest achievements:

Justice of the Supreme Court [of New York] 1885
Member Second Division of the Court of Appeals
Member General Term First Department

Chief Judge of the Court of Appeals
Democratic Presidential Nominee 1904
President American Bar Association 1907
President New York County Lawyers Association 1909–1911
President State Bar Association 1913–1914

Parker's will left to the City of Kingston, New York, a unique collection of letters, documents, and books belonging to or signed by New York state governors, complete from Governor George Clinton to Governor Alfred E. Smith, as well as a score of parchments dating back to 1669 from the British colonial governors. His will also left the city the sum of ten thousand dollars to build a fireproof room to house the valuable collection. Through the efforts of several prominent Kingston citizens and Governor Alfred E. Smith, the state allocated an additional ninety thousand dollars and built a New York State Museum in Kingston to house Parker's collection and several other priceless treasures belonging to the town dating back to the early Dutch occupation and the Revolutionary War days.[16]

On June 11, 1927, a boulder and bronze tablet marking Parker's birthplace was unveiled and dedicated on the old farm near Cortland, New York (see figure 14.2). The marker was a gift of the Tiooghnioga

Figure 14.2. Dedication of the Alton B. Parker birthplace marker, June 11, 1927. From the Alton B. Parker Papers, Manuscript Division, Library of Congress, Washington, DC. Public domain.

Chapter of the Daughters of the American Revolution.[17] Although the marker notes that Parker served as the chief judge of the court of appeals, it fails to mention that he ran for president in 1904.

After Parker's death, Amelia Parker returned to their lodgings at the Ambassador Hotel in New York City. She spent the last several years of her life living at the Wyndham Hotel on West 58th Street.[18] She remained active in a number of patriotic, historical, and genealogical societies, including the American Heraldry Society, the Order of the Crown of America, the National Society of Magna Charta Dames, the Society of Mayflower Descendants (she could trace her ancestry back to Miles Standish), the National Society of Colonial Dames of the State of New York, the National Society Daughters of Founders and Patriots, Daughters of American Colonists, and the New York Chapter of the Daughters of the American Revolution.[19] Amelia was also a trustee of the New York State Historical Association, a trustee of Schuyler Mansion, a governor of the Thomas Jefferson Memorial Association, a member of the American Historical Association, a member of the New England Historic and Genealogical Society, and a member of the New York Biographical and Genealogical Society.[20] In the early days of August 1960, Mrs. Parker suffered a stroke.[21] She died on Saturday, August 20, 1960, at the age of eighty-nine.[22] She is buried near her husband in Wiltwyck Cemetery.

15

What Kind of President Would Parker Have Made?

What kind of president would Alton Parker have made? Not surprisingly, it depends on whom you ask. Prior to 1904, there had, perhaps, never been a presidential campaign in the country's history where both candidates were men of such a high level of character and courage.[1] According to Irving Stone:

> Both [men] were powerfully built champions of "the vigorous life"; both had the intestinal fortitude to stand by their convictions; both . . . had alert, penetrating brains, the same kind of social conscience. Both commanded the respect of their country and their confreres. Both were dynamos of energy for work and play. Though Theodore Roosevelt appeared to be the more dashing figure in the eyes of the people, Alton Brooks Parker would have achieved the same results with less fanfare, less spectacular means: instead of crying "Charge!" at San Juan Hill, he would have said quietly to his troops, "Gentlemen, shall we proceed?"[2]

In Stone's estimation, because there were no major incidents to cope with during Roosevelt's second term, and because it was a quiet period in American development, there would have been little appreciable difference between the administration of President Roosevelt and the administration of a President Parker.[3] Noted another commentator, "Parker was an even-tempered man, not prone to descend into attacks on personalities no matter what the provocation. He had good political instincts . . . Parker was incorruptible, and saw service as far more important than personal gain . . . [H]e had excelled in every other demand made upon him in his long and varied career, and there is good reason to believe the presidency would have been graced by his presence."[4]

In 1998, Mississippi Court of Appeals Judge Leslie Southwick asked forty-two historians and five biographers to rank presidential also-rans on how they might have fared had they actually won their election for the presidency.[5] Of the forty-one also-rans who were ranked by the historians and biographers, Parker occupied the number thirty-four slot, the lead candidate in the "unsatisfactory" category. Parker's relatively low ranking was likely the result of his historical obscurity and the lack of scholarly writing about Parker and his life (indeed, only thirty-one of the historians and biographers who were asked to rank the also-rans claimed that they were sufficiently familiar with Parker to provide a rating).[6]

A review of some of the pressing national issues of the early part of the first decade of the 1900s, along with Parker's prior statements or reactions to these or similar issues, indicates that Parker was more likely to be the type of president envisioned by Stone or Southwick than by the polled historians. Parker was no isolationist, but he was a staunch opponent of US imperialism. During the campaign he decried the mismanagement of the Philippines and urged that the Filipino people be granted independence from US rule. Philippine independence most likely would have been a cornerstone of Parker's foreign policy program (and may have led to Philippine independence long before the end of World War II). In addition, Parker's opposition to rampant military spending undoubtedly would have been a serious impediment to the rapid expansion of the US Navy between 1904 and 1907 (during that time frame, eleven new battleships were commissioned and launched).

Parker recognized during the campaign that he likely would be burdened with a Republican Congress and that some issues, such as the revision of the tariff, likely were never going to meet with congressional approval. But Parker had demonstrated, from the time he was first elected as a county surrogate, a willingness to work with members of the opposition as well as his own party to get things accomplished. There is no reason to believe that he would have let personal feelings or party animosity interfere with his efforts to enact a legislative program for the benefit of all Americans.

In November 1907, the owners and operators of a mine in Goldfield, Nevada, announced that they would begin paying the miners who worked in the mine in scrip instead of cash. When the miners asked for security to back up the scrip and a date for resumption of cash payments, the operators refused to provide either. The miners then went on strike.[7]

In December the mine owners and operators met with Nevada Governor John Sparks and asked Sparks to request federal assistance to handle the strike. Sparks sent a request to Roosevelt, and, in response, Roosevelt directed his acting secretary of war to send a detachment of soldiers to Goldfield. There is no evidence that Roosevelt consulted with his advisors or made any attempt to ascertain whether persons or property were actually in danger in Goldfield before committing federal troops. There is, however, evidence that he reacted rashly and instinctively based on his prejudices against the unions involved in the dispute.[8]

Once the federal troops arrived in Goldfield, the owners and operators felt secure enough to press for an advantage. They reduced wages by one dollar per day and demanded that the miners return to work. Eventually the strike was broken, and the miners' union was destroyed in the process.[9]

Parker was a progressive when it came to labor issues. As a judge, he authored opinions upholding a union's right to strike, imposing limits on the number of hours that could be worked in a day, and upholding the constitutionality of prevailing wage laws. As a lawyer he defended the American Federation of Labor in the trial courts and on appeal and personally represented Samuel Gompers in criminal and civil proceedings. Given his history with labor issues and labor leaders, it is almost unthinkable that Parker would have committed federal troops in support of the Goldfield mine owners and operators. And given his long history of patiently and judiciously analyzing the issues presented to him before acting, he most assuredly would not have strengthened the hand of the owner/operators without gathering all the facts and consulting with his advisors.

In November and December 1907, the country faced its worst financial crisis in its history. The Panic of 1907 was triggered by the failed attempt in October 1907 to corner the market on stock in the United Copper Company. When this bid failed, two of the largest brokerage firms in New York City declared bankruptcy. Those bankruptcies resulted in a six-week stretch of runs on banks in New York City and other American cities.[10] Given Parker's prior involvement in averting the closure of the Ulster

County Savings Institution, he likely would have handled the Panic of 1907 in much the same way Roosevelt did: by directing his secretary of the treasury to infuse the banks with millions in cash and by asking J. P. Morgan to work with bank executives to shore up the banking system.[11]

In the closing days of the 1904 campaign, Parker railed against the dangerous influence of corporate money in the election contest. He worried about the corrupting influence of corporate contributions on elections and campaigned against them in the hope that it would help ensure cleaner elections in the future. He was still talking about the issue two decades later.[12] It is doubtful that a Republican-controlled Congress would have passed any legislation designed to curb the use and influence of corporate campaign contributions, but given Parker's disdain for Roosevelt's Wall Street "shakedown," had he won the election, he presumably would have kept the issue of campaign finance reform front and center.

In a memorial address eulogizing the assassinated William McKinley, Parker provided some idea of the type of president—and the presidential qualities—he most admired: "His mind was judicial, and would not be drawn from a patient search for the evidence that would show in which direction truth and justice lay by the clamor of those who insistently demanded that the President should always lead the people instead of working their will. He submitted without a murmur to undeserved criticism, and kept his counsel when unjustly assailed, apparently content that his deeds should in the end speak for themselves."[13] What kind of president would Parker have made? In this author's estimation, he would have been judicious. He would have been patient. He would have been cautious. He would have been temperate. He would have been thoughtful. And he would have been good.

Notes

Foreword

1. Richard B. Doss, "Democrats in the Doldrums: Virginia and the Democratic National Convention of 1904," *Journal of Southern History* 20, no. 4 (November 1954): 513.
2. "Bourbon" Democrats were opposed to high-tariff protectionism and American imperialism. They supported fiscal discipline, fought for the gold standard, and were strong supporters of states' rights.
3. John W. Davis was the lone conservative Democrat to win his party's nomination for president between 1908 and 1948. Davis was nominated as a compromise candidate on the 103rd ballot in 1924 after supporters of progressive candidate Alfred E. Smith and supporters of the more conservative William Gibbs McAdoo refused to yield their votes to settle on a presidential candidate.
4. Irving Stone, *They Also Ran* (New York: Doubleday, 1966), 99.

Chapter 1

1. Robert M. Mandelbaum, "Alton Brooks Parker," in *The Judges of the New York Court of Appeals: A Biographical History*, ed. Albert M. Rosenblatt (New York: Fordham University Press, 2007), 293-94.
2. John R. Grady, *The Lives and Public Services of Parker and Davis* (Philadelphia: National Publishing,1904), 52, 55-56.
3. Mandelbaum, "Alton Brooks Parker," 294; "Memoirs" of Alton Brooks Parker, 1, Container 16, Alton B. Parker Papers, Manuscript Division, Library of Congress, Washington, DC.
4. "Memoirs" of Alton Brooks Parker, 56; see also Norman H. Westerdahl, *Judge for President: Alton Parker and His Times* (Peoria, IL: Jonsson Jo Books, 1976), 1. Fred, as it turns out, was not as stable in the employment field as his older brother Alton. He bounced around from job to job until he finally landed

a position in a New York bank. He got the job thanks to a recommendation from his brother and the fact that he was excellent with numbers and could quickly add up columns of values. Things went well until it came time to add up the year-end bank statement totals. In doing so, Fred made a single mistake. Unfortunately, that one mistake happened to be in the millions column. Fred was forced to give up the banking business. Westerdahl, *Judge for President*, 3. At the time of the 1904 presidential campaign, Fred was working as an insurance examiner in New York City. Grady, *The Lives and Public Services of Parker and Davis*, 56.

    5. "Judge Alton B. Parker's Life Story Told by Photographs—His Birthplace and Present Home," *St. Louis Post-Dispatch Sunday Magazine*, April 24, 1904, 7.

    6. "Woman Whipped Chief Justice Parker," *New York Daily Tribune*, April 3, 1904, Alton B. Parker scrapbook, Container 23, Alton B. Parker Papers, Manuscript Division, Library of Congress, Washington, DC.

    7. "Judge Alton B. Parker's Life Story Told by Photographs—His Birthplace and Present Home," *St. Louis Post-Dispatch Sunday Magazine*, April 24, 1904, 7.

    8. "Judge Alton B. Parker's Life Story Told by Photographs—His Birthplace and Present Home," *St. Louis Post-Dispatch Sunday Magazine*, April 24, 1904, 7.

    9. Louis Albert Banks, ed., *Capital Stories About Famous Americans* (New York: Christian Herald, 1905), 416.

    10. Grady, *The Lives and Public Services of Parker and Davis*, 61–62.

    11. *Alton B. Parker of Esopus* (New York: Klyne Esopus Museum, 2004), 1.

    12. Grady, *The Lives and Public Services of Parker and Davis*, 57.

    13. *Alton B. Parker of Esopus*, 1.

    14. *Alton B. Parker of Esopus*, 1; see also Grady, *The Lives and Public Services of Parker and Davis*, 57; "Memoirs" of Alton B. Parker, 3, Container 16, Alton B. Parker Papers, Manuscript Division, Library of Congress, Washington, DC.

    15. Grady, *The Lives and Public Services of Parker and Davis*, 58–61.

    16. "Memoirs" of Alton B. Parker, 4–5.

    17. Mandelbaum, "Alton Brooks Parker," 294.

    18. Westerdahl, *Judge for President*, 4; Mandelbaum, "Alton Brooks Parker," 294. August Schoonmaker Jr., the firm's senior partner, was a distant relative of Parker's future father-in-law.

    19. Amelia Campbell Parker, "Alton Brooks Parker," *Proceedings of the Ulster County Historical Society, 1934–1935* (Kingston, NY: Ulster County Historical Society, 1935), 32.

    20. James K. McGuire, ed., *The Democratic Party of the State of New York*, Vol. II (New York: United States History Company, 1905), 196–97.

    21. Parker, "Alton Brooks Parker," 33.

    22. Westerdahl, *Judge for President*, 4; "Memoirs" of Alton B. Parker, 6.

    23. "Memoirs" of Alton B. Parker, 7. During the course of his lifetime, Parker would be awarded an honorary doctor of laws degree four times. He received

his first LLD from Union College in 1901. He also received LLD degrees from McGill University, the University of Toronto, and The College of William and Mary. "Memoirs" of Alton B. Parker, 66; Parker, "Alton Brooks Parker," 54–55.

24. "Memoirs" of Alton B. Parker, 7.

25. Mandelbaum, "Alton Brooks Parker," 294.

26. "Memoirs" of Alton B. Parker, 10–11.

27. James Grafton Rogers, *American Bar Leaders: Biographies of the Presidents of the American Bar Association 1878–1928* (Chicago: American Bar Association, 1932), 141.

28. "Memoirs" of Alton B. Parker, 8.

29. "Memoirs" of Alton B. Parker, 25.

30. Grady, *The Lives and Public Services of Parker and Davis,* 56–57.

31. Banks, *Capital Stories,* 416.

32. Banks, 417.

33. Banks, 417.

34. Stone, *They Also Ran,* 100.

35. Stone, 100. M. G. Cunniff, in his profile of Parker published in *The World's Work,* described Parker this way: "His mustache is brown, with a tinge of red. His hair, turning a little gray, is a darker brown. His eyes, alive with light, are brown with hazel colorings. Morning plunges in the Hudson, horseback rides at dawn in winter snow-storms, and the August sun that beats on his hayfields have tanned his unfurrowed face to the lasting glow of superabundant health." M. G. Cunniff, "Alton Brooks Parker," *The World's Work,* June 1904, 4923. For a time, Cunniff served as Parker's private secretary. "Mike Cunniff Dead," *The Graham Guardian* (Graham, AZ), December 25, 1914, 11.

36. Stone, *They Also Ran,* 100–1.

37. "A Short Range Picture of Parker, the Man," *New York Times,* July 11, 1904.

38. Charles S. Morris and Edward S. Ellis, *Men and Issues of 1904* (Philadelphia: J.C. Winston, 1904), 165.

39. "Judge Parker, the Man, at His Esopus Residence," *Los Angeles Herald,* July 17, 1904, 3.

40. Westerdahl, *Judge for President,* 31–32.

41. Morris and Ellis, *Men and Issues of 1904,* 171.

42. Westerdahl, *Judge for President,* 30; see also Morris and Ellis, *Men and Issues of 1904,* 169–71.

43. Stone, *They Also Ran,* 101; Morris and Ellis, *Men and Issues of 1904,* 171.

44. Ulster County Savings institution addendum to "Memoirs" of Alton B. Parker, 12, Container 16, Alton B. Parker Papers, Manuscript Division, Library of Congress, Washington, DC.

45. Reminiscences of Bertha Parker Hall, 59, Container 16, Alton B. Parker Papers, Manuscript Division, Library of Congress, Washington, DC.

46. Mandelbaum, "Alton Brooks Parker," 303.

47. Westerdahl, *Judge for President*, 5.

48. Westerdahl, 37–38.

49. Westerdahl, 39; Reminiscences of Bertha Parker Hall, 65.

50. Westerdahl, *Judge for President*, 35.

51. Correspondence between Mary Hall and Alton B. Parker and between Alton Parker Hall and Alton B. Parker, Containers 5–6, 8, Alton B. Parker Papers, Manuscript Division, Library of Congress, Washington, DC.

52. "Pen Portrait of a Possible President," *New York Times*, April 3, 1904.

53. "Pen Portrait of a Possible President," *New York Times*, April 3, 1904.

54. Westerdahl, *Judge for President*, 28.

55. National Register of Historic Places Registration Form, dated July 8, 2016, 5.

56. National Register of Historic Places Registration Form, dated July 8, 2016, 5.

57. Westerdahl, *Judge for President*, 27.

58. Mandelbaum, "Alton Brooks Parker," 297; National Register of Historic Places Registration Form, dated July 8, 2016, 15, 26.

59. Westerdahl, *Judge for President*, 26.

60. "Pen Portrait of a Possible President," *New York Times*, April 3, 1904.

61. Morris and Ellis, *Men and Issues of 1904*, 169.

62. Westerdahl, *Judge for President*, 27.

63. Mandelbaum, "Alton Brooks Parker," 297.

64. Morris and Ellis, *Men and Issues of 1904*, 167.

65. Morris and Ellis, 169.

66. Mandelbaum, "Alton Brooks Parker," 295; "Memoirs" of Alton B. Parker, 18–19.

67. "Memoirs" of Alton B. Parker, 20.

68. *Utica Saturday Globe*, September 18, 1897, Alton B. Parker scrapbook, Container 21, Alton B. Parker Papers, Manuscript Division, Library of Congress, Washington, DC.

69. "Memoirs" of Alton B. Parker, 24.

70. Westerdahl, *Judge for President*, 8–9.

71. Mandelbaum, "Alton Brooks Parker," 295–96. *The Ellenville Journal* wrote, "Surrogate Alton B. Parker has leaped suddenly into national fame, as the great American decliner. Henceforth his name will shine in our list of eminent personages along with Daniel Pratt and Sammy Tilden. Mr. Cleveland called our Surrogate to Washington recently, it seems, and proposed to lay him away on the shelf labeled First Assistant Postmaster General. But Mr. Parker was not to be caught with such chaff. He is capable, popular with his party, and ambitious of political preferment. He knows well enough that the way to the honors he covets lies not through the cubby-holes of an 'assistant' at Washington. It was

a put-up-job of the old party stagers to get a dangerous young rival out of the way. But Mr. Parker was too smart for them: he is not yet ready to be retired on hard work and half his present income: he will see them later." "Memoirs" of Alton B. Parker, 28.

72. Henry Bacon to Alton B. Parker, August 27, 1902, Container 2, Alton B. Parker Papers, Manuscript Division, Library of Congress, Washington, DC. See also Thomas H. Dowd to Alton B. Parker, August 11, 1902, Container 2, Alton B. Parker Papers, Manuscript Division, Library of Congress, Washington, DC, and Thomas H. Dowd to Alton B. Parker, August 16, 1902, Container 2, Alton B. Parker Papers, Manuscript Division, Library of Congress, Washington, DC ("I appreciate the fact that it would be a great sacrifice on your part to accept the nomination of our party for Governor; and if the only thing I could see in sight for you would be your election to the office of Governor, I would not urge it; but I am firmly convinced that with your nomination and election as Governor of this state, that the presidency of this country is within your grasp . . .").

73. "The Call to Judge Parker," *New York Evening Sun,* August 2, 1901.

74. "Memoirs" of Alton B. Parker, 82.

75. Fred C. Shoemaker, "Alton B. Parker: The Images of a Gilded Age Statesman in an Era of Progressive Politics" (master's thesis, The Ohio State University, 1983), 39.

Chapter 2

1. "Memoirs" of Alton B. Parker, 13.
2. "Memoirs" of Alton B. Parker, 14.
3. Mandelbaum, "Alton Brooks Parker," 295.
4. Charles J. Hailes, "Alton Brooks Parker: Pen Portrait of the Distinguished Jurist Who Is Likely to Be Called to Lead His Party in the Presidential Contest of 1904," *Albany Law Journal* 66 (May 1904): 137.
5. "Memoirs" of Alton B. Parker, 34.
6. "Memoirs" of Alton B. Parker, 36–37.
7. Mandelbaum, "Alton Brooks Parker," 296.
8. "Memoirs" of Alton B. Parker, 44.
9. Parker, "Alton Brooks Parker," 38; Alton B. Parker Speech at Columbia Law School, March 18, 1903, Container 2, Alton B. Parker Papers, Manuscript Division, Library of Congress, Washington, DC.
10. Mandelbaum, "Alton Brooks Parker," 296; Parker, "Alton Brooks Parker," 39; Governor Hill himself asked Parker if he would give up his position on the bench to go to the Senate. Parker replied, "Indeed I would not Governor. The law is to be my life work." "Memoirs" of Alton B. Parker, 49.
11. Mandelbaum, "Alton Brooks Parker," 296.

12. Parker, "Alton Brooks Parker," 39.

13. "Memoirs" of Alton B. Parker, 54.

14. "Memoirs" of Alton B. Parker, 54–55.

15. Parker, "Alton Brooks Parker," 39; see also David B. Hill to Alton B. Parker, September 15, 1897, Container 1, Alton B. Parker Papers, Manuscript Division, Library of Congress, Washington, DC.

16. *The Kingston Leader,* undated article, Alton B. Parker scrapbook, Container 21, Alton B. Parker Papers, Manuscript Division, Library of Congress, Washington, DC.

17. *The Kingston Leader,* undated article, Alton B. Parker scrapbook, Container 21, Alton B. Parker Papers, Manuscript Division, Library of Congress, Washington, DC.

18. Container 1, Alton B. Parker Papers, Manuscript Division, Library of Congress, Washington, DC.

19. Container 1, Alton B. Parker Papers, Manuscript Division, Library of Congress, Washington, DC.

20. "Memoirs" of Alton B. Parker, 55–57.

21. Parker, "Alton Brooks Parker," 39; see also James K. McGuire, ed., *Democratic Party of the State of New York,* Vol. II (New York: United States History Company, 1905), 198.

22. M'Cready Sykes, "Alton B. Parker, Chief Judge of the New York Court of Appeals," *Green Bag* 16, no. 3 (March 1904): 145.

23. David B. Hill to Alton B. Parker, telegram, November 3, 1897, Container 1, Alton B. Parker Papers, Manuscript Division, Library of Congress, Washington, DC.

24. Parker, "Alton Brooks Parker," 39–40; November 4, 1897, letter from David B. Hill to Alton B. Parker, November 4, 1897, Container 1, Alton B. Parker Papers, Manuscript Division, Library of Congress, Washington, DC.

25. Mandelbaum, "Alton Brooks Parker," 297.

26. Hon. Morgan J. O'Brien, "Alton Brooks Parker," *ABA Journal* 12 (1926): 454.

27. "Memoirs" of Alton B. Parker, 15–16.

28. O'Brien, "Alton Brooks Parker," 454.

29. Westerdahl, *Judge for President,* 17.

30. Cunniff, "Alton Brooks Parker," 4923.

31. Cunniff, 4925.

32. Westerdahl, *Judge for President,* 18.

33. Westerdahl, 18.

34. Hailes, "Alton Brooks Parker: Pen Portrait of the Distinguished Jurist," 138.

35. "The Trend of Chief Judge Alton B. Parker's Mind, as Indicated by His More Important Judicial Opinions," Alton B. Parker scrapbook, Container 23, Alton B. Parker Papers, Manuscript Division, Library of Congress, Washington, DC.

36. Shoemaker, "Alton B. Parker: The Images of a Gilded Age Statesman," 36.

37. James O. Wheaton, "The Genius and the Jurist: A Study of the Presidential Campaign of 1904" (PhD diss., Stanford University, 1965), 108.

38. Westerdahl, *Judge for President*, 39.

39. As we shall see in just a few pages, in 1905, the US Supreme Court declared a New York law setting maximum working hours for bakers unconstitutional, holding that the Constitution prohibits states from interfering with most employment contracts because the right to buy and sell labor is a fundamental freedom protected by the Fourteenth Amendment. *Lochner v. New York*, 198 U.S. 45 (1905). Parker wrote the New York Court of Appeals opinion finding the maximum hours law was a proper exercise of the state's power to protect workers and consumers.

40. Hailes, "Alton Brooks Parker: Pen Portrait of the Distinguished Jurist," 139.

41. Leslie H. Southwick, *Presidential Also-Rans and Running Mates, 1788 through 1996* (Jefferson, NC: McFarland & Company, 1998), 442.

42. *Tisdell v. New Hampshire Fire Insurance Co.*, 155 N.Y. 163, 166 (1898).

43. *Tisdell*, 168–69.

44. *Tisdell*, 171.

45. *Sternaman v. Metropolitan Life Insurance Co.*, 170 N.Y. 13, 28 (1902).

46. Ray Stannard Baker, "Parker and Roosevelt on Labor: Real Views of the Two Candidates on the Most Vital National Problem," *McClure Magazine*, November 1904, 42.

47. Baker, 43.

48. Baker, 43–44.

49. Baker, 44.

50. Baker, 45.

51. Baker, 46–47.

52. Baker, 47.

53. *National Protective Association of Steam-Fitters and Helpers v. Cumming*, 170 N.Y. 315, 334 (1902).

54. *Cumming*, 324, 328–29.

55. Baker, "Parker and Roosevelt on Labor," 49.

56. *Bohmer v. Haffen*, 161 N.Y. 390 (1900).

57. *People ex rel. Rodgers v. Coler*, 166 N.Y. 1, 25 (1901).

58. *Coler*, 27.

59. *Ryan v. City of New York*, 177 N.Y. 271 (1904).

60. *People v. Orange County Road Construction Co.*, 175 N.Y. 84, 94 (1903).

61. *People v. Lochner*, 177 N.Y. 145, 162 (1904).

62. Bruce W. Dearstyne, *The Crucible of Public Policy: New York Courts in the Progressive Era* (Albany, NY: State University of New York Press, 2022), 56.

63. Dearstyne, *The Crucible of Public Policy*, 58.

64. *People v. Lochner*, 177 N.Y. 145, 149, 154 (1904).

65. *Lochner*, 162.

66. *Lochner*, 163.
67. Dearstyne, *The Crucible of Public Policy*, 64–65.
68. Dearstyne, 68; *Lochner v. New York*, 198 U.S. 45, 57 (1905).
69. Dearstyne, 56.
70. Dearstyne, 56.
71. James Creelman, "Alton B. Parker: A Character Sketch," *The American Monthly Review of Reviews*, August 1904, 169.
72. "In the Mirror of the Present: The Trusts and Judge Parker," *The Arena*, September 1904, 313.
73. *Cohen v. Berlin Jones Envelope Co.*, 166 N.Y. 292, 299, 304 (1901).
74. *John D. Park & Sons Co. v. The National Wholesale Druggists Assoc.*, 175 N.Y. 1, 21–22 (1903).
75. *Hamer v. Sidway*, 124 N.Y. 538, 545 (1891).
76. *Hamer*, 551.
77. Leslie Southwick, "A Judge Runs for President: Alton Parker's Road to Oblivion," *Green Bag 2d* 5 (Autumn 2001): 38.
78. Southwick, "A Judge Runs for President," 38.
79. *Roberson v. Rochester Folding Box Co.*, 171 N.Y. 538, 542–43 (1902).
80. *Roberson v. Rochester Folding Box Co.*, 64 A.D. 30, 35 (N.Y. App. Div. 1901).
81. Dearstyne, *The Crucible of Public Policy*, 44.
82. *Roberson v. Rochester Folding Box Co.*, 171 N.Y. 538, 547 (1902).
83. Mandelbaum, "Alton Brooks Parker," 298.
84. *Roberson v. Rochester Folding Box Co.*, 171 N.Y. 538, 559 (1902).
85. *Roberson*, 561–62.
86. Mandelbaum, "Alton Brooks Parker," 298.
87. Mandelbaum, 298.
88. Mandelbaum, 298.
89. Mandelbaum, 298.
90. Mandelbaum, 298; "Memoirs" of Alton B. Parker, 85–86.
91. Theodore Roosevelt to Alton B. Parker, May 25, 1900, Container 1, Alton B. Parker Papers, Manuscript Division, Library of Congress, Washington, DC.
92. Alton B. Parker to Theodore Roosevelt, May 28, 1900, Container 1, Alton B. Parker Papers, Manuscript Division, Library of Congress, Washington, DC.
93. Nathan Miller, *Theodore Roosevelt: A Life* (New York: William Morrow, 1992), 346.
94. Shoemaker, "Alton B. Parker: The Images of a Gilded Age Statesman," 14–15.
95. Theodore Roosevelt to Alton B. Parker, March 16, 1901, Container 2, Alton B. Parker Papers, Manuscript Division, Library of Congress, Washington, DC.
96. Joseph B. Bishop, *Theodore Roosevelt & His Time Shown in His Own Letters* (New York: Charles Scribner's Sons, 1920), 147.

97. Shoemaker, "Alton B. Parker: The Images of a Gilded Age Statesman," 15; Theodore Roosevelt to Alton B. Parker, May 31, 1901, Container 2, Alton B. Parker Papers, Manuscript Division, Library of Congress, Washington, DC.

Chapter 3

1. Herbert J. Bass, *"I Am a Democrat": The Political Career of David Bennett Hill* (Syracuse, NY: Syracuse University Press, 1961), 1.
2. Edward S. Ellis, "Political Giants of the Present Day," *The Great Leaders and National Issues of 1896* (Philadelphia: Monarch Publishing, 1896), 295.
3. Bass, *"I Am a Democrat,"* 1.
4. Westerdahl, *Judge for President*, 10.
5. Grady, *The Lives and Public Services of Parker and Davis*, 85–86.
6. Edgar L. Murlin, *The Red Book: An Illustrated Legislative Manual of the State* (Albany, NY: James R. Lyon, 1895), 68.
7. Ellis, "Political Giants of the Present Day," 296.
8. Westerdahl, *Judge for President*, 10; McGuire, *The Democratic Party of the State of New York*, 79.
9. Bass, *"I Am a Democrat,"* 2.
10. Bass, 2.
11. Bass, 3.
12. Bass, 3.
13. McGuire, *The Democratic Party of the State of New York*, 79; Grady, *The Lives and Public Services of Parker and Davis*, 82.
14. Bass, *"I Am a Democrat,"* 3–4.
15. Alton B. Parker, *Address by Alton B. Parker, In Memoriam David Bennett Hill"* (n.p.: Wentworth Press, 2019), 3.
16. Bass, *"I Am a Democrat,"* 5.
17. Bass, 5.
18. Grady, *The Lives and Public Services of Parker and Davis*, 83.
19. Bass, *"I Am a Democrat,"* 8.
20. "Cornell Loses a Legacy," *New York Times*, May 20, 1890, 9.
21. *People v. Patrick*, 182 N.Y. 131 (1905).
22. Bass, *"I Am a Democrat,"* 9.
23. Bass, 11; Parker, "In Memoriam David Bennett Hill," 3.
24. Bass, *"I Am a Democrat,"* 12.
25. Bass, 12–13.
26. "His Last Day as Governor," *New York Times*, January 6, 1885, 1.
27. Bass, *"I Am a Democrat,"* 19.
28. Bass, 19.
29. Bass, 19–20.

30. Bass, 39.
31. Southwick, *Presidential Also-Rans*, 441.
32. Cunniff, "Alton Brooks Parker," 4925.
33. Mandelbaum, "Alton Brooks Parker," 295; "Memoirs" of Alton B. Parker, 32.
34. "Memoirs" of Alton B. Parker, 32.
35. Bass, *"I Am a Democrat,"* 51, 112, 114.
36. Bass, 125.
37. Parker, "In Memoriam David Bennett Hill," 11–12.
38. T. S. Williams, memorandum, January 28, 1891, Container 5, Alton B. Parker Papers, Manuscript Division, Library of Congress, Washington, DC.
39. Bass, *"I Am a Democrat,"* 159, 171, 174, 213.
40. Parker, "In Memoriam David Bennett Hill," (1911), 13; Bass, *"I Am a Democrat,"* 214.
41. Parker, "In Memoriam David Bennett Hill," 13.
42. Parker, "In Memoriam David Bennett Hill," 20.
43. *Pollack v. Farmers' Loan & Trust Co.*, 157 U.S. 429 (1895) (holding that an unapportioned tax on income from real estate was unconstitutional); *Pollock v. Farmers' Loan & Trust Co.*, 158 U.S. 601 (1895) (extending the principle to income from personal property and holding that the Income Tax Act of 1894 was unconstitutional).
44. David B. Hill to Alton B. Parker, December 7, 1893, Container 1, Alton B. Parker Papers, Manuscript Division, Library of Congress, Washington, DC.
45. Bass, *"I Am a Democrat,"* 224.
46. Bass, 201, 222.
47. Bass, 232, 235.
48. Bass, 236–37.
49. Bass, 238.
50. Bass, 238–39.
51. Bass, 243.
52. Bass, 244.
53. Ellis, "Political Giants of the Present Day," 298.
54. *Official Report of the Proceedings of the Democratic National Convention* (n.p.: Democratic National Committee, 1896), 68d.
55. *Official Report of the Proceedings of the Democratic National Convention (1896)*, 72.
56. *Official Report of the Proceedings of the Democratic National Convention (1896)*, 78–79.
57. *Official Report of the Proceedings of the Democratic National Convention (1896)*, 73–74.
58. *Official Report of the Proceedings of the Democratic National Convention (1896)*, 96.

59. Michael Kazin, *A Godly Hero: The Life of William Jennings Bryan* (New York: Anchor Books, 2006), 56–58.

60. Kazin, *A Godly Hero,* 59–61; *Official Report of the Proceedings of the Democratic National Convention (1896),* 210–211, 218, 241, 249.

61. Bass, *"I Am a Democrat,"* 245.

62. Bass, 245.

63. "Many Senators Selected," *New York Times,* January 20, 1897, 1.

64. *Official Report of the Proceedings of the Democratic National Convention* (n.p.: Democratic National Committee, 1900), 86.

65. *Official Report of the Proceedings of the Democratic National Convention (1900),* 132.

66. *Official Report of the Proceedings of the Democratic National Convention (1900),* 158.

67. *Official Report of the Proceedings of the Democratic National Convention (1900),* 182–83.

68. *Official Report of the Proceedings of the Democratic National Convention (1900),* 185–86.

69. Wheaton, "The Genius and the Jurist," 94.

70. "All for Parker," *Rockland County Times* (Nanuet, NY), April 23, 1904, 1.

71. "New York Has Spoken," *Rockland County Times* (Nanuet, NY), April 23, 1904, 7.

Chapter 4

1. Douglas A. Irwin, "Higher Tariffs, Lower Revenues? Analyzing the Fiscal Aspects of 'The Great Tariff Debate of 1888,'" *The Journal of Economic History* 58, no. 1 (March 1998): 61.

2. Irwin, "Higher Tariffs, Lower Revenues?" 61.

3. Michael McGerr, "The Guilded Age: 1873–1896," in *Of the People . . . The 200 Year History of the Democratic Party,* ed. Ronald H. Brown (Los Angeles: General Publishing Group, 1992), 88.

4. McGerr, "The Guilded Age," 90.

5. McGerr, 88.

6. McGerr, 89–90.

7. McGerr, 90–91.

8. Mandelbaum, "Alton Brooks Parker," 299.

9. Not all Democrats were in favor of bimetallism. In fact, throughout the Northeast and upper Midwest, Democrats who couldn't stand the party's new platform and the rhetoric of its new leader made plans to defeat them. In early September they convened the National Democratic Party to nominate a ticket committed to the gold standard. They nominated Illinois senator John M. Palmer

for president and former Kentucky governor Simon B. Buckner for vice president. Kazin, *A Godly Hero*, 63; *Campaign Text Book of the National Democratic Party* (Chicago: National Democratic Committee, 1896).

10. Kazin, *A Godly Hero*, 61; see also Thomas R. Ross, *Henry Gassaway Davis: An Old-Fashioned Biography* (Elkins, WV: T.R. Ross, 1994), 237.

11. Kazin, *A Godly Hero*, 53, 62.

12. Kazin, 62.

13. Kazin, 66, 68–69.

14. C. Carter Smith, ed., *A Sourcebook on the U.S. Presidency: Presidents of a Growing Country* (Brookfield, CT: Millbrook Press, 1993), 84.

15. Smith, *A Sourcebook on the U.S. Presidency*, 70; Donald A. Ritchie, "The Election of 1896," in *Running for President: The Candidates and Their Images 1789–1896*, ed. Arthur M. Schlesinger (New York: Simon & Schuster, 1994), 430.

16. "United States Presidential Election of 1896," Encyclopedia Britannica, last modified August 19, 2014, http://www.britannica.com.

17. Ritchie, "The Election of 1896," 425, 432.

18. John Milton Cooper Jr., "The Best . . . and Worst of Times 1897—1920," in *Of the People . . . The 200 Year History of the Democratic Party*, ed. Ronald H. Brown (Los Angeles: General Publishing Group, 1992), 96.

19. Cooper, "The Best . . . and Worst of Times," 96.

20. Ted Hake, *Encyclopedia of Political Buttons: United States 1896–1972* (York, PA: Hake's Americana & Collectibles, 1985), 30.

21. Cooper, "The Best . . . and Worst of Times," 96.

22. Cooper, 96.

23. Cooper, 96–97.

24. Cooper, 97.

25. Cooper, 96; John Milton Cooper Jr., "The Election of 1900," in *Running for President: The Candidates and Their Images 1900–1992*, ed. Arthur M. Schlesinger (New York: Simon & Schuster, 1994), 3.

26. Cooper, "The Best . . . and Worst of Times," 96.

27. Westerdahl, *Judge for President*, 44–45.

28. Larry J. Sabato and Howard R. Ernst, *Encyclopedia of American Political Parties and Elections* (New York: Checkmark Books, 2007), 335.

29. Sabato and Ernst, *Encyclopedia*, 335–36.

30. In 1884, Cleveland won 219 electoral votes by carrying the solid South and most of the Northeastern states, including New York, Rhode Island, Connecticut, New Jersey, Delaware, and Maryland. He also won Indiana and Missouri. Cleveland's results in the 1892 election were substantially similar to those in 1884, except he also picked up Illinois, Wisconsin, and California.

31. *Puck*, May 4, 1904.

Chapter 5

1. Cleveland was elected president in 1884. He was renominated by the Democrats in 1888, but lost to the Republican nominee, Benjamin Harrison. Cleveland was again nominated by the Democrats in 1892 and won a second non-consecutive term as president, the only person ever to do so. Roosevelt himself was excited about the possibility of running against Cleveland. He welcomed the opportunity in a letter sent to Massachusetts Senator Henry Cabot Lodge, writing, "I like the old fellow, I think he would be a formidable candidate." Clifford Smyth, *Builders of America: Theodore Roosevelt* (New York: Funk & Wagnalls, 1931), 132.

2. "The Progress of the World," *The American Monthly Review of Reviews*, January 1904, 21.

3. "The Progress of the World," 21–22.

4. "The Progress of the World," 22; McKelway said in his editorial endorsing Parker, "There is another man who, while Mr. Cleveland was the first choice of this paper, has always been the second choice of the Eagle for the nomination, and, indeed, has been himself the first choice of many other Democrats . . . The other man is Alton Brooks Parker, Chief Judge of the Court of Appeals of New York, the highest judicial body in this state." "Memoirs" of Alton B. Parker, 97.

5. Southwick, "A Judge Runs for President," 41; Stone, *They Also Ran*, 112. On March 29, 1904, Cleveland said of Parker, "He is clean, decent, and conservative, and ought on those grounds to inspire confidence in quarters where it is sadly needed if our party is ever going to be a political power again." Allan Nevins, ed., *Letters of Grover Cleveland, 1850–1908* (Boston: Houghton Mifflin, 1933), 576.

6. Westerdahl, *Judge for President*, 62–63.

7. Grady, *The Lives and Public Services of Parker and Davis*, 87.

8. Grady, 87.

9. Wheaton, "The Genius and the Jurist," 129.

10. "George Gray (Delaware politician)," Wikipedia, last modified December 22, 2022, http://en.m.wikipedia.org/wiki/Special:History/George_Gray_(Delaware_politician).

11. "George Gray (Delaware politician)."

12. "George Gray (Delaware politician)."

13. Wheaton, "The Genius and the Jurist," 146.

14. "Richard Olney Dies," *New York Times*, April 10, 1917, 13.

15. "Richard Olney Dies."

16. *Encyclopedia Britannica*, 11th ed. (1910), s.vv. "Olney, Richard."

17. *Encyclopedia Britannica*.

18. *Encyclopedia Britannica*.

19. Wheaton, "The Genius and the Jurist," 146.

20. Wheaton, 148.

21. In 1894, Olney wrote a letter to the United States Circuit Court in Philadelphia in relation to a petition of the Brotherhood of Railroad Trainmen asking for relief against the receivers of the Philadelphia & Reading Railroad, who had threatened to discharge all members of the brotherhood unless they resigned from the organization within a specified time. In his letter to the court, Olney argued in favor of the right of labor to organize and added, "No better mode for the settlement of contests between labor and capital has yet been devised or tried than arbitration." "Richard Olney Dies," *New York Times,* April 10, 1917, 13.

22. Wheaton, "The Genius and the Jurist," 148–49.

23. Hartley Davis, "Our Next President," *Munsey's Magazine,* October 1903, 10.

24. "Former Senator Cockrell Is Dead," *Washington, D.C. Evening Star,* December 13, 1915, 2.

25. "Former Senator Cockrell Is Dead."

26. John H. Eicher and David J. Eicher, *Civil War High Commands* (Palo Alto, CA: Stanford University Press, 2001), 179.

27. Eicher, *Civil War High Commands,* 179.

28. "Former Senator Cockrell Is Dead," *Washington, D.C. Evening Star,* December 13, 1915, 2.

29. "Former Senator Cockrell Is Dead."

30. Wheaton, "The Genius and the Jurist," 151.

31. *Republican Campaign Text Book* (n.p.: Republican National Committee, 1904), 531.

32. *Republican Campaign Text Book,* 534.

33. Arthur Krock, *The Editorials of Henry Watterson* (New York: George H. Doran, 1923), 92–95.

34. W. A. Swanberg, *Citizen Hearst* (New York: Bantam Books, 1961), 8.

35. Swanberg, 28.

36. Swanberg, 33, 39.

37. Swanberg, 41.

38. Swanberg, 26, 40.

39. Swanberg, 40.

40. Swanberg, 43–44.

41. Swanberg, 88.

42. Swanberg, 216.

43. Swanberg, 223.

44. Swanberg, 242.

45. Swanberg, 248.

46. Westerdahl, *Judge for President,* 109.

47. "The Progress of the World," *The American Monthly Review of Reviews,* January 1904, 23.

48. Wheaton, "The Genius and the Jurist," 159–60.
49. Wheaton, 160.
50. "The Election Results," *Harper's Weekly*, accessed June 1, 2022, https://elections.harpweek.com/1904/overview-1904-4.asp.
51. Swanberg, *Citizen Hearst*, 257–58.
52. Swanberg, 258.
53. Dearstyne, *The Crucible of Public Policy*, 78.
54. Dearstyne, 78; Wheaton, "The Genius and the Jurist," 119–20.
55. Privately, Parker doubted that he could get elected. As early as 1902, he stated to David Bennett Hill, "Senator, there is no more chance for a sound money Democrat to be elected to the Presidency two years hence than there is to go to Heaven without dying, unless that sound money Democrat shall be advocated as the Democratic nominee by Williams Jennings Bryan before the Convention is held." Bryan, of course, would advocate no such thing. Mandelbaum, "Alton Brooks Parker," 300.
56. Although Parker was not "actively" seeking the nomination, there were plenty of newspapers, as early as 1902, who were banging the drum for Parker. See, e.g., "Talk of Judge Alton B. Parker and the Democratic Presidential Nomination," *New York Tribune*, March 23, 1902; "Judge Parker Has the Pole," *Saugerties Telegram*, March 27, 1902; "J.W. Kern on Judge Parker: New Yorker That Is Talked of for President," *The Indianapolis News*, May 1, 1902; "A Presidential Feeler from Texas," *The Evening Sun*, May 3, 1902; "Parker for President," *The Richmond Dispatch*, June 19, 1902; "No Enthusiasm Over Olney. Washington Politicians Do Not Regard Him as a Presidential Possibility—Justice Parker Suggested," *New York Tribune*, July 11, 1902; Alton B. Parker scrapbooks, Containers 21 and 22, Alton B. Parker Papers, Manuscript Division, Library of Congress, Washington, DC.
57. Southwick, "A Judge Runs for President," 43.
58. Westerdahl, *Judge for President*, 64; Stone, *They Also Ran*, 104.
59. Stone, *They Also Ran*, 104.
60. Erving Winslow to Alton B. Parker, January 15, 1903, Container 2, Alton B. Parker Papers, Manuscript Division, Library of Congress, Washington, DC.
61. Alton B. Parker to Erving Winslow, January 17, 1903, Container 2, Alton B. Parker Papers, Manuscript Division, Library of Congress, Washington, DC.
62. "Parker Campaign Fairly Launched," *The New York Herald*, February 7, 1904, Alton B. Parker scrapbook, Container 22, Alton B. Parker Papers, Manuscript Division, Library of Congress, Washington, DC.
63. "Parker Campaign Fairly Launched."
64. "Parker Campaign Fairly Launched."
65. "Parker Campaign Fairly Launched."
66. Stone, *They Also Ran*, 104–5.
67. Dearstyne, *The Crucible of Public Policy*, 80; Westerdahl, *Judge for President*, 69.

68. "A Heart's Desire," Container 22, Alton B. Parker Papers, Manuscript Division, Library of Congress, Washington, DC.
69. "Parker's Views Set Forth by Danforth," *New York Times*, May 6, 1904.
70. Stone, *They Also Ran*, 105.
71. Again, although Parker was not "actively" seeking the nomination in 1903, he was receiving letters from supporters all over the country urging him to run for President. See, e.g., James Creelman to Alton B. Parker, January 14, 1903 ("For some time I have been carefully investigating the political situation and I am now convinced that your nomination for President is reasonably certain."); Arkansas Supreme Court Justice C. D. Wood to Alton B. Parker, February 28, 1903 ("Your shown popularity in New York, and the belief among your friends that you are eminently qualified for the presidency, has turned the eyes of the South, especially, toward you as their next National Democratic leader."); J. P. Gray, Dean of the University of Tennessee Department of Dentistry, to Alton B. Parker, September 26, 1903 ("I want to assure you that I have not heard a man in the city who has not thought you were the man to be nominated for president. I understand that all over the State they are of the same opinion."); David E. Poer to Alton B. Parker, October 9, 1903 ("You will pardon me for writing at this time, yet Indiana democrats are looking to you as their standard bearer in the campaign of 1904."); Charles Jackson to Alton B. Parker, December 24, 1903 ("The vast majority of the people clamor for your nomination—shall you disappoint them?"). Container 2, Alton B. Parker Papers, Manuscript Division, Library of Congress, Washington, DC.
72. Wheaton, "The Genius and the Jurist," 126.
73. U. S. Const. amend. XIV, § 1.
74. Westerdahl, *Judge for President*, 52.
75. Shoemaker, "Alton B. Parker: The Images of a Gilded Age Statesman," 44.
76. "Judge Parker Speaks," *New York Times*, July 4, 1903, 4.
77. "Fourteenth Amendment: Judge Alton B. Parker Addresses Georgia Lawyers," *The Times Dispatch* (Richmond, VA), July 4, 1903, 10.
78. James Gerard, *My First Eighty-three Years in America* (Garden City, NJ: Doubleday, 1951), 101–2.
79. "Memoirs" of Alton B. Parker, 90.
80. "Memoirs" of Alton B. Parker, 90.
81. *New York Evening Sun*, February 8, 1903.
82. "Judge Parker and the Presidency," *Brooklyn Daily Eagle*, February 15, 1903, 14.
83. "Parker Boomed by Guggenheimer," *New York World*, March 16, 1903, 2.
84. "Choice of a Leader," *Buffalo Enquirer*, November 20, 1903.
85. J. M. Page to Alton B. Parker, December 1, 1903, Container 2, Alton B. Parker Papers, Manuscript Division, Library of Congress, Washington, DC.
86. "Pointing to Parker," *Houston Post*, December 20, 1903.

87. Terry Golway, *Machine Made: Tammany Hall and the Creation of Modern American Politics* (New York: Liveright Publishing, 2014), 4–5; Richard F. Welch, *King of the Bowery* (Albany, NY: State University of New York Press, 2008), 23.

88. Golway, *Machine Made*, 4–5.

89. Golway, 6.

90. Golway, 6.

91. Golway, 6.

92. Golway, 6; Welch, *King of the Bowery*, 23.

93. Golway, *Machine Made*, 6.

94. Welch, *King of the Bowery*, 23.

95. Welch, 24, 31.

96. Welch, 31, 70.

97. Welch, 70, 193.

98. Oliver E. Allen, *The Tiger: The Rise and Fall of Tammany Hall* (Reading, MA: Addison-Wessley, 1993), 207–31.

99. "The leader of the Democratic party in New York City, Mr. Murphy, who has consistently believed that the cause of the party would best be served by a delegation to St. Louis left free to use its own judgment, at once declared that in his opinion it would be unwise at this early date to prejudge the issue by declaring for any one choice." "Tammany Issues a Statement," *Brooklyn Eagle*, March 6, 1904, Alton B. Parker scrapbook, Container 22, Alton B. Parker Papers, Manuscript Division, Library of Congress, Washington, DC.

100. "Judge Lynn Denounces Murphy Opposition," *New York Times*, July 9, 1904, 6; "Murphy is Aroused by Patriotism Issue," *New York Times*, October 3, 1917, 6; "Traitor! Cried Chief Murphy to Belmont 'You Aided Enemy.'" ("Murphy—I am looking for a candidate who is sure of carrying New York and enough other states to assure Democratic victory in the nation. I regard Parker as weak"), *New York American*, May 24, 1904, Alton B. Parker scrapbook, Container 23, Alton B. Parker Papers, Manuscript Division, Library of Congress, Washington, DC.

101. "Bright Augury for Parker," *New York Times*, April 5, 1904, 8.

102. "Murphy Fighting for His Political Life," *New York Times*, April 19, 1904, 2.

103. "George Raines for Chairman," *New York Times*, April 10, 1904, 1.

104. "Parker and Hill Split on Platform," *New York Times*, April 10, 1904, 1.

105. "Parker and Hill Split on Platform."

106. "Say Hill Yielded to Parker," *New York Times*, April 11, 1904, 2.

107. "Convention Organized After Wild Scramble," *New York Times*, April 19, 1904, 1.

108. "Convention Organized After Wild Scramble."

109. "New York Platform Drops Radicalism," *New York Times*, April 19, 1904, 1.

110. "Parker Men Win First Skirmish of the Day," *New York Times*, April 19, 1904, 2.

111. "Parker Men Win First Skirmish of the Day."

112. "Tammany Struggles in Vain," *New York Times*, April 19, 1904, 2.

113. "Tammany Struggles in Vain."

114. "New York Democratic Convention Instructs Delegates for Parker," *Los Angeles Herald*, April 19, 1904, 1–2.

115. "Bryan Wanted Parker to Be His Running Mate in Campaign of 1900," *The World*, May 1, 1904, Alton B. Parker scrapbook, Container 23, Alton B. Parker Papers, Manuscript Division, Library of Congress, Washington, DC.

116. "Bryan Wanted Parker to Be His Running Mate in Campaign of 1900."

117. "Bryan Brands Parker Story False," *New York American*, May 2, 1904, Alton B. Parker scrapbook, Container 23, Alton B. Parker Papers, Manuscript Division, Library of Congress, Washington, DC.

118. Wheaton, "The Genius and the Jurist," 244–45; "Mississippi Delegates Bound Fast to Parker; Arkansas Also for Parker," *New York Times*, June 16, 1904, Alton B. Parker scrapbook, Container 23, Alton B. Parker Papers, Manuscript Division, Library of Congress, Washington, DC.

119. Southwick, "A Judge Runs for President," 43.

120. "The Progress of the World," *The American Monthly Review of Reviews*, June 1904, 654; "Other Democratic Conventions," *The Outlook*, June 11, 1904, 338; Wheaton, "The Genius and the Jurist," 231–32, 247.

121. Wheaton, "The Genius and the Jurist," 244.

122. "Democrats Fail to Concentrate," *The Outlook*, June 18, 1904, 387.

123. "Democratic Indications," *The Outlook*, May 21, 1904, 145.

124. Wheaton, "The Genius and the Jurist," 245.

125. *Puck*, May 25, 1904.

126. Stone, *They Also Ran*, 105; Doss, "Democrats in the Doldrums," 514; Wheaton, "The Genius and the Jurist," 156. The Democratic National Committee met on January 12, 1904, to choose the site of the Democratic National Convention. It was expected that the committee would choose Chicago as the site of the convention. Once the committee met and realized the strength of the Hearst movement, it abandoned Chicago, where Hearst published one of his daily newspapers and Hearst clubs proliferated, believing that it afforded too favorable an environment for that candidate. St. Louis was then named as the host city. "The Progress of the World," *The American Monthly Review of Reviews*, February 1904, 148.

127. "The Democratic Convention," *The Outlook*, July 16, 1904, 638.

Chapter 6

1. "The March of Events," *The World's Work*, May 1904, 4723.

2. Thomas H. McKee, *The National Conventions and Platforms of All Political Parties, 1789 to 1905* (Baltimore, MD: Friedenwald, 1906), 393. The Socialist Party was the first party to hold its national convention, from May 1–5, 1904. The Socialist Party nominated Eugene V. Debs for president and Benjamin Hanford for vice president. McKee, *The National Conventions*, 409.

3. Morris and Ellis, *Men and Issues of 1904*, 39–40.

4. Morris and Ellis, 40–43.

5. Westerdahl, *Judge for President*, 74.

6. "The Progress of the World," *The American Monthly Review of Reviews*, July, 1904, 9.

7. Wheaton, "The Genius and the Jurist," 293–94.

8. Morris and Ellis, *Men and Issues of 1904*, 45–46.

9. Morris and Ellis, 52.

10. Morris and Ellis, 45–64.

11. Westerdahl, *Judge for President*, 76.

12. "The Democratic Convention," *The Outlook*, June 25, 1904, 432.

13. *The Outlook*, 432.

14. "Bryan on Parker's Chances," *New York American*, June 21, 1904, Alton B. Parker scrapbook, Container 23, Alton B. Parker Papers, Manuscript Division, Library of Congress, Washington, DC.

15. "Bryan on Parker's Chances."

16. McKee, *The National Conventions*, 382.

17. *Collier's St. Louis Convention Extra*, July 12, 1904, 2.

18. *Collier's St. Louis Convention Extra*, 2.

19. Richard B. Doss, ed., "Inside the Democratic National Convention of 1904," *Virginia Magazine of History & Biography* 64, no. 3 (July 1956): 291.

20. Doss, "Inside the Democratic National Convention of 1904," 291.

21. Doss, 291.

22. *Official Report of the Proceedings of the Democratic National Convention* (n.p.: Democratic National Committee, 1904), 1–3. Missouri Congressman Champ Clark was elected permanent chairman of the convention on Thursday, July 7, 1904. *Official Report of the Proceedings of the Democratic National Convention (1904)*, 123.

23. *Official Report of the Proceedings of the Democratic National Convention (1904)*, 44–46.

24. At this point in time it was not unusual for the nominees to not attend the convention in person. Most of the "electioneering" was conducted by surrogates.

25. Westerdahl, *Judge for President*, 78; "Judge Parker Caught Out in a Hurricane," *The World*, July 6, 1904, Alton B. Parker scrapbook, Container 23, Alton B. Parker Papers, Manuscript Division, Library of Congress, Washington, DC.

26. Westerdahl, *Judge for President*, 83.

27. Westerdahl, 83.

28. A party's platform is designed to appeal to the general public for the ultimate purpose of garnering support—and votes—for the party's candidate (or candidates) for office.

29. Doss, "Inside the Democratic National Convention of 1904," 296–97.

30. Wheaton, "The Genius and the Jurist," 327.

31. Doss, "Inside the Democratic National Convention of 1904," 299–300.

32. Doss, 300–1, 303.

33. McKee, *The National Conventions,* 384–93.

34. *Official Report of the Proceedings of the Democratic National Convention (1904),* 145–55; Westerdahl, *Judge for President,* 84.

35. Westerdahl, *Judge for President,* 84–85.

36. *Official Report of the Proceedings of the Democratic National Convention (1904),* 155.

37. "The March of Events," *The World's Work,* August 1904, 5203.

38. Westerdahl, *Judge for President,* 117.

Chapter 7

1. Doss, "Democrats in the Doldrums," 527.

2. Grady, *The Lives and Public Services of Parker and Davis,* 48–49; *Official Report of the Proceedings of the Democratic National Convention (1904),* 208.

3. *Official Report of the Proceedings of the Democratic National Convention (1904),* 168, 170, 175–76.

4. *Official Report of the Proceedings of the Democratic National Convention (1904),* 189.

5. Westerdahl, *Judge for President,* 112.

6. Westerdahl, 112.

7. William Jennings Bryan, *The Speeches of William Jennings Bryan* (New York: Funk & Wagnalls, 1909), 2:50.

8. *Official Report of the Proceedings of the Democratic National Convention (1904),* 236.

9. Westerdahl, *Judge for President,* 113; *Official Report of the Proceedings of the Democratic National Convention (1904),* 242. In his memoirs, Bryan said the following about why he seconded the nomination of Cockrell: "I was somewhat in a quandary as to what to do. My main objective was to prevent the nomination of Judge Parker, who was so closely identified with the men who had defeated the party in two campaigns that I felt sure he would be so handicapped by this support as to make his election impossible. I had no particular choice in selecting Senator Cockrell, but was governed by two considerations. First, he stood for everything that I had been fighting for and I could therefore urge his nomination without surrendering or abandoning anything. In the second place,

he was an ex-Confederate soldier and I thought that there was a possibility that with him we might break the Southern support of Judge Parker, and I believed that Senator Cockrell would poll a very much larger vote than Judge Parker could possibly poll." William Jennings Bryan and Mary Baird Bryan, *Memoirs of William Jennings Bryan* (Chicago: John C. Winston, 1925), 152.

10. *Official Report of the Proceedings of the Democratic National Convention (1904)*, 241–42.

11. *Official Report of the Proceedings of the Democratic National Convention (1904)*, 184; 200–7, 210–15, 218–25, 226–28.

12. *Official Report of the Proceedings of the Democratic National Convention (1904)*, 161–65.

13. Westerdahl, *Judge for President*, 106.

14. *Official Report of the Proceedings of the Democratic National Convention (1904)*, 165–68.

15. Westerdahl, *Judge for President*, 114.

16. *Official Report of the Proceedings of the Democratic National Convention (1904)*, 247–49.

17. Westerdahl, *Judge for President*, 114; *Official Report of the Proceedings of the Democratic National Convention (1904)*, 247–49.

18. *Official Report of the Proceedings of the Democratic National Convention (1904)*, 247–49.

19. *Official Report of the Proceedings of the Democratic National Convention (1904)*, 247–49.

20. Stone, *They Also Ran*, 106; Grady, *The Lives and Public Services of Parker and Davis*, 48; *Official Report of the Proceedings of the Democratic National Convention (1904)*, 249.

21. Westerdahl, *Judge for President*, 114.

22. Westerdahl, 114–15.

23. *Official Report of the Proceedings of the Democratic National Convention (1904)*, 251.

24. "Judge Parker Makes a Speech," *Chicago Tribune*, July 10, 1904, 5.

25. *Official Report of the Proceedings of the Democratic National Convention (1904)*, 254.

26. *Official Report of the Proceedings of the Democratic National Convention (1904)*, 254–55.

27. Doss, "Inside the Democratic National Convention of 1904," 305.

28. Doss, 305.

29. Doss, 307.

30. Doss, 307.

31. Doss, 307.

32. Doss, 308.

33. Doss, 308.

34. Doss, 308.
35. Doss, 308.
36. Doss, 308.
37. Doss, 309.
38. *Official Report of the Proceedings of the Democratic National Convention (1904)*, 256–68.
39. *Official Report of the Proceedings of the Democratic National Convention (1904)*, 273.
40. *Official Report of the Proceedings of the Democratic National Convention (1904)*, 273
41. *Official Report of the Proceedings of the Democratic National Convention (1904)*, 276.
42. *Official Report of the Proceedings of the Democratic National Convention (1904)*, 314.
43. McGuire, *Democratic Party of the State of New York*, 192.
44. Louis W. Koenig, *Bryan: A Political Biography of William Jennings Bryan* (New York: Putnam, 1971), 390.
45. Westerdahl, *Judge for President*, 122.
46. Westerdahl, 122.
47. Westerdahl, 120–21.
48. Westerdahl, 121.
49. "Why Parker Decided to Send His Message," *New York Times*, July 12, 1904, 1.
50. "Why Parker Decided to Send His Message."
51. "Why Parker Decided to Send His Message."
52. "Judge Parker Gives Facts Connected with 'Gold Telegram,'" undated article, Container 8, Alton B. Parker Papers, Manuscript Division, Library of Congress, Washington, DC.
53. "The March of Events," *The World's Work*, August 1904, 5204.
54. Westerdahl, *Judge for President*, 123.
55. The Democratic leaders who met to discuss what should be done in response to Parker's telegram included Virginia Senator John W. Daniel, delegate Allen Caperton Braxton, chairman of the executive committee of the Democratic National Committee William F. Sheehan, Mississippi Congressman and House Minority Leader John Sharp Williams, former New York Senator David B. Hill, former New York Senator Edward Murphy, delegate and New York State legislator Patrick H. McCarren, Louisiana Senator Murphy James Foster, delegate Benjamin F. Shively, Tennessee Senator Edward W. Carmack, Virginia Senator Thomas S. Martin, Nevada Senator Francis G. Newlands, South Carolina Senator Benjamin Tillman, former Kentucky Governor John Crepps Wickliffe Beckham, former Colorado Governor Charles S. Thomas, delegate James R. Gray, delegate John P.

Poe, and Utah Senator Frank J. Cannon. Doss, "Inside the Democratic National Convention of 1904," 311.

56. Westerdahl, *Judge for President*, 123.
57. Westerdahl, 123.
58. Westerdahl, 123.
59. Westerdahl, 123.
60. *Official Report of the Proceedings of the Democratic National Convention (1904)*, 276.
61. Doss, "Inside the Democratic National Convention of 1904," 315.
62. Doss, 315–16.
63. Doss, 316.
64. Doss, 316.
65. Doss, 316.
66. Doss, 316.
67. Doss, 316.
68. Doss, 316–17.
69. *Official Report of the Proceedings of the Democratic National Convention (1904)*, 314, 317–18.
70. Creelman, "Alton B. Parker: A Character Sketch," 171.
71. "Cockran Tells How Situation Changed," *New York Times*, July 12, 1904.
72. "A Man at Last," *New York Evening Post*, in *Boston Evening Transcript*, July 12, 1904, 9.
73. "The March of Events," *The World's Work*, August 1904, 5203.
74. "Approval of Parker's Stand," *New York Times*, July 11, 1904.
75. Leonard Schlup, "Alton B. Parker and the Presidential Campaign of 1904," *North Dakota Quarterly* 49, no. 1 (Winter 1981), 54–55.
76. Champ Clark, *My Quarter Century of American Politics* (New York: Harper & Bros., 1920), 2:150.
77. Westerdahl, *Judge for President*, 125.
78. *San Francisco Bulletin*, in *Boston Evening Transcript*, July 12, 1904, 9.
79. "The Democratic Ticket—Parker and Davis," *Public Opinion*, July 1904, 40.
80. "Simply a Sharp Political Trick," *New-York Tribune*, in *Boston Evening Transcript*, July 12, 1904, 9.
81. "Alton B. Parker," *Oklahoma Law Journal* 3, no. 1 (July 1904): 27–28.
82. *Official Report of the Proceedings of the Democratic National Convention (1904)*, 321.
83. *Official Report of the Proceedings of the Democratic National Convention (1904)*, 321.
84. Krock, *The Editorials of Henry Watterson*, 96–100.
85. "Are They Both Democrats?," *The Outlook*, July 30, 1904, 723–24.
86. "Are They Both Democrats?," *The Outlook*, July 30, 1904, 723–24.

87. Westerdahl, *Judge for President,* 128B.

88. Leonard Champ Clark, "Alton B. Parker and the Presidential Campaign of 1904," *North Dakota Quarterly* 49, no. 1 (Winter 1981): 53.

89. "Mr. Bryan's Position," *The Outlook,* July 23, 1904, 673.

90. "Mr. Bryan's Position," *The Outlook,* July 23, 1904, 673.

91. "Mr. Bryan's Position," *The Outlook,* July 23, 1904, 673.

92. "Mr. Bryan's Position," *The Outlook,* July 23, 1904, 673.

93. Frank R. Kent, *The Democratic Party: A History* (New York: Century Co., 1928), 366.

Chapter 8

1. "Henry G. Davis, Democratic Candidate for Vice-President," *The American Monthly Review of Reviews,* August 1904, 171–72.

2. Ross, *Henry Gassaway Davis,* 13.

3. "Henry G. Davis, Democratic Candidate for Vice-President," *The American Monthly Review of Reviews,* August 1904, 172.

4. "Henry G. Davis, Democratic Candidate for Vice-President," *The American Monthly Review of Reviews,* August 1904, 172.

5. Ross, *Henry Gassaway Davis,* 13.

6. Ross, 13.

7. Ross, 13.

8. Ross, 14–15.

9. Charles M. Pepper, *The Life and Times of Henry Gassaway Davis* (New York: The Century Co., 1920), 13.

10. Pepper, *Henry Gassaway Davis,* 14.

11. Pepper, 14.

12. Pepper, *Henry Gassaway Davis,* 15.

13. Ross, 15–16.

14. Ross, 16.

15. Pepper, *Henry Gassaway Davis,* 18.

16. Pepper, 22.

17. Pepper, 23.

18. Pepper, 30.

19. "Henry G. Davis, Democratic Candidate for Vice-President," *The American Monthly Review of Reviews,* August 1904, 176.

20. Ross, *Henry Gassaway Davis,* 166.

21. Ross, 247.

22. Ross, 215.

23. Ross, 25.

24. Ross, 25.

25. Ross, 26.
26. Ross, 26.
27. Ross, 30–31.
28. Pepper, *Henry Gassaway Davis,* 32.
29. Ross, *Henry Gassaway Davis,* 34.
30. Ross, 38–40.
31. Ross, 40.
32. Ross, 46.
33. Ross, 55–56.
34. Ross, 61. Prior to the 1913 ratification of the Seventeenth Amendment to the US Constitution, senators were chosen by state legislatures.
35. Pepper, *Henry Gassaway Davis,* 55.
36. Ross, *Henry Gassaway Davis,* 69.
37. "Henry G. Davis, Democratic Candidate for Vice-President," *The American Monthly Review of Reviews,* August 1904, 173.
38. Ross, *Henry Gassaway Davis,* 109.
39. Pepper, *Henry Gassaway Davis,* 96.
40. Ross, *Henry Gassaway Davis,* 71, 72, 79, 82, 89, 94, 105, 126.
41. Ross, 132.
42. Ross, 138.
43. Ross, 140.
44. Pepper, *Henry Gassaway Davis,* 97.
45. Ross, *Henry Gassaway Davis,* 164.
46. Pepper, *Henry Gassaway Davis,* 186, 188–89, 192.
47. Pepper, 106–7.
48. Pepper, 108.
49. Ross, *Henry Gassaway Davis,* 194.
50. Pepper, *Henry Gassaway Davis,* 111–12; Ross, *Henry Gassaway Davis,* 263.
51. Pepper, 119.
52. Pepper, 126–27.
53. Pepper, 40.
54. Pepper, 57.
55. Pepper, 70.
56. Pepper, 80.
57. Pepper, 137.
58. "Henry G. Davis, Democratic Candidate for Vice-President," *The American Monthly Review of Reviews,* August 1904, 176.
59. Pepper, *Henry Gassaway Davis,* 139.
60. Pepper, 142, 146.
61. Pepper, 147, 168.
62. "Henry G. Davis, Democratic Candidate for Vice-President," *The American Monthly Review of Reviews,* August 1904, 175; Ross, *Henry Gassaway Davis,* 212.

63. Pepper, *Henry Gassaway Davis,* 213; Ross, *Henry Gassaway Davis,* 297.
64. Ross, *Henry Gassaway Davis,* 282.
65. Ross, 282.
66. "Henry G. Davis, Democratic Candidate for Vice-President," *The American Monthly Review of Reviews,* August 1904, 174.

Chapter 9

1. Schlup, "Alton B. Parker," 54; Grover Cleveland to Alton B. Parker, July 14, 1904, Container 2, Alton B. Parker Papers, Manuscript Division, Library of Congress, Washington, DC.
2. Grover Cleveland, "Steady, Democrats, Steady!," *Collier's,* July 23, 1904, 6.
3. Cleveland, "Steady, Democrats, Steady!," 6.
4. Cleveland, 6.
5. Cleveland, 6.
6. "Candidates Meet at Rosemount," *New York Herald,* July 21, 1904, Alton B. Parker scrapbook, Container 24, Alton B. Parker Papers, Manuscript Division, Library of Congress, Washington, DC.
7. Ross, *Henry Gassaway Davis,* 281.
8. "Candidates Meet at Rosemount," *New York Herald,* July 21, 1904, Alton B. Parker scrapbook, Container 24, Alton B. Parker Papers, Manuscript Division, Library of Congress, Washington, DC.
9. Mandelbaum, "Alton Brooks Parker," 300.
10. Mandelbaum, 300.
11. "Parker Taken to Task by an Indignant Woman," *New York Times,* July 27, 1904, 1.
12. "Parker Taken to Task by an Indignant Woman."
13. "Taggart Will Head National Committee," *New York Times,* July 27, 1904, 3.
14. "Taggart Will Head National Committee."
15. "Sheehan for Head of Executive Committee," *New York Times,* August 4, 1904, 1.
16. Wheaton, "The Genius and the Jurist," 362–63. Although Minton was still reported as head of the Press Bureau in the October 29, 1904, issue of *New York Times,* the *Chicago Record-Herald* reported in mid-September that Thomas B. Fielders was in charge of the Democratic Press Bureau. "Leaders at National Headquarters," *Chicago Record-Herald,* September 11, 1904.
17. "Judge Parker Resigns from the Bench," *The World,* August 6, 1904, Alton B. Parker scrapbook, Container 24, Alton B. Parker Papers, Manuscript Division, Library of Congress, Washington, DC.

18. Southwick, "A Judge Runs for President," 40; Wheaton, "The Genius and the Jurist," 391.

19. "The Progress of the World," *The American Monthly Review of Reviews,* September 1904, 268.

20. "Judge Parker Resigns from the Bench," *The World,* August 6, 1904, Alton B. Parker scrapbook, Container 24, Alton B. Parker Papers, Manuscript Division, Library of Congress, Washington, DC.

21. Not until Franklin Roosevelt flew to the Democratic National Convention in Chicago in 1932 and acknowledged his nomination did any candidate make an acceptance speech before the assembled delegates. Westerdahl, *Judge for President,* 115–16.

22. Edmund Morris, *Theodore Rex* (New York: Random House, 2001), 349.

23. Morris, *Theodore Rex,* 349.

24. Morris, 349.

25. Morris, 349.

26. Morris, 349.

27. *Campaign Text Book of the Democratic Party of the United States* (New York: Metropolitan Printing Co., 1904), 30–31.

28. *Campaign Text Book of the Democratic Party of the United States (1904),* 31.

29. *Campaign Text Book of the Democratic Party of the United States (1904),* 32.

30. Westerdahl, *Judge for President,* 131.

31. "Judge Parker's Acceptance," *The Outlook,* August 20, 1904, 922.

32. Grady, *The Lives and Public Services of Parker and Davis,* 289.

33. Grady, 290.

34. Grady, 291.

35. Grady, 292.

36. Grady, 292.

37. Grady, 293.

38. Grady, 293.

39. Grady, 294.

40. Grady, 295.

41. Grady, 296.

42. Grady, 296.

43. Grady, 297.

44. Grady, 299.

45. Grady, 299.

46. Grady, 301.

47. Grady, 301.

48. August Belmont to Alton B. Parker, August 9, 1904, Container 2, Alton B. Parker Papers, Manuscript Division, Library of Congress, Washington, DC.
49. Shoemaker, "Alton B. Parker: The Images of a Gilded Age Statesman," 65.
50. Morris, *Theodore Rex,* 350; "Comments on Judge Parker's Speech," *Chicago Tribune,* August 12, 1904, Alton B. Parker newspaper clippings, Container 31, Alton B. Parker Papers, Manuscript Division, Library of Congress, Washington, DC.
51. Shoemaker, "Alton B. Parker: The Images of a Gilded Age Statesman," 67.
52. "Comment," *Harper's Weekly,* August 1904, 1304.
53. Shoemaker, "Alton B. Parker: The Images of a Gilded Age Statesman," 68.
54. "The Democratic Campaign to Date," *Boston Evening Transcript,* August 27, 1904, 16.
55. "The Sphinx Speaks," *The Chronicle Paragraph,* August 11, 1904, Container 31, Alton B. Parker Papers, Manuscript Division, Library of Congress, Washington, DC.
56. "Comment on Judge Parker's Speech of Acceptance," *The Nation,* August 18, 1904.
57. "Comment on Judge Parker's Speech of Acceptance."
58. "Comment on Judge Parker's Speech of Acceptance."
59. Creelman, "Alton B. Parker," 163, 165, 168–69.
60. Creelman, 169.
61. Creelman, 171.
62. Albert Stickney, *The Records* (n.p.: printed by the author, 1904), 1.
63. Stickney, 5.
64. Stickney, 8.
65. Stickney, 68.
66. Stickney, 68.
67. Correspondence with county Democratic Committees, Container 11, Alton B. Parker Papers, Manuscript Division, Library of Congress, Washington, DC.
68. "Parker Leaders Don't See How He Can Win," *Philadelphia Press,* August 31, 1904, Alton B. Parker newspaper clipping, Container 31, Alton B. Parker Papers, Manuscript Division, Library of Congress, Washington, DC.
69. "The Progress of the World," *The American Monthly Review of Reviews,* October 1904, 392.
70. "The Progress of the World."
71. "The Progress of the World."
72. Don C. Sietz, *Joseph Pulitzer: His Life and Letters* (New York: Simon & Schuster, 1924), 262.
73. *Letter of Judge Alton B. Parker of New York, Accepting the Democratic Nomination for President of the United States* (New York: Literary Dept. of the Democratic National Committee, 1904), 9.
74. *Letter of Judge Alton B. Parker,* 15.
75. *Letter of Judge Alton B. Parker,* 16.

76. *Letter of Judge Alton B. Parker,* 16.

77. "Paralyzed by Parker Letter," *New York Press,* September 27, 1904, Alton B. Parker scrapbook, Container 25, Alton B. Parker Papers, Manuscript Division, Library of Congress, Washington, DC.

78. "Paralyzed by Parker Letter."

79. "Paralyzed by Parker Letter."

80. Pepper, *Henry Gassaway Davis,* 176.

81. Grady, *The Lives and Public Services of Parker and Davis,* 302–4.

82. Grady, 304.

83. Grady, 304.

84. "Fear of Hill Trick," *The Globe,* August 29, 1904, Alton B. Parker scrapbook, Container 25, Alton B. Parker Papers, Manuscript Division, Library of Congress, Washington, DC; "Removal of a Handicap: Hill's Announcement Helpful to Parker," *The New York Evening Post,* August 29, 1904, Alton B. Parker newspaper clipping, Container 31, Alton B. Parker Papers, Manuscript Division, Library of Congress, Washington, DC.

85. Pepper, *Henry Gassaway Davis,* 178.

86. Finley Peter Dunne, "Mr. Dooley on the Duties of a Vice President," *Jackson Evening News,* July 23, 1904, 6.

87. Ross, *Henry Gassaway Davis,* 286.

88. Westerdahl, *Judge for President,* 168.

89. *Alton B. Parker of Esopus,* 69–73.

90. "Iroquois Campaign Song," Anonymous (1904).

91. Danny O. Crew, *Presidential Sheet Music: An Illustrated Catalogue of Published Music Associated with the American Presidency and Those Who Sought the Office* (Jefferson, NC: McFarland, 2001), 35.

92. "Alton Parker," *The Evansville Courier,* September 27, 1904, 4.

93. Container 2, Alton B. Parker Papers, Manuscript Division, Library of Congress, Washington, DC.

94. "Rabbi Writes Poem Eulogizing Parker," *New York American,* July 16, 1904, Alton B. Parker scrapbook, Container 24, Alton B. Parker Papers, Manuscript Division, Library of Congress, Washington, DC.

Chapter 10

1. Wheaton, "The Genius and the Jurist," 277–78.

2. "The Progress of the World," *The American Monthly Review of Reviews,* October 1904, 390.

3. "The Progress of the World."

4. J. G. van Slyke, "Judge Parker's Personality: A Neighbor's Appreciation," *The Outlook,* July 16, 1904, 645.

5. Gil Troy, *See How They Ran: The Changing Role of the Presidential Candidate* (New York: Maxwell Macmillan International, 1991), 115.

6. Wheaton, "The Genius and the Jurist," 365.

7. "Will Urge Parker to Speak in West," *The World*, August 13, 1904, Alton B. Parker scrapbook, Container 24, Alton B. Parker Papers, Manuscript Division, Library of Congress, Washington, DC.

8. Stone, *They Also Ran*, 113. Colonel Henry Watterson, editor of the *Louisville Courier-Journal*, advised Parker not to "swing round the circle." According to Watterson, "Horace Greeley made some of the finest speeches ever delivered, and he was weaker after each speech. Horatio Seymour lost votes every time he spoke. James G. Blaine would have been elected President if he had remained quietly in his home in Augusta, as Garfield did at Mentor in 1880, and as McKinley did at Canton in 1896 and 1900." "Judge Parker and the Stump," *The Evening Sun*, September 3, 1901, Alton B. Parker scrapbook, Container 25, Alton B. Parker Papers, Manuscript Division, Library of Congress, Washington, DC.

9. "The Progress of the World," *The American Monthly Review of Reviews*, November 1904, 524.

10. Shoemaker, "Alton B. Parker: The Images of a Gilded Age Statesman," 71–72.

11. *Puck*, October 19, 1904, 1.

12. "The Progress of the World," *The American Monthly Review of Reviews*, November 1904, 519.

13. "The Progress of the World."

14. Lewis L. Gould, *The Presidency of Theodore Roosevelt* (Lawrence, KS: University of Kansas Press, 1991), 139. Within two weeks of Parker's nomination, the West Shore Railroad had laid a long siding for the special trains of voters expected to visit Parker. Southwick, "A Judge Runs for President," 46. Few came, however, as shown by an article in the *New York Times* titled "No Boom for Esopus." *New York Times,* October 9, 1904, 7.

15. Bruce W. Dearstyne, "Alton B. Parker: New York's Neglected Statesman," New York Almanack, last modified June 8, 2022, https://www.newyorkalmanack.com/2022/06/alton-b-parker-new-yorks-neglected-statesman/.

16. Schlup, "Alton B. Parker," 59.

17. Koenig, *Bryan*, 396.

18. Shoemaker, "Alton B. Parker," 74.

19. Wheaton, "The Genius and the Jurist," 371; "Tammany Will Taboo Hearst for Congress," *New York Times*, August 1, 1904, 5.

20. Westerdahl, *Judge for President*, 169.

21. Ross, *Henry Gassaway Davis*, 285, 292.

22. Ross, 287. Parker's son-in-law, Charles Mercer Hall, did not cast his vote for Parker for president. "Parker and Davis Even—Neither's Son-in-Law Will Vote Democratic Ticket," *New York Daily Tribune*, August 3, 1904, Alton B.

Parker scrapbook, Container 24, Alton B. Parker Papers, Manuscript Division, Library of Congress, Washington, DC.

23. Wheaton, "The Genius and the Jurist," 396.
24. Shoemaker, "Alton B. Parker," 71.
25. "The Election Results," *Harper's Weekly*, accessed June 1, 2022, https://elections.harpweek.com/1904/overview-1904-4.asp.
26. Gould, *Theodore Roosevelt*, 139–40.
27. Wheaton, "The Genius and the Jurist," 441.
28. Wheaton, 442.
29. Wheaton, 443.
30. Wheaton, 438–39.
31. Shoemaker, "Alton B. Parker," 71.
32. Wheaton, "The Genius and the Jurist," 440–41.
33. Wheaton, 420.
34. Wheaton, 429.
35. Wheaton, 418.
36. Wheaton, 446.
37. Wheaton, 447.
38. Wheaton, 447.
39. Wheaton, 458.
40. Wheaton, 458.
41. Wheaton, 458–59.
42. Wheaton, 403, 407.
43. Westerdahl, *Judge for President*, 157.
44. Wheaton, "The Genius and the Jurist," 403–4, 407.
45. Carl Schurz, "To the Independent Voter: An Open Letter" (New York: Parker Independent Clubs, 1904), 5.
46. Schurz, "To the Independent Voter," 7.
47. Schurz, 18–20.
48. Schurz, 25–32, 34.
49. Schurz, 42. Interestingly, Schurz was one of the few people who believed that Parker did the right thing in refusing to leave his home and go out and speak to the American people. He wrote to Parker in August 1904 congratulating him on his "very wise decision not to deliver a dinner speech at Chicago and to abstain from stump speaking during the campaign." Carl Schurz to Alton B. Parker, August 1, 1904, Container 2, Alton B. Parker Papers, Manuscript Division, Library of Congress, Washington, DC.
50. The article was based on an address delivered by Judge Parker at the commencement ceremonies at Union College in Albany, New York, in 1901.
51. Alton B. Parker, "Educated Men in Politics," *Success*, September 1904, 550.
52. Parker, "Educated Men," 550.
53. Parker, 550.

54. Parker, 551.

55. Parker, 551.

56. Wheaton, "The Genius and the Jurist," 411. The Democrats highlighted Roosevelt's unflattering statements about many of his predecessors, including McKinley. Among the quotes: Thomas Jefferson was "that slippery demagogue" who was "less fit to conduct the country in troublous times than any president we have ever had"; James Madison was "a mere pale shadow of Jefferson" and a "ridiculously incompetent leader for a war with Great Britain"; James Monroe was described as "an honorable man with a very unoriginal mind"; of John Tyler he said, "Tyler has been called a mediocre man; but this is unwarranted flattery. He was a politician of monumental littleness"; Benjamin Harrison was "a genial little runt; . . . an absolute mediocrity"; McKinley "[had] no more backbone than a chocolate eclair." Daniel Ruddy, *Theodore Roosevelt's History of the United States: His Own Words* (New York: Smithsonian Books/HarperCollins, 2010), 84, 104–5, 108, 136, 222–23, 238.

57. Wheaton, "The Genius and the Jurist," 411.

58. Shoemaker, "Alton B. Parker: The Images of a Gilded Age Statesman," 74.

59. Lewis L. Gould, *Reform and Regulation: American Politics, 1900–1916* (New York: Wiley, 1978), 47.

60. "Parker the Silent," *Boston Evening Transcript*, October 12, 1904, 16.

Chapter 11

1. Wheaton, "The Genius and the Jurist," 478.

2. Wheaton, 478.

3. Wheaton, 478–79.

4. Notes for "Memoirs" of Alton B. Parker, Container 16, Alton B. Parker Papers, Manuscript Division, Library of Congress, Washington, DC.

5. Notes for "Memoirs."

6. Notes for "Memoirs."

7. Alton B. Parker, "Political Corruption by the Trusts" (New York: Parker Independent Clubs, 1904), 6–8; "Parker Attacks Campaign Graft," *The Press*, October 25, 1904, Alton B. Parker newspaper clipping, Container 32, Alton B. Parker Papers, Manuscript Division, Library of Congress, Washington, DC.

8. October 28, 1904 speech, Alton B. Parker Papers, Container 12, Manuscript Division, Library of Congress, Washington, DC.

9. October 28, 1904, speech.

10. Troy, *See How They Ran,* 116.

11. "Judge Parker Urged to Take the Stump," *The World,* September 25, 1904, Alton B. Parker scrapbook, Container 25, Alton B. Parker Papers, Manuscript Division, Library of Congress, Washington, DC. Parker was still pushing back, arguing that "letters and statements to newspapers would be just as effective."

Notes to Chapter 11 | 293

12. "Alton B. Parker to Go On Stump," *Chicago Tribune,* September 24, 1904, 1.

13. "The Progress of the World," *The American Monthly Review of Reviews,* November 1904, 522.

14. "Managers Hope Parker's Speeches May Put Ginger Into Campaign," *The New York Daily Tribune,* October 5, 1904, 3.

15. Stone, *They Also Ran,* 114.

16. Mandelbaum, "Alton Brooks Parker," 301.

17. Morris, *Theodore Rex,* 357.

18. Morris, 362.

19. "15,000 Cheer Judge Parker 26 Minutes," *New York Herald,* November 1, 1904, Alton B. Parker scrapbook, Container 25, Alton B. Parker Papers, Manuscript Division, Library of Congress, Washington, DC.

20. "15,000 Cheer Judge Parker 26 Minutes."

21. "15,000 Cheer Judge Parker 26 Minutes."

22. "Jersey Throngs Hear Parker on Trusts," *New York Times,* November 2, 1904, 1–2; "Parker Speaks Three Times in a Night in Jersey," *The Journal,* November 2, 1904, Alton B. Parker newspaper clipping, Container 32, Alton B. Parker Papers, Manuscript Division, Library of Congress, Washington, DC.

23. "Parker, the Orator, Cheered by Throngs," *New York Times,* November 3, 1904, 1.

24. "Parker, the Orator," 2.

25. "Parker, the Orator," 2.

26. "Parker, the Orator," 1.

27. "Parker, the Orator," 1.

28. "Parker on Standing Pat," *New York Times,* November 4, 1904, 1.

29. "Connecticut Turns Out to Meet Parker," *New York Times,* November 4, 1904, 2.

30. "Connecticut Turns Out to Meet Parker."

31. Bishop, *Theodore Roosevelt and His Time,* 1009.

32. "Roosevelt Brands Parker Charges False," *Galena Daily Gazette,* November 5, 1904, 1.

33. Westerdahl, *Judge for President,* 182; Shoemaker, "Alton B. Parker: The Images of a Gilded Age Statesman," 81.

34. "The Progress of the World," *The American Monthly Review of Reviews,* December 1904, 645.

35. Oswald Garrison Villard, *Fighting Years: Memoirs of a Liberal Editor* (New York: Harcourt, Brace, 1939), 179.

36. "The Fall of Parker," *Chicago Tribune,* November 4, 1904, 8.

37. "His Certificate of Virtue," *New York Sun,* in *New York Times,* November 7, 1904, 2.

38. "What the Public Remembered," *The American Monthly Review of Reviews,* December 1904, 645.

39. Mandelbaum, "Alton Brooks Parker," 301.

40. Morris, *Theodore Rex*, 359.

41. Miller, *Theodore Roosevelt*, 440.

42. Miller, 359–60; Alton B. Parker to Tom R. Wells, October 1, 1925, Container 10, Alton B. Parker Papers, Manuscript Division, Library of Congress, Washington, DC.

43. Westerdahl, *Judge for President*, 187.

44. Westerdahl, 188.

45. "Democrats Quake at Exposure of Parker," *New York Press*, November 5, 1904, Alton B. Parker scrapbook, Container 25, Alton B. Parker Papers, Manuscript Division, Library of Congress, Washington, DC.

46. "Democrats Quake at Exposure of Parker."

47. "Democrats Quake at Exposure of Parker."

48. Krock, *The Editorials of Henry Watterson*, 100–2.

49. "Hon. David B. Hill to Speak Here," *Evansville Courier*, September 27, 1904, 2.

50. Wheaton, "The Genius and the Jurist," 600.

51. "Cleveland Scores Republican Shams," *The St. Paul Globe*, October 22, 1904, Alton B. Parker newspaper clipping, Container 32, Alton B. Parker Papers, Manuscript Division, Library of Congress, Washington, DC.

52. "Cleveland Scores Republican Shams."

53. Grover Cleveland, "Parker," *McClure's Magazine*, November 1904, 3–8.

54. "Cleveland at Newark Lashes the Trusts," *New York Times*, November 5, 1904, 1.

55. "Cleveland at Newark Lashes the Trusts."

56. "Cleveland at Newark Lashes the Trusts."

57. Westerdahl, *Judge for President*, 197.

58. George Thayer, *Who Shakes the Money Tree? American Campaign Financing Practices from 1789 to the Present* (New York: Simon and Schuster, 1973), 53.

59. Southwick, "A Judge Runs for President," 46; Finley Peter Dunne, "Mr. Dooley's Last Words to Voters," *Jackson Evening News* (Jackson, MS), November 5, 1904, 2.

Chapter 12

1. Westerdahl, *Judge for President*, 198.

2. Shoemaker, "Alton B. Parker: The Images of a Gilded Age Statesman," 85.

3. Wheaton, "The Genius and the Jurist," 518–19.

4. "Parker to Roosevelt," *New York Times*, November 9, 1904, 1.

5. "Parker to Roosevelt," *New York Times*, November 9, 1904, 1.

6. "Conceded and Doubtful States," *The American Monthly Review of Reviews*, November 1904, 518.

7. "Conceded and Doubtful States."
8. "Conceded and Doubtful States."
9. "Conceded and Doubtful States."
10. Bass, *"I am a Democrat,"* 246.
11. "1904 Presidential General Election Data—National," Dave Leip's Atlas of U.S. Presidential Elections, last modified February 14, 2018, http://www.uselectionatlas.org.
12. Wheaton, "The Genius and the Jurist," 520.
13. David Nasaw, *The Chief: the Life of William Randolph Hearst* (Boston: Houghton Mifflin, 2000), 185.
14. Wheaton, "The Genius and the Jurist," 520.
15. Maryland ultimately split its electoral votes, seven for Parker and one for Roosevelt. "The Election Results," *Harper's Weekly*, accessed June 1, 2022, https://elections.harpweek.com/1904/overview-1904-4.asp.
16. Ray Ginger, *The Age of Excess: the United States from 1877 to 1914* (New York: Macmillan, 1965), 267.
17. "Personal Triumph for Roosevelt," *New York Times*, in *Boston Evening Transcript*, November 9, 1904, 4.
18. John Milton Cooper Jr., "The Election of 1904," in *Running for President: The Candidates and Their Images 1900-1992*, ed. Arthur M. Schlesinger (New York: Simon & Schuster, 1994), 32.
19. Westerdahl, *Judge for President*, 199. Grant received 286 electoral votes to Greeley's 66 electoral votes. Greeley died after the election but before the Electoral College could meet to cast its votes, and the electors pledged to Greeley voted for four candidates for president and eight candidates for vice president.
20. Cooper, "The Election of 1904," 32. Toward the end of October, Parker's managers were telling the press that according to their internal calculations, Parker was going to wind up with 256 electoral votes on election day—17 more than need to capture the presidency. Amazingly, they reported that in addition to the solid South, Parker was going to win New York, New Jersey, Connecticut, Delaware, Maryland, West Virginia, Indiana, Montana, Colorado, Idaho, and Wyoming. They were only right about Maryland. "256 Parker Votes in Electoral College," *The Brooklyn Eagle*, October 20, 1904, "Figures Proclaim Parker's Election," *The St. Paul Globe*, October 21, 1904, Alton B. Parker newspaper clippings, Container 32, Alton B. Parker Papers, Manuscript Division, Library of Congress, Washington, DC.
21. Cooper, "The Election of 1904," 32.
22. Cooper, 32.
23. Cooper, 32.
24. Cooper, 32.
25. Cooper, 32.
26. Cooper, 32.

27. Kent, *The Democratic Party,* 366.

28. Norbert H. Mahnken, "Bryan Country," in *William Jennings Bryan: A Profile,* ed. Paul W. Glad (New York: Hill and Wang, 1967), 145.

29. Kenneth W. Leish, ed., *The American Heritage Book of the Presidents and Famous Americans* (New York: Dell Publishing, 1967), 8:672.

30. *New York Times,* November 9, 1904, 1.

31. Cooper, "The Election of 1904," 33.

32. Cooper, 33.

33. Cooper, 33.

34. Cooper, 33.

35. "Parker Urges Party to Work for Future," *New York Times,* November 10, 1904, 1.

36. McGuire, *The Democratic Party of the State of New York,* 200.

37. McGuire, 200–1.

38. "American Politics," *The Forum,* January 1905, 336.

39. "American Politics."

40. Champ Clark to Alton B. Parker, November 20, 1904, Container 2, Alton B. Parker Papers, Manuscript Division, Library of Congress, Washington, DC.

41. "American Politics," *The Forum,* January 1905, 324.

42. *Life,* November 24, 1904, 498.

43. "American Politics," *The Forum,* January 1905, 328.

44. "American Politics," 324.

Chapter 13

1. *Alton B. Parker of Esopus,* 5.

2. Rogers, *American Bar Leaders,* 145; D. P. Bergheimer to Claude T. Dawes, July 2, 1907, Container 2, Alton B. Parker Papers, Manuscript Division, Library of Congress, Washington, DC; Alton B. Parker to Bertha Parker, February 12, 1919, Container 5, Alton B. Parker Papers, Manuscript Division, Library of Congress, Washington, DC.

3. *The Yale Alumni Weekly,* April 23, 1920, 721; October 1, 1920 letter to Alton B. Parker, Container 5, Alton B. Parker Papers, Manuscript Division, Library of Congress, Washington, DC.

4. Alton B. Parker to Bertha P. Hall, February 21, 1921, Container 6, Alton B. Parker Papers, Manuscript Division, Library of Congress, Washington, DC.

5. Alton B. Parker, "The Lawyer in Public Affairs," *Green Bag* 17 (1905): 342.

6. Parker, "The Lawyer in Public Affairs," 343.

7. Parker, 344.

8. "The Progress of the World," *The American Monthly Review of Reviews,* December 1904, 654.

9. Container 2, Alton B. Parker Papers, Manuscript Division, Library of Congress, Washington, DC.

10. Swanberg, *Citizen Hearst,* 283.

11. *Matter of Hearst v. Woelper,* 183 N.Y. 274 (N.Y. 1905). Not surprisingly, Hearst was not willing to take no for an answer. He convinced the state legislature to enact a statute requiring a judicial recount and recanvass of the votes cast for mayor in the 1905 election. That statute was declared unconstitutional by the New York Court of Appeals on November 17, 1907. *Matter of Metz v. Maddox,* 82 N.E. 507 (N.Y. 1907).

12. *Loewe v. Lawlor,* 208 U.S. 274 (1908).

13. *Loewe.*

14. *Loewe.*

15. *Lawyers Against Labor: From Individual Rights to Corporate Liberalism,* Daniel R. Ernst (1995), 151.

16. *Lawlor v. Loewe,* 235 U.S. 522, 534 (1915).

17. *Lawlor,* 534.

18. William B. Gould, IV, *A Primer on American Labor Law,* 4th ed. (Cambridge, MA: MIT Press, 2004), 14.

19. *Gompers v. Bucks Stove & Range Company,* 221 U.S. 418 (1911).

20. *Gompers v. Bucks Stove.*

21. *Gompers v. Bucks Stove.*

22. *Gompers v. Bucks Stove.*

23. *Gompers v. United States,* 233 U.S. 604 (1914).

24. *Gompers v. U.S.*

25. *Gompers v. U.S.*

26. *Dr. Miles Medical Co. v. John D. Park & Sons,* 220 U.S. 373, 374, 381–82 (1911).

27. *Dr. Miles Medical Co.,* 373.

28. Joseph McNamara, "Here's Why William Sulzer Was the First—And Still Only—NY Governor to Be Impeached," *New York Daily News,* August 14, 2017.

29. McNamara, "Here's Why William Sulzer Was the First."

30. Ray B. Smith, ed., *History of the State of New York, Political and Governmental,* Vol. 4 (Syracuse, NY: Syracuse Press, 1922), 242.

31. Westerdahl, *Judge for President,* 212.

32. Westerdahl, 212–13.

33. Westerdahl, 212–13; "Sulzer Gives Graft Clues," *New York Times,* January 22, 1914, 1–2.

34. Westerdahl, *Judge for President,* 214.

35. Wsterdahl, 214.

36. McNamara, "Here's Why William Sulzer Was the First."

37. *Proceedings of the Court for the Trial of Impeachments: The People of the State of New York by the Assembly Thereof Against William Sulzer, as Governor* (Albany, NY: J.B. Lyon, 1913), 1:46.

38. *Proceedings of the Court*, 46–55; Westerdahl, *Judge for President*, 215.

39. Westerdahl, 215.

40. Westerdahl, 215.

41. *Proceedings of the Court*, 3, 5–6.

42. Francis Bergan, *The History of the New York Court of Appeals, 1847–1932* (New York: Columbia University Press, 1985), 237.

43. Bergan, *New York Court of Appeals*, 237.

44. *Proceedings of the Court*, 18.

45. *Proceedings of the Court*, 114–15.

46. *Proceedings of the Court*, 131.

47. *Proceedings of the Court*, 18.

48. *Proceedings of the Court*, 26.

49. *Proceedings of the Court*, 28.

50. *Proceedings of the Court*, 44.

51. *Proceedings of the Court*, 45.

52. Bergan, *New York Court of Appeals*, 239.

53. Bergan, 239.

54. *Proceedings of the Court*, 176–77, 181.

55. Bergan, *New York Court of Appeals*, 241.

56. *Proceedings of the Court*, 235.

57. Bergan, *New York Court of Appeals*, 242.

58. *Proceedings of the Court*, 432.

59. *Proceedings of the Court*, 435–749, 1413, 1437.

60. *Proceedings of the Court*, 1449.

61. *Proceedings of the Court*, 1448–49.

62. *Proceedings of the Court*, 1686.

63. *Proceedings of the Court*, 1698.

64. *Proceedings of the Court*, 1700.

65. *Proceedings of the Court*, 1739.

66. *Proceedings of the Court*, 1742–43.

67. *Proceedings of the Court*, 1748.

68. *Proceedings of the Court*, 1748, 1759, 1762, 1765.

69. "Alton Brooks Parker," *Harper's Weekly*, accessed June 6, 2022, http://elections.harpweek.com/elections/1904 Biographies.

70. "Judge Parker in City Again: Former Presidential Candidate Argues Shawmut Railroad Case Before Justice Woodward Here," *Jamestown Evening Journal* (Jamestown, NY), July 18, 1918, "Case Ends Today," *Jamestown Evening Journal* (Jamestown, NY), July 19, 1918, Alton B. Parker scrapbook, Container 29, Alton B. Parker Papers, Manuscript Division, Library of Congress, Washington, DC.

71. *Smith v. Pacific Improvement Co.,* 104 Misc. 481 (N.Y. Sup. Ct. 1918).

72. Biographical notes, Container 16, Alton B. Parker Papers, Manuscript Division, Library of Congress, Washington, DC; "Cryptic Deals Laid to Gould," Alton B. Parker newspaper clipping, Container 32, Alton B. Parker Papers, Manuscript Division, Library of Congress, Washington, DC.

73. *Gould v. Gould,* 126 Misc. 54 (N.Y. Sup. Ct. 1925); "Ten Million Spent in Gould Legal Wars," *New York Times,* April 19, 1925, Alton B. Parker newspaper clipping, Container 33, Alton B. Parker Papers, Manuscript Division, Library of Congress, Washington, DC.

74. "Gould Case Enters Argument Stage," *New York Times,* March 21, 1925, Alton B. Parker newspaper clipping, Container 33, Alton B. Parker Papers, Manuscript Division, Library of Congress, Washington, DC.

75. "Jay Gould Trustees Lauded as Faithful," *New York Evening Post,* March 31, 1925, Alton B. Parker newspaper clipping, Container 33, Alton B. Parker Papers, Manuscript Division, Library of Congress, Washington, DC.

76. "Gould Heirs Liable for $50,000,000 Loss in Father's Estate," *New York Times,* November 12, 1925, 1.

77. *In re Gould,* 148 A. 731 (N.J. 1930).

78. Rogers, *American Bar Leaders,* 140; Container 2, Alton B. Parker Papers, Manuscript Division, Library of Congress, Washington, DC.

79. Alton B. Parker, "The Congestion of Law," *Report of the Twenty-Ninth Annual Meeting of the American Bar Association* (Philadelphia: Dando Printing & Publishing, 1906), 384.

80. Parker, "The Congestion of Law," 384, 387.

81. Parker, 383.

82. Parker, 394.

83. "The James Wilson Memorial," *The American Law Register* 55, no. 1 (1907): 26–27.

84. "Lawyers Won't Censure Roosevelt," *New York Times,* August 29, 1907, 6.

85. "Lawyers Won't Censure Roosevelt"; John Austin Matzko, "The Early Years of the American Bar Association, 1878–1928" (PhD diss., University of Virginia, 1984), 124–25.

86. Matzko, "The Early Years," 145.

87. Alton B. Parker, "President's Annual Address," *The Green Bag* 19, no. 10 (October 1907): 590.

88. Parker, "President's Annual Address," 592.

89. Dearstyne, *The Crucible of Public Policy,* 92.

90. Parker, "President's Annual Address," 582.

91. Susan D. Carle, "Lawyers' Duty to Do Justice: A New Look at the History of the 1908 Canons," *Law and Social Inquiry* 24, no. 1 (Winter 1999): 9.

92. Carle, "Lawyers' Duty to Do Justice," 31.

93. James M. Alterman "Considering the A.B.A.'s 1908 Canon of Ethics," *Fordham Law Review* 71, no. 6 (2003), 2395–96.

94. Edwin David Robertson, *Brethren and Sisters of the Bar: A Centennial History of the New York County Lawyers' Association* (New York: Fordham University Press, 2008), 3.

95. Robertson, *Brethren and Sisters*, 4, 9, 381.

96. Robertson, 9–10.

97. Robertson, 11, 13.

98. Robertson, 356, 358.

99. Robertson, 15.

100. Robertson, 26.

101. Robertson, 30–36.

102. "For Lawyers' Club, an Era Is Vanishing with Its Home," *New York Times*, December 20, 1979, B11.

103. William Allan Butler, *History of The Lawyers Club* (New York: Lawyers Club, 1921), 41–42, 44, 77, 79.

104. "Lawyers Praise Peckham," *New York Times*, December 19, 1909, 16; *Address of Alton B. Parker, Memorial Exercises of the Late Mr. Justice Peckham*, Container 13, Alton B. Parker Papers, Manuscript Division, Library of Commerce, Washington, DC.

105. Westerdahl, *Judge for President*, 206.

106. Dearstyne, *The Crucible of Public Policy*, 29–30.

107. Dearstyne, 30.

108. Dearstyne, 29–30; *Proceedings of the Thirty-Sixth Annual Meeting of the New York State Bar Association Held at Utica, January 24–25, 1913* (Albany, NY: The Argus Co., 1913), 223–24, 225, 226.

109. Dearstyne, *The Crucible of Public Policy*, 30; *Thirty-Sixth Annual Meeting*, 205.

110. Dearstyne, *The Crucible of Public Policy*, 30.

111. "A. B. Parker Chosen State Bar's Head," *New York Herald*, January 25, 1913, Alton B. Parker scrapbook, Container 28, Alton B. Parker Papers, Manuscript Division, Library of Congress, Washington, DC.

112. *Report of the Committee on Uniform Judicial Procedure to the American Bar Association* (1922), 383.

113. Mandelbaum, "Alton Brooks Parker," 302, see also, for example, *Fordham Law School Bulletin of Information, 1908–1909*.

114. "Parker Praises the Common Law," *New York Times*, July 12, 1907, 6; *Address of Hon. Alton B. Parker before the State Bar Association of North Carolina*, Container 13, Alton B. Parker Papers, Manuscript Division, Library of Congress, Washington, DC.

115. *Address by Alton B. Parker at Jamestown on Constitution Day*, Container 13, Alton B. Parker Papers, Manuscript Division, Library of Congress, Washington, DC.

116. *Address by Alton B. Parker at Jamestown on Constitution Day*.

117. *Address of Hon. Alton B. Parker before the Law Academy of Philadelphia*, Container 13, Alton B. Parker Papers, Manuscript Division, Library of Congress, Washington, DC.

118. *An Address Delivered at the University of Virginia on Washington's Birthday, An Address Delivered in the Armory of the 7th Regiment, N.G.N.Y., The Tariff—A Moral Issue, an Address Delivered at Princeton University*, Container 13, Alton B. Parker Papers, Manuscript Division, Library of Congress, Washington, DC.

119. *Address of Alton B. Parker before New Hampshire Bar Association*, 10, Container 13, Alton B. Parker Papers, Manuscript Division, Library of Congress, Washington, DC.

120. *Address of Alton B. Parker before New Hampshire Bar Association*, 18.

121. Alton B. Parker, *Annual Address before the South Carolina Bar Association delivered by Alton B. Parker on Thursday Evening, January 25, 1912 at Columbia* (n.p., 1912), 9.

122. Parker, *Annual Address*, 13.

123. Parker, *Annual Address*, 18.

124. Parker, *Annual Address*, 19.

125. Alton B. Parker, *Annual Address by Hon. Alton B. Parker before the Ohio State Bar Association, Ohio Law Bulletin* (July 28, 1913), 275.

126. Parker, *Annual Address*, 280.

127. Alton B. Parker, "The Citizen and the Constitution," *Yale Law Journal* 23, no. 8 (June 1914): 632.

128. Parker, "The Citizen and the Constitution," 632.

129. Parker, "The Citizen and the Constitution," 639.

130. Alton B. Parker, *The Foundations in Virginia: An Address Delivered at the College of William and Mary, Williamsburg, Virginia, on Wednesday, October 6, 1920* (n.p., 1920), 4.

131. Parker, *The Foundations in Virginia*, 8.

132. Parker, 8.

133. Parker, 9–13.

134. *Address of Alton B. Parker before the Vermont Bar Association, January 3, 1921*, 26, Container 14, Alton B. Parker Papers, Manuscript Division, Library of Congress, Washington, DC.

135. "School to Teach Constitution Open," *New York Times*, January 15, 1922, 16.

136. "School to Teach Constitution Open."

137. "Judge Parker on Future of Party," *Richmond Times Dispatch* (Richmond, VA), April 14, 1905, 1.

138. "Judge Parker on Future of Party," 1.

139. "Judge Parker on Future of Party," 8.

140. "Judge Parker on Future of Party," 8.

141. "Back to Jefferson," *New York Daily Tribune*, April 15, 1905, 4.

142. *Address of Hon. Alton B. Parker, Permanent Chairman, Democratic State Convention, 1908*, Container 13, Alton B. Parker Papers, Manuscript Division, Library of Congress, Washington, DC.

143. *Official Report of the Proceedings of the Democratic National Convention* (Chicago: Press of Western Newspaper Union, 1908), 77.

144. *Official Report of the Proceedings of the Democratic National Convention* (Chicago: Peterson Linotyping Co., 1912), 12; *Official Report of the Proceedings of the Democratic National Convention (1908)*, 30.

145. *Official Report of the Proceedings of the Democratic National Convention (1908)*, 33–35.

146. "Parker Sees Mack and Dodges a Boom," *New York Times*, September 4, 1908, 3.

147. William Jennings Bryan to Alton B. Parker, telegram, October 7, 1908, Container 3, Alton B. Parker Papers, Manuscript Division, Library of Congress, Washington, DC.

148. "Parker to Go on Stump," *New York Times*, July 15, 1908, 1; *Official Report of the Proceedings of the Democratic National Convention (1912)*, 11.

149. Alton B. Parker speeches, Container 13, Alton B. Parker Papers, Manuscript Division, Library of Congress, Washington, DC.

150. *Official Report of the Proceedings of the Democratic Conference Held in Saratoga Springs, September 9 and 10, 1909, Resulting in the Declaration of Principles and the Organization of the New York State Democratic League* (Auburn, NY: Citizen Printers, 1909), 3.

151. *Official Report Saratoga Springs*, 42.

152. *Official Report Saratoga Springs*, 6; "Judge Parker Sounds Keynote in Opening Address Today at the Democratic Conference," *The Daily Saratogian*, September 9, 1909, Alton B. Parker newspaper clipping, Container 32, Alton B. Parker Papers, Manuscript Division, Library of Congress, Washington, DC.

153. *Official Report Saratoga Springs*, 6, 8–9.

154. *Official Report Saratoga Springs*, 12.

155. *Official Report Saratoga Springs*, 71.

156. *Official Report Saratoga Springs*, 73.

157. "Refuse to Follow Democratic League," *New York Times*, October 31, 1911, 6.

158. *Address of Alton B. Parker as Temporary Chairman, Democratic State Convention, Rochester, New York, September 29, 1910*, 15, Container 13, Alton B. Parker Papers, Manuscript Division, Library of Congress, Washington, DC.

159. Westerdahl, *Judge for President*, 206.

160. Claude Moore Fuess, "Political Episode: Henry L. Stimson and the New York Campaign of 1910," *Proceedings of the Massachusetts Historical Society* 68 (1944): 400.

161. Fuess, "Political Episode," 399.

162. Fuess, "Political Episode," 401.

163. See, e.g., Thomas Spratt to Alton B. Parker, November 5, 1910 (thanking Parker for speaking in Ogdensburg, NY); C. E. Treman to Alton B. Parker, November 9, 1910 (thanking Parker for speaking in Ithaca, NY); O. U. Kellogg to Alton B. Parker, November 15, 1910 (thanking Parker for speaking in Cortland, NY), Container 3, Alton B. Parker Papers, Manuscript Division, Library of Congress, Washington, DC; see also "Parker Here for Tonight's Meeting," *The Watertown Times* (Watertown, NY), October 25, 1910; "Large Audience Hears Mr. Parker in Binghamton," *Buffalo Times,* October 20, 1910; "Parker Uses Scripture—Judge Speaks at Oswego," *New York Tribune,* October 27, 1910, Alton B. Parker scrapbook, Container 27, Alton B. Parker Papers, Manuscript Division, Library of Congress, Washington, DC; "John A. Dix Dissected Boss Roosevelt in New York; Alton B. Parker Discussed Leading Issues in Albany," *The Argus,* November 3, 1910, Alton B. Parker newspaper clipping, Container 32, Alton B. Parker Papers, Manuscript Division, Library of Congress, Washington, DC.

164. Fuess, "Political Episode," 402.

165. See, e.g., Thomas N. Dowd to Alton B. Parker, November 9, 1910 ("Why don't you ask [to be elected United States Senator]?"); Hal Bell to Alton B. Parker, November 9, 1910 ("I desire . . . to express the earnest hope that you will be selected as the party's nominee for United States Senator."); George W. Johnston to Alton B. Parker, November 9, 1910 ("If you would consent to serve the Party and the State as United States Senator, in spite of the sacrifices involved, it would be a patriotic act."); Elbridge L. Adams to Alton B. Parker, November 10, 1910 ("This morning's SUN says that you are too busy to accept an election to the Senate. Of course it would involve a considerable financial sacrifice, but it would be a fine thing for the State of New York, if you could be induced to make that sacrifice."). Container 3, Alton B. Parker Papers, Manuscript Division, Library of Congress, Washington, DC.

166. Undated newspaper clipping, Container 3, Alton B. Parker Papers, Manuscript Division, Library of Congress, Washington, DC; see also "Parker Would Decline," *New York Tribune,* November 10, 1910, Alton B. Parker scrapbook, Container 27, Alton B. Parker Papers, Manuscript Division, Library of Congress, Washington, DC.

167. Dearstyne, *The Crucible of Public Policy,* 70.

168. "Parker Defends Courts," *New York Tribune,* September 1, 1910, 2.

169. Parker, "In Memoriam David Bennett Hill," 23.

170. "Another Boom for Alton B. Parker Started," *The Buffalo Commercial* (Buffalo, NY), January 19, 1912, 1.

171. Westerdahl, *Judge for President,* 207.

172. Westerdahl, 207.

173. Westerdahl, 208.

174. "Bryan's Declaration of War," *New York Times,* June 25, 1912, 1.

175. Westerdahl, *Judge for President*, 208.
176. Westerdahl, 209.
177. Westerdahl, 209.
178. Kent, *The Democratic Party*, 394.
179. "Wilson Talks of Parker," *New York Times*, June 25, 1912, 2.
180. Kent, *The Democratic Party*, 395.
181. *Official Report of the Proceedings of the Democratic National Convention (1912)*, 3.
182. Westerdahl, *Judge for President*, 209.
183. *Official Report of the Proceedings of the Democratic National Convention (1912)*, 3.
184. Westerdahl, *Judge for President*, 209.
185. *Official Report of the Proceedings of the Democratic National Convention (1912)*, 5–7.
186. *Official Report of the Proceedings of the Democratic National Convention (1912)*, 9.
187. *Official Report of the Proceedings of the Democratic National Convention (1912)*, 10.
188. *Official Report of the Proceedings of the Democratic National Convention (1912)*, 17.
189. *Official Report of the Proceedings of the Democratic National Convention (1912)*, 19.
190. *Official Report of the Proceedings of the Democratic National Convention (1912)*, 21.
191. *Official Report of the Proceedings of the Democratic National Convention (1912)*, 23.
192. *Official Report of the Proceedings of the Democratic National Convention (1912)*, 27.
193. *Official Report of the Proceedings of the Democratic National Convention (1912)*, 28–29.
194. *Official Report of the Proceedings of the Democratic National Convention (1912)*, 198.
195. *Official Report of the Proceedings of the Democratic National Convention (1912)*, 197, 201, 204, 206, 210, 213–14, 216, 218.
196. *Official Report of the Proceedings of the Democratic National Convention (1912)*, 221.
197. *Official Report of the Proceedings of the Democratic National Convention (1912)*, 232–37.
198. *Official Report of the Proceedings of the Democratic National Convention (1912)*, 351.
199. *Official Report of the Proceedings of the Democratic National Convention (1912)*, 388.

200. *Official Report of the Proceedings of the Democratic National Convention (1912)*, 391.

201. *Official Report of the Proceedings of the Democratic National Convention (1912)*, 416.

202. "75 Injured at Marshall Rally," *New York Times*, August 21, 1912, 1; "Platform Sinks Carrying 450; Deaths Likely," *Indianapolis Star*, August 21, 1912, Alton B. Parker scrapbook, Container 28, Alton B. Parker Papers, Manuscript Division, Library of Congress, Washington, DC.

203. "75 Injured at Marshall Rally," *New York Times*, August 21, 1912, 1, 3; *Official Report of the Proceedings of the Democratic National Convention (1912)*, 416–22.

204. Stenographic report of the 1912 New York Democratic State Convention, 1–2, Container 13, Alton B. Parker Papers, Manuscript Division, Library of Congress, Washington, DC.

205. Stenographic report, 3.

206. Stenographic report, 3.

207. Schlup, "Alton B. Parker," 60.

208. In January 1916, before Wilson nominated Brandeis to replace Lamar, Parker publicly urged Wilson to "disregard party lines" and appoint William Howard Taft to the court. "Parker Urges Taft for Supreme Court," *New York World*, January 6, 1916, Alton B. Parker scrapbook, Container 29, Alton B. Parker Papers, Manuscript Division, Library of Congress, Washington, DC.

209. When nominating McReynolds, Wilson erroneously believed that McReynolds was a liberal, but during his time on the court he became "best remembered as a stalwart conservative and a foe of economic regulatory power by government." Over his twenty-six years on the court McReynolds was known for his open racism and anti-Semitism. James W. Ely Jr., "McReynolds, James C. (1862–1946)," in *Encyclopedia of American Civil Liberties,* ed. Paul Finkelman, vol. 1 (New York: Taylor & Francis, 2006), 992–93.

210. *American Bar Association Journal* 7, no. 9 (September 1921): 499; Biographical notes, Container 16, Alton B. Parker Papers, Manuscript Division, Library of Congress, Washington, DC.

211. Biographical notes.

212. "League to Enforce Peace Is Launched," *New York Times*, June 18, 1915, 4.

213. Westerdahl, *Judge for President*, 218.

214. "All Look to Wilson, Promising Support," *New York Times*, May 11, 1915, 4.

215. "World Court Urged for Lasting Peace," May 13, 1915, Alton B. Parker scrapbook, Container 28, Alton B. Parker Papers, Manuscript Division, Library of Congress, Washington, DC.

216. "World Court Urged for Lasting Peace."

217. *Official Program, Citizens' Preparedness Parade, New York City, May 13, 1916* (New York: Citizens Preparedness Parade,1916), 1, 3; "New York Ready for Big Parade," *New York Times,* May 13, 1916, 1, 4.

218. Westerdahl, *Judge for President,* 37.

219. *Official Program of the Citizens' Preparedness Parade,* 14.

220. Westerdahl, *Judge for President,* 37; Reminiscences of Bertha Parker Hall, 59, Container 16, Alton B. Parker Papers, Manuscript Division, Library of Congress, Washington, DC.

221. Westerdahl, *Judge for President,* 220.

222. Westerdahl, 220.

223. Westerdahl, 220; "Democrats Hold Old Time Rally in Associate Hall," *The Lowell Sun,* November 1, 1916; "Parker Lauds Wilson; Tells of His Burdens," *The Baltimore Sun,* November 3, 1916, Alton B. Parker scrapbook, Container 29, Alton B. Parker Papers, Manuscript Division, Library of Congress, Washington, DC.

224. "Mrs. Alton B. Parker," *New York Times,* April 3, 1917, 13.

225. Dearstyne, *The Crucible of Public Policy,* 90.

226. Alton B. Parker, "Roosevelt's Americanism," *The Journal of American History* 13, nos. 3 & 4 (1919): 315.

227. Parker, "Roosevelt's Americanism," 316.

228. Parker, 316.

229. Dearstyne, *The Crucible of Public Policy,* 93.

230. "Committee of 150 Appointed to Hunt Disloyalty in U.S.," *New-York Tribune,* March 11, 1920, 20.

231. "Committee of 150."

232. "Committee of 150."

233. Dearstyne, *The Crucible of Public Policy,* 93.

234. "Clergy Criticised by Alton B. Parker," *San Francisco Chronicle,* January 30, 1920, 3.

235. William A. Dalton to Alton B. Parker, October 26, 1920, Container 5, Alton B. Parker Papers, Manuscript Division, Library of Congress, Washington, DC.

236. James M. Cox to Alton B. Parker, November 8, 1920, Container 5, Alton B. Parker Papers, Manuscript Division, Library of Congress, Washington, DC.

237. "Alton B. Parker, 70, Takes Bride of 51," *New York Times,* January 17, 1923, 22; February 23, 1923 letter from Alton B. Parker to Mary Hall, February 23, 1923, Container 8, Alton B. Parker Papers, Manuscript Division, Library of Congress, Washington, DC.

238. "Alton B. Parker, 70, Takes Bride of 51."

239. "Alton B. Parker, 70, Takes Bride of 51."

240. Parker had an opportunity to visit England in 1919 while serving as chancellor of the Sulgrave Institution. While he was in the country, he unveiled a statue of Abraham Lincoln in the town of Manchester and visited Sulgrave Manor and presented the caretakers of the house with a replica of the famous portrait of

George Washington by Charles Willson Peale and a two-thousand dollar donation on behalf of the National Society of Colonial Dames of America. "Gift of Statue of Lincoln to Manchester," *Newcastle Chronicle,* September 16, 1919; "The Home of George Washington—American Gift to Sulgrave Manor," *Yorkshire Post,* September 15, 1919, Alton B. Parker scrapbook, Container 30, Alton B. Parker Papers, Manuscript Division, Library of Congress, Washington, DC.

241. Parker resigned as the chancellor of the Sulgrave Institution on September 14, 1922. In his letter of resignation to John A. Stewart, chairman of the Board of Governors, Parker explained that he was resigning because Stewart was asking the American members of the Sulgrave Institution to help defray the costs of a recent trip incurred by English members of the Institution and because Stewart had sent out an appeal for funds, under Parker's name, without first obtaining Parker's consent. Alton B. Parker to John A. Stewart, September 14, 1922, Container 7, Alton B. Parker Papers, Manuscript Division, Library of Congress, Washington, DC.

242. Biographical notes, Container 16, Alton B. Parker Papers, Manuscript Division, Library of Congress, Washington, DC.

243. "Alton B. Parker Weds Following Brief Romance," undated newspaper clipping, Container 32, Alton B. Parker Papers, Manuscript Division, Library of Congress, Washington, DC.

244. Biographical notes; "Alton B. Parker Weds Following Brief Romance."

245. "Judge Parker's Wife Revealed as Republican," *San Francisco Examiner,* July 12, 1924, 2.

246. "Alton B. Parker, 70, Takes Bride of 51."

247. November 23, 1923, *New York Times* article; December 2, 1923, *New York Herald* article, Alton B. Parker to Burton K. Wheeler, November 23, 1923, Container 8, Alton B. Parker Papers, Manuscript Division, Library of Congress, Washington, DC.

248. Robert Dallek, *Franklin D. Roosevelt and American Foreign Policy, 1932-1945* (New York: Oxford University Press, 1979), 78–81.

249. *Church and College Denounce Pacifist Pledge* (New York: National Civic Federation, 1924), 3–4.

250. *Church and College,* 5–6.

251. *Church and College,* 4, 8, 10, 12, 33–34, 36–37, 47–51.

252. *Church and College,* 54.

253. *Church and College,* 54.

254. Biographical notes, Container 16, Alton B. Parker Papers, Manuscript Division, Library of Congress, Washington, DC.

255. Biographical notes.

256. Parker, "Alton Brooks Parker," 54.

257. Parker, "Alton Brooks Parker," 55; Henry Alan Johnston to Alton B. Parker, June 8, 1923, Container 8, Alton B. Parker Papers, Manuscript Division, Library of Congress, Washington, DC.

308 | Notes to Chapter 14

258. Parker, "Alton Brooks Parker," 55; November 19, 1918, letter from the Sulgrave Institution, Charles D. Orth to Alton B. Parker, September 10, 1920, F. Cunliffe-Owen to Alton B. Parker, October 14, 1920, Ralph W. Wescott to Alton B. Parker, March 23, 1921, Containers 4 and 5, Alton B. Parker Papers, Manuscript Division, Library of Congress, Washington, DC.

259. Schlup, "Alton B. Parker," 59; Arthur J. Brown to Alton B. Parker, December 8, 1920, A. Fitz Roy Anderson to Alton B. Parker, August 17, 1992, February 4, 1922, Stanley H. Howe to Alton B. Parker, February 4, 1922, Linley V. Gordon to Alton B. Parker, April 24, 1924, Containers 5, 6 and 9, Alton B. Parker Papers, Manuscript Division, Library of Congress, Washington, DC.

260. William Draper Lewis to Alton B. Parker, June 16, 1923, Container 8, Alton B. Parker Papers, Manuscript Division, Library of Congress, Washington, DC.

Chapter 14

1. Medical records of Alton B. Parker, Container 20, Alton B. Parker Papers, Manuscript Division, Library of Congress, Washington, DC.

2. Medical records.

3. Medical records; Westerdahl, *Judge for President*, 221.

4. Westerdahl, 221.

5. "Judge Parker Dies in His Auto in Park," *New York Times*, May 11, 1926, 1.

6. "Some Who Drop the Mantle of Leadership," *American Monthly Review of Reviews*, June, 1926, 648.

7. Parker, "Alton Brooks Parker," 41.

8. Morgan J. O'Brien, "Alton Brooks Parker," *ABA Journal* 12, no. 7 (July 1926), 454.

9. "Tributes Paid by Coolidge, Gov. Smith," *San Francisco Chronicle*, May 11, 1926, Alton B. Parker newspaper clipping, Container 34, Alton B. Parker Papers, Manuscript Division, Library of Congress, Washington, DC.

10. "Judge Parker Dies in His Auto in Park," *New York Times*, May 11, 1926, 1.

11. O'Brien, "Alton Brooks Parker," 454–55.

12. Parker, "Alton Brooks Parker," 56.

13. Parker, "Alton Brooks Parker," 56.

14. "Alton B. Parker Buried Yesterday," *New York American*, May 13, 1926, Container 30, Alton B. Parker Papers, Manuscript Division, Library of Congress, Washington, DC; "City Pays Tribute to Judge Parker," *Kingston Daily Freeman*, May 13, 1926, Alton B. Parker newspaper clipping, Container 33, Alton B. Parker Papers, Manuscript Division, Library of Congress, Washington, DC.

15. "City Pays Tribute to Judge Parker."

16. Genealogical notes, Container 16, Alton B. Parker Papers, Manuscript Division, Library of Congress, Washington, DC; "Alton B. Parker Memorial Will

be Built at Kingston," *Knickerbocker Press,* November 12, 1927, Alton B. Parker scrapbook, Container 30, Alton B. Parker Papers, Manuscript Division, Library of Congress, Washington, DC.

17. "Alton B. Parker Memorial Will be Built at Kingston."
18. Death Notice of Amelia Day Campbell Parker, *Kingston Daily Freeman* (Kingston, NY), August 22, 1960, 2.
19. Death Notice of Amelia Day Campbell Parker; Biographical notes, Container 16, Alton B. Parker Papers, Manuscript Division, Library of Congress, Washington, DC.
20. Biographical notes.
21. Death Notice of Amelia Day Campbell Parker.
22. Death Notice of Amelia Day Campbell Parker.

Chapter 15

1. *The World's Work,* August 1904, 5203.
2. Stone, *They Also Ran,* 115–16.
3. Stone, 116.
4. Southwick, *Presidential Also-Rans and Running Mates,* 444–45.
5. Southwick, "A Judge Runs for President," 50; Hampton Sides, "Ones Who Got Away," *New York Times Magazine,* July 19, 1998, 13; Jack Elliott Jr., "Among Also-Rans: Clay Hot, Perot Not," *Jackson Clarion-Ledger,* August 10, 1998, 3B.
6. Southwick, "A Judge Runs for President," 47, 50.
7. Peter R. Perry, "Theodore Roosevelt and the Labor Movement" (master's thesis, California State University, Hayward, 1991), 56–57.
8. Perry, "Theodore Roosevelt and the Labor Movement," 58, 60–61.
9. Perry, 61, 71.
10. Abigail Tucker, "The Financial Panic of 1907: Running from History," Smithsonian Magazine, accessed February 5, 2023, http://www.smithsonianmag.com.
11. Tucker, "The Financial Panic of 1907." Morgan chartered a series of working groups to gather the facts surrounding the financial crisis and then deployed the information they gathered to organize successive rescues of the major banking and financial institutions. Tucker, "The Financial Panic of 1907."
12. "Parker Names Underwriters of Col. Roosevelt's Campaign as Revealed by Dan Lamont," *New York World,* January 13, 1924, 1.
13. Shoemaker, "Alton B. Parker: The Images of a Gilded Age Statesman," 5.

Bibliography

Manuscript Collections

Parker, Alton B. Papers, Manuscript Division, Library of Congress, Washington, DC.

Books and Book Chapters

Allen, Oliver E. *The Tiger: The Rise and Fall of Tammany Hall.* Reading, MA: Addison-Wesley, 1993.
Banks, Louis Albert, ed. *Capital Stories About Famous Americans.* New York: Christian Herald, 1905.
Bass, Herbert J. *"I Am a Democrat": The Political Career of David Bennett Hill.* Syracuse, NY: Syracuse University Press, 1961.
Bishop, Joseph B., ed. *Theodore Roosevelt & His Time Shown in His Own Letters.* New York: Charles Scribner's Sons, 1920.
Bergan, Francis. *The History of the New York Court of Appeals, 1847–1932.* New York: Columbia University Press, 1985.
Bryan, William Jennings. *The Speeches of William Jennings Bryan, Volume II.* New York: Funk & Wagnalls, 1909.
Bryan, William Jennings, and Mary Baird Bryan. *The Memoirs of William Jennings Bryan.* Chicago: John C. Winston, 1925.
Butler, William Allen. *History of the Lawyers Club.* New York: Lawyers Club, 1921.
Campaign Text Book of the Democratic Party of the United States. Chicago: National Democratic Committee, 1896.
Campaign Text Book of the Democratic Party of the United States. New York: Metropolitan Printing Co., 1904.
Church and College Denounce Pacifist Pledge. New York: National Civic Federation, 1924.
Clark, Champ. *My Quarter Century of American Politics.* New York: Harper & Bros., 1920.

Cooper, John Milton, Jr. "The Best . . . and Worst of Times 1897–1920." In *Of the People . . . The 200 Year History of the Democratic Party,* edited by Ronald H. Brown. Los Angeles: General Publishing Group, 1992.

———. "The Election of 1900." In *Running for President: The Candidates and Their Images 1900–1992,* edited by Arthur M. Schlesinger. New York: Simon & Schuster, 1994.

———. "The Election of 1904." In *Running for President: The Candidates and Their Images 1900–1992,* edited by Arthur M. Schlesinger. New York: Simon & Schuster, 1994.

Crew, Danny O. *Presidential Sheet Music: An Illustrated Catalogue of Published Music Associated with the American Presidency and Those Who Sought the Office.* Jefferson, NC: McFarland, 2001.

Dallek, Robert. *Franklin D. Roosevelt and American Foreign Policy 1932–1945.* New York: Oxford University Press, 1979.

Dearstyne, Bruce W. *The Crucible of Public Policy: New York Courts in the Progressive Era.* Albany, NY: State University of New York Press, 2022.

Eicher, John H., and David J. Eicher. *Civil War High Commands.* Palo Alto, CA: Stanford University Press, 2001.

Ellis, Edward S. *The Great Leaders and National Issues of 1896.* Philadelphia: Monarch Publishing Co., 1896.

Ely, James W., Jr. "McReynolds, James C. (1862–1946)." In *Encyclopedia of American Civil Liberties,* edited by Paul Finkelman. Vol. 1. New York: Taylor & Francis, 2006.

Ernst, Daniel R. *Lawyers Against Labor: From Individual Rights to Corporate Liberalism.* Urbana: University of Illinois Press, 1995.

Gerard, James W. *My First Eighty-Three Years in America.* Garden City, NJ: Doubleday, 1951.

Ginger, Ray. *The Age of Excess: the United States from 1877–1914.* New York: Macmillan, 1965.

Golway, Terry. *Machine Made: Tammany Hall and the Creation of Modern American Politics.* New York: Liveright Publishing, 2014.

Gould, William B., IV. *A Primer on American Labor Law.* 4th ed. Cambridge, MA: MIT Press, 2004.

Gould, Lewis L. *The Presidency of Theodore Roosevelt.* Lawrence: University of Kansas Press, 1991.

———. *Reform and Regulation: American Politics, 1900–1916.* New York: Wiley, 1978.

Grady, John R. *The Lives and Public Services of Parker and Davis.* Philadelphia: National Publishing, 1904.

Hake, Theodore L. *Encyclopedia of Political Buttons: United States 1896–1972.* York, PA: Hake's Americana & Collectibles, 1985.

Kazin, Michael. *A Godly Hero: The Life of William Jennings Bryan.* New York: Anchor Books, 2006.

Kent, Frank R. *The Democratic Party: A History.* New York: Century Co., 1928.

Klyne Esopus Museum. *Alton B. Parker of Esopus.* New York: Klyne Esopus Museum, 2004.

Koenig, Louis W. *Bryan: A Political Biography of William Jennings Bryan.* New York: Putnam, 1971.

Krock, Arthur, ed. *The Editorials of Henry Watterson.* New York: George H. Doran, 1923.

Leish, Kenneth W., ed. *The American Heritage Book of the Presidents and Famous Americans.* Vol. 8. New York: Dell Publishing, 1967.

Letter of Judge Alton B. Parker of New York, Accepting the Democratic Nomination for President of the United States. New York: Literary Dept. of the Democratic National Committee, 1904.

Mahnken, Norbert H. "Bryan Country." In *William Jennings Bryan: A Profile,* edited by Paul W. Glad. New York: Hill and Wang, 1967.

McGerr, Michael. "The Guilded Age: 1873–1896." In *Of the People . . . The 200 Year History of the Democratic Party,* edited by Ronald H. Brown. Los Angeles: General Publishing Group, 1992.

McGuire, James K., ed. *The Democratic Party of the State of New York, Vol. II.* New York: United States History Company, 1905.

McKee, Thomas H. *The National Conventions and Platforms of All Political Parties, 1789 to 1905.* Baltimore, MD: Friedenwald, 1906.

Miller, Nathan. *Theodore Roosevelt: A Life.* New York: William Morrow, 1992.

Morris, Charles, and Edward S. Ellis. *Men and Issues of 1904.* Philadelphia: J.C. Winston, 1904.

Morris, Edmund. *Theodore Rex.* New York: Random House, 2001.

Murlin, Edgar L. *The Red Book: An Illustrated Legislative Manual of the State.* Albany, NY: James R. Lyon, 1895.

Nasaw, David. *The Chief: The Life of William Randolph Hearst.* Boston: Houghton Mifflin, 2000.

Nevins, Allan, ed. *Letters of Grover Cleveland, 1850–1908.* Boston: Houghton Mifflin, 1933.

Official Report of the Proceedings of the Democratic Conference Held in Saratoga Springs, September 9 and 10, 1909, Resulting in the Declaration of Principles and the Organization of the New York State Democratic League. Auburn, NY: Citizen Printers, 1909.

Official Report of the Proceedings of the Democratic National Convention. N.p.: Democratic National Committee, 1896.

Official Report of the Proceedings of the Democratic National Convention. N.p.: Democratic National Committee, 1900.

Official Report of the Proceedings of the Democratic National Convention. N.p.: Democratic National Committee, 1904.

Official Report of the Proceedings of the Democratic National Convention. Chicago: Press of Western Newspaper Union, 1908.

Official Report of the Proceedings of the Democratic National Convention. Chicago: Peterson Linotyping Co., 1912.

Parker, Alton B. *Address by Alton B. Parker, In Memoriam David Bennett Hill.* N.p.: Wentworth Press, 2019.

Pepper, Charles M. *The Life and Times of Henry Gassaway Davis.* New York: The Century Co., 1920.

Proceedings of the Court for the Trial of Impeachments: The People of the State of New York by the Assembly Thereof Against William Sulzer, as Governor. Albany, NY: J.B. Lyon, 1913.

Proceedings of the Thirty-Sixth Annual Meeting of the New York State Bar Association Held at Utica, January 24–25, 1913. Albany, NY: The Argus Co., 1913.

Report of the Committee on Uniform Judicial Procedure to the American Bar Association, American Bar Association, 1922.

Republican Campaign Text Book. N.p.: Republican National Committee, 1904.

Ritchie, Donald A. "The Election of 1896." In *Running for President: The Candidates and Their Images 1789–1896,* edited by Arthur M. Schlesinger. New York: Simon & Schuster, 1994.

Robertson, Edwin David. *Brethren and Sisters of the Bar: A Centennial History of the New York County Lawyers' Association.* New York: Fordham University Press, 2008.

Rogers, James Grafton. *American Bar Leaders: Biographies of the Presidents of the American Bar Association 1878–1928.* Chicago: American Bar Association, 1932.

Rosenblatt, Albert M., ed. *The Judges of the New York Court of Appeals: A Biographical History.* New York: Fordham University Press, 2007.

Ross, Thomas R. *Henry Gassaway Davis: An Old-Fashioned Biography.* Elkins, WV: T.R. Ross, 1994.

Ruddy, Daniel. *Theodore Roosevelt's History of the United States: His Own Words.* New York: Smithsonian Books/HarperCollins, 2010.

Sabato, Larry J., and Howard R. Ernst. *Encyclopedia of American Political Parties and Elections.* New York: Checkmark Books, 2007.

Seitz, Don C. *Joseph Pulitzer: His Life & Letters.* New York: Simon & Schuster, 1924.

Smith, C. Carter. *A Sourcebook on the U.S. Presidency: Presidents of a Growing Country.* Brookfield, CT: Millbrook Press, 1993.

Smith, Ray B., ed. *History of the State of New York, Political and Governmental.* Vol. 4. Syracuse, NY: The Syracuse Press, 1922.

Smyth, Clifford. *Builders of America: Theodore Roosevelt.* New York: Funk & Wagnalls, 1931.

Southwick, Leslie H. *Presidential Also-Rans and Running Mates, 1788 through 1996.* Jefferson, NC: McFarland & Company, 1998.
Stone, Irving. *They Also Ran.* New York: Doubleday, 1966.
Swanberg, W. A. *Citizen Hearst.* New York: Bantam Books, 1961.
Thayer, George. *Who Shakes the Money Tree? American Campaign Financing Practices from 1789 to the Present.* New York: Simon and Schuster, 1973.
Troy, Gil. *See How They Ran: The Changing Role of the Presidential Candidate.* New York: Maxwell Macmillan International, 1991.
Villard, Oswald Garrison. *Fighting Years: Memoirs of a Liberal Editor.* New York: Harcourt, Brace, 1939.
Welch, Richard F. *King of the Bowery.* Albany, NY: State University of New York Press, 2008.
Westerdahl, Norman N. *Judge for President; Alton Parker and His Times.* Peoria, IL: Jonsson Jo Books, 1976.

Articles and Periodicals

"75 Injured at Marshall Rally." *New York Times,* August 21, 1912.
"A Man at Last." *Boston Evening Transcript,* July 12, 1904.
"A Short Range Picture of Parker, the Man." *New York Times,* July 11, 1904.
"All for Parker." *Rockland County Times* (Nanuet, NY), April 23, 1904.
"All Look to Wilson, Promising Support." *New York Times,* May 11, 1915.
"Alton B. Parker, 70, Takes Bride of 51." *New York Times,* January 17, 1923.
"Alton B. Parker: A Character Sketch." *American Monthly Review of Reviews,* August 1904.
"Alton B. Parker to Go On Stump." *Chicago Tribune,* September 24, 1904.
"Alton B. Parker." *Oklahoma Law Journal* 3, no. 1 (July 1904): 27–28.
"Alton Parker." *Evansville Courier* (Evansville, IN). September 27, 1904.
Alterman, James M. "Considering the A.B.A.'s 1908 Canon of Ethics." *Fordham Law Review* 71, no. 6 (2003): 2395–2508.
"American Politics." *The Forum,* January 1905.
"Another Boom for Alton B. Parker Started." *Buffalo Commercial* (Buffalo, NY), January 19, 1912.
"Approval of Parker's Stand." *New York Times,* July 11, 1904.
"Are They Both Democrats?," *The Outlook,* July 30, 1904.
"Back to Jefferson." *New York Daily Tribune,* April 15, 1905.
Baker, Ray Stannard. "Parker and Roosevelt on Labor: Real Views of the Two Candidates on the Most Vital National Problem." *McClure Magazine,* November 1904.
"Bright Augury for Parker." *New York Times,* April 5, 1904.
"Bryan's Declaration of War." *New York Times,* June 25, 1912.

"The Call to Judge Parker." *New York Evening Sun,* August 2, 1901.
"Career of Mr. McClellan." *New York Times,* October 2, 1903.
Carle, Susan D. "Lawyers' Duty to Do Justice: A New Look at the History of the 1908 Canons." *Law and Social Inquiry* 24, no. 1 (Winter 1999): 1–44.
Cleveland, Grover. "Parker." *McClure's Magazine,* November 1904.
———. "Steady, Democrats, Steady!" *Collier's,* July 23, 1904.
"Choice of a Leader." *Buffalo Enquirer* (Buffalo, NY), November 20, 1903.
"Clergy Criticized by Alton B. Parker." *San Francisco Chronicle,* January 30, 1920.
"Cleveland at Newark Lashes the Trusts." *New York Times,* November 5, 1904.
"Cockran Tells How Situation Changed." *New York Times,* July 12, 1904.
Collier's St. Louis Convention Extra. July 12, 1904.
"Comment on Judge Parker's Speech of Acceptance." *The Nation,* August 18, 1904.
"Comment." *Harper's Weekly,* August 1904.
"Committee of 150 Appointed to Hunt Disloyalty in U.S." *New York Tribune,* March 11, 1920.
American Monthly Review of Reviews, November 1904.
"Connecticut Turns Out to Meet Parker." *New York Times,* November 4, 1904.
"Convention Organized After Wild Scramble." *New York Times,* April 19, 1904.
"Cornell Loses a Legacy." *New York Times,* May 20, 1890.
Creelman, James. "Alton B. Parker: A Character Sketch." *American Monthly Review of Reviews,* August 1904.
Cunniff, M. G. "Alton Brooks Parker." *The World's Work,* June 1904.
Davis, Hartley. "Our Next President." *Munsey's Magazine,* October 1903.
"The Democratic Campaign to Date." *Boston Evening Transcript,* August 27, 1904.
"The Democratic Convention." *The Outlook,* July 16, 1904.
"The Democratic Convention." *The Outlook,* June 25, 1904.
"Democratic Indications." *The Outlook,* May 21, 1904.
"The Democratic Ticket—Parker and Davis." *Public Opinion,* July 1904.
"Democrats Fail to Concentrate." *The Outlook,* June 18, 1904.
Doss, Richard B. "Democrats in the Doldrums: Virginia and the Democratic National Convention of 1904." *The Journal of Southern History* 20, no. 4 (November 1954): 511–29.
———., ed. "Inside the Democratic National Convention of 1904." *The Virginia Magazine of History & Biography* 64, no. 3 (July 1956): 291–323.
Dunne, Finley Peter. "Mr. Dooley on the Duties of a Vice President." *Jackson Evening News* (Jackson, MS), July 23, 1904.
———. "Mr. Dooley's Last Words to Voters." *Jackson Evening News* (Jackson, MS), November 5, 1904.
Elliott, Jack, Jr. "Among Also-Rans: Clay Hot, Perot Not." *Jackson Clarion-Ledger* (Jackson, MS), August 10, 1998.
"The Fall of Parker." *Chicago Tribune,* November 4, 1904.

"For Lawyers' Club, an Era Is Vanishing with Its Home." *New York Times*, December 20, 1979.

"Former Senator Cockrell Is Dead," *Washington, D.C. Evening Star*. December 13, 1915.

"Fourteenth Amendment: Judge Alton B. Parker Addresses Georgia Lawyers," *The Times Dispatch* (Richmond, VA), July 4, 1903.

Fuess, Claude Moore. "Political Episode: Henry L. Stimson and the New York Campaign of 1910." *Proceedings of the Massachusetts Historical Society* 68 (1944): 392–406.

Hailes, Charles J. "Alton Brooks Parker: Pen Portrait of the Distinguished Jurist Who Is Likely to Be Called to Lead His Party in the Presidential Contest of 1904." *Albany Law Journal* 66, no. 5 (May 1904):136–40.

"George McClellan Is Stricken at 75." *New York Times*, December 1, 1940.

"George Raines for Chairman." *New York Times*, April 10, 1904.

"Gould Heirs Liable for $50,000,000 Loss in Father's Estate." *New York Times*, November 12, 1925.

Harper, Fred, Alex Troy, Henry V. Borst, William M. Chadbourne, Alton B. Parker, Alfred H. Bright, letters from Bar Association Members, *American Bar Association Journal* 7, no. 9 (September 1921): 499.

"Henry G. Davis, Democratic Candidate for Vice-President." *American Monthly Review of Reviews*, August 1904.

"His Certificate of Virtue." *New York Times*, November 7, 1904.

"His Last Day as Governor." *New York Times*, January 6, 1885.

"Hon. David B. Hill to Speak Here." *Evansville Courier* (Evansville, IN), September 27, 1904.

"In the Mirror of the Present: The Trusts and Judge Parker." *The Arena*, September 1904.

Irwin, Douglas A. "Higher Tariffs, Lower Revenues? Analyzing the Fiscal Aspects of 'The Great Tariff Debate of 1888.'" *The Journal of Economic History* 58, no. 1 (March 1998): 59–72.

"The James Wilson Memorial." *The American Law Register* 55, no. 1 (1907): 26–27.

"Judge Alton B. Parker's Life Story Told by Photographs—His Birthplace and Present Home." *St. Louis Post-Dispatch Sunday Magazine*, April 24, 1904.

"Judge Parker and the Presidency." *Brooklyn Daily Eagle*, February 15, 1903.

"Judge Parker Dies in His Auto in Park." *New York Times*, May 11, 1926.

"Judge Parker Makes a Speech." *Chicago Tribune*, July 10, 1904.

"Judge Parker on Future of Party." *Richmond Times Dispatch*, April 14, 1905.

"Judge Parker Speaks." *New York Times*, July 4, 1903.

"Judge Parker, the Man, at His Esopus Residence." *Los Angeles Herald*, July 17, 1904.

"Judge Parker's Acceptance." *The Outlook*, August 20, 1904.

"Judge Parker's Wife Revealed as Republican." *San Francisco Examiner*, July 12, 1924.

"Lawyers Praise Peckham." *New York Times,* December 19, 1909.
"Lawyers Won't Censure Roosevelt." *New York Times,* August 29, 1907.
"Leaders at National Headquarters." *Chicago Record-Herald,* September 11, 1904.
"League to Enforce Peace Is Launched." *New York Times,* June 18, 1915.
Life, November 24, 1904.
"Managers Hope Parker's Speeches May Put Ginger Into Campaign." *New York Daily Tribune,* October 5, 1904.
"Many Senators Selected." *New York Times,* January 20, 1897.
"The March of Events," *The World's Work.* August 1904.
"The March of Events," *The World's Work.* May 1904.
McNamara, Joseph. "Here's Why William Sulzer Was the First—and Still Only—NY Governor to Be Impeached." *New York Daily News,* August 14, 2017.
"Mike Cunniff Dead." *Graham Guardian* (Graham, AZ), December 25, 1914.
"Mr. Bryan's Position." *The Outlook,* July 23, 1904.
"Mrs. Alton B. Parker." *New York Times,* April 3, 1917.
"Murphy Fighting for His Political Life." *New York Times,* April 19, 1904.
"New York Democratic Convention Instructs Delegates for Parker." *Los Angeles Herald,* April 19, 1904.
"New York Has Spoken." *Rockland County Times* (Nanuet, NY), April 23, 1904.
"New York Platform Drops Radicalism." *New York Times,* April 19, 1904.
"New York Ready for Big Parade." *New York Times,* May 13, 1916.
"No Boom for Esopus." *New York Times,* October 9, 1904.
O'Brien, Morgan J. "Alton Brooks Parker." *ABA Journal* 12, no. 7 (July 1926): 453–55.
"Olney, Richard." *Encyclopedia Britannica,* 11th ed. (1910), s.vv.
"Other Democratic Conventions." *The Outlook,* June 11, 1904.
Parker, Alton B. "Educated Men in Politics." *Success,* September 1904.
———. "President's Annual Address." *The Green Bag* 19, no. 10 (October 1907): 581–93.
———. "Roosevelt's Americanism." *The Journal of American History* 13, nos. 3–4 (1919): 314–16.
———. "The Citizen and the Constitution." *Yale Law Journal* 23, no. 8 (June 1914): 631–40.
———. "The Congestion of Law." *Report of the Twenty-Ninth Annual Meeting of the American Bar Association.* Philadelphia: Dando Printing & Publishing, 1906.
———. "The Lawyer in Public Affairs." *The Green Bag* 17, no. 6 (June 1905): 338–44.
Parker, Amelia Campbell. "Alton Brooks Parker." *Proceedings of the Ulster County Historical Society, 1934–1935.* Kingston, NY: Ulster County Historical Society, 1935.
"Parker and Hill Split on Platform." *New York Times,* April 10, 1904.
"Parker Boomed by Guggenheimer." *New York World,* March 16, 1903.
"Parker Defends Courts." *New York Tribune,* September 1, 1910.

"Parker Men Win First Skirmish of the Day." *New York Times*, April 19, 1904.
"Parker Names Underwriters of Col. Roosevelt's Campaign as Revealed by Dan Lamont." *New York World*, January 13, 1924.
"Parker on Standing Pat." *New York Times*, November 4, 1904.
"Parker Praises the Common Law." *New York Times*, July 12, 1907.
"Parker Sees Mack and Dodges a Boom." *New York Times*, September 4, 1908.
"Parker Taken to Task by an Indignant Woman." *New York Times*, July 27, 1904.
"Parker the Silent." *Boston Evening Transcript*, October 12, 1904.
"Parker to Go on Stump." *New York Times*, July 15, 1908.
"Parker to Roosevelt." *New York Times*, November 9, 1904.
"Parker Urges Party to Work for Future." *New York Times*, November 10, 1904.
"Parker, the Orator, Cheered by Throngs." *New York Times*, November 3, 1904.
"Parker's Views Set Forth by Danforth." *New York Times*, May 6, 1904.
"Pen Portrait of a Possible President." *New York Times*, April 3, 1904.
"Personal Triumph for Roosevelt." *Boston Evening Transcript*, November 9, 1904.
"Pointing to Parker." *Houston Post*, December 20, 1903.
"The Progress of the World." *American Monthly Review of Reviews*, December 1904.
"The Progress of the World." *American Monthly Review of Reviews*, February 1904.
"The Progress of the World." *American Monthly Review of Reviews*, January 1904.
"The Progress of the World." *American Monthly Review of Reviews*, July 1904.
"The Progress of the World." *American Monthly Review of Reviews*, June 1904.
"The Progress of the World." *American Monthly Review of Reviews*, November 1904.
"The Progress of the World." *American Monthly Review of Reviews*, October 1904.
"The Progress of the World." *American Monthly Review of Reviews*, September 1904.
Puck, May 25, 1904.
Puck, May 4, 1904.
Puck, October 19, 1904.
"Refuse to Follow Democratic League." *New York Times*, October 31, 1911.
"Richard Olney Dies." *New York Times*, April 10, 1917.
"Roosevelt Brands Parker Charges False." *Galena Daily Gazette* (Galena, IL), November 5, 1904.
"Say Hill Yielded to Parker." *New York Times*, April 11, 1904.
Schlup, Leonard, "Alton B. Parker and the Presidential Campaign of 1904." *North Dakota Quarterly* 49, no. 1 (Winter 1981): 48–60.
"School to Teach Constitution Open." *New York Times*, January 15, 1922.
"Sheehan for Head of Executive Committee." *New York Times*, August 4, 1904.
Sides, Hampton. "Ones Who Got Away." *New York Times Magazine*, July 19, 1998.
"Simply a Sharp Political Trick." *Boston Evening Transcript*, July 12, 1904.
"Some Who Drop the Mantle of Leadership." *American Monthly Review of Reviews*, June 1926.
Southwick, Leslie. "A Judge Runs for President: Alton Parker's Road to Oblivion." *Green Bag 2d* 5 (Autumn 2001): 37–50.

"Sulzer Gives Graft Clues." *New York Times*, January 22, 1914.
Sykes, M'Cready. "Alton B. Parker, Chief Judge of the New York Court of Appeals." *Green Bag* 16, no. 3 (March 1904): 145–52.
"Taggart Will Head National Committee." *New York Times*, July 23, 1904.
"Tammany Struggles in Vain." *New York Times*, April 19, 1904.
"Tammany Will Taboo Hearst for Congress." *New York Times*, August 1, 1904.
"What the Public Remembered." *American Monthly Review of Reviews*, December 1904.
"Why Parker Decided to Send His Message." *New York Times*, July 12, 1904.
"Wilson Talks of Parker." *New York Times*, June 25, 1912.
"Woman Whipped Chief Justice Parker." *New York Daily Tribune*, April 3, 1904.
The Yale Alumni Weekly 29, no. 31 (April 23, 1920): 721.
van Slyke, J. G. "Judge Parker's Personality: A Neighbor's Appreciation." *The Outlook*, July 16, 1904.

Court Opinions

Bohmer v. Haffen, 161 N.Y.2d 390 (1900).
Cohen v. Berlin Jones Envelope Co., 166 N.Y. 292 (1901).
Dr. Miles Medical Co. v. John D. Park & Sons, 220 U.S. 373 (1911).
Gompers v. Bucks Stove & Range Company, 221 U.S. 418 (1911).
Gompers v. United States, 233 U.S. 604 (1914).
Gould v. Gould, 126 Misc. 54 (N.Y. Sup. Ct. 1925).
Hamer v. Sidway, 124 N.Y. 538 (1891).
In re Gould, 148 A. 731 (N.J. 1930).
John D. Park & Sons Co. v. The National Wholesale Druggists Assoc., 175 N.Y. 1 (1903).
Lawlor v. Loewe, 235 U.S. 522 (1915).
Lochner v. New York, 198 U.S. 45 (1905).
Loewe v. Lawlor, 208 U.S. 274 (1908).
Matter of Hearst v. Woelper, 183 N.Y. 274 (N.Y. 1905).
Matter of Metz v. Maddox, 82 N.E. 507 (N.Y. 1907).
National Protective Association of Steam-Fitters and Helpers v. Cumming, 170 N.Y. 315 (1902).
People v. Lochner, 177 N.Y. 145 (1904).
People v. Orange County Road Construction Co., 175 N.Y. 84 (1903).
People v. Patrick, 182 N.Y. 131 (1905).
People ex rel. Rodgers v. Coler, 166 N.Y. 1 (1901).
Pollack v. Farmers' Loan & Trust Co., 157 U.S. 429 (1895).
Pollack v. Farmers' Loan & Trust Co., 158 U.S. 601 (1895).
Roberson v. Rochester Folding Box Co., 64 A.D. 30 (N.Y. App. Div. 1901).
Roberson v. Rochester Folding Box Co., 171 N.Y. 538 (1902).

Ryan v. City of New York, 177 N.Y. 271 (1904).
Smith v. Pacific Improvement Co., 104 Misc. 481 (N.Y. Sup. Ct. 1918).
Sternaman v. Metropolitan Life Insurance Co., 170 N.Y. 13 (1902).
Tisdell v. New Hampshire Fire Insurance Co., 155 N.Y. 163 (1898).

Unpublished Materials

Matzko, John Austin. "The Early Years of the American Bar Association." PhD diss., University of Virginia, 1984.
National Register of Historic Places Registration Form. July 8, 2016.
Perry, Peter R. "Theodore Roosevelt and the Labor Movement." Master's thesis, California State University, Hayward, 1991.
Shoemaker, Fred C. "Alton B. Parker: The Images of a Gilded Age Statesman in an Era of Progressive Politics." Master's thesis, The Ohio State University, 1983.
Wheaton, James O. "The Genius and the Jurist: A Study of the Presidential Campaign of 1904." PhD diss., Stanford University, 1965.

Online Sources

"Alton Brooks Parker." *Harper's Weekly*. Accessed June 6, 2022. http://elections.harpweek.com/elections/1904 Biographies.
Dearstyne, Bruce W. "Alton B. Parker: New York's Neglected Statesman." New York Almanack. Last modified June 8, 2022. https://www.newyorkalmanack.com/2022/06/alton-b-parker-new-yorks-neglected-statesman/.
"George Gray (Delaware Politician)." Wikipedia. Last modified December 22, 2022. http://en.m.wikipedia.org/wiki/Special:History/George_Gray_(Delaware_politician).
"The Election Results." *Harper's Weekly*. Accessed June 1, 2022. https://elections.harpweek.com/1904/overview-1904-4.asp.
Tucker, Abigail. "The Financial Panic of 1907: Running from History." *Smithsonian Magazine*. Accessed February 5, 2023. http://www.smithsonianmag.com.
"United States Presidential Election of 1896." Encyclopedia Britannica. Last modified August 19, 2014. http://www.britannica.com.
"1904 Presidential General Election Data—National." Dave Leip's Atlas of U.S. Presidential Elections. Last modified February 14, 2018. http://www.uselectionatlas.org.

Other Sources

Death Notice of Amelia Day Campbell Parker. *The Kingston Daily Freeman*. August 22, 1960.

Encyclopedia Britannica, 11th ed. (1910). S.vv. "Olney, Richard."
Fordham Law School Bulletin of Information, 1908–1909.
"Iroquois Campaign Song." Anonymous. 1904.
Official Program, Citizens' Preparedness Parade, New York City, May 13, 1916. New York: Citizens Preparedness Parade, 1916.
Parker, Alton B. *Annual Address by Hon, Alton B. Parker before the Ohio State Bar Association, Ohio Law Bulletin.* July 28, 1913.
———. *Annual Address before the South Carolina Bar Association delivered by Alton B. Parker on Thursday Evening, January 25, 1912 at Columbia.* 1912.
———. "Political Corruption by the Trusts." New York: Parker Independent Clubs, 1904.
———. *The Foundations in Virginia: An Address Delivered at the College of William and Mary, Williamsburg, Virginia, on Wednesday, October 6, 1920.* N.p., 1920.
Schurz, Carl. "To the Independent Voter: An Open Letter." New York: Parker Independent Clubs, 1904.
Stickney, Albert. *The Records.* N.p.: printed by the author, 1904.
U. S. Const. amend. XIV.

Index

acceptance speech of ABP, 140; press reaction, 140, 144–147
Accord, New York, 12
Accord school, 8
Alabama, 56, 74, 97, 110, 191, 231
Albany Law School, 8, 249
Albany, New York, 28, 52, 57, 81, 87, 121, 136, 206, 230
Albany platform, 75, 226
Albany Times, 23
Alderson, John D., 111
Ambassador Hotel, 251, 252
American Bar Association (ABA), 214, 215, 216, 217, 239, 246, 248, 253, 255
American Bar Association Journal, 253
American Can, 188
American Committee for Armenian Independence, 249
American Committee on the Rights of Religious Minorities, 249
American Federation of Labor (AFL), 203, 204, 213, 259
American Heraldry Society, 256
American Historical Association, 256
American Law Institute, 249
American Monthly Review of Reviews, 115, 147, 167, 180
American Tobacco Company, 163

Andrews, James D., 220
Arizona, 92, 101
Arkansas, 191, 276n71
Armenian-Republican clubs, 170
Arriago, Antonio Lazo, 129
Association of the Bar of the City of New York, 217
Auchincloss, Gordon, 201, 254
Aycock, Charles B., 110
Azpiroz, Don Manuel de, 129

Baldwin, Simeon, 231
Ball, David A., 113
Baltimore & Ohio Railroad, 124, 125, 126
Baltimore, Maryland, 123, 125, 129, 231, 238
Baltimore Sun, 84
Bar Association of the City of New York, 254
Barrett, George C., 24
Barrett, John, 129
Barnard, George G., 50
Bartlett, Willard, 230
Bayard, Thomas F., 70, 127, 128
Beckham, John Crepps Wickliffe, 110, 282n55
Beekman, John J., 158
Belknap, William, 128

323

Belles, Ruth, 251
Belmont, August, xiii, 58, 64, 136, 137, 143–144, 163, 190, 191, 232, 234
Belmont Banking House, 163
Bennett, Ruth Campbell, 245
Bermuda, 246
Betts, James A., 25
Beveridge, Albert J., 98, 173
Bijur, Nathan, 171
bimetallism, 54, 56, 60, 61
Birder, Jacob P., 110
Black, Frank S., 24, 97
Blaine, James G., 128, 154, 290n8
Blake, George W., 207
Bland-Allison Act, 128
Bland, Richard P., 61
Bliss, Cornelius N., 129, 164
Board of Indian Commissioners, 172
Board of Supervisors, 8, 9
Boardman, Albert, 254
Boies, Horace, 61
Boston Advertiser, 179
Boston American, 77
Boston Evening Transcript, 144
Boston Herald, 84
Boston, Massachusetts, 104, 144
Boston Pilot, 172
bourbon Democrat, xiii, 261n2
Brackett, Edgar T., 208
Brandeis, Louis D., 239, 305n208
Bratton, J. W., 156
Braxton, Allen Caperton, 282n55
Brent, Bishop Charles H., 244
Bridgeport, Connecticut, 183
Bromby, George Haydn, 156
Brooklyn Academy of Music, 177
Brooklyn Daily Eagle, 84, 180
Brooklyn Eagle, 19, 158, 177. *See also*, *Brooklyn Daily Eagle*
Brotherhood of Railroad Trainmen, 274n21

Brown, Robert M. G., 125
Brown, Roscoe, 206
Bryan, William Jennings, xiii, 25, 45, 57, 64, 65, 72, 78, 81, 84, 95, 101, 102, 113, 114, 115, 118, 119, 121, 133, 155, 163, 166, 172, 173, 193, 194, 226, 237, 238, 275n55, 280n9; call for a new presidential nominee, 112; comparing himself to Aaron and Parker to Moses, 169; condemnation of the Albany platform, 75; credential fight at the 1904 convention, 100; "Cross of Gold" speech, 56, 61; efforts to insert silver plank and income tax plank into 1904 platform, 101; first campaign for president, 61–62, 64; "I Have Kept the Faith" speech, 104; open letter in opposition to Parker's candidacy, 98; opposition to Parker's selection as temporary chairman of the 1912 Democratic National Convention, 232–235; Parker as his potential running mate in 1900, 91–92; possible run for the presidency in 1904, 74, 75; professed support for Parker and Davis, 120–121; response to Parker's gold telegram, 115, 121; second campaign for president, 62, 64; speeches on behalf of Parker & Davis, 169; thoughts on Parker's fitness to be the Democratic nominee, 91; thoughts on why Parker lost, 197
Buchanan, James, 59
Buchanan, W. I., 129
Buckner, Simon B., 271n9
Bucks Stove & Range Company, 204
Buffalo Enquirer, 85
Buffalo, New York, 51, 63, 211
Bureau of Corporations, 177

Burr, Aaron, 86, 154
Byrne, John M., 172

Cable, Benjamin T., 101
Calderon, Manuel Alvarez, 129
California, 64, 76, 77, 92 100, 103, 104, 129, 192, 272n30
Camden, J. N., 128
Cameron, Simon, 127
campaign paraphernalia, 156–157, 161
campaign poems, 158–161
campaign songs, 156–158
Campbell, Amelia Day, 246
Campbell, Andrew Arthur, 246
Campbell, Frank, 89
Cannon, Frank J., 282n55
Cannon, Rev. John F., 99
Cannon, Joseph, 96, 98
Canton, Ohio, 166–167, 227
Carlisle, John G., 79
Carmack, Edward, 84, 100, 113, 114, 115, 282n55; seconds nomination of Parker for president, 107–108; purported receipt of telegram from Parker demanding a gold plank in the Democratic Party platform, 112
Carnegie, Andrew, 129, 131, 164
Carnegie Hall, 182, 189
Carnegie Lyceum, 217
Carnegie Steel Company, 164
Chaffee, Jerome B., 128
Charleston, West Virginia, 128, 130
Charlottesville, Virginia, 249
Chemung County Democratic Committee, 50
Chicago American, 77
Chicago, Illinois 19, 51, 55, 56, 91, 95, 129, 130, 189, 278n126, 291n49
Chicago Record-Herald, 286n16
Chicago Tribune, 180, 187
Chronicle Telegraph, 145
Church, Sanford E., 27–28

Cincinnati Enquirer, 69, 110, 136
Cincinnati, Ohio, 129, 227
Cincinnati Times-Star, 118
Citizens Committee of America, 249
Citizens' Preparedness Parade, 241; Lawyers' Division, 241; Lower Wall Street Business Mens' Association, 241; Jewelry Trades Division, 241
Civil Service Act, 152
Civil War, 73, 74, 104, 126, 127, 149, 152, 153, 192
Clarke, John Hessin, 239
Clark, James Beauchamp ("Champ"), 103, 104, 114, 137, 231, 232, 233, 237, 279n22; advice provided regarding recission of Parker's nomination, 112–113; notification address to Parker, 138–139; response to Parker's gold telegram, 117–118; thoughts on why Parker lost, 197
Clark, Roger P., 208
Clay, Henry, 154
Clayton, Henry D., 56
Clearwater, A. T., 22
Cleveland, Grover, 19, 51, 54–55, 57, 64–65, 72, 84, 95, 103, 115, 116, 117, 133, 136, 151, 154, 165, 176, 177, 226, 272n30, 273n1, 273n4, 273n5; article in support of Parker, 189; campaign for the presidency in 1888, 59; campaign for the presidency in 1892, 60; endorsement of Parker, 68; letter in support of Parker's candidacy, 134; promotion of Parker as ideal candidate, 120; refusal to run for president in 1904, 67–68; speeches on behalf of Parker, 189–190; tariff revision, 60
Cleveland Leader, 166
Cleveland, Ohio, 240

Clinton, George, 255
Clinton, Hillary Rodham, 122
Coal & Coke Railway Company, 128
Cockran, Bourke, 90, 91, 189; response to Parker's gold telegram, 116
Cockrell, Francis, 73, 103, 104, 108, 110, 280n9; early life, 73; political career, 74; service in the Civil War, 73–74
Cockrell, Joseph, 73
Cockrell, Nancy, 73
Cohen v. Berlin Jones Envelope Co., 40
Cole, E. E., 104
Coler, Bird S., 20, 108, 244
College of William and Mary, 223; Marshall-Wythe School of Government and Citizenship, 224
Collier's Weekly, 120, 134
Collins, Patrick, 104
Colonial Club of New York City, 81–82
Colorado, 192, 229, 282n55, 295n20
Columbia, 64
Committee on Criminal Courts, 219
Committee on Custom Relations, 129
Committee on Platform & Resolutions, 100, 102, 226
Congress, 59, 77, 78, 83, 128, 146, 174, 220; investigation into corporate campaign contributions, 187–188, 197, 221, 226, 258, 260
Conkling, Roscoe, 127
Connecticut, xiii, 47, 52, 56, 77, 92, 119–120, 170, 180, 183, 192, 231, 272n30, 295n20
Coolidge, Calvin, 253
Coolidge, T. Jefferson, 129
Cooper Union, 98, 171, 181, 182
Cortelyou, George, 171, 188; alleged solicitation of campaign donations from corporations, 177, 180–181, 184, 185–186
Cortland Academy, 4
Cortland County, New York, 1
Cortland, New York, 1, 4, 12, 255
county surrogate, 9, 21–22, 23
Cowen, Philip, 171
Cox, James M., 244
Crawford, Marcus, 49
Creelman, James, 81, 115, 276n71; character sketch of Parker, 147–149; urges Parker to address the issues of the day, 81
Croker, Richard, 87
Crum, W. D., 173
Culberson, Charles, 111
Cullen, Edgar M., 208, 209, 210
Cumberland, Maryland, 125, 128
Cummings v. Union Blue Stone Company, 39
Czolgosz, Leon, 63

Danbury Hatters case, 203–204. See also, *Loewe v. Lawlor*.
Danforth, Elliott, 25, 80; reports Parker's views on various issues, 81
Daniel, John W., xiii, 56, 101, 102, 282n55
Darrow, Clarence, 103
Daughters of American Colonists, 256
Daughters of the American Revolution, 246, 256
Davis, Ada Kate (daughter of HGD and KAD), 125
Davis & Elkins College, 130
Davis, Anderson Cord (son of HGD and KAD), 125
Davis, Caleb (father of HGD), 123, 124
Davis, Eliza Ann (sister of HGD), 124
Davis, Elizabeth (sister of HGD), 124

Davis, Grace Thomas (Daughter of HGD and KAD), 125
Davis, Henry G. (HGD), 100, 101, 120, 139, 158, 161, 163, 172, 173, 192; acceptance speech, 153–154; attendance at Democratic National Conventions, 129–130; business ventures, 125–126; campaign speeches, 169; childhood, 123–124; commissioner on the Intercontinental Railway Commission, 129; committee assignments in US Senate, 127; delegate to the First Pan-American Conference, 128–129; delegate to the Second Pan-American Conference, 129; early jobs, 124; education, 124; election to US Senate, 127; election to West Virginia Senate, 127; expressed willingness to serve as vice president, 111; financial contributions to the campaign, 155; first meeting with Parker, 134; important votes as a US senator, 127–128; letter of acceptance, 155; nomination for vice president, 119; notification of nomination for vice president, 153; philanthropy, 130; physical appearance, 130–131; reasons for his nomination as vice president, 119; re-election to US Senate, 127; service as chairman of the Pan-American Railway Committee, 129; start of his political career, 126; work as a state senator, 127; work at Waverly plantation, 124; work for the Baltimore & Ohio Railroad, 125
Davis, Henry G., Jr. (son of HGD and KAD), 125, 130
Davis, John (brother of HGD), 123
Davis, John Thomas (son of HGD and KAD), 125
Davis, John W., 214, 246, 252, 254, 261n3
Davis, Kate Bantz (daughter of HGD and KAD), 125
Davis, Katharine Ann Bantz (KAD), 125
Davis, Louisa Brown (mother of HGD), 123, 124
Davis, Mary Louise ("Hallie") (daughter of HGD and KAD), 125, 130
Davis Memorial Hospital, 130
Davis Memorial Presbyterian Church, 130
Davis, Thomas (brother of HGD), 124, 125, 126, 130
Davis, William (brother of HGD), 124, 126
Debs, Eugene V., 193, 279n2
Declaration of Independence, 223
Delaware, xiii, 69, 70, 104, 127, 170, 191, 231, 272n30, 295n20
Delmas, Delphin M., 100, 103
D. E. Loewe & Company, 203
Democrat, xiii, 21, 22, 25, 49, 56, 57, 59, 76, 105, 107, 121, 136, 139, 196, 198, 232, 246, 275n55
Democratic, 11, 22, 23, 24, 25, 26, 43, 47, 50, 52, 53, 54, 55, 57, 58, 61, 62, 64, 67, 68, 71, 75, 77, 78, 79, 81, 84, 85, 86, 87, 88, 92, 93, 95, 98, 99, 100, 101, 102, 103, 104, 105, 109, 110, 114, 116, 117, 119, 120, 121, 130, 131, 134, 136, 139, 141, 145, 149, 150, 151, 152, 152, 153, 158, 169, 171, 172, 173, 175, 177, 180, 187, 189, 191, 192, 193, 197, 198, 206, 226, 227, 228, 229,

Democratic *(continued)*
237, 252, 275n55, 277n99, 277n100, 282n55
Democratic campaign literature, 175–176
Democratic Club of New York, 183, 225
Democratic Literary Bureau, 136
Democratic National Campaign Song, 156
Democratic National Convention, 19, 51, 55, 57, 58, 92, 98, 100, 129, 130, 154, 165, 226, 231, 242, 278n126
Democratic National Committee, 56, 69, 99, 136, 137, 151, 153, 156, 194, 226, 232, 234, 278n126, 282n55; campaign debt, 190
Democratic National Headquarters, 191
Democratic Party, xiii, xiv, 20, 24, 25, 55, 57, 60, 64, 72, 77, 81, 83, 93, 113, 117, 118, 121, 156, 163, 172, 174, 195, 225, 228, 231, 235, 237
Democratic Party platform (1904), 101–102, 103, 113, 144, 156, 165, 171, 280n28; adoption of, 102
Democratic Presidential March, 156
Democratic Press Bureau, 136, 286n16
Democratic Speakers' Bureau, 136
Democrats, 26, 27, 50, 51, 52, 53, 54, 55, 59, 60, 61, 62, 63, 75, 81, 84, 85, 89, 95, 111, 114, 118, 119, 120, 127, 133, 134, 142, 168, 169, 170, 171, 176, 192, 193, 196, 197, 198, 227, 228, 229, 231, 236, 239, 273n1, 273n4, 292n56; courting the labor vote, 172; efforts to win the youth vote, 172–173
Denver, Colorado, 226
Denver platform, 226
Department of Commerce & Labor, 184
Depew, Chauncey, 98, 187
Dewey, Thomas, 122
DeWitt, C. N., 23
Dillon, John Forrest, 217, 218
District of Columbia Law School, 46
Dix, John A., 206, 229, 238
Dockery, Alexander M., 108, 110, 113, 114
Dolliver, Jonathan P., 98
Douglas, Stephen A., 154
Dresser, Paul, 157
Dr. Miles Medical Company, 205
Dublin, Ireland, 249
DuBois, Fred T., 101
Dunne, Finley Peter, 155

economic turmoil, 60
electoral college, 62, 151, 192
Elkins, Stephen B., 125, 128, 130; support for Roosevelt & Fairbanks, 168–169
Elkins, West Virginia, 128, 130
Elks' Hall, 181
Ellenville Journal, 19
Elmira Gazette, 50
Elmira, New York, 49
Enterprise Association of Steam-fitters, 33, 34
Equitable Life Insurance Company, 188
Esopus, New York, 14, 83, 88, 113, 134, 138, 145, 147, 151, 165, 166, 167, 168, 169, 178, 179, 198
Essex Troop Armory, 181
Estee, M. M., 129
Europe, 239, 241, 242, 246, 248
Evansville Courier, 158
Evansville, Indiana, 189

Fairbanks, Charles W., 98, 155, 170
Fellows, John R., 56
Field, Marshall, 110
Fielders, Thomas B., 286n16

Fifth Maryland Regiment Armory, 231
First Pan-American Conference, 128
First Voters Democratic Association of Essex County, 190
Fletcher, E. O., 156
Flint, Charles R., 129
Florida, 107, 191, 246
Flowers, Roswell P., 24
Fordham University School of Law, 220
Fort Wayne, Indiana, 189
Forum, 198
Foss, Eugene, 231
Foster, Murphy James, 282n55
Foster, Volney W., 129
Fourteenth Amendment, 28, 38, 141, 229; Parker's speech concerning, 82–83
Fox, Austen G., 208
Frawley, James J., 208, 209, 210, 213
Frick, Henry Clay, 164, 186, 188
Frost, Rev. Timothy P., 95
Frugone, Frank L., 170

Garfield, James A., 290n8
General Committee, 86–87
General Committee of the Democratic-Republican Party, 86–87. *See also,* General Committee
General Electric, 163, 188
Georgia, 72, 82, 92, 129, 191, 223
Georgia Bar Association, 82
Gerard, James W., 83; propaganda campaign on Parker's behalf, 83
Germany, 240
Gold Democratic party, 57
Gold Democrats, 57
Goldfield, Nevada, 259
gold plank, 101, 111, 112, 113, 114, 115, 121
gold standard, 56, 60, 61, 62, 101, 102, 113, 114, 118, 119, 134, 165

gold telegram, 113–114, 144, 145, 153; convention response to same, 114–115; press coverage, 115–119
Gompers, Samuel, 203, 204, 205, 244, 259
Gorman, Arthur P., 64, 84, 95, 108, 128, 155, 156, 176; early life, 68; opposition to Panama Canal Treaty, 69; political career, 68
Gould, Edwin, 214, 254
Gould, George J., 188, 214
Gould, Howard, 214
Gould, Jay, 214
Grace, Emmeline, 13
Grady, Thomas F., 57, 91
Grant County, West Virginia, 126
Grant, Ulysses S., 154, 193, 295n19
Gray, Andrew C., 69
Gray, George, 69, 104, 108; consideration for vice president, 110; early life, 69; judicial career, 70; political career, 70
Gray, James R., 282n55
Gray, John C., 43, 230
Gray, J. P., 276n71
Great Northern Railway, 188
Greeley, Horace, 154, 193, 290n8, 295n19
Green Bag, 201
Guam, 63
Guardian, 146
Guffey, James M., 136
Guggenheimer, Randolph, 84; endorsement of Parker, 85
Guthrie Daily Leader, 193

Hall, Alton Parker ("Parker") (grandson of ABP and MSP), 13, 242
Hall, Alton Parker, III (great-grandson of ABP and MSP), 13
Hall, Bertha Schoonmaker Parker (daughter of ABP and MSP), 13

Hall, Charles Mercer, 13, 290n22
Hall, J. K. P., 69
Hall, Penny (great-granddaughter of ABP and MSP), 13
Hamer, Louisa, 41–42. *See also, Hamer v. Sidway*
Hamer v. Sidway, 41–42
Hamilton, Alexander, 86
Hamlin, Charles Sumner, 101
Hamlin, Hannibal, 127
Hampshire County, West Virginia, 126
Handy, Irwin L., 104
Hanford, Benjamin, 279n2
Hanna, Mark, 166
Hanson, John F., 129
Hardenburgh, Jacob, 8
Harding, Warren, 239
Hardy County, West Virginia, 126
Harmon, Judson, 110, 231, 237
Harper's Weekly, 144, 171
Harriman, Edward, 186, 187, 188
Harris, William A., 111, 119
Harrison, Benjamin, 59, 60, 125, 128, 129, 239, 273n1, 292n56
Harrity, William F., 56
Hartford, Connecticut, 184
Hatch, Edward W., 201
Hawaii, 92
Hay, John, 97
Hayes, Rutherford B., 128, 174
Hazen, L. M., 159
H. C. Frick & Company, 164
Healy, Timothy, 249
Hearst clubs, 77
Hearst, George, 76, 77
Hearst, Phoebe Apperson, 76
Hearst, William Randolph, 62, 64, 88, 93, 95, 103, 104, 108, 110, 163, 202, 278n126, 297n11; bid for New York gubernatorial nomination, 242–243; education, 76; foundation of his newspaper empire, 77; instructed delegations for, 92; pros and cons of his candidacy for the presidency, 77–78; support for Parker, 169
Henderson, John B., 128
Hennessy, John A., 207
Henry, Robert L., 233
Herrick, Charles, 208
Herrick, D-Cady, 25, 189, 208; defense of New York governor William Sulzer, 209–212
H. G. Davis & Company, 125, 126
Higgins, Frank, 188
Hill, Caleb, 47
Hill, C. B., 119
Hill, David B., 20, 22, 64, 80, 81, 84, 91, 92 93, 95, 100, 118, 144, 155, 172, 189, 226, 275n55, 282n55; accomplishments as governor, 53; accomplishments as senator, 54; appointment of Parker as campaign manager, 52; battle with Parker over content of New York state platform, 88; campaigning for Cleveland, 51, 52–53; death, 230; early life, 47–49; education, 47–48; election as alderman, 51; election as city attorney, 49; election as lieutenant governor, 51; election as mayor of Elmira, 51; election to New York state legislature, 50; election to US Senate, 53; failure to win election as governor of New York, 55; failure to win election as temporary chairman of Democratic National Convention, 56; failure to win reelection as US senator, 57; governor of New York, 51–53; legal education, 49; legal practice, 49; nominating Bryan for president, 57; nomination for vice president, 57–58; Parker's

election as chief judge of the New York Court of Appeals, 26–27; physical appearance, 47–48; political philosophy, 54; retirement from politics, 154; seeks presidential nomination, 54–55; speech on behalf of minority report supporting the gold standard at the Democratic National Convention, 56; time in New York state legislature, 50; urges Parker not to run for chief judge of the New York Court of Appeals, 25
Hill, Muller & Stanchfield, 50
Hinman, Harvey, 208
Hiscock, Frank H., 252
Holmes, Oliver Wendell, 153, 203
Home Music Company, 158
Hotel Knickerbocker, 217
House Foreign Affairs Committee, 206
Houston Post, 86
Howard, George, 124
Hudson River, 14, 17, 29, 100, 116, 138
Hughes, Charles Evans, 238, 239, 245, 248, 254
Hundley, Oscar R., 97
Hurley, New York, 8

Idaho, 92, 101, 192, 295n20
Illinois, 62, 72, 75, 86, 92, 100, 101, 111, 127, 129, 192, 225, 271n9, 272n30
imperialism, 63
Indiana, 52, 62, 75, 92, 98, 101, 111, 129, 136, 172, 180, 189, 192, 231, 272n30, 295n20
Indianapolis, Indiana, 173, 189, 227, 237
Ingersoll v. Nassau Electric Railroad, 42

In re Gould, 299n77
instructed delegation, 87, 88, 90, 277n99; fight for an instructed delegation in New York, 91–92; in states other than New York, 92
Intercontinental Railway Commission, 129
Interior Department, 152
International Harvester, 188
Interstate Commerce Commission, 19
Iowa, 61, 64, 92, 98, 192
Ireland, 240
Iroquois Campaign Song, 158

Jackson, Andrew, 154
Jackson, Charles, 276n71
Jamestown, Virginia, 220
Jarvis, William C., 141
Jefferson Day banquet, 225
Jefferson, Thomas, 141, 154, 194, 223, 226, 235, 292n56
Jersey City, New Jersey, 181
Jersey County Democrat, 86
John D. Park & Sons Co., 40, 205. See also, *John D. Park & Sons Co. v. The National Wholesale Druggists Association*
John D. Park & Sons Co. v. The National Wholesale Druggists Association, 40–41
Johnson, Andrew, 208
Johnston, Rev. John T. M., 110
Jones, James K., 69

Kansas, 64, 104, 111, 192
Kansas City platform, 85, 101
Kelly, John, 87
Kentucky, 110, 119, 136, 192, 205, 271n9, 282n55
Kenyon, William, 9
Kenyon, William S., 22
Kern, John W., 110, 226, 234

Kilbourne, James, 110
Kingston Daily Freeman, 22
Kingston, New York, 8, 9, 14, 160, 191, 254, 255
Kishinev pogrom, 171
Kitchener Memorial Fund, 249
Knight, George A., 173
Knox, Philander C., 179
Kresel, Isidor J., 208
Ku Klux Klan, 127

Lafayette, Indiana, 189
Lamar, Joseph Rucker, 238, 239, 305n208
Lamont, Daniel S., 57, 163; discussion with Parker regarding corporate campaign contributions to Roosevelt, 177–178, 186
Latin-American Republican National League, 171
Law Academy of Philadelphia, 221
Lawton, William, 22
Lawyer's Club, 218, 254; Board of Governors, 218; Committee on Meetings and Speakers, 218; Sub-Committee on Finance, 218; War Committee, 218
Lea, Luke, 235
League to Enforce Peace, 239
Leavitt, John Brooks, 217
Lee, Arthur, 125
Lee, Stan, 202
Lewiston, Montana, 159
Life, 198
Lincoln, Abraham, 97, 126, 154, 175, 221, 306n240
Lincoln-McKinley Association of Missouri, 97
Littleton, Martin W., 104; nomination of Parker for president, 105–107
Lochner, Joseph, 38. *See also, People v. Lochner; Lochner v. New York*

Lochner v. New York, 39, 218, 219, 229, 267n39
Lodge, Henry Cabot, 96, 120, 273n1
Loewe v. Lawler, 203–204. *See also,* Danbury Hatters case.
Logansport, Indiana, 158
Los Angeles Examiner, 77
Los Angeles Herald, 11
Louisiana, 192, 282n55
Louisville Courier-Journal, 75, 173, 290n8
Loyal Democratic League of New York, 25
Lurton, Horace Harmon, 238, 239
Lusitania, 240

Mack, Norman E., 234, 235
Madison, James, 223, 235, 292n56
Madison Square Garden, 181
Malloy, F. J., 25
Maine, 127, 192
Manhattan Club, 79
Manhattan Elevated Railroad, 214
Manhattan, New York, 182, 206
Marshall, John, 215
Marshall, Louis, 208
Marshall, Thomas, 231, 233, 237, 238, 242
Martin, Thomas S., 136, 282n55
Martin, Timothy, 136
Maryland, xiii, 68, 108, 124, 126, 169, 170, 192, 272n30, 295n15, 295n20
Mason-Dixon line, 153
Massachusetts, 71, 72, 96, 120, 127, 129, 192, 231, 273n1
Matter of Hearst v. Woelper, 297n11
Matter of Metz v. Maddox, 297n11
Mayflower Compact, 223
McAdoo, William G., 261n3
McCall, Edward E., 207
McCall, John A., 172

Index | 333

McCarran, Patrick H., 79, 88, 89, 91, 282n55
McCausland, Arthur, 10, 17, 113, 244, 254
McClellan, George B., 95
McClellan, George B., Jr., 108, 202, 225
McClure's Magazine, 189
McConville, Daniel, 136
McDermott, Allen L., 56
McDonough, John T., 172
McKelway, St. Clair, 67; editorial support for Parker, 84
McKinley, William, 45, 61, 62, 63, 70, 96, 129, 148, 166, 167, 192, 240, 260, 290n8, 292n56
McLean, John R., 69, 110, 136
McMahon, John D., 238
McQueed, Charles, 33. *See also, National Protective Association of Steam Fitters and Helpers v. Cumming*
McReynolds, James Clark, 239, 305n209
Menden, Connecticut, 184
Merrill, J. T. Woods, 91
Messmer, S. G., 172
Metropolitan Life Insurance Company, 218
Michigan, 75, 192
Milburn, John G., 254
Miles, Nelson Appleton, 104, 108
Miller, David, 201, 254
Miller, Nathan L., 254
Mineral County, West Virginia, 126
Minnesota, 64, 75, 108, 192
Minton, Maurice M., 83, 136, 286n16
Mississippi, 100, 105, 114, 115, 192, 282n55
Missouri, 61, 69, 73, 77, 103, 108, 110, 112, 113, 128, 174, 192, 272n30, 279n22

Missouri Pacific Railroad, 214
Monroe Doctrine, 72, 101, 174
Monroe, James, 176, 223, 235, 292n56
Montana, 192, 295n20
Monticello, 249
Moore, J. Hampton, 173
Morgan, J. P., 63, 173, 187, 260, 309n11
Morris, Free, 111
Morton, Levi, 38, 55
Mott, Frank, 238
Mr. Dooley, 155, 190
Mt. Vernon, Virginia, 246
Muller, William, 50
Murphy, Charles, 55, 86, 232, 277n99, 277n100; disputes with New York governor William Sulzer, 206–207; political power, 87; refusal to support an instructed delegation for Parker, 88
Murphy, Edward, 282n55
Murray Hill Lyceum, 188
Mutual Life Insurance Company, 188

Nashville, Tennessee, 227
Nation, 146
National Association of Democratic Clubs, 77, 172, 173
National Budget Committee, 249
National City Life, 188
National Civic Federation, 243, 244, 246, 247, 248, 254
National Committee on American Japanese Relations, 249
National Committee on Foreign Relations and National Defense, 246
National Council of Religions in Higher Education, 249
National Democratic Club, 244, 254
National Democratic Party, 271n9

334 | Index

National League of Republican Clubs, 173
National Protective Association of Steam Fitters and Helpers v. Cumming, 33–36, 172
National Security League, 249
National Society Daughters of Founders and Patriots, 256
National Society of Colonial Dames of America, 306n240
National Society of Colonial Dames of the State of New York, 256
National Society of Magna Charta Dames, 256
National Wholesale Druggists Association, 40. See also, *John D. Park & Sons Co. v. The National Wholesale Druggists Association*
Nebraska, 63, 64, 104, 133, 192
Nevada, 92, 101, 192, 225, 259, 282n55
Newark, New Jersey, 181, 190
Newcomb, Alvah S., 113, 114
New England Anti-Imperialist League, 79
New England Historic and Genealogical Society, 256
New Hampshire, 192, 221
New Hampshire Bar Association, 221
New Haven, Connecticut, 184
New Jersey, xiii, 56, 77, 119, 136, 170, 180, 181, 192, 231, 272n30, 295n20
Newlands, Francis G., 101, 225, 282n55
New Mexico, 92, 101–102
New York, xiii, xiv, 13, 14, 19, 26, 27, 28, 37, 42, 43, 44, 45, 47, 49, 50, 51, 52, 53, 55, 56, 57, 58, 63, 75, 79, 82, 83, 84, 85, 86, 87, 89, 90, 91, 92, 97, 98, 105, 106, 107, 108, 111, 116, 119, 120, 122, 127, 129, 136, 149, 150, 168, 170, 171, 172, 173, 178, 180, 187, 188, 189, 192, 205, 209, 211, 218, 226, 227, 229, 232, 234, 237, 242, 243, 249, 255, 272n30, 276n71, 277n100, 282n55, 295n20
New York American, 44, 77
New York Biographical and Genealogical Society, 256
New York Bolletino, 170
New York Central Railroad, 163, 187
New York City Board of Aldermen, 243
New York Civil Service Commission, 18
New York County Lawyers' Association, 217, 218, 254, 255
New York Court of Appeals, 24, 84, 136, 198, 202, 208, 209, 219, 230, 252, 253, 273n4, 297n11; importance of, 27
New York Court of Appeals, Second Division, 23–24
New York Daily Graphic, 52
New York Daily Tribune, 226
New York Evening Journal, 77
New York Evening Post, 116
New York Evening Sun, 19
New York Evening Telegram, 81
New York Herald, 83, 239
New York Law Journal, 217
New York Life Insurance Company, 163, 172, 188
New York Municipal Council, 84
New York, New York, 13, 27, 36, 129, 138, 151, 163, 178, 180, 181, 201, 225, 237, 241, 244, 251, 254, 259, 277n99
New York State Bar, 9
New York State Bar Association, 219, 220, 254, 255; Committee of Fifteen, 219–220
New York State Democratic Committee, 24, 88, 229

Index | 335

New York State Democratic Convention, 54, 87, 89, 91, 226, 228, 238
New York State Democratic League, 227–228
New York State Historical Association, 256
New York state platform (1904), 89–90, 91, 98
New York Stock Exchange, 208, 213
New York Sun, 52, 84, 98, 144, 187
New York Sunday Democrat, 172
New York Supreme Court, 22, 225, 253
New York Supreme Court, First Department, Appellate Division, 24
New York Supreme Court, First Department, General Term, 24
New York Times, 10, 80, 117, 135, 245, 252
New York Transcript, 252
New-York Tribune, 118, 244
New York World, 19, 81, 180
Nicholas II (czar), 242
Nicoll, De Lancey, 136, 191, 254
Norfolk Landmark, 179
North Carolina, 110, 192, 220
North Dakota, 64, 104, 110, 192
Northern Pacific Railway Company, 163, 177
Northern Securities Company, 149, 173
notification ceremonies, 137
notification committee, 137, 138

O'Brien, Denis, 36, 230
O'Brien, Jimmie, 26
O'Brien, John F., 137
O'Brien, Morgan J., 219, 228, 254
Odell, Benjamin, 89, 251; allegation that Parker profited from involvement in the trusts, 188

Odell, William, 20
O'Gorman, James A., 214, 254
Ohio, 75, 110, 127, 136, 192, 231, 237
Ohio Bar Association, 222
Oklahoma, 101, 193
Oklahoma Law Journal, 118
Olney, Richard, 64, 84, 104, 108, 171, 274n21; early life, 71; physical description, 72; political career, 71–72; pros and cons of his candidacy for the presidency, 72–73
Olney, Wilson, 71
Order of the Crown of America, 256
Oregon, 64, 192
O'Reilly, John Boyle, 170
Outlook, 92, 93, 140
Overmyer, David, 104, 111
Oxholm, Anne Mercer (great-granddaughter of ABP and MSP), 13
Oxholm, Mary Louise (great-granddaughter of ABP and MSP), 13
Oxholm, Mary McAlister Hall (granddaughter of ABP and MSP), 13
Oxholm, Theodore, 13
Oxholm, Theodore, Jr. (great-grandson of ABP and MSP), 13
Oyster Bay, New York, 191

Page, J. M., 86
Page, Kirby, 246, 247, 248
Palmer, John M., 271n9
Panama, 64, 174, 182
Panama Canal, 64, 101, 152, 173
Panama Canal Treaty, 69, 182
Pan-American Exhibition, 63
Pan-American Railway Committee, 129
Panic of 1837, 124
Panic of 1907, 259, 260

336 | Index

Paris, France, 249
Parker, Alton B. (ABP), xiii, xiv; acceptance speech, 140–144, 165; activities on the opening day of the 1904 convention, 100; address to Democratic newspaper editors, 151; advice to Roosevelt regarding law school, 45–46; advice to Roosevelt regarding vice presidency, 44–45; appearance on the bench, 28; appointment to New York Court of Appeals, Second Division, 23; appointment to New York Supreme Court, 22; appointment to New York Supreme Court, First Department, Appellate Division, 24; appointment to New York Supreme Court, First Department, General Term, 24; attacks Roosevelt's "stand pat" policy, 183; attraction as a candidate for president, 78; becoming a lawyer, 3; birth, 1; birthplace, 1, 3; burial, 254–255; call for a return to Jeffersonian ideals, 182–183; campaign for chief judge of the New York Court of Appeals, 24–26; campaign speeches at Rosemount, 168–169; casting his vote for president, 191; chief judge New York Court of Appeals, xiii; childhood, 2; civic engagement, 249; death, 252; death of son, 13; decision to leave Rosemount and make campaign speeches, 180; demand for privacy during the campaign, 135; discussion with D. Lamont regarding corporate campaign contributions to Roosevelt, 177–178, 186; drafting the ABA's canon of ethics, 216–217; education, 4; efforts to include Bryan in the 1904 campaign, 133; election as county surrogate, 9, 21–22; election as permanent chairman of New York State Democratic Convention, 238; election as temporary chairman of the 1912 Democratic National Convention, 235; election to New York Supreme Court, 23; electoral vote totals, 192–193; entry into politics, 18; eulogy of David Hill, 230–231; first meeting with Davis, 134; first speech following nomination, 109; founding the New York County Lawyers' Association, 217; funeral, 254; health, 251; hobbies, 17; impeachment of New York governor William Sulzer, 208–213; initial reluctance to actively campaign, 166–167, 168; involvement in the Jay Gould estate case, 214; involvement in the League to Enforce Peace, 239–240; involvement with Ulster County Savings Association, 12–13; judicial philosophy, 28, 30–31; keynote speech at the 1912 Democratic National Convention, 235–236; letter of acceptance, 151–152; management of John Dix's mayoral campaign, 229; need for educated men in politics, 175; nomination for president, 105–108; nomination to be temporary chairman of the 1912 Democratic National Convention, 234; notification of nomination for president, 138–139; notifies Thomas Marshall of his nomination for vice president, 237–238; offer of post of first assistant postmaster general, 19, 264n71; one term pledge, 143; oratorical skills, 164; outlook on life, 10; parenting, 13–14; participation

in New York State Democratic League, 227–228; physical appearance, 2, 10–12, 263n35; pledged delegate count, 92; popular vote, 192; possible campaign for governor, 19–20, 24; president of the American Bar Association, 215–216; president of the New York County Lawyers' Association, 218; president of the New York State Bar Association, 220; press response to allegations of corporate campaign contributions, 187; press support for his initial reluctance to actively campaign, 179–180; public statement in support of Wilson following the sinking of the *Lusitania*, 240; reasons behind and drafting of his gold telegram, 113–114, 115; refusal to be considered a candidate for president in 1912, 231; refusal to run for US Senate, 229, 265n10; refusal to second guess the legislature, 36, 37, 43; refusal to speak about issues of the day, 79–80, 81; relationship with grandchildren, 14; reluctance to seek the presidential nomination, 78–79; remarks praising Roosevelt following his death, 243; representation of Mayor McClellan, 202; representation of Samuel Gompers and the AFL, 203–205; resignation as county surrogate, 23; resignation from the New York Court of Appeals, 136–137; response to Roosevelt's criticism of the courts, 229–230; routine when the Court of Appeals was in session, 28–29; ruling concerning invasion of privacy, 42–44; rulings in contract cases, 31, 41–42; rulings in insurance cases, 31–33; rulings in labor cases, 31, 33–39, 259; rulings in trust cases, 31, 39–41; sadness in leaving the bench, 184–185; service as marshal of the Lawyers' Division in the WWI Citizens' Preparedness Parade, 241; speaks out against corporate contributions to campaign funds, 178–179, 180–181, 184, 186–187, 226, 228, 235, 237–238, 260; speech at the World Court Conference, 241; speech concerning the Fourteenth Amendment, 82–83; speeches on behalf of Bryan and Kern, 226–227; speech on the future of the Democratic Party, 225–226; statement following his defeat, 194–196; support of Grover Cleveland, 19; teaching, 4–8; telegram conceding defeat, 191; thoughts on a lawyer's role in public affairs, 201–202; thoughts on what it would take for the Democrats to win, 196–197; thoughts on why he lost, 196; treatment of young lawyers, 27–28; work as president of the National Civic Federation, 244, 246–248; work on the Committee of Fifteen, 219–220; work on the Committee on Criminal Courts, 219; work to elect David Hill governor, 52; writing style, 28

Parker, Amelia Day Campbell ("Amy"), 244, 248, 249, 251, 253; death, 256; early life, 246; first marriage, 246

Parker Campaign Songster, 158

Parker Constitutional Club, 173

Parker, Frederick (brother of ABP), 2, 14, 261n4 (chap. 1)

Parker, George F., 136

Parker, Gilbert (brother of ABP), 2

Parker, Harriett ("Hattie")(sister of ABP), 2
Parker, Harriett Stratton (mother of ABP), 1, 2
Parker, John Brooks (father of ABP), 1, 9–10
Parker, John M. (son of ABP and MSP), 13
Parker & Kenyon, 9
Parker Marshall & Randall, 201
Parker, Marshall, Miller & Auchincloss, 201
Parker, Marshall, Miller, Auchincloss & Randall, 201
Parker, Mary (sister of ABP), 2
Parker, Mary Louise Schoonmaker (MSP), 8, 9, 10, 229, 242; death, 242
Patrick, Albert T., 50
Patterson, Charles E., 25
Pattison, Robert E., 61, 101, 108
Payne, Henry C., 95
Peabody, George Foster, 136
Peck, Henderson, 208
Peckham, Rufus W., 39, 218, 219
Pendleton Act, 128
Pennsylvania, 61, 63, 69, 101, 127, 136, 192
People ex rel. Rodgers v. Coler, 36–37
People v. Place, 44
People v. Lochner, 37–39, 172, 230
People v. Orange County Road Construction Co., 37
Pepper, Charles M., 129
Perkins, George W., 186, 188
Philadelphia and Reading Railroad, 274n21
Philadelphia Enquirer, 164
Philadelphia North American, 121
Philadelphia, Pennsylvania, 239
Philadelphia Press, 144
Philippine Islands, 63

Philippines, 63, 64, 72, 143, 166, 170, 172, 258; independence for, 143, 173. *See also,* Philippine Islands
Piedmont Savings Bank, 126
Piedmont, Virginia, 125
Piedmont, West Virginia, 126, 130
Place, Martha, 44. *See also, People v. Place*
Platt, Thomas C., 57
Poe, John P., 101, 282n55
Poer, David E., 276n71
Pollock v. Farmers' Loan & Trust Co., 270n43
Populist Party, 169, 193
Porter, Logan S., 158
Portland, Maine, 216
post-election toast, 198
Potomac & Piedmont Coal & Railroad Company, 126
Poughkeepsie, New York, 238
Princeton, Indiana, 189
Princeton University, 221
Prohibitionists, 193
Progressive Democratic League of New York, 25
Progressive Party, 231
Puck, 64, 65, 92, 167, 174
Puerto Rico, 63
Pulitzer, Joseph, 62, 151, 176, 180
Pullman strike, 60

Raines, George, 88, 89, 91
Rainey, Henry T., 225
Ramsperger, Samuel J., 208, 209, 210
Rehnquist, William, 39
Republican, 9, 19, 20, 22, 23, 24, 25, 26, 38, 49, 51, 52, 55, 57, 59, 61, 63, 70, 78, 85, 89, 98, 102, 110, 118, 120, 125, 137, 141, 142, 143, 144, 147, 151, 154, 155, 163, 164, 165, 169, 170, 171, 172, 173, 174, 175, 177, 179, 181, 186, 187, 188, 192,

194, 195, 226, 228, 229, 231, 238, 239, 246, 258, 260
Republican campaign literature, 175–176
Republican Inter-State League, 171
Republican National Committee, 95, 164, 168, 171, 177, 179, 184, 186
Republican Party, 63, 89, 119, 121, 141, 147, 149, 165, 174, 181, 195, 196, 231, 235, 236
Republican platform (1904), 96–97
Republicans, 22, 23, 25, 26, 27, 52, 53, 56, 57, 59, 60, 61, 62, 63, 69, 95, 120, 127, 141, 171, 175, 189, 190, 191, 192, 194, 225, 228, 231, 273n1; courting ethnic voting blocks, 170–171; courting the African-American vote, 171; courting the Catholic vote, 172; courting the Jewish vote, 171; courting the labor vote, 172; courting the youth vote, 173
Review of Reviews, 187
Revolutionary War, 124, 201, 255
Rhode Island, 77, 92, 192, 272n30
Rice, William Marsh, 50
Richards, Eugene L., 208
Roberson, Abigail, 42, 135; response to Parker's demand for privacy, 135–136. *See also, Roberson v. Rochester Folding Box Co.*
Roberson v. Rochester Folding Box Co., 42–44, 135
Roberts, John, 39
Robertson, F. C., 111
Rochester, New York, 9
Rocky Mountain Club of New York, 243
Roosevelt, Franklin, 122, 244, 287n21
Roosevelt, Theodore, xiv, 63, 72, 79, 95, 96, 98, 103, 104, 114, 115, 117, 119, 120, 122, 141, 143, 146, 147, 149, 151, 157, 164, 168, 169, 170, 171, 172, 173, 174, 175, 176, 178, 180, 181, 184, 188, 189, 190, 192, 193, 197, 198, 216, 221, 235, 237, 241, 245, 257, 259, 260, 273n1, 292n56; alleged extortion of campaign contributions from corporations, 177; campaign for the presidency in 1912, 231; casting his vote for president, 191; criticism of the courts, 229; death, 243; domestic policies, 63–64; electoral vote totals, 192; foreign policy, 64; nomination to run for president, 97–98; popular vote, 192; promise to not seek a third term, 194; public endorsements, 172; response to Parker's allegations of campaign finance misfeasance, 185–186; response to Parker's gold telegram, 117; seeks advice from Parker regarding vice presidency, 44–45; seeks advice from Parker regarding law school, 45–46; Wall Street support of, 163–164
Root, Elihu, 95, 164, 220
Rose, David S., 104, 110
Rosemount, 2, 14, 17, 81, 109, 134, 136, 137, 138, 151, 166, 167, 168, 178, 251; crops, 17; dock, 17; grounds 16; livestock, 16–17; main house, 14–16
Russell, E. L., 110
Russia, 242
Russo-Japanese War, 169
Ryan, Thomas Fortune, xiii, 58, 111, 163, 190, 232, 234
Ryan v. City of New York, 37

Sague, John K., 238
San Francisco Bulletin, 118
San Francisco, California, 76, 144, 178
San Francisco Examiner, 76

San Juan, Cuba, 138
San Juan Hill, 63, 116, 149, 257
Sanner, Felix J., 208, 209, 210
Saratoga, New York, 215
Schoonmaker, Augustus, Jr., 8, 18, 19, 27, 262n18
Schoonmaker & Hardenburgh, 8
Schoonmaker, Moses, 8
Schoonmaker, Phoebe, 8
Schurz, Carl, 174, 175, 291n49; open letter to the independent voter, 174
Schwab, Charles M., 254
Scott, Walter, 254
Searing, John W., 22
Seattle, Washington, 217
Second Pan-American Conference, 129
Serumgard, Siver, 110
Seymour, Horatio, 290n8
Sharp, Severyn, 254
Shaw, Albert, 176
Shaw, Leslie M., 173
Sheehan, William F., 53, 64, 100, 113, 114, 136, 144, 191, 201, 282n55
Shelton, Thomas W., 220
Shepard, Edward, 84, 177
Shepard, Helen Gould, 214
Sherman Anti-Trust Act, 60, 63, 203, 205
Sherman, James S., 231
Sherman Silver Purchase Act, 60
Shipbuilding Trust, 188
Shively, Benjamin F., 101, 111, 282n55
Siam, 129
Sidway, Franklin, 41. See also, Hamer v. Sidway
Smith, Alfred E., 243, 253, 255, 261n3
Smith & Hill, 49
Smith, Gabriel L., 49, 50
Smith, James F., 172
Smith, James, Jr., 136
Socialist Party, 222; 279n2

Society of Mayflower Descendants, 246, 256
South Carolina, 112, 115, 118, 129, 192, 223, 282n55
South Carolina Bar Association, 221, 222
South Dakota, 64, 92, 192
Southwick, Leslie, 258
Soviet Union, 246
Spanish-American war, 63, 104, 143, 149, 168
Sparks, John, 259
Springfield, Ohio, 227
Springfield Republican, 144
Stable Money League, 249
Stanchfield, John B., 50, 208
Standard Oil, 163, 188
State Normal School, 4
St. Clair, J. W., 56
Sternaman v. Metropolitan Life Insurance Co., 33
Stevenson, Adlai E., 58, 189
Stevenson, Adlai E., II, 58
Stewart, John A., 307n241
Stickney, Albert, 149; commentary on the records of Parker and Roosevelt, 149–150
Stillman, James, 186
Stimson, Henry L., 229
Stires, Rev. Ernest M., 254
St. Louis, Missouri, 58, 81, 90, 91, 93, 98, 114, 121, 129, 130, 133, 138, 165, 167, 173, 242, 277n99, 278n126
Stone, Irving, 257, 258
Stone, William J., 69
Story, Joseph, 215
Story, William, 41–42. See also, Hamer v. Sidway
Story, William, II, 41–42. See also, Hamer v. Sidway
St. Peter's Hall, 181

Straus, Oscar, 171
Strauss, Charles, 217
Studebaker, Clement, 129
Styles, Edward Burton, 246
Success, 175
Sulgrave Institution, 245, 254, 306n240, 307n241; National Women's Committee, 245
Sulgrave Manor, 248, 306n240
Sullivan, Roger, 100
Sulzer, William, 205; articles of impeachment against, 207–208; disputes with Tammany leader Charles Murphy, 207; early political career, 206; impeachment trial, 208–213; removal from office, 213; running for governor, 206; votes on the articles of impeachment, 213
Sumner, Charles, 127
Supplementary Republican Text Book, 171
Supreme Court of the District of Columbia, 204, 205
Syracuse, New York, 3, 238

Tabor, Charles F., 25
Taft, William Howard, 170, 173, 220, 231, 239, 245, 305n208
Taggart, Thomas, 136, 137
Tammany Hall, 50, 88, 91, 169, 205, 206, 237; bosses, 87; founding, 86; transformation into a political machine, 86–87
tariff, 59, 60, 62, 101, 147, 148, 155, 173, 174, 175, 178, 182, 183, 195, 196, 221, 225, 226, 228, 235, 237, 238; need for revision, 141–142, 179, 190
Taylor, Zachary, 223
Ten Eyck Hotel, 28
Tennessee, 74, 84, 100, 107, 108, 112, 192, 235, 282n55

Terre Haute, Indiana, 189
Texas, 77, 111, 192
Third Regiment Armory, 183
Thomas, Benjamin Franklin, 71
Thomas, Charles S., 282n55
Thomas Jefferson Memorial Association, 249, 256
Thurman, Allen G., 127
Thurston, Hart & McGuire, 49
Tilden, Samuel J., 50, 128, 175
Tillman, "Pitchfork" Ben, xiii, 112, 115, 189, 282n55; response to Parker's gold telegram, 118
Tisdell v. New Hampshire Fire Insurance Co., 31–33
Todd, Hiram C., 208
Towne, Charles A., 108
Treaty of Washington, 127
Trescott, William H., 129
Trumball, Lyman, 127
Trump, Donald J., 122
trusts, 31, 59, 62, 77, 81, 89, 90, 101, 104, 148, 149, 174, 178, 179, 182, 183, 184, 190, 195, 196, 225, 228, 235, 237, 238; enforcement of laws to limit same, 142
Turner, George, 110, 111, 119
Tweed, William Marcy, 87
Tyler, John, 223, 292n56

Ulster County Bar Association, 254
Ulster County, New York, 8, 9, 12, 21, 109
Ulster County Savings Association, 12–13, 259–260
Underwood, Oscar, 231
Union Pacific Railroad, 163, 187
United Copper Company, 259
United Hatters of North America, 203
United States Court of Appeals for the Second Circuit, 203

United States Supreme Court, 27, 28, 39, 50, 54, 83, 127, 202, 203, 204, 205, 215, 218, 219, 220, 229, 231, 238, 239
unit rule, 87, 88, 91
University of Virginia, 221
Untermyer, Samuel, 188
US Constitution, 29, 30, 38, 46, 81, 83, 106, 108, 139, 141, 147, 154, 175, 201, 220, 221, 223, 224, 229, 230, 235
US House of Representatives, 59, 104, 206, 220
US Senate, 53, 54, 55, 57, 61, 68, 69, 70, 74, 77, 127, 128, 133, 142, 176
USS *Maine*, 62
Utah, 64, 192, 282n55

Van Etten, John, 22
Vann, Irving G., 24, 28, 208, 230; urges Parker to run for chief judge of the New York Court of Appeals, 24; thoughts on Parker's judicial philosophy, 30–31
Van Wyck, Augustus, 225
Vardaman, James K., 115
Vermont, 192
Vermont Bar Association, 224
Vilas, William F., 19
Virginia, 56, 77, 102, 111, 112, 126, 127, 136, 192, 282n55

Wagner, Robert F., 209, 210
Waldorf Astoria Hotel, 243
Wall, Edward C., 104, 108, 110
Wallace, William W., 25
Waller, Thomas M., 56
Wall Street, 80, 121, 122, 163, 164, 187, 188, 234, 237, 260
War of 1812, 124
Washington, 64, 92, 110, 111, 192
Washington, DC, 19, 129, 191, 246

Washington, George, 201, 221, 235, 245, 246, 306n240
Washington Post, 69, 110
Watson, Thomas E., 169
Watterson, Henry, 75, 119, 173, 188, 189, 290n8
Waverly plantation, 124
Wende, Gottfried, 211
Werner, William, 28
Westbrook, Theodore R., 22
Western Union, 163, 188, 214
West, Paul, 156
West Shore Railroad, 290n14
West Virginia, xiii, 56, 68, 101, 111, 119, 120, 125, 126, 127, 128, 129, 155, 156, 169, 170, 192, 295n20
West Virginia Central & Pittsburgh Railway, 128
West Virginia House of Delegates, 126
Wheeler, Burton K., 246
Wheeling Register, 128
White, Henry, 164
White Sulphur Springs, West Virginia, 153
White, William Pinckney, 128
Whitlock, George, 216
Williamsburg, Virginia, 224
Williams, James Robert, 111, 119
Williams, John Sharp, xiii, 64, 100, 104, 108, 114, 115, 189, 282n55; notification address to Davis, 153
Williams, T. S., 53
Wilson, James, 215
Wilson, Woodrow, 206, 231, 237, 238, 239, 241, 242, 305n208, 305n209; opposition to Parker's selection as temporary chairman of the 1912 Democratic National Convention, 233–234; refusal to appoint Parker to the US Supreme Court, 238–239
Wiltwyck Cemetery, 254, 256

Windom, William, 128
Winslow, Erving, 79
Wisconsin, 62, 75, 104, 110, 136, 192, 272n30
Wood, C. D., 276n71
Wood, Leonard, 45, 241
Woodson, Urey, 136, 190, 191
Woodstock, Maryland, 123, 124
World, 91
World Court Conference, 240
World War I, 218, 239, 240, 241, 244
World's Work, 72, 95, 116
Wyndham Hotel, 256
Wyoming, 64, 92, 192, 295n20

Yale Law School, 222
yellow journalism, 62
YMCA, 130

Milton Keynes UK
Ingram Content Group UK Ltd.
UKHW010514250624
444652UK00005B/373